THE CATHOLIC ALL YEAR COMPENDIUM

Kendra Tierney

The Catholic All Year Compendium

Liturgical Living for Real Life

IGNATIUS PRESS   SAN FRANCISCO

Cover art and design by Tricia Hope Dugat

© 2018 by Ignatius Press, San Francisco
All rights reserved
ISBN 978-1-62164-159-9
Library of Congress Control Number 2018939526
Printed in the United States of America ♾

To my children
Jack, Betty, Bobby, Gus, Anita, Frankie, Lulu,
Mary Jane, and George.
And to my godchildren
Ava, Lucy, Clementine, John, Alaina, Agnes, Mike, and Maryam.
I pray that this book will inspire you to
a lifetime of crazy Catholic fun.

CONTENTS

PREFACE

When my publisher suggested that I write this second book (my first book, *A Little Book about Confession for Children*, was published in 2014), it seemed like a great idea. Now, I couldn't be happier that it finally exists, because it has been a crazy ride. During the proposing and writing process, I was pregnant, packed up to move, accidentally had a baby at home, sold the old house, moved, entered the exciting world of construction supervising and do-it-yourself remodeling and feeding a family of ten from a makeshift kitchen in the garage, found out I was pregnant again, got super morning sickness, got better, fell off a ladder while painting and broke my tailbone, had a kid hospitalized after a freak accident, and somehow managed to fulfill my dream of getting this written. And here I am, typing a preface with a different snoozing newborn on my lap. It has really been something.

This book has been a long time coming. My intention when I started my blog in 2013 was to document all the Church's feast days and our crazy Catholic life. But then it turned out that there were about a million other things I also wanted to blog about. So it's a good thing this part is now a book. My blog and its social media babies are still around and have become a place for Catholics to come together and chat about saints and feast days and the pope and parenting and what we're watching on TV. Come find me and say hey. Just search for "Catholic All Year" or "Kendra Tierney".

INTRODUCTION

I wrote this book because of International Talk Like a Pirate Day. Not that this book will help you talk like a pirate. Alas, ye scurvy landlubber, it won't. But the fact that there is a Talk Like a Pirate Day (September 19) and an Ice Cream for Breakfast Day (first Saturday of February) and a Clean Out Your Refrigerator Day (November 15) tells us something. When my social media feeds fill up with photos of donuts on the first Friday of June (National Donut Day), I can see that we as a society are hungry for community and shared experiences (and donuts, of course).

And while I'm not here to tell you that you shouldn't observe Compliment Day on January 24 (I would *never*, and your hair looks great like that), I *am* here to tell you that, for Catholics, there is a whole *world* of days we could be celebrating together—days that have been marked by crazy community fun long before you could put a hashtag on it. We did it before. And there's no reason we can't do it again.

The Catholic Church recognizes more than ten thousand canonized saints, and each one has a feast day. A fraction of those show up on the free calendars they hand out at church, but for almost every day of the year, there are at least three saints from which to choose! Somewhere in the world, there are activities and foods and events traditionally used to celebrate each of those saints.

Saints' days plus days celebrating the founding of particular churches, the approved Marian apparitions, and the important events in the lives of Jesus, his mother Mary, and the first Christians make up the feasts of the year. Combined with days of fasting and seasons of preparation and celebration, you've got the liturgical year.

The calendar of the Catholic Church has, for centuries, set a rhythm for the year for the faithful. Planting particular crops and paying rent were associated with specific saints' days. Entire towns would fast together and feast together. Somewhere along the way, we have lost that cultural inheritance. Many of us have only the vaguest notion that the liturgical year even exists, let alone any idea of how to incorporate those days and that rhythm into our family life.

That's where I was as a young wife and a new mother. I was starting to rediscover the faith in which I grew up but into which I never really delved. I hoped to create for my family a home full of joy and faith and Catholic traditions, but I didn't know where to begin.

This book will not teach you how to talk like a pirate. But it will teach you what I have learned and discovered and compiled and invented over the last decade, during my slow and steady journey into liturgical living in the home.

Despite being the person writing this book, I do not claim to be an expert in theology, history, cooking, baking, crafting, party planning, or home decorating. I am, however, a very enthusiastic amateur practitioner of all the above. I am not a perfect mother or a perfect wife or a perfect Catholic. And while perfection is always the goal (see Mt 5:48), that's not what this book is about. This book isn't about Catholic perfection; it's about celebrating our common faith with family and friends.

Sometimes all you really need is a little enthusiasm and the willingness to give things a try. The easiest way is to start when your children are young enough to be dazzled by even your less successful endeavors. Case in point: I stood in my kitchen one Friday afternoon, looking at a slightly runny red gelatin heart, decorated with orange segments and pretzel sticks, sitting somewhat off-center on a cake plate. It was supposed to look like the Sacred Heart of Jesus, but it had looked better in my head—less oozy. My four-year-old daughter, however, took one look at it and gasped in wonder at its beauty. She called the other kids in to see it. They agreed that it was awesome but could use some whipped cream.

So that's what we did. We put some whipped cream on it. Over dinner, we talked about St. Margaret Mary Alacoque and her visions. We talked about the burning love that Jesus has for each one of us and the pain that he suffers because of the sin and the ingratitude of mankind. Then we ate the weepy heart. And now my kids can't imagine a feast of the Sacred Heart without one. That's what living the liturgical year looks like in our home.

In this book you will get that can't-miss dessert idea (obviously) plus dozens more ideas for activities, foods, crafts, and family adventures for the whole liturgical year, all of which require very little planning. I'll share the fun and heroic stories that the husband and I tell our kids to help them to love our favorite saints, and I'll explain how we talk to our kids about the less fun stuff, such as Judas' betrayal and the Passion of Our Lord.

You do not have to do everything in this book. You can be a good Catholic and do these things to celebrate the liturgical year. You can also be a good Catholic and do other things or no things at all to celebrate the liturgical year. Our family doesn't do everything in this book every year. And we certainly didn't do it all in the beginning. Start slowly. Add one observance at a time. If you love it, do it again next year. If you don't love it, wait a couple of years and try again. Or just chuck it entirely.

In addition to offering liturgical-living inspiration, this book peeks at the basics of Catholic life in a family, surrounded by schoolwork and commutes and cell phones and TV. Whether we are converts to Christianity or have come over to Catholicism from another denomination or are cradle Catholics who just never learned any of this stuff, there's a lot to learn. But together, maybe we can make it happen!

Sixteen years ago, when I first became a mother, I had no idea that it was possible for a regular family to live a full Catholic life in the midst of today's world with today's demands and expectations. But it is. It definitely is. You just need to know when to add whipped cream.

Something to keep in mind as you read: the Catholic Church is big and wide. It encompasses the whole world and many cultural traditions and liturgical rites. It is for all people in all circumstances. I've done my best to make this book useful and accessible to (and supportive of) *all* Catholics, but my family and I are American, Ordinary Form, Latin Rite, Roman Catholics, and I'm a stay-at-home mom. This identity has shaped my personal knowledge and experience, and you'll see that reflected in the book. It's my hope that you'll be able to adapt for yourself and your circumstances what has worked for me and mine.

Liturgical Living for Life

Making the Liturgical Year Your Own

One of the many things I love about the Catholic Church is how she manages to be universal and particular at the same time. When I attend Mass in a different parish, or even a different country, the order and the parts of the Mass are the same. Even though there might be unique traditions and practices and languages particular to that part of the world, the Mass still feels familiar. I love that artists in every age often render Jesus and Our Lady and the saints with the artists' own ethnic features and in their own local dress, yet they are still recognizable to all of us.

Liturgical living in the home is a lot like that. It can look different but *be* the same in different homes. Your time and budget constraints, your abilities and preferences will inform how you choose to bring the rhythm of the Church year into your family life. And that's a *good* thing. Working or stay-at-home, homeschooling or brick-and-mortar, rich or poor, big or small—no matter what terms apply to you and your family, you can find a way to bring a bit of the tradition of our beautiful faith into your home.

One important note: for a Catholic, all of this stuff can be very fun and meaningful, but it is secondary to getting to Mass on Sundays and holy days of obligation and participating in the sacraments. That is the meal. This is just the garnish.

Remember that you don't have to do it all, and you definitely don't have to do it all at once. I grew up Catholic, but liturgical living in the home is something I discovered as an adult and slowly began incorporating into our family culture. So, here at the beginning of this book, I want to give you a practical guide for implementation.

The resources you have on hand—picture books from the library or from your own collection, craft supplies, movies, local places to go on family outings, and prayers you already have or can find online—can be chosen to celebrate whichever saints' days happen to be coming up. Whether dining out, ordering takeout, or cooking and baking in your own kitchen, the things your family eats can be selected to fit the feast. In other words, *whatever* you have available and usually do can be liturgically tweaked a bit. If crafts or baking or outings aren't feasible for you right this second, don't sweat it. Do the things that work for your family.

How to Begin

If I were starting completely from scratch, I would follow the steps below. How quickly you go from one step to the next will depend entirely on how well each step goes. Feel free to hang out at any step for however many days, weeks, months, or years it takes for that practice to feel like a part of your family routine. These steps are listed not in order of importance but in what I think is the order of "doability" for a family with no liturgical-living experience.

1. Start with the liturgical living you're doing already.

Choose a couple of practices to add to your family routine for the liturgical seasons that come before and after the two major feasts you're already observing: Christmas and Easter. Do them. See if you like them. If you do, do them again next year. If you don't, try something else next year. As you get more comfortable, try adding additional practices as well.

2. Begin celebrating baptismal anniversaries.

Find out the baptismal date of each person in your family. Dig out your kids' baptismal certificates or call your parish office and ask for copies (you'll need copies for the rest of your kids' sacraments anyway). For your own baptismal date, call your mom or your hometown parish or see if you can figure it out. If you can't, just say a prayer, choose a random date, write it down, and use that. In our house on a person's baptismal anniversary, he chooses a special meal and a dessert, and he holds a candle while the whole family renews their baptismal promises and are sprinkled with holy water. Ideally, he holds the candle he received at his baptism, because you wrote his name on the box and put it where you could find it again. But if you're not one of those magical unicorn moms who does that sort of thing, any candle will do. Add those dates to your family calendar (with a reminder ahead of time) so you will remember to remember them each year.

3. Begin celebrating name days.

Choose a patron saint for each person in your family. Usually this would be a saint whose name a person shares, but it could also be a confirmation saint or just a saint the person particularly likes. Look up some information about the saint and find out his feast day. Add the feast days of your family's patrons to your calendar with reminders. On each person's name day, either let that person choose a special meal and dessert or have a special meal in honor of the saint.

4. Remember Fridays and Sundays.

If it isn't already a part of your family culture, somewhere amongst these early steps, begin observing Fridays and Sundays in your home. Every Friday is a mini–Good Friday. Consider abstaining from meat on Fridays.[1] When that isn't possible, make an alternate Friday sacrifice, if that's permitted by your bishop. Every Sunday is a mini-Easter. Have a feast on Sundays. Use the good dishes, spend time together as a family, refrain from your usual work as much as possible, consider not patronizing businesses, and eat dessert. Consider cutting out desserts on days that aren't Sundays or feast days, so that Sundays and feast days will feel special.

5. Start observing days that have better-known traditions associated with them.

- St. Nicholas' Day: December 6
- Fat Tuesday (Mardi Gras): the day before Ash Wednesday

---

[1] See appendix A for more information on fasting and abstinence.

- Ash Wednesday: forty-six days before Easter
- St. Patrick's Day: March 17
- Spy Wednesday, Holy Thursday, Good Friday, Holy Saturday: the week before Easter
- Michaelmas: September 29
- All Souls' Day: November 2

6. Begin observing solemnities in your home.

Solemnities mark the most important days of the liturgical year. On a solemnity, Mass is celebrated as on a Sunday, with readings proper to the feast. Some solemnities are also holy days of obligation, and these vary from country to country.

There are feasts that are raised to the rank of solemnities for some Catholics, but not universally. The feast of the patron of a religious order, parish, city or country is raised to a solemnity for members of that order or parish, or residents of that place. For instance, the feast of St. Dominic is a solemnity for the Dominican Order, the feast of St. George is a solemnity in England, the feast of St. Thérèse of Lisieux is a solemnity for members of St. Thérèse parishes, and the feast of Our Lady, Queen of Angels, is a solemnity for people who live in Los Angeles.

If a solemnity falls on a Friday, Catholics are not required to abstain from meat or to do a different act of penance. It's a Meat Friday, and we get to celebrate without making an alternate sacrifice.

There are twenty-three solemnities on the universal calendar. That averages out to a couple of days per month. Many of them fall on Sundays or are days you probably already celebrate (such as Christmas). These are celebrations of the most important people, events, and mysteries of our long faith tradition.

- The Immaculate Conception of the Blessed Virgin Mary: December 8
- The Nativity of the Lord (Christmas): December 25
- Mary, Mother of God: January 1
- The Epiphany of the Lord: traditionally January 6, transferred in the United States to the Sunday between January 2 and 8, inclusive
- St. Joseph, Spouse of the Blessed Virgin Mary: March 19

- The Annunciation of the Lord: March 25
- Resurrection of the Lord (Easter): the first Sunday after the first full moon that falls on or after March 21, eight solemnities, Sunday to Sunday
- Ascension of the Lord: the Thursday forty days after Easter; transferred in most dioceses in the United States to the following Sunday
- Pentecost: the Sunday fifty days after Easter
- The Most Holy Trinity: the Sunday after Pentecost
- The Most Holy Body and Blood of Christ (Corpus Christi): the Sunday after Trinity Sunday (formerly celebrated on a Thursday, but now mostly observed on a Sunday)
- The Most Sacred Heart of Jesus: the Friday after Corpus Christi
- The Nativity of St. John the Baptist: June 24
- SS. Peter and Paul: June 29
- The Assumption of the Blessed Virgin Mary: August 15
- All Saints: November 1
- Our Lord Jesus Christ, King of the Universe: the last Sunday before Advent

Add these dates to your family calendar, with reminders. You can find liturgical calendars for your phone or tablet that will add the movable feasts on the correct date each year. If you prefer paper, there are beautiful Catholic calendars and planners that include feast days. Definitely get to Mass if the solemnity is also a holy day of obligation. Try to get to Mass even if it isn't.

Use our family's traditions or create some of your own that your kids can look forward to each year. These celebrations can be as complicated as throwing a bonfire for the neighborhood on the Nativity of St. John the Baptist or putting on a pageant and carnival for your child's school for All Saints' Day, or as simple as having cookies and discussing with your kids the importance of the feast.

I recommend beginning to observe baptismal anniversaries and name days before solemnities. Even though those days are perhaps not as important to the *universal* Church, I found it easier to begin liturgical-living celebrations by focusing on our family first and then widening our focus to the Church.

7. After that, it's really all gravy.

We observe the seasons and the feast days in steps 1 through 6 every year, unless illness or scheduling conflicts prevent us. We observe other feast days as we are able.

Some Thoughts on Planning

As I plan my meals and make my grocery list for the week, I peek at the upcoming feasts, note our family schedules, and plan to have a meal associated with a saint's day whenever we can.

We might schedule a family activity, such as a hike or a trip to a museum, that fits in somehow with the feast day. We talk about the saint or the event over dinner. If we have a book about the saint, we'll read it at story time.

There are many traditional prayers associated with particular feast days, and all the saints on the universal calendar have a special Collect (pronounced *kol*-ekt), the prayer said by the priest to conclude the introductory rite of the Mass. You can find the words to the Collect in a daily missal. If there is a special prayer associated with the day, we'll add it to our Grace before Meals or to our morning or evening prayers.

All the fun stuff is really a jumping-off point. It's a way for all of us to learn about the lives of Jesus and the saints, the events of the Bible, and the history and the tradition of Christianity. It's a way to bring our faith into our dinnertime and story time and conversations. Trying to answer my kids' questions is how I have learned just about everything I know about the saints. Through our discussions about theological concepts and heroic martyrdoms, our whole family has grown in our understanding of and appreciation for our Church. It's my hope that liturgical living in the home will mean that the Catholic faith will continue to be a part of the daily lives and the yearly routines of my children as they grow into adulthood.

In Short

This is what living the liturgical year looks like in our home, after a decade of baby steps:

- I decorate our home to reflect the current liturgical season.
- We do special practices throughout each season.
- We celebrate three special days each year for each person in the family: birthday, name day, baptism day. On those days the special person gets to choose what we have for dinner and dessert.
- We observe a mini-Lent each Friday.
- We celebrate a mini-Easter each Sunday.
- We remember family traditions for Christmas and Easter and for the other solemnities of the year. Whenever possible, we involve friends and family members in our solemnity celebrations. Whenever convenient, we eat fun food and have fun discussions on other feast days as well.

That's it, and somehow it manages not to be overwhelming, although it does seem like a lot when it's all written down! I have found liturgical living in the home to be a beautiful way to connect with my family, my faith, my community, and the long history of our Church.

2

Advent

In the Latin Catholic Church, the liturgical calendar begins on the first Sunday of Advent, which means we begin each year with our preparations for celebrating the birth of baby Jesus! It seems very fitting. Advent is traditionally a time of prayer, fasting, and almsgiving (it is sometimes called "little Lent"), during which we prepare our hearts and our homes for the coming of Christ at Christmas. In our family we make a point of celebrating Advent during Advent and Christmas during Christmas, rather than celebrating Christmas during Advent and nothing at all during Christmas, even though such observances have become more and more countercultural over the past few decades.

Keeping Advent

Even before the liturgical year was a part of our family's day-to-day life, I "got" Lent. I'm not saying I did it right, but I at least understood the concept. I knew that Lent was a time of penitence in preparation for Easter. And since the more secular, cultural, bunny parts of Easter are not as popular as the more secular, cultural, elf parts of Christmas, it was easy for me to maintain whatever little focus I had on the penitential part of Lent then, and it's a no-brainer to focus on that stuff with my kids now.

But Advent? Finding the balance in Advent is harder. As I began to love my faith more and more, I wanted to show that love by going all out for Christmas. But as I began to understand my faith more and more, I got the feeling we were putting the cart before the horse.

Learning how much the liturgical year was a part of the daily life of Catholics in earlier eras motivated me to start incorporating it into my family life. There are so many lovely classic children's books, such as *The Children of Noisy Village*[1] and *The Twenty-Four Days Before Christmas*,[2] that detail how the weeks before Christmas used to be observed as a time of waiting and mindful preparation.

Advent, after all, recalls specifically the wait for the birth of a baby. It can be fun. It can be joyful. But it's all expectant joy. Mary and Joseph waited and prepared for nine months for the birth of Jesus, and the Jewish people had been waiting and preparing for thousands of years for the birth of the Savior! My second child was born in the winter, and I remember how poignant it was to be very pregnant during Advent. It was clear that there could be no skipping ahead, no matter how weary I was with the waiting.

But skipping ahead is what I was doing with Christmas. The day after Thanksgiving we would get our tree and crank the carols and string the lights and watch the TV specials and eat the cookies. We would host Christmas parties and attend Christmas parties. And by the time Christmas arrived, I was pooped and about ready to be done with it all. The tree was a dried-out fire hazard, and I was sick of Christmas carols and of the kids being crazed candy-cane-and-sugar-cookie-fueled maniacs.

But my free Church liturgical calendar said we were supposed to be just starting Christmas. We were supposed to celebrate Christmas for the next eight days or twelve days or even twenty-something days, depending on whom you ask—and then still kind of celebrating it for a few weeks after that. So, eventually, even though everyone around us was celebrating Christmas in November, we decided to make a mindful effort to back away from Christmas until Christmas has arrived and really observe Advent in our home and in our hearts.

Here's what we do to keep Advent.

I do my Christmas shopping before Advent begins.

For some, shopping for gifts might feel like an important part of the preparation for Christmas that belongs in Advent. Making

---

[1] Astrid Lindgren, *The Children of Noisy Village* (Oxford: Oxford University Press, 2014).

[2] Madeleine L'Engle and Jill Weber, *The Twenty-Four Days before Christmas: An Austin Family Story* (New York: Farrar, Straus and Giroux, 2010).

homemade presents feels like that for me, but shopping never has. It feels busy and crowded and stressful. Also, it's easy for the idea of what kids *want* for Christmas to take over their hearts and minds as Christmas approaches.

So getting the shopping done early has been really helpful for our family. Between the husband and me, I'm the more impulsive and the more likely to overdo Christmas presents. Of course, you get to a certain number of kids, and it's all you can do to make sure you remembered to get each of them *something*, but, still, I'm the one of us more likely to keep thinking of new things I would like to get for the kids. So it's really good for me to get the shopping out of the way early. I make a list and check it twice, and then *I do not* let myself buy more stuff.

It's good for me, and it's really good for the kids. They talk about what they would like to get and make their lists for Santa, but then it's over, and we don't talk and talk about what they *want*. Instead their focus is on making gifts for siblings and other family members, doing good deeds, and making crafts and decorations for the house.

And I get to avoid all the crazy last-minute shopping madness!

Of course, I shop for all the food and fixings we need for Christmas dinner, and for the supplies we need for Christmas baking. But other than that, I try to limit even food shopping. I use Advent to clean out the freezer and the pantry by using up all the stuff that, for whatever reason, I haven't felt like cooking. And we eat pretty simply—lots of soup—except for our saint's day meals. So I cut down some on my normal food shopping.

We consider decorating a process rather than a box to check.

I am a generally festive person. I don't think I could bear to come home to a completely bare house when the rest of the town is decorated, even if I agreed with the principle of it. Fortunately, I don't think that's necessary.

We decorate throughout Advent. At the beginning all the Nativity sets come out, and the pieces are added a few at a time. We also get out the Advent calendars, of course, and the Christmas books (we love to read aloud as a family, and we have a special focus on it during Advent). Then we slowly add things here and there over the days and weeks.

I've come to appreciate homemade paper- and nature-based decorations that can be made and tossed each year. It means less stuff to store and more family traditions and family togetherness. It means they're a little different each year and always charmingly imperfect. Making wreaths and garlands and snowflakes takes more time than slapping up store-bought decorations, but one of my goals for Advent is to spend that time with and for my family. It won't necessarily happen the same way every year, and some years it will barely happen at all. But we can count on some family baking and crafting together every Advent, even though we don't necessarily do a whole lot of that the rest of the year.

We hold off on Christmas stuff until Christmastime, as much as possible.

The *General Instruction of the Roman Missal* (*GIRM*) is a book of rules and instructions governing how Mass is to be celebrated in just about every possible circumstance. It doesn't specifically apply to our homes, but it does give us an understanding of how the Church hopes that we, the faithful, will observe and experience the various liturgical seasons. It tells us, "During Advent the floral decoration of the altar should be marked by a moderation suited to the character of this season, without expressing prematurely the full joy of the Nativity of the Lord."[3] In other words, inside the church we are supposed to be holding back on the decorations. While our decorating decisions at home are not bound by these instructions, I keep them in mind. That's why we wait until Christmas Eve to do our final decorating, hang the stockings, and trim the tree.

We wait on the Christmas stuff because it creates in all of us a feeling of excitement and expectation and longing—not just for presents, but for the great event. Christmas is a time of year, but it also marks a historical event that happened at an actual moment on a particular night. Observing Advent has helped us to remember that and to keep from getting burned out.

[3] United States Conference of Catholic Bishops, *General Instruction of the Roman Missal* (Washington, D.C.: United States Conference of Catholic Bishops, 2010), no. 305, http://www.vatican.va/roman_curia/congregations/ccdds/documents/rc_con_ccdds_doc _20030317_ordinamento-messale_en.html#DECREE_OF_PUBLICATION.

We enjoy what Advent has to offer.

Even though Advent is a season of preparation and not-yet celebration, I still think it might be my favorite time of year. I love getting ready for something as much as, if not more than, celebrating it. I don't think my kids would say the same, but I do know that they would tell you they really enjoy Advent.

The big kids have a hand in all the decorating and baking, which they really like. And everyone in the family loves our Christmas Novena. We make an Advent wreath and light the candles and say the prayers each evening at dinner. We celebrate the feasts that fall during Advent, and those traditions are especially meaningful for us, because they are part of the lead-up to Christmas!

We keep Advent (mostly) quiet.

Keeping all our Advent traditions would be really hard if we were watching television and listening to the radio, since the rest of the world is pretty much celebrating Christmas already. So we don't watch television or listen to the radio. We'll watch an occasional football or hockey game that we care about, but other than that, I just don't turn on the television. For us, the point of avoiding television and radio isn't penitential; it's just to help us focus. And we're usually so busy with worthwhile activities that we don't miss it.

If you have only little kids, I do not necessarily suggest that you do this. In our home, I was able to manage keeping the TV off only when I had older kids who could help entertain the little ones. But even if you have only little children, you could try to avoid the Christmas versions of their favorite shows until Christmas has arrived.

A newish bump in the road of keeping Advent is the recent proliferation of all-Christmas-music radio stations. My town now has two of them. I would really, *really* love them, if only the timing weren't completely wrong. The carols begin before Thanksgiving and end *on Christmas Day.* And that, in a nutshell, is what's wrong with letting the secular culture tell us how to celebrate Christmas.

Just as the *GIRM* calls for sparsely decorated churches during Advent, it also says that church music should be "consistent with the season's character" and should not "anticipate the full joy of the Nativity of the

Lord".[4] Unlike during Lent, we still sing the Alleluia during Masses in Advent, but we do not sing the Gloria. Why? Because that hymn begins with the words that the angels sang when they announced the birth of Christ to shepherds: "Glory to God in the highest, and on earth peace" (Lk 2:14). We don't sing it during Advent, because we are awaiting the celebration of that announcement.

I understand why the mall is decorated for Christmas by Halloween and Christmas music is playing in all of the stores beginning in November. They are trying to get you to buy stuff, and that's fine. But the fact that the TV stations are playing Christmas movies and the radio stations are playing Christmas music throughout Advent and then *not at all* during Christmas is a problem for Catholics who are trying to live liturgically.

The good news is twofold. First, with DVRs and DVDs and video streaming, we can watch Christmas movies whenever we want to, not just when the powers that be decide to put them on the air. And with CDs and music streaming, we aren't stuck listening to Christmas music only when it's on the radio. Second, there are really great Advent carols! Here are some of our favorites:

- "O Come, O Come, Emmanuel"
- "Come, Thou Long-Expected Jesus"
- "Creator of the Stars of Night"
- "O Come, Divine Messiah"
- "Lo! How a Rose E'er Blooming"
- "Let All Mortal Flesh Keep Silent"
- "The Angel Gabriel from Heaven Came"
- "People, Look East"
- "Ave Maria"
- "It's Beginning to Look a Lot Like Christmas"
- "I'll Be Home for Christmas"
- "Christmas Is Coming"
- "Silver Bells"
- "Santa Claus Is Coming to Town"

That's our Advent, really. We focus on the preparation, on the waiting. We talk about it with the kids. They know that we are

[4] Ibid., no. 313.

celebrating differently from other families during Advent, but they also know that once Christmas comes, they'll get twelve days of it instead of just one.

Here's what we *don't* do.

We don't refuse party invitations.

We're not Scrooges. Even traditional Catholic organizations to which we belong have their Christmas parties during Advent. Of course, *they* call them Advent parties instead of Christmas parties, but they *look* an awful lot like Christmas parties to me. That's fine. I don't expect everyone to celebrate the way we do. We are grateful for the invitations we receive, and we go where we are invited.

When we go to parties, we don't make our kids eat only vegetables.

We go where we are invited, *and* we allow our kids to enjoy themselves. We don't eat Christmas cookies at our house during Advent (although we do celebrate quite a few Advent saints' days that involve cookies), but when we are at someone else's house, we happily eat what's put before us (see Lk 10:8). Likewise, we don't give the kids presents early, but if a neighbor comes by with a little something for the kids, they get to open it in front of the giver and say thank you and enjoy it.

We don't think people who celebrate Advent differently are wrong.

We have arrived at this way of celebrating in a slow, steady way. Neither the husband nor I grew up observing Advent the way we do now, but we think it works. It is in keeping with the long tradition of the Catholic Church. We have seen the benefits in our family, both spiritually and practically. But nowhere in the *Catechism of the Catholic Church* or canon law is there anything telling Catholics that they must observe Advent, or any other liturgical season, in any particular way in their homes. I always suggest, especially to people just starting out, that families start slowly, keep doing what works, and don't keep doing stuff that doesn't work.

Giving and Receiving Gifts

We all know that we want the focus of our Christmas celebrations to be the birth of Jesus. But if there are children involved, and especially if there are children *and* extended families involved, we also have to figure out how to handle presents.

I grew up in a family with two kids and a bonkers number of presents under the tree. It wasn't that my parents were overly indulgent; it's just that they are very, very festive. So anything that would be purchased for anyone in the house during the month of December would be wrapped and put under the tree. There would be toys and clothes. There would be socks if we needed socks, and notebook paper if we needed notebook paper. I have a very clear memory of my mom unwrapping a set of windshield wipers with a tag indicating that they were a gift to her from her car.

It was fun. But it was also overwhelming and exhausting and time-consuming. We would wake up early, open presents, have breakfast, open more presents, go to Mass, and open more presents. It was an all-day process. My parents kept stopping us from playing with things so that we could get back to opening things.

When our oldest kids were little, the husband and I headed right down that same path. As the years went by and we found ourselves with more and more children and more and more stuff, we began to realize that all those toys weren't making our kids happier. They weren't making our home happier or our Christmases happier either.

I started getting really bold in our Lenten and Advent clean-outs. I determined which toys were useful and enjoyable, and which were just causing clutter and unhappiness. (Mother-of-two me wouldn't believe how few toys it takes to satisfy the children of mother-of-nine me.) Now the kids are old enough to take the lead in the clean-outs themselves. Advent is a good time both to make room for any new things that might be coming our way and to think about needy kids who might appreciate some of our toys that we haven't used in a while. Talking about how toys that aren't our favorites might go to another kid who could love and cherish them makes a huge difference in terms of how my kids handle toy clean-outs.

In addition to donating toys and clothes that we don't use anymore, we also budget each year to buy new gifts for needy kids and donate them to a charity gift program. We buy one new gift for each of our kids to donate to someone his own age. The kids get to come shopping with me to choose something that they would like to receive but is for giving instead.

We scaled back on giving stuff to our kids. We became mindful about not bringing new toys into the house when it wasn't a specifically gift-giving holiday. We also started setting limits on the number of gifts we gave to each kid at Christmas. Whenever possible, we give activities and experiences rather than stuff. We ask the grandparents to consider giving the kids a group gift such as a big outdoor toy, a trip to an amusement park, or passes to the zoo.

These changes required growth from all of us. It was just as hard for me to learn to be patient in giving as it was for the kids to learn to be patient in receiving. And I had to learn to let go of my desire to be the one to find the perfect, most awesome present ever. To help with this, if there's something I know a particular kid will be really excited to receive, I try to pass that gift idea along to the grandparents, so they get to be the heroes.

We made sure that our families know that we are struggling to manage clutter and stuff, and they've been amazingly receptive to it all. But I know that not all extended families are as understanding. And even with an understanding extended family, we still end up with stuff in the house that isn't a good fit for us. Our policy is to let people know our preferences ahead of time, if that's possible, and always to accept gifts gratefully. But then we get to decide what stays in our home and what doesn't. Most things get to stay in the house at least until the next seasonal clean-out. But if I believe something is dangerous, immoral, or might wake a sleeping baby, I reserve the right to get rid of it immediately.

So that the children will become good givers as well as receivers, we do several things. I help them to create homemade cards or gifts for their grandparents and other extended family members. The husband and I usually take turns helping the kids to make or buy something as a gift for the other parent. For sibling gift giving, we organize a Secret Santa exchange amongst the kids. At the beginning of Advent, each kid draws the name of one sibling. Then each prays for and does secret good deeds for his chosen sibling throughout Advent. He also buys a Christmas present for only that sibling. I give the little kids a budget, but the older kids spend their own money. On Christmas morning they find out who has been sneaking around making their beds or putting their dishes in the dishwasher or leaving them notes in their backpacks. And the kids are still welcome to make presents for any other siblings.

Christmas Cards

We love receiving Christmas cards featuring beautiful religious art or smiling family photos, or both. I come from a long line of family-photo-Christmas-card types. My dad's parents sent out a photo Christmas card every single year, through wars and everything. My parents have sent one out every year, and they have them all in an album on their coffee table, so we can flip through it and see my entire life, year by year, from babyhood and childhood through perms and graduations and my wedding, and now my kids and their cousins are in the photos too. It's great!

Even better, my parents have also been in every photo. Moms, I know you think people don't want to see you in photos; they just want to see your cute kids. But when I look back at our family photos from my youth, the ones my kids and I cherish are the ones with my mom in them! So get in that photo; your future grandchildren will thank you.

It can be tough in a big family to keep up with baby books and studio portraits for so many kids. But making it a priority to put on clean clothes and take a family photo once a year is pretty doable for us. We've made looking at the camera and smiling a part of our family culture. We take a few, use the best one, and that's that. I like our cards to include a religious image or a quote, plus a short update about our family for the year.

Christmas cards are especially meaningful for us, because we have so many far-flung friends and family members. We hang every card we receive on the wall of our living room throughout Advent and Christmas. Then, when we take them down, we put them in a basket under our home altar table. All year long, we take out a few when we say our family Rosary and pray for the intentions of those families.

Advent Calendars

When you are observing Advent as a time of waiting, your kids are sure to want to know *how much longer?* They will probably want to know how much longer a couple of times per day. A good way to satisfy that desire and to thwart at least a few of the questions, is to have an Advent calendar (or ten) around the house.

There are dozens of types from which to choose—homemade or store-bought, disposable or reusable—and we've had quite a few over the years. The key, I think, is finding one that encourages the spirit of waiting and preparing that we are hoping to foster, rather than a spirit of receiving.

For a few years, we got the German-style Advent calendars with a little door to rip open each day, revealing a small piece of chocolate. There were two problems for us with this kind of Advent calendar. First, eating a piece of candy every day for twenty-five days pretty much killed the feeling of waiting for Christmas treats. Second, when Christmas arrived, all they had to show for Advent was a piece of trash and a hankering for chocolate every morning.

Now we prefer Advent calendars that build to something or that *actually* build something! Those have seemed to fit better with the season. For the family, we have what we call the "Puffy Tree". It's a tree made of stuffed fabric triangles that hangs on the wall. Each day, someone in the family gets to hang an inch-high wooden ornament on one of the triangles. You can see that as the days get closer to Christmas, the tree gets more and more filled in, and we get closer to the blessed event. Then it stays there as a decoration for the Christmas season.

A good one for little kids to do themselves, and a good specific alternative to candy Advent calendars, is a sticker calendar. Kids get to add a sticker to a scene each day, and on Christmas, the scene is complete. We've had Victorian Christmas Village ones and Nativity ones. Both are very cute. One (crazy) note: in a case of liturgical living coming back to bite me, my kids balked at the idea of putting the Wise Men and their gifts into the scene before it was liturgically appropriate to do so. I had a twelve pack of the sticker sets and didn't have twelve kids, so I was able to provide them with extra animal stickers. But really, Mary and Joseph and the shepherds and the angels don't belong there before Christmas Eve either. So, while I usually recommend going with Jesus-themed stuff over village-themed stuff, the village one ended up being more of a success for us.

I've got two boys with Advent-adjacent birthdays, and their birthday requests for the last five years straight have been LEGO Advent calendars. They aren't religious, of course, but LEGO blocks have been our family's favorite toy for ten years running, and these calendars are a fun addition to our Advent. Each day, the child gets to open one window and put together one little figure. But the catch is, all the little figures come together to create a scene, so they all have to stay there together on the fold-down base. When Christmas comes, they've built a fun little world. *Then* they can finally have all the LEGOs. My kids like to leave the scene up through the Christmas season and then break each figure down, put it into a baggie, stuff it back into the window, and tape the door shut, and then a different kid gets to use that one next year. If you have many children, it ends up taking up a lot of space. We set up a large folding table for them all. And when other families with little kids come to visit, we cover the whole thing with a sheet, to avoid temptation for little hands.

Advent Wreaths

I have very strong memories of our family Advent wreath when I was growing up. Perhaps it's because that was really the only liturgical-living-in-the-home tradition my family observed, or maybe it's because I was a preteen in the late eighties and had a very hairsprayed two-layers-of-bangs hairdo, which I once set ablaze while leaning over a lit front candle to light a back candle. Not a good technique, but memorable. Fortunately, it didn't sour me on the tradition. There's something really magical about the smell of the greenery and the flickering candlelight and the repetition of the prayers each evening as we slowly build to Christmas.

The exact origins of the Advent wreath are unknown. It appears that pre-Christian Germanic peoples used wreaths lit with candles during the wintertime as a sign of hope that warmer and longer days would return in the spring. During the Middle Ages, some Christians were using wreaths with candles to prepare for the coming of

Christmas, and the practice was observed by both Protestants and Catholics in the 1600s.[5] Advent wreaths were brought to the United States by German immigrants.

The Advent wreath is really an archetype of liturgical living in the home. It was used in Catholic homes and schools for decades before an official blessing of the Advent wreath was included in the 1976 revision of the *Rituale Romanum*, the Church's official book of prayers and blessings, which meant it could be used in churches. Pope St. John Paul II was the first to bring the tradition of the Advent wreath to the Vatican, since it's not a historically Italian tradition, and the Vatican has had one ever since.

An Advent wreath is a beautiful way to talk about religious symbolism with kids. The circle of the wreath, with no beginning or end, symbolizes God's eternal nature. The evergreen branches signify the immortality of the soul. Decorative pine cones or seed pods represent new life and resurrection. The four candles remind us of the four weeks of Advent and also the four thousand years from the creation of Adam and Eve to the birth of Jesus Christ.[6] The candle flames symbolize the light of Christ.

The four candles are red in Germany and also in the wreath used at the Vatican. In the United States, it is customary to use three purple candles and one pink candle. The pink candle is lit on the third Sunday of Advent, Gaudete Sunday, one of the two Sundays of the year when the priest may wear rose-colored vestments. Gaudete Sunday is celebrated as a day of rejoicing because we have reached the halfway point of Advent and are that much closer to Christmas! On Christmas Eve, the four Advent candles are traditionally replaced with one large white Christ candle in the center of the wreath, to light during the Christmas season.

When choosing or creating an Advent wreath for your home, it's good to be mindful of all that great symbolism associated with the traditional shape and materials, so you don't accidentally end up with one that's missing any of it.

---

[5] William Saunders, "The History of the Advent Wreath", *Arlington Catholic Herald*, November 28, 2017, https://www.catholicherald.com/Faith/Your_Faith/Straight_Answers/The_history_of_the_Advent_wreath-10737406815.

[6] As time is reckoned in the Bible, which might not be meant literally.

It's also good to remember that there is a strong preference (but not an official mandate) in various Church documents for the use of natural rather than artificial materials for religious purposes whenever possible. "Fake" greenery and "fake" candles are not ideal for use in a sacramental. "Human minds and hearts are stimulated by the sounds, sights, and fragrances of liturgical seasons, which combine to create powerful, lasting impressions of the rich and abundant graces unique to each of the seasons."[7]

Our children love going out to cut whatever greenery we can find in the yard to create our wreath. We use a combination of small pine boughs, juniper branches, rosemary clippings—whatever we can find. It means our home still has that evergreen smell, even though we don't have a tree up yet. Do-it-yourself anything with kids can be overwhelming, but this one really is pretty easy. Even very young kids can successfully create an Advent wreath with just a little help.

I know that the very thought of children plus fire will make some folks uncomfortable. I know that some would prefer to use battery-operated safety candles instead, especially since we sometimes see push-button votive candles in churches. But the Catholic Church has consistently required the use of real candles for religious purposes and especially for the celebration of the Mass. As recently as 2018, the United States bishops stated that for the sake of authenticity, electric candles should not be used in church.[8]

So we use real candles. Real candles mean that Advent offers a chance for my kids to learn how to strike matches or flick a lighter in a supervised environment. (It also offers a chance to learn when it is appropriate to use matches or a lighter and why it's not appropriate to do so at any other time!) The youngest kids get to light candles with help from a grown-up, but by the time they are five or six, most of my kids can light candles themselves without incident, and they take a lot of pride in it. And we always teach them to light the back candle before the front one—and to take it easy on the hair spray.

[7] National Conference of Catholic Bishops, *Built of Living Stones: Art, Architecture, and Worship* (Washington, D.C.: United States Conference of Catholic Bishops, 2000), 26.

[8] "Composition of Candles for Use in the Liturgy", United States Conference of Catholic Bishops, http://www.usccb.org/prayer-and-worship/sacred-art-and-music/architecture-and-environment/composition-of-candles.cfm.

We've made different kinds of Advent wreaths over the years, but a few years back we started using the eight-inch glass votive candles available online, at many dollar stores, and in the Latin-food section of many grocery stores. With the glass votives, there's no dripping candle wax and less of a chance of kids or their stuff encountering flames. But, of course, we don't leave lit candles unattended. Also the candles burn longer than regular tapers.

These votive candles come in various colors with various images. If I can't find candles without images, I just get the right colors (three purples and a pink) and soak the candles in cold water for about five minutes. Then we scrape the paper labels off using our fingers, table knives, and steel wool to remove the last of the glue. It does feel strange to scrape an image of Mary or one of the saints off a candle, but there's nothing officially inappropriate about it, and it's for a good cause! We just blow them a kiss good-bye and get on with the job.

If you can find only white votive candles, you can paint the glass jars, tie colored ribbons around them, tape colored paper on them, or decoupage them with colored tissue paper squares. It just depends on how crafty you're feeling!

We head out into the yard and gather whatever evergreens we can find, and we especially keep an eye out for seed pods, cones, and berries. If you don't have evergreens in your yard, a walk to a neighborhood park with a pair of kitchen shears might do the trick, and Christmas-tree lots often let you take trimmings for free. We place the four candles on a round tray and arrange the branches around the candles, attempting to keep a bit of open space in the middle. The branches can be wrapped with floral wire, which keeps them in the wreath shape, or left loose. I spray the branches with water each day, and if they start looking too dry, I replace them with a few new branches.

The traditional Advent wreath prayers can be found online and in some Catholic prayer books. We say the prayer and light the candles together as a family each night before dinner, or at breakfast if that's the meal when we'll all be together. Most wreath prayers include the suggestion that the youngest child, then the oldest child, then the mother, then the father light the candles for one entire week. But in a family with more than two children, it seems to me that method would cause unnecessary discord. So we just take turns lighting the candles. Usually the father of the family, as head of the household, would lead the prayers, but the mother or an older child can take over if that's what works. We keep the candles burning throughout the meal. One set of candles has always lasted all through Advent for us.

Straw for Baby Jesus

Another Advent tradition we love is Straw for Baby Jesus. The idea is for kids to learn about Jesus' words in the parable: "And the King will answer them, 'Truly, I say to you, as you did it to one of the least of these my brethren, you did it to me'" (Mt 25:40). Their sacrifices and good works during Advent, done for parents or friends or siblings, can help to create a soft, comfy bed for the baby Jesus when he is born on Christmas.

My dad built us a little wooden manger, but a small wooden crate or a shoe box wrapped in brown paper would work just as well. We put the manger on our altar table along with a jar of pieces of brown and yellow yarn—real straw would be great too. During Advent, if the husband or I see one of the kids doing a good job on a task or being kind to a sibling or doing right away what we've asked them to do, we tell him he can put a piece of straw in baby Jesus' manger. We also let the kids award pieces of straw to each other at evening prayers, if they've witnessed or been on the receiving end of acts of kindness. Then, last thing before bed on Christmas Eve, we bring the baby Jesus out (at first he was one of the girls' baby dolls, but we have a fancier breakable one now) and place him in the straw and sing "Away in a Manger".

It's amazing how motivating the straw is. The kids are getting *no* reward for themselves. They're not earning points toward a big prize. They're merely getting to put a piece of yarn in a box. That's it. But all our children, from toddlers to teenagers, appreciate being recognized for good behavior. We do systems like this twice a year, during Advent and Lent, and it's really helpful for resetting if the kids have fallen into bad habits and for reinforcing good behaviors. I think it's more effective, and it doesn't create a sense of entitlement, because it happens only twice a year, and for a set time.

The Jesse Tree

The Jesse Tree is an Advent activity that traces salvation history from Creation through the Incarnation using Bible readings and ornaments featuring associated traditional symbols, one for each day of Advent.

I support the Jesse Tree, but it's not a part of our family's Advent traditions. I made a whole set of ornaments and we tried it one year, but we've found that the Christmas Novena and the St. Andrew's Christmas Anticipation Prayer, which I discuss later in this chapter, have been a better fit for us than the Jesse Tree. But some folks love it, so you might want to give it a try and see if it's a good custom for your family.

Catholic New Year's Eve

The beginning of the liturgical year is the first Sunday of Advent. So *Catholic* New Year's Day isn't January 1; it's at the end of November or the beginning of December (it moves around a bit), when the season of Advent begins. "Advent is a period beginning with the Sunday nearest to the feast of St. Andrew the Apostle on November 30 and embracing four Sundays."[9] The first Sunday of Advent can fall as early as November 27 or as late as December 3, either during the weekend of American Thanksgiving or the weekend afterward.

I find it helpful that Advent doesn't usually start exactly on December 1, as it does on Advent calendars. It means we often get a bit of a window between the first Sunday of Advent and December 1 to get out the books and the calendars and the decorations and to make the wreath. It means Advent can have a rolling start.

We live near Pasadena, California, home to a very famous January 1 parade; and since we moved to Los Angeles over ten years ago, we've never missed one. We try to get the kids in bed at a reasonable hour on December 31, so we can get them up and going bright and early on the first. That means no countdown to midnight on that night for us. Instead, we raise our glasses and count the final

[9] Francis Mershman, "Advent", *Catholic Encyclopedia*, vol. 1 (New York: Robert Appleton, 1907), New Advent, http://www.newadvent.org/cathen/01165a.htm.

ten seconds before midnight on Catholic New Year's Eve, which is always on a Saturday.

The Mass readings on the first Sunday of Advent are all about vigilance and waking up and staying awake.

> Besides this you know what hour it is, how it is full time now for you to wake from sleep. For salvation is nearer to us now than when we first believed. (Rom 13:11)

> Watch therefore, for you do not know on what day your Lord is coming. But know this, that if the householder had known in what part of the night the thief was coming, he would have watched and would not have let his house be broken into. Therefore you also must be ready; for the Son of man is coming at an hour you do not expect. (Mt 24:42–44)

> Take heed, watch and pray; for you do not know when the time will come. It is like a man going on a journey, when he leaves home and puts his servants in charge, each with his work, and commands the doorkeeper to be on the watch. Watch therefore—for you do not know when the master of the house will come, in the evening, or at midnight, or at cockcrow, or in the morning—lest he come suddenly and find you asleep. And what I say to you I say to all: Watch. (Mk 13:33–37)

It really is the perfect night to try to stay up late!

A fun, easy, and relatively cheap way to celebrate is with a cocktail party. It is also very retro—and sophisticated. We offer a fun cocktail, ask guests to bring some appetizers to share, and play board games or card games or music. It's very low stress for a party.

Whether we're throwing an adult party, an all-ages party, a teenager party, or a just-family party, our one constant is a toast to the new year with champagne or some other bubbly beverage. One Catholic New Year's Eve, we were on a family camping trip in a national park for Thanksgiving weekend. I brought champagne and sparkling apple cider so that we could toast the new year after dinner. We did, but then we were all sound asleep by 9:30 P.M. So much for staying alert!

FEAST OF ST. ANDREW: NOVEMBER 30

The feast of St. Andrew the apostle is closely associated with the beginning of Advent and the new liturgical year. Because of where

he happens to fall on the Church calendar, St. Andrew is also associated with the Christmas Anticipation Prayer, also known as the St.
Andrew Christmas Novena—which is confusing because it's not a
novena (a prayer said for nine days straight) and it doesn't really have
anything to do with St. Andrew, other than that it begins on his feast
day. It is traditionally recited fifteen times per day, ending on Christmas Eve.

The prayer is as follows:

> Hail and blessed be the hour and moment
> In which the Son of God was born of the most pure Virgin
>   Mary at midnight,
> in Bethlehem, in the piercing cold.
> In that hour vouchsafe, I beseech Thee, O my God,
> to hear my prayer and grant my desires,
> through the merits of Our Savior Jesus Christ and of His Blessed
>   Mother. Amen.[10]

I have spent most of my Christmases living in Southern California,
where the weather can rarely be accurately described as "piercing
cold". The average low temperature for December in Los Angeles is
around forty-five degrees, which, as it turns out, is exactly the same
as the average low temperature in Bethlehem in December. So, not
"piercing cold" in the way folks are used to in Russia or Canada or
New York (where the prayer received its imprimatur in 1897), but
still cold enough that I would hardly like to be out in a stable having
a baby.

In any case, this prayer always gets me right in the gut. I love it.
Somehow it makes it all feel so real to me, how Christmas was an
actual historical event, this one amazing moment in time, in which a
very special baby was born to a very special mother, in very humble
surroundings.

The Christmas Anticipation Prayer is unique in liturgical traditions in that the prayer is said fifteen times per day for twenty-five
straight days. I don't know another tradition like it. But, even fifteen
times, it's short and quick. I keep a printout of the prayer in the car,
so we can say it if we're driving around. Sometimes we tack it onto

---

[10] Imprimatur: Michael Augustine, Archbishop of New York, February 6, 1897.

our family Rosary or say it instead of our family Rosary on a really busy day. We manage to memorize it pretty quickly again each year, and we've found that it's something we can do during the whole of Advent without much effort or planning.

To make it more meaningful, we keep a written list of all our intentions for the prayer. That way, all through Advent, we're focused on people and issues we care about and on using prayer as a gift to others.

If we forget one day, maybe we'll say it thirty times the next day, or maybe we won't. It's not a magic spell that you have to say just right to get what you want. The effort and the intent are what is important. Perhaps God will think it would benefit us to grant our requests, perhaps not; that's up to him. The goal of prayers like these isn't to conform God's will and desire to ours, but to conform our will and desire to God's.

And now, back to St. Andrew.

In St. John's Gospel, we learn that St. Andrew was a Galilean fisherman and a disciple of St. John the Baptist. As the two were standing together one day, they saw Jesus walk by. John the Baptist exclaimed, "Behold, the Lamb of God." And Andrew immediately began to follow Jesus, who said to him, "Come and see." That's just what Andrew did. He went. He saw. He spent the afternoon with Jesus. Then he rushed off to find his brother Simon and tell him, "We have found the Messiah." Simon went to meet Jesus, who immediately gave him a new name: "So you are Simon the son of John? You shall be called Cephas (which means Peter)" (Jn 1:35–42).

Andrew was one of first of the original twelve apostles. It was Andrew who told Jesus about the boy with the loaves and fishes when Jesus fed the five thousand (Jn 6:8–9). He was there at the Last Supper. After Jesus' Ascension, Andrew is reported to have preached the gospel in Romania, Ukraine, Russia, Istanbul, and Greece, where he was martyred in A.D. 60, by being bound—instead of nailed, to prolong his suffering—to a cross. He is said to have requested to be crucified on a saltire, or X-shaped, cross, because he felt unworthy to die in the same manner as Christ.

It's an impressive resume, for sure, but despite all of that, Andrew's most lasting contribution to the Christian faith was bringing his brother Peter to meet Jesus. Peter's important contributions to the life story of Jesus are well known, as is his selection by Jesus as the first leader of the Church, or pope. A few years after Andrew, Peter was crucified—not sideways—but upside down! It's rather symbolic of the way that Peter's accomplishments seem to overshadow Andrew's in every way. But none of what Peter did would have been possible if Andrew hadn't introduced him to Jesus.

The feast of St. Andrew is a great day to think about God's plan for our lives and how little things we do can have a huge impact on other people and on the whole world! Whom does Jesus want us to bring to him, so that he can say, "Come and see"?

St. Andrew is the patron saint of all sorts of things and places, but he is perhaps most famously the patron saint of Scotland. So in our family, our celebration of his feast day comes from the Scottish tradition. The Scots have a great devotion to St. Andrew. Their flag even features a white St. Andrew's cross on a blue sky!

For dinner, I make—and here's where I start losing you guys, and, really, it's a shame because we're just getting started—I make ... haggis. Wait, come back! Seriously, it's got rather a poor reputation outside Scotland, but it's nothing to be scared of. It's basically just meatloaf, with more presentation value. And more offal (organ meats), but since here in the United States you would have to get most of the really weird stuff off the black market, don't worry about it. Instead make your haggis with a couple of types of ground meat, some liver (or a heart if you're feeling adventurous and live near an international grocery store), and some oats. Totally not scary.

Now, if you want an *exciting* haggis, you have to cook it sewn up in a sheep's stomach or a beef bung; that way, when you stab it with your sword, it shoots out a stream of meat juices at you. I haven't felt the need to be quite that adventurous, so I just make the meatloaf part, form it into a dome, and cook it in the slow-cooker. It doesn't shoot juices at the boys, but that hasn't stopped them from enthusiastically stabbing it with a kitchen knife (because Dad won't let them use his Marine Corps sword, for reasons they choose not to be able to comprehend) as they cut and serve it. I've also steamed it, wrapped in parchment paper, in a pressure cooker, which makes for a slightly more satisfying first stabbing. The traditional accompaniment to haggis is *neeps* and *tatties*, and a dram; that's mashed turnips and potatoes, and a glass of Scotch whiskey. For dessert, Scottish shortbread cookies are tasty whether homemade or from a lovely plaid box bought at the grocery store.

Stir-Up Sunday

Stir-Up Sunday is a very British tradition. It's founded on the words "stir up thy might" in a traditional opening prayer (a Collect) of the Mass that we shared with the services of our Anglican brethren until the more recent revisions of the Roman Missal. Previously, the prayer was recited on the Sunday *before* the first Sunday of Advent, when Stir-Up Sunday is observed in the Anglican tradition. In our house, we observe Stir-Up Sunday on the first Sunday of Advent, when we recite the following Advent wreath prayer: "O Lord, stir up thy might, we beg thee, and come, that by thy protection we may deserve to be rescued from the threatening dangers of our sins and saved by thy deliverance. Who livest and reignest forever. Amen."

The story behind Stir-Up Sunday is that as wives and mothers and cooks and housekeepers sat in church and heard the words "stir up thy might", they were reminded to stir up their Christmas pudding (essentially a steamed fruitcake), so it would have time for the flavors to blend and mature. Back at home, everyone would partake in stirring up the batter, always from east to west, in honor of the Wise Men's journey in that direction. A traditional Christmas pudding has thirteen ingredients, one for each of the twelve apostles and Jesus.

I have to admit here that I have never made, or even tasted, a traditional English pudding. As an American, the idea of baking a dessert and leaving it to sit on the counter for a few weeks to improve is foreign to me. Perhaps one of these years I'll give it a try. But in the meantime, not wanting to miss out on Stir-Up Sunday entirely, I've used it as a chance to get a jump on the seasonal baking. We bake small loaves of quick breads, such as coffee cake and gingerbread, which I wrap up and store in the freezer as easy-to-grab gifts for teachers, neighbors, delivery guys, and so forth. And if I've got a couple of loaves left over, we've got our Christmas breakfast covered.

Choosing Saints for the Year

As a family activity for the beginning of Advent, we like to choose patron saints for the year. Each member of the family chooses one saint he already knows, usually his name saint, and one saint at random to get to know during the year. We have a four-volume set of *Butler's Lives of the Fathers, Martyrs, and Other Principle Saints* containing (often amusingly gruesome) biographies of nearly fifteen hundred saints. It can be pretty hilarious when the kids pick a volume, open to a random page, select a saint, and then read aloud the antiquated language. In this way we have learned about the "complication of other distempers from the inward bruises, which brought on a dropsy", which were suffered by Bl. Lidwina when she fell while ice skating;[11] and about St. Tarasius, whose virtue was truly great because it was "constant and crowned with perseverance, though exposed to continual dangers of illusion or seduction amidst the artifices of hypocrites and a wicked court".[12] Good times.

If you don't happen to own a nineteenth-century multivolume set of saints' lives, you can use other resources, such as the online Saint's Name Generator (http://saintsnamegenerator.com/), although I can't be sure you'll bump into Bl. Lidwina and her dropsy.

The next step is to write down the name of the saint, and his feast day, so it's not forgotten three minutes later. We keep the names of our patron saints for the year in a basket of holy cards and other sacramentals on our family altar table in the living room; some years I type them up and put them in a frame.

Saints of the Advent Season

The season of Advent has a *bunch* of saints to celebrate, one right after the other. Upon first look, it can seem like too much to honor them all, especially if we're trying to have a quiet Advent, focused on preparation and waiting. If you're just getting started on liturgical

[11] Alban Butler, *Lives of the Fathers, Martyrs, and Other Principal Saints*, ed. Rev. F.C. Husenbeth (Great Falls, Mont.: St. Bonaventure Publications, 1997), 1:456.
[12] Ibid., 255.

living, I would recommend starting with one or two of the Advent saints this year, and then adding more as it works with your schedule and as one of these saints gives you a little poke here or there to say hello.

Some years, with new babies or illnesses or big life changes or traveling, we don't get around to observing all these feast days. And that's okay. But many years we do celebrate them all, while still trying to keep our Advent quiet. The reason it works for us is that I try to tie many of the Advent preparations that I would be doing already (such as baking and decorating) to a particular saint's day. The goal is not to add extra stuff, but rather to give a little more meaning to the things I want to get done anyway, and to have a particular day on which I remember to do those things.

There's nothing like writing something down to give you a little self-awareness. I *say* that we avoid extra treats during Advent. My kids and I have always believed that we do. Yet, as I am about to describe how we celebrate the saints of Advent, the season seems like one long cookie party. But somehow, in practice, it really doesn't feel like that. The focus of all the baking is giving gifts and stowing away treats for Christmas. Usually when we finish making cookies for a Sunday dessert around here, we each have a couple right then, and we somehow manage to finish up the whole batch that day. But with our Advent cookies, we save one or two for each person in the family and eat them after dinner, after we talk about the saint. Then we save the rest for Christmas.

FEAST OF ST. NICHOLAS: DECEMBER 6

And now ... here comes Santa Claus. For faithful Catholics, there's a desire to get this right and a concern that getting it wrong will ruin our kids' faith forever. I've been asked the question countless times over the years in the lead-up to Advent and Christmas: Do our children "believe" in Santa Claus? But I don't think that's the right question. Not believing in Santa Claus is like not believing in George Washington, because both are actual historical persons.

Kids, and other people, are free not to believe in leprechauns or fairies (although I happen to want to believe in them myself) since the evidence for the existence of those creatures is tenuous at best.

But not believing in Santa isn't like not believing in unicorns; it's like not believing in Secretariat. I mean, you can doubt the existence of Secretariat if you want, but I would think it was weird if you did.

Santa Claus was born in what is now Turkey in the third century. He became bishop of Myra (more of his story later). Santa Claus was real. And he continues to be real and to exist because, as Catholics believe, he has an everlasting soul that never dies. The Catholic Church has recognized Nicholas, bishop of Myra, as a canonized saint, which means we believe that he is in heaven, where he can hear our prayers and intercede with God the Father for us.

This brings us to the follow-up question I am sometimes asked, which is whether we celebrate St. Nicholas instead of Santa Claus. And, if you'll forgive me, that's an even odder question than the first. Asking if we celebrate St. Nicholas *or* Santa Claus is like asking if we prefer St. John Paul II or Santo Juan Pablo II. In both cases, the two names belong to the same person, just in different languages. Santa Claus was derived from Sinterklaas, the Dutch nickname for St. Nicholas.

So, now that we have addressed the questionable questions, let's address the question people really *mean*, which is: Do we and should we allow our children to believe that Santa brings them presents?

We do. I think we should.

When Santa brings gifts to my kids on December 6 for St. Nicholas Day and on Christmas, it allows *me* to toil in secret and to experience giving without receiving anything in return. Not even the thanks. I think that's a good thing. "And you will be blessed, because they cannot repay you. You will be repaid at the resurrection of the just" (Lk 14:14).

I also think that getting gifts from St. Nicholas helps our children to understand that the saints are real and that prayers to them are efficacious—maybe not exactly in the put-chocolate-in-your-shoes way it might seem now, but it's a good start.

Here's exactly how we talk to our kids about Santa Claus:

- Santa and St. Nick and Father Christmas are all the same guy.
- He is a saint, so, like all the saints, he lives in heaven with Jesus.
- Folks say he also has a workshop at the North Pole, where he makes toys. (Maybe he has elf helpers; we can't know that part for sure. I've never seen an elf in real life myself.)

- He loves Jesus, so he wants to bring birthday presents to all the good boys and girls on Christmas Eve (and probably the naughty ones too), to help us all celebrate Jesus' birthday. Jesus is very generous, and, like hobbits, he likes other people to get the presents on his birthday.
- Reports are that he has reindeer that fly. Saints are sometimes able to do miraculous things, with the help of God. It is said that St. Pio could bilocate, St. Francis could reason with a ravenous wolf, and St. Joseph of Cupertino could fly all on his own! It's really not that big a stretch for us that Santa could have reindeer that fly and somehow manage to visit houses all over the world in one night. But, like St. Margaret of Antioch and St. George and their dragons, it's possible that it all means something else somehow.
- When Santa lived on earth, he was a priest and a bishop. Bishops can't be married now, but when St. Nicholas lived, that was allowed, so it's possible that there was a Mrs. Claus. But it's also possible that whoever made that book or show featuring a Mrs. Claus just doesn't know that he was really a bishop.
- Santa seems to visit most houses on Christmas Eve only, but, for kids who are waiting for Christmas and observing Advent, he also visits on his feast day, December 6, and leaves some extra little treats as an attaboy.
- Many countries, and many families, have different Christmas traditions. Santa is cool with that and abides by the customs and preferences of individuals. We are cool with that, too.
- We don't have to understand exactly how all this stuff works right now. Some things are mysterious. That's okay. Some mysterious things we won't be able to understand until we are in heaven with Jesus; other mysterious things we'll be able to understand better when we're older.

The key for us is to have Santa be a part of our celebration but not to make him the focus of our celebration or allow the commercial aspects of his secular character to overtake the most important message of Christmas, which is the Incarnation, that is, God's becoming man and dwelling among us. After all, we celebrate *many* saints in the lead-up to Christmas, not just St. Nicholas. This has meant that Santa makes our Christmas more fun and more reverent at the same time.

The truth of Christianity has a long history of *not* being defeated by fun customs and stories. It's only since the rise of some very vocal Evangelical Protestant sects that American Catholics have begun to worry that fun childhood traditions are somehow a threat to their children's long-term faith in Jesus and in truth in general. Historical anti-Santa sentiment is, in general, more rooted in anti-Catholicism than in pro-baby-Jesus-ness.

St. Thérèse of Lisieux, a saint who is the daughter of two saints, remembered enjoying presents from St. Nicholas on Christmas morning. "I knew that when we reached home after Midnight Mass I should find my shoes in the chimney-corner, filled with presents, just as when I was a little child, which proves that my sisters still treated me as a baby. Papa, too, liked to watch my enjoyment and hear my cries of delight at each fresh surprise that came from the magic shoes, and his pleasure added to mine."[13]

It has not been our personal experience that Santa's bringing presents to our children has made them less reverent or less trusting. It is my hope that fun Catholic traditions such as receiving gifts from Santa Claus, and all the other saints' day traditions we celebrate in our home, will make my kids understand and appreciate their Catholic faith all the more.

We now have older kids who know who's really bringing the presents, and it has been a painless and trauma-free transition from Team Little Kid to Team Parents and Big-Kid Helpers. My biggest kids now get to stay up late on Christmas Eve and help wrap presents in the special Santa paper, and help fill stockings, and help eat the cookies left for Santa, and so forth. So it's fun for them too, and they get to share in the joy of secret giving!

I have a general parenting strategy of avoiding Big Important Conversations whenever possible and instead handing out small pieces of the puzzle, one by one, and letting kids connect them. We allow our kids to figure out exactly how this whole Santa thing works on their own, just by giving them knowing looks and whatnot. We try to protect their belief in Santa until seven or eight or nine, depending on the child, and then we move them over to the Santa's Helpers

---

[13] *Story of a Soul: The Autobiography of St. Thérèse of Lisieux*, ed. Rev. T. N. Taylor, 8th ed. (London: Burns, Oates and Washbourne, 1922), 70.

team. Before then, we encourage their belief and keep up the fun by answering their questions in an open-ended way with possible explanations. After that age, if questions come up, I just give them a kiss and a smile and say, "That's a very good question.... What do *you* think?" We view it as a family game, in which everyone eventually gets to move from one side of the field to the other.

I love this quote from G. K. Chesterton, from an article he wrote for the magazine *Black and White*:

> What has happened to me has been the very reverse of what appears to be the experience of most of my friends. Instead of dwindling to a point, Santa Claus has grown larger and larger in my life until he fills almost the whole of it. It happened in this way.
>
> As a child I was faced with a phenomenon requiring explanation. I hung up at the end of my bed an empty stocking, which in the morning became a full stocking. I had done nothing to produce the things that filled it. I had not worked for them, or made them or helped to make them. I had not even been good—far from it.
>
> And the explanation was that a certain being whom people called Santa Claus was benevolently disposed toward me.... What we believed was that a certain benevolent agency did give us those toys for nothing. And, as I say, I believe it still. I have merely extended the idea.
>
> Then I only wondered who put the toys in the stocking; now I wonder who put the stocking by the bed, and the bed in the room, and the room in the house, and the house on the planet, and the great planet in the void.
>
> Once I only thanked Santa Claus for a few dollars and crackers. Now, I thank him for stars and street faces, and wine and the great sea. Once I thought it delightful and astonishing to find a present so big that it only went halfway into the stocking. Now I am delighted and astonished every morning to find a present so big that it takes two stockings to hold it, and then leaves a great deal outside; it is the large and preposterous present of myself, as to the origin of which I can offer no suggestion except that Santa Claus gave it to me in a fit of peculiarly fantastic goodwill.[14]

And now, back to the biography of St. Nicholas. There is a surprising amount of historical record about him. We know that he was

---

[14] G. K. Chesterton, "The Other Stocking", quoted in "Meeting of the WPA Chesterton Society", Western Pennsylvania Chesterton Society, December 11, 2015, http://wpachesterton .blogspot.com/2015/12/december-2015-meeting-wpa-chesterton.html.

born in 270 to a Greek family in the Roman Empire, in what is today Turkey. After his parents died, he was raised by his uncle, an archbishop, and he had a reputation for being a very devout child. He was ordained a priest at a young age. In the year 312, he visited the Holy Land; the Greek Orthodox Church in Jerusalem still has in its care a text written by St. Nicholas during that visit! He was consecrated bishop of Myra in 317. He is remembered as a good, faithful bishop, who helped the poor and needy and had a special love for mariners and children. He attended the First Council of Nicaea, where he was a staunch defender of Christianity in the face of the Arian heresy, which denied the full divinity of Jesus. He, like all but two of the bishops in attendance, signed the Nicene Creed, confirming what we believe as Christians. We still say the Nicene Creed at Mass each Sunday.

That's what we know.

Legends of St. Nicholas

There are also many, *many* legends about St. Nicholas. Maybe they are true; maybe they aren't. Maybe some parts are true, and other parts are exaggerated to make the stories more fun to hear. We can't know for sure, but we do know that these stories have been passed down from generation to generation because they can help us to understand something that *is* true, about the character of the saint or about our Catholic faith. It's also fun to know these stories because we can often recognize elements from them on holy cards, in stained-glass windows, statues, mosaics, icons, and other depictions of the saint. So here are some things you might see in a picture of St. Nicholas.

A baby turning away from his mother, holding up his hand to her

One story says that St. Nicholas was so devout that even as a baby, he would nurse only once on fasting days.

A bare head

In old images of St. Nicholas, he is almost always depicted as an old man with a beard, dressed as a bishop, with a crozier (the hooked staff a bishop carries to symbolize his role as a shepherd of his people) but no miter (the tall, pointed hat a bishop wears).

The saint's head is bare because at the Council of Nicaea Nicholas debated with the heretic Arius over whether Jesus is fully God (true) or whether he was created by God at some fixed point in time and is therefore only partly divine (false). St. Nicholas became so angry at Arius that he lost his temper and smacked him right across the face. Well, the other bishops knew Nicholas was right and Arius was wrong in the debate, but they were still shocked and disappointed in St. Nicholas' behavior, which wasn't fitting for a bishop. So, they confiscated his miter. He was put in jail, where the Virgin Mary appeared to him, gave him a talking to, then removed his chains, restored his miter, and sent him back to the council to make sure they got everything right about the divinity of Christ when they wrote the Nicene Creed.

A sailing ship

St. Nicholas lived in Myra, an ancient Greek town on what is now the coast of Turkey. Many people who lived in Myra would have made their living on the sea, as fishermen or merchants. There are stories of St. Nicholas praying to calm a storm while he was on a sea voyage and praying to make the grain last when they were nearly out. After he died, many sailors continued to pray for his intercession when they faced trouble at sea.

Three naked little boys in a wooden tub

If you've seen naked little boys with St. Nicholas in a statue or on a holy card, you've probably wondered what in the world could be going on. In the Middle Ages, the story was told that three little boys ran away from their homes in search of food for their families during a famine. An evil butcher saw them and tricked them into coming into his shop, where he stripped them down and trapped them in barrels of salt, intending to sell them as meat! St. Nicholas came to the shop, rescued the boys, and returned them to their families. And the butcher became Black Peter, St. Nicholas' servant, for the rest of his life.

Three golden balls

This is the story that is probably most familiar to us. When St. Nicholas was a child, his parents died, and he inherited their fortune. He preferred to live simply and eat little, so he spent hardly any of all that money on himself; instead he sought out people who needed his help and gave to them in secret. He learned of a man who had three daughters who were of marriageable age but couldn't afford to provide dowries for them. The man was poor and sick, and he knew that if he died and his daughters weren't married, there would be no one to take care of them. He prayed and prayed for a miracle.

St. Nicholas wanted to help, but he didn't want anyone to know it was he. So, late at night, he threw three bags of gold into the house, through the window or down the chimney, and the coins fell into the daughters' stockings, which were hanging by the fire to dry, or into their shoes, which were sitting by the door. In the morning the family found the gold coins, and the daughters were able to be married. In statues and paintings, the money is usually depicted as three gold balls.

Our St. Nicholas Customs

Letters to Santa

On the eve of the feast of St. Nicholas (December 5) our kids finalize their letters to Santa Claus. Now, if you'll recall, my goal is to get all my Christmas shopping done before Advent. As the toy catalogues start arriving in November, I let the kids look through them and start making their lists, so I have an idea of what they would like. By December 5, I'm finished shopping (I hope!), and it doesn't really make a difference what they write down. But it's still good to have the letters done. That way the children can quit talking about what *they want* for Christmas and focus on doing anonymous good deeds, St. Nicholas–style, for their Secret Santa sibling, and on making presents and decorations for the house.

They put their letters to Santa and one of their shoes—usually the biggest one they can find—near the front door or the fireplace, and then off to bed they go. When they wake up on December 6, they find that their letters to Santa have been replaced by a few little treats: some golden chocolate coins, a candy-cane crozier, a chocolate Santa, and so forth, and a new book. Often, it's a Christmas book, which is a good way to add to our collection of saint books and other Christmas storybooks, but sometimes it's just a fun new chapter book for an older kid, good for reading over Christmas break.

Portrait with Santa

December 5 or 6 is usually when I take little kids to visit Santa at the mall and have a picture taken with him (if I do so at all). Now, it could be awkward, because almost certainly the Santa at the mall doesn't know that it's his feast day, but my kids *do* know and want to congratulate him on it. But we just tell the kids that the Santa at the mall isn't the real Santa, of course. He's one of Santa's helpers.

St. Nicholas Cookies

Our main activity for the day is making and decorating gingerbread cookies. The tradition comes from such northern European countries as Belgium, the Netherlands, and Germany, and the cookies are called *speculaas* or *speculoos*. For St. Nicholas Day, *speculaas* are traditionally made using a detailed, hand-carved wooden cookie mold in the shape of the saint. You can still get those or less expensive resin versions, both of which create amazing-looking cookies. But you can also use regular outline-type cookie cutters to make plenty of shapes that would be appropriate for the day. Or you can create your own cardboard templates and use a knife to cut out the shapes you want.

I let the kids help make them—even though I would rather not. Most of our recurring liturgical-living-in-the-home traditions involve my cooking a regional food for dinner or a dessert or both, dinner conversation, and maybe a picture book. Involved crafting-with-kids projects aren't in our usual repertoire. During Advent, however, there are quite a few family baking and crafting projects that we come back to year after year. I always think that if we're *ever* going to do this kind of stuff, Advent is the time to do it. I want the kids to be involved in creating gifts for others, and *they* want to be involved in it too. So, even though it's messier and more time-consuming, and sometimes there is complaining or losing interest and wandering off, we keep doing it. Because kids don't remember that part, they just remember that for St. Nicholas Day they get to help make the cookies, and no matter how it may have gone last year, they seem to have fond memories of it.

Since we homeschool in the primary grades, I've always been able to adjust our school schedule to allow for seasonal projects during the day. Now that we also have kids in regular school and teenagers with complicated schedules of their own, however, I'm trying to find a new balance. Some activities I go ahead and do with just the homeschooled kids, which is fine, since the older kids got to do those things when they were younger, and now it's the little kids' turn. But activities we want to do as a family we schedule for a day and time that works for everyone. Remember, there really are no rules when it comes to liturgical living in the home. You get to do what works for you. I'm just *certain* the saints don't mind.

Back to cookie baking. I like to make a really big batch of dough (any gingerbread or sugar-cookie dough will work, even the pre-made tubes of it from the grocery store) so we can make lots of cookies. We eat some on St. Nicholas Day, freeze some for giving to friends and neighbors, and freeze some for ourselves for one of our twelve-days-of-Christmas treats. And, if it feels like a particularly do-it-yourself year, I put a chunk of the dough in the fridge (well wrapped in plastic wrap) for the feast of Our Lady of Loreto on December 10. More on that to come.

If you don't feel like baking, you can choose one or more store-bought cookies to decorate. Packaged peanut-shaped cookies or madeleines can be decorated to look like St. Nicholas' head and miter. Or you can use icing to draw whatever pictures or symbols you would like on square or rectangular cookies.

Once they're all cut out, baked, and cooled, you can decide whether you want to decorate them, and how. Some years we leave them plain, but most of the time we decorate them with royal icing, which is easy to work with and dries to the touch. For a traditional gingerbread-cookie look, you need only white. For a traditional St. Nicholas–cookie look, you need red and white. You can also go crazy and make multiple gourmet colors.

After dinner, we read a book about St. Nicholas—my kids like a creepy one about the evil butcher and the boys in the barrel the best, but something else might work better for your family. Then we recite the Nicene Creed and eat our *speculaas* with *bishopswyn* (bishop's wine), which is hot mulled wine for grown-ups and warm grape juice or apple cider with a cinnamon stick for the children.

We put all the leftover cookies in plastic storage containers, between layers of wax paper, and put them in the freezer. We'll take them out as needed, along with the little loaves of bread we made on Stir-Up Sunday and the other cookies we'll make for upcoming Advent feasts, to make up gift plates. And we'll save some for us for Christmastime.

FEAST OF ST. AMBROSE: DECEMBER 7

St. Ambrose was born to a Roman Christian family in A.D. 340. Legend has it that when Ambrose was a baby, a swarm of bees settled on his face while he was lying in his cradle, leaving behind a drop of honey when they flew away. His father thought it was a good sign and indicated his son's future eloquence and "honeyed tongue". I'm not sure that would be my exact reaction to a swarm of bees on my baby's face, but to each his own. St. Ambrose is usually pictured with a beehive and is the patron saint of beekeepers, bees, and candlemakers.

As a young man, Ambrose studied in Rome, impressed the emperor, and was appointed governor of Milan. In 374, the bishop of Milan died. Remember the heretical Arians who gave St. Nicholas so much trouble at the Council of Nicaea in 325? Well, those guys were still around, causing trouble and heated disagreements in the Church. Ambrose, as the governor of Milan, had a reputation for wisdom and good counsel, so he was asked to speak to both sides in the hopes of bringing them together.

He did. He spoke so eloquently, and with such respect for all involved, that both sides immediately called for *Ambrose* to be appointed bishop. The only problem was that Ambrose wasn't a priest, or even a Christian yet. He was a catechumen, which means he was preparing to be baptized. He tried to decline the honor, but even the emperor supported the decision, and within a week he was baptized a Christian, ordained a priest, and consecrated the bishop of Milan.

It was all part of God's plan, apparently, because Ambrose became an excellent bishop, supporting the poor, composing hymns, writing important theological documents, and effectively arguing against heresy. It was through his sermons, counsel, and friendship that St.

Augustine was converted. He and St. Augustine were two of the first Doctors of the Church.

Because of St. Ambrose's association with candlemakers, this is a good day to do a candle-related craft. We've rolled our own candles from beeswax sheets. These are available as kits, and you can even get them in pink and purple to use in your Advent wreath. They burn more quickly than regular taper candles, so if we burn them during dinner each night, we usually go through more than one set during Advent.

If you've got a box of old candle stubs (we do), a great way to use them up is to melt them down and make them into new candles by dipping or by pouring the wax into candle or candy molds. Added bonus: you get to feel like Ma Ingalls from *Little House on the Prairie*.

Another good craft for the day is tissue-paper candle transfers. These are easy and turn out looking quite professional, and they make great Christmas gifts for grandparents. It's also a good way to make a decorated Christ candle to replace the Advent candles once Christmas comes.

A tissue-paper transfer candle can be created using a white pillar candle of any size. Let your child write or draw with permanent marker on a piece of white tissue paper, taped to a piece of regular paper. (Be sure to protect the table and the kids' clothes from the marker.) Remove the tissue from the paper backing and trim the excess tissue paper from around the drawing. Position the tissue paper, right side out, on the candle, and use a piece of wax paper, pinched closed in back, to hold the design tightly around the candle. Using a heat gun or a hair dryer, heat the candle until the tissue paper melts into it, usually thirty seconds or so. Peel the wax paper back to check if the tissue needs more heat and proceed accordingly.

The Penitential Prayer of St. Ambrose of Milan is short and sweet and profound and excellent for any day, but especially for this feast day:

> O Lord, who hast mercy upon all,
> take away from me my sins,
> and mercifully kindle in me
> the fire of thy Holy Spirit.
> Take away from me the heart of stone,

and give me a heart of flesh,
a heart to love and adore Thee,
a heart to delight in Thee,
to follow and enjoy Thee, for Christ's sake, Amen[15]

For food, any dessert with honey in it would be quite appropriate. And, of course, there's always ambrosia "salad", if you're looking for a way to feed your kids more canned fruit, whipped cream, and marshmallows. Because December 7 is the vigil of the solemnity of the Immaculate Conception, it's traditionally a day of fasting and abstinence—like Ash Wednesday and Good Friday.[16] For a simple, meat-free dinner, if you add rice to minestrone soup, it becomes "Milanese-style". True story. Fitting for the bishop of Milan.

SOLEMNITY OF THE IMMACULATE CONCEPTION OF THE BLESSED VIRGIN MARY (HOLY DAY OF OBLIGATION): DECEMBER 8

The Immaculate Conception is a solemnity, one of the most important feast days of the Church calendar. And because Our Lady Immaculately Conceived is the patroness of the United States, it's also a holy day of obligation in this country. That means the faithful are required to attend Mass, as on a Sunday.

This feast can be confusing because many people think it refers to the conception of Jesus. The title Immaculate Conception, however, refers only to Mary and the belief that from the first moment of her existence she was preserved from original sin in order to be the mother of Jesus.

The original (or first) sin committed by the first human beings (named Adam and Eve in the book of Genesis) separated them and their descendants from God. Man, therefore, is born in a weakened state, prone to evil—you may have noticed.

Catholics believe that before God entered the world as a man, he first prepared his mother. Instead of being cleansed of original sin and

---

[15] "Penitential Prayer of St. Ambrose of Milan", Catholic Online, https://www.catholic.org/prayers/prayer.php?p=3082.

[16] See appendix A for more information on fasting and abstinence.

infused with grace at baptism, like the rest of us, Mary, like Eve, was created pure, in view of the foreseen merits of Jesus Christ. For this reason, Mary is often called "the New Eve".

The early Church Fathers believed that Mary had been "purified beforehand in both soul and flesh by the Spirit".[17] But it wasn't until 1854 that the Immaculate Conception was defined dogmatically by Pope Pius IX. It's a slow Church. A dogma of the Catholic Church, by the way, is a truth that has been revealed by God and recognized by the Magisterium as something in which all Catholics *must* believe.

In our home, we celebrate the Immaculate Conception by going to Mass and having a dinner of all white foods, such as chicken alfredo, cauliflower, and white dinner rolls. For dessert, I either pick up store-bought meringue cookies or make cream cheese mints (they're like the inside of a York Peppermint Pattie). The latter is a really quick and easy treat that doesn't require baking. Older kids can make them by themselves. The dough can be split and tinted in different colors, if desired. I like to leave them all white for the feast day; then I drizzle melted chocolate and red and green candy melts on top of the left-over mints and add them to the cookie stash in the freezer.

Our feast of the Immaculate Conception activity is a family procession. Processions are the *best*. We really should bring them back to parishes and neighborhood streets! But in the meantime, they are a fun, festive, and very easy way to honor Our Lady in the home. A traditional Catholic procession features one statue or image and a trail of people following behind it. My kids enjoy it a lot more, however, if everyone gets to carry something. We have a shelf of various figurines of Our Lady, collected in our travels over the years. So everyone chooses a Mary, and we parade around the house or the yard or both, grown-ups included, singing "Immaculate Mary" or "Ave Maria" and lifting up our little statues for the chorus.

Traditional prayers for the day are the Litany of the Blessed Virgin Mary (also known as the Litany of Loreto), which we pray on all Marian feast days, and the Collect from the Mass for this solemnity:

[17] Saint Gregory of Nazianzus, *Festal Orations*, trans. Nonna Verna Harrison (Crestwood, N.Y.: St. Vladimir's Seminary Press, 2008), 71.

O God,
who by the Immaculate Conception of the Blessed Virgin
prepared a worthy dwelling for your Son,
grant, we pray,
that as you preserved her from every stain
by virtue of the Death of your Son, which you foresaw,
so, through her intercession,
we, too, may be cleansed and admitted to your presence.
Through our Lord Jesus Christ, your Son,
who lives and reigns with you in the unity of the Holy Spirit,
one God, for ever and ever.[18]

FEAST OF ST. JUAN DIEGO: DECEMBER 9 AND FEAST OF OUR LADY OF GUADALUPE: DECEMBER 12

It seems appropriate to discuss the feasts of St. Juan Diego and Our Lady of Guadalupe together, even though they fall on different days. Their story is beautiful and touching. Every year we read Tomie dePaola's version, *The Lady of Guadalupe*. We also have CCC of America's cartoon video *Juan Diego: Messenger of Guadalupe*.

Juan Diego was a middle-aged Aztec peasant who lived during the Spanish conquest of Mexico. He became a Christian and, by all accounts, was a humble, pious man. He often walked many miles from his home in the hills to his parish church.

On one of these walks, on December 9, 1531, Mary appeared to Juan, looking like a beautiful Aztec lady. She asked him—in his native Nahuatl language—to tell the archbishop that she wished him to build a church for her. Juan said that he wasn't the kind of guy archbishops were in the habit of listening to, but she wouldn't take no for an answer.

As Juan predicted, the archbishop didn't seem to believe him when he related Mary's message. But none of that matters if God has chosen you to do something, especially if he's sent Mama Mary after you.

The archbishop told Juan to ask Mary for a sign, and Juan intended to do so. But then his uncle fell deathly ill, and he decided to care for

---

[18] "Proper of Saints", *The Roman Missal*, English trans. according to the 3rd typical ed. by the International Commission on English in the Liturgy (Yonkers, N.Y.: Magnificat, 2011), 1007.

him instead. He knew he would be in the soup if he bumped into Mary again, so he took the long way around the mountain.

Mary appeared to him anyway, with arms folded and one eyebrow raised, I assume. She chided him for not coming to her for help. "Am I not here," she asked him, "who am your mother?" She told him not to worry about his uncle and directed him to gather some roses he would find growing, unseasonably, on the mountaintop and to take them to the archbishop.

With roses wrapped in his tilma, or cloak, Juan Diego arrived before Archbishop Juan de Zumárraga on December 12. When Juan released the bottom of his tilma, everyone in the room saw not only the miraculous roses but also an image of Our Lady embedded within the fibers of his cloak. The archbishop was astonished and immediately knelt to venerate the image. Two weeks later, the first chapel was built on the site of the apparitions, and Juan's tilma was installed inside.

Our Lady of Guadalupe has become an important part of the religious culture of the Americas and has inspired millions of conversions to the Catholic faith. The image imprinted by Our Lady, despite being nearly five hundred years old, shows no signs of deterioration.

We have been fortunate enough to visit the shrine, which is just outside of Mexico City. It's a wild mishmash of priests and religious, people dressed in traditional Aztec costumes, pilgrims shuffling toward the basilica on their knees, music and dancing, colorful paper flowers, and photo opportunities with fiberglass donkeys. We saw the tilma and enjoyed the striking contrast of the new Basilica of Our Lady of Guadalupe, consecrated in 1976, next to the old one, finished in 1709. But the most moving thing for me was seeing the small dirt-floor room, adjacent to the first chapel on the site, where Juan spent the rest of his life, as the caretaker of the tilma.

St. Pope John Paul II visited the shrine in 1979 and prayed a beautiful prayer to Our Lady of Guadalupe. It's available online, and we like to recite it on this feast day.

Tamales

Because I grew up in Southern California, Our Lady of Guadalupe has always been familiar to me, as are many other Mexican traditions.

If you live anywhere in the southwestern United States, you probably know that Christmastime means tamales for those of Mexican descent. If you don't have a Mexican *tiá* (aunt) who throws an annual *tamalada*, a giant all-day tamale-making party, you try to find someone else's *tiá* who will invite you to hers or give you some tamales.

So, if you're looking for something *really* great to celebrate St. Juan Diego and Our Lady of Guadalupe, you can't do better than throwing a *tamalada*, in which different families bring different prepared elements and everyone hangs out while assembling and eating tamales. Enough tamales are made so that every family one can bring some home for later.

I've been lucky enough to be invited to a *tamalada* but haven't ever thrown one. Not having a *tiá* of my own makes me nervous about getting all the elements right. There *are* store-bought tamales available (but don't let a *tiá* hear you say that!), and there are plenty of other delicious Mexican dishes that don't take all day and the whole neighborhood to make. I'm pretty sure Juan Diego would approve of a taco night.

As a sweet treat, we like to have cookies and Mexican hot chocolate. Around my home in Southern California, you can find packaged Mexican hot chocolate in the grocery store. It's easy to prepare with hot milk and especially tasty if you take the time to froth it with a whisk or a hand blender. Regular hot chocolate with some cinnamon would do as an American approximation.

For one of the two feast days, I like to make a big batch of Mexican wedding cookies. My Midwestern mother-in-law is the one who introduced me to them, but she called them "snowballs". They are a fun, powdered-sugary treat and make a great addition to the freezer stash of Christmas goodies. For the other feast day, I might go authentic and make *polvorones de canele* or go slightly less authentic and make snickerdoodles; both are cinnamon-sugary delicious.

If you're looking for a fun group activity for kids, our favorite is a tilma-making party. I've seen crafty tilmas made of brown paper bags, cut to go over the child's head and hang over the chest and back, with no sides. Kids can decorate them with a printout of Our Lady of Guadalupe that they've colored. At a party we attended, the hostess provided inexpensive white kid-sized aprons with iron-on transfers of Our Lady of Guadalupe. The kids decorated around Our Lady with tubes of fabric paint. While the paint dried, everyone enjoyed some Mexican snacks and watched the video *Juan Diego: Messenger of Guadalupe*. It was a great time, and nearly ten years later, my kids still have their aprons!

It's a nice day to deliver some roses to a local shrine or statue or image of Our Lady of Guadalupe or to your mom. Probably there aren't a whole lot of dads reading this. But maybe if you moms happen to leave this book out, open to this page, with a subtle sticky note pointing right to this part, your husband will see it and help the kids find you some roses. After all, *are you not there—who are their mother?*

Last, and least, is something I learned from our beloved family babysitter when *I* was little, which is always to wear your hair in peasant braids on the feast of Our Lady of Guadalupe. I have no idea if this is actually a custom, or if she just made it up, but my girls and I are keeping up the tradition!

FEAST OF OUR LADY OF LORETO: DECEMBER 10

Let's discuss the baptizing of traditions for a moment. The Catholic Church is a universal church. In fact, the word "catholic" *means* "universal". Catholic missionaries have, through the ages, traveled all over the globe to bring to all people the mercy of Christ through the One True Church he founded.

When missionaries would arrive at a new place, however, the people there would already have customs and traditions, right? Some of them (human sacrifice, polygamy, etc.) would have to go. But others, such as a big yearly town festival or a custom of lighting candles in a wreath during the winter, aren't inherently bad and wouldn't need to be abolished. So the missionaries would find customs that could be reinterpreted in the light of Christ, and voilà! They became Catholic traditions.

There are some secular practices in the lead-up to Christmas that I don't want. Consumerism, greed, movies that glorify that stuff—we don't need any of that in our Advent. On the other hand, there are all the overtly religious traditions that I work hard to make sure my kids understand and that I want to be part of our Advent each year. We make those things a priority. But there's also the middle stuff—not important, but not wrong: snowmen, reindeer, gifts, particular stories, special cookies, and so forth. Those are things of which many people, with or without a religious tradition, have fond childhood memories.

I'm totally fine with my kids having fond childhood memories of that stuff too. But, if possible, I want to take a page out of the missionaries' playbook and baptize it. Enter the feast of Our Lady of Loreto ... and gingerbread houses.

The Virgin Mary was from Nazareth in Galilee. She lived in the home of her parents, whom we traditionally call SS. Anne and Joachim. This is the house where she was born, where Joseph would come to pick her up for dates—or however that sort of thing used to work. It was where the Annunciation took place. After traveling to Bethlehem and giving birth to Jesus there, the Holy Family fled to Egypt. When Jesus was still young, they resettled in Nazareth. During Jesus' public ministry, which began after he turned thirty, Mary was often present with him in and around Jerusalem, but we have it from his own mouth that "foxes have holes, and birds of the air have nests; but the Son of man has nowhere to lay his head" (Mt 8:20). So, Mary would likely have kept her home in Nazareth.

After Jesus, from the cross, gave his mother and St. John into the care of one another, tradition holds that they lived in Ephesus, and it is from there that Mary is believed to have been assumed into heaven. The house in Ephesus is believed by some of the faithful to have been found on the outskirts of the town, and you can go there to visit it if you'd like.

But what of Mary's house in Nazareth? *That* is believed to be ... in Loreto, Italy.

The story goes that after Jesus' Ascension, the apostles converted the home in Nazareth into a chapel, which was discovered in 336 by St. Helena (feast day: August 18), mother of the Roman emperor Constantine. A basilica was built around the house, and there are records of Christians worshipping there for nearly a thousand years.

During the Crusades in the late thirteenth century, Jerusalem and the surrounding areas were destroyed, and Our Lady's home was threatened with destruction by the Turks. So four angels picked up the house and moved it from Nazareth to a hill in Loreto, Italy, where it arrived, safe and sound, in 1295. In the sixteenth century a new, grand basilica was built around the small stone house, and pilgrims can visit both today.

While the Magisterium has yet to offer an opinion on the legitimacy of the possible home of Our Lady and St. John in Ephesus, there have been several papal bulls (official decrees) in favor of the shrine at Loreto. The earliest came in 1491, and in 2012 Pope Benedict XVI visited the shrine. St. Francis of Assisi and St. Thérèse of Lisieux both made pilgrimages to the house. Since 1920, Our Lady of Loreto has been officially the patroness of air travel, which is just awesome, if you ask me.

Despite getting the thumbs-up from various popes, there is no requirement for Catholics to have a devotion to Our Lady of Loreto or to believe in the miraculous angelic transfer of her house. Unlike with a dogma (such as the Immaculate Conception), Catholics are free to choose whether to believe in a particular apparition or miracle or personal revelation—even if it involved a saint. In fact, at least one pope thought it more likely that the other local story was true, the one that says the house was moved by the members of the Angelo *family* who on their return from the Crusades dismantled the house and brought it by ship to Loreto as a pile of stones. They then carefully rebuilt the house on a hilltop. That story isn't *quite* as fun, but it's still pretty cool.

Gingerbread Houses

Either story works for our activity for the day, which is making gingerbread houses. This is one of those activities that doesn't happen every Advent. It only started happening at all when some well-intentioned person gave us a bunch of gingerbread-house kits (and hiding them in the back of the pantry didn't make my kids forget about them).

On occasion we have made gingerbread houses from scratch with leftover St. Nicholas–cookie dough. This undertaking has been mostly a disaster that somehow comes together, kinda, at the end. Afterward I usually vow to use kits or graham crackers from then on. But after the memory of the craziness has faded a little, I'll think to myself, "Hey, we should make them from *scratch* this year."

The kids are game for however we end up making them, and they love the story of angels flying about, carrying houses. I like gingerbread houses as an Advent activity because we *make* them now, and use them as a decoration, but we don't get to *eat* them until they become one of our twelve-days-of-Christmas treats. It's all about the waiting, although a few candy decorations and fingers-full of icing have been known to make their way into little mouths.

FEAST OF ST. LUCY: DECEMBER 13

The name Lucy (or Lucia) means "light", which makes St. Lucy's Day a particularly welcome celebration for a dark mid-December day. What we know for sure about St. Lucy is that she was martyred in Sicily in 304, when the Roman emperor Diocletian was persecuting Christians. She is one of seven holy women who, along with the Blessed Virgin Mary, are commemorated by name in the Canon of the Mass.

Lucy was born to wealthy Christian parents, but after her father died, her mother fell very ill and, fearing that there would be no one to take care of Lucy after she was gone, promised her hand in marriage to a young man from a noble—but pagan—family.

After Lucy prayed to God that her mother would be healed, St. Agatha appeared to Lucy in a dream and said it would be so, because of Lucy's great faith. Lucy and her mom were pretty excited about it all, as you can imagine, and then and there decided to give away their fortune to the poor and to dedicate the rest of their lives to serving Christ.

But they had forgotten about Lucy's fiancé—dun, dun, *dun*!

He was furious that Lucy now refused to marry him, but he was especially furious that even if he could make her marry him, she had already given away her fortune. He denounced her to the Sicilian governor as a Christian, and she was brought to trial.

Governor Paschasius himself came to see what all the ruckus was about, and St. Lucy looked him right in the eye and announced that he and Diocletian would be removed from power and dead within three years. The governor was so angered by her predictions that he had her eyeballs poked out and handed to her before having her executed.

When Lucy's body was presented for burial, all of her wounds had been miraculously healed. And everything she had told the governor came to pass. Just a few years later, the Roman Empire was under the rule of Constantine (son of St. Helena), who in 313 legalized Christianity.

St. Lucy Crowns

There are celebrations associated with St. Lucy in Sicily and all over the world. But perhaps most familiar to Americans are the Scandinavian St. Lucy traditions. In the depths of winter in northern Europe, it's dark almost all day long, with just a few hours of twilight when the sun peeks over the horizon before setting again. It's easy to understand why they would seek out the saint of light!

In Norway and Sweden, girls dressed as St. Lucy, in white dresses with red sashes, march in procession carrying palms to symbolize her martyrdom. On their heads they wear a crown of evergreen branches, lingonberry sprigs, and tall white candles. The candles are lit. On fire. On their heads. Little girls. I love it!

You can make your own crown—starting, if you like, with a store-bought wreath or a specially made Lucia-crown frame—out of branches and floral wire. These days, you can get felt or battery-operated-candle versions of the crown. I think you know by this point how I feel about that sort of thing, but it's your call.

St. Lucy Buns

We have yet to make any flaming head wreaths around here. It's on my list. But we do really enjoy making the traditional breakfast treat of the day: *lussebullar* (Lucy buns). They are saffron-flavored sweet rolls, formed into shapes, the most common of which is a rolled *S*, with a raisin added in the center of each furl so that they look like ... Lucy's *eyeballs!* My kids love these. Funny, pious, educational, gruesome, and tasty all at the same time.

A real *lussebullar* recipe requires saffron threads, yeast dough, kneading, rising, and whatnot. I used to be very intimidated by the idea of yeast breads. But really, they're not *hard*, per se. They just require following the directions exactly and being around the house to complete the various steps between letting the dough rise. When

I was a homeschool-only mom, it really wasn't a problem for our schedule. And biting into a real yeast roll that I made with my own two hands—when I could barely boil water as a newlywed—well, it feels like quite an accomplishment.

Some years, there isn't time for homemade everything. But that doesn't mean we can't have our *lussebullar*. I have had great success using canned cinnamon-roll dough (be sure to choose a brand with dough that is actually rolled in there). Just open the can, separate the rolls, carefully unroll each one halfway, and then roll it up in the other direction to make an *S*. Place a raisin in the center of each furl—toddlers are great at this—and they're ready for the oven. It takes ten minutes. After they come out of the oven, we swirl on the frosting that comes with the rolls. They won't taste like saffron, but they'll remind you of eyeballs, and that's really the point. Mmmmmm.

Even without a white dress and a red sash and a candle crown, my oldest daughter and I have had fun getting up before dawn to make the rolls and then carrying them upstairs on a tray to serve the rest of the family *lussebullar* in bed! Of course, they also make a fun snack or dessert any time of day.

Baptizing another secular tradition, in honor of the saint of light, we light our outdoor Christmas lights for the first time on the feast of St. Lucy. We go for a drive around the neighborhood after dinner, singing Advent songs and admiring all the festive Christmas lights.

The week after the feast of St. Lucy is one of the four Ember Weeks, traditionally days of fasting and abstinence.[19]

FEAST OF ST. JOHN OF THE CROSS: DECEMBER 14

St. John of the Cross lived in Spain in the sixteenth century. As we can tell by his name, he had a love for austerity and a great devotion to the Crucifixion. While praying one day, he was granted a vision of Christ Crucified, in which St. John saw Jesus from above, as God the Father would have seen him. He drew a small sketch of it, which can still be seen today in Avila, Spain. In 1951, Salvador Dalí used this sketch as the inspiration for his well-known painting *Christ of Saint John of the Cross*.

---

[19] See appendix A for more information on fasting and abstinence.

Along with his friend and fellow mystic St. Teresa of Avila, St. John of the Cross founded an order of priests, nuns, and religious, called the Discalced (barefoot) Carmelites. Before starting a new order, they had tried to reform the existing Carmelite Order, whose rules and standards had become more relaxed over the previous two hundred years—what with wearing shoes and all. His attempts at reform, though approved by his superiors, were met with great resistance. Eventually, he was captured by a group of Carmelites opposed to his reforms and imprisoned in a six-by-ten-foot cell, with no lamp and no bed and no change of clothes. There he was beaten often and fed a meager diet of bread, water, and scraps of salt fish. He was kept there for nine months, until he managed to pry the cell door off its hinges and escape through a window in an adjoining room!

St. John of the Cross is considered one of the greatest Spanish poets. He composed his "Spiritual Canticle of the Soul and the Bridegroom Christ" during his imprisonment and wrote it by the light of a small hole in the wall, on scraps of paper that a guard slipped him. It's short enough to be read aloud as an activity for his feast day. Pope St. John Paul II decided to learn Spanish so he could read the poem in its original language. So, maybe that for next year.

I grew up with old-world foodie grandparents who regularly served things such as caviar and steak tartare and beef tongue and, once, an entire sheep's head at our weekly extended-family Sunday brunch. Our family also did some international traveling. And even though we were regular spoiled little American kids in many ways, it was part of our family culture to eat whatever weird stuff was on our plates. Food was always viewed as an adventure in our house. If you can eat only chicken nuggets and macaroni and cheese, your survival is dependent on your being able to find those particular foods. There is a cool kind of power in being able to eat pretty much whatever. The husband and I are trying to raise our kids that way too. (We have the benefit of, so far, not having any complicating food allergies or health issues in our family.) Saints' days give us a chance to try new and crazy—to us—foods together as a family activity.

Since St. John of the Cross had to survive for nine months on crusts of bread and scraps of salt fish, I like to serve a "dare you to eat it" appetizer of salt fish on crackers. Probably St. John had dried fish, but a tin of anchovies (fishier) or sardines (chewier and saltier) makes an easy-to-find-at-the-grocery-store substitute. The first time we tried it, we were all pretty wary of those little fish. Anchovies are whole, with the heads and everything! But everyone tried some, and most of the kids really liked them.

For dinner, you can't go wrong with a traditional Spanish soup. We like the Castilian *sopa de ajo* (garlic soup). It's a tomato and garlic soup with ham and whole poached eggs. It's quite different from standard American fare but not particularly challenging taste-wise.

For dessert, I like to add to our Advent cookie stash by making peanut butter kisses. The brown peanut butter cookie reminds us of the wooden cross, and the chocolate kiss on the top is for the particular love St. John of the Cross had for it. (Brown and black are also the colors of the Carmelite habit.) A good activity during family prayers is to venerate the cross, kneeling one by one to kiss a crucifix placed on the floor.[20] Usually we associate this practice with Lent, specifically Good Friday, but this day is a chance to remember that Jesus was born in order that he might suffer and die for our sins.

GAUDETE SUNDAY—BAMBINELLI SUNDAY

Somewhere amongst these feast days will fall the third Sunday of Advent, known as Gaudete Sunday because of the first word of the entrance antiphon for Mass: *Gaudete!* (Rejoice!) This is a day to celebrate that Advent is more than halfway over and Christmas is close at hand. It is one of the two days of the year on which the priest may wear rose-colored vestments, and *we* can wear pink to Mass as well! At home, we light the pink candle on the Advent wreath.

Since 2008, when Pope Benedict XVI revived an old Vatican tradition—which has been continued by Pope Francis—Gaudete Sunday has also been known as Bambinelli Sunday. On the third Sunday of Advent, children from all over Rome come to St. Peter's Square with a little baby Jesus in their hands, either homemade or from their family Nativity sets, and the pope blesses all the baby Jesuses!

Some parishes in Europe and the United States are picking up the tradition and encouraging children to bring a baby Jesus to church to be blessed after Mass (hopefully not during Mass: extra blessings like

---

[20] For more on how to do this, see the feast of the Exaltation of the Holy Cross on September 14.

that aren't properly performed as part of the Mass). Even if it's not something your parish does, there is no reason you can't bring your Jesus with you and track down Father after Mass to ask him to give you a blessing. Then, bring Jesus home and put him someplace safe until Christmas Eve.

We usually set up our Nativity scenes at the beginning of Advent, but with just the stable, the manger, the animals, and a shepherd. On Gaudete Sunday we like to add Mary and Joseph to the display. The journey from Nazareth to Bethlehem is about a hundred miles! Joseph was on foot and Mary was nine months pregnant, so we can figure the journey would have taken them between eight and fourteen days. If Jesus was born shortly after their arrival in Bethlehem, Bambinelli Sunday is a good guess as to when they would have departed from Nazareth. We wait until Christmas Eve to add Jesus, and we wait until Epiphany to add the Wise Men.

A fun dinner for Bambinelli Sunday is a traditional British meat pie. Meat pies can range from pie-shaped pies with a beef stew–type filling, to individual empanada-type handheld pies, to very tall, very decorated, very, *very* complicated concoctions filled with unusual game meats. But the thing that makes them appropriate for the day is that, before the Protestant schism, meat pies in England were made in an oval or rectangular shape, to look like the manger, and topped with a wavy crust, to look like the swaddling clothes.

If you've got a chicken potpie or a shepherd's pie recipe that you like, you can make it in a loaf pan, instead of in a pie pan, and voilà! You've got a manger, just waiting for the baby Jesus. Or you can make or buy individual meat pies or empanadas, and they're swaddling clothes, waiting for the same.

Any pink dessert is fun for Gaudete Sunday, and for the occasion I like to make a big batch of Christmas sugar cookies as the last of my Advent baking. We decorate some of them with pink frosting and sprinkles for Gaudete Sunday, which is always funny because we end up with pink Santa hats, pink reindeer, and pink Christmas trees. The rest are decorated as Christmas cookies and added to the freezer stash. If I've managed to do all the saint-day baking on my list, I now have mini-loaves, gingerbread cookies, cream cheese mints, snickerdoodles, snowballs, peanut butter kisses, and sugar cookies, and I can make up gift plates or tins for neighbors, friends, teachers, and delivery persons and, I hope, still have enough to serve a treat for each night of the twelve days of Christmas.

Christmas Novena: December 16–24

Of all the many things our family does during Advent each year, the Christmas Novena is the most meaningful and memorable. We've found the nine-day format to be much more manageable for our family than the twenty-five-day Jesse Tree. The set of prayers and readings we use in our family was composed by an Italian priest, Rev. Charles Vachetta, C.M., in 1721. I love the feeling of being united with the billions of Catholics who have prayed these prayers over the centuries.

A novena is any prayer or set of prayers said for nine days consecutively, usually ending on the vigil of a feast day and often prayed with a particular intention in mind. So a Christmas novena could be anything from a Memorare or a Rosary prayed each day for nine days, to a nine-day set of prayers and readings like the one we use, done in preparation for Christmas. It would normally begin on December 16 and end on December 24. But, because we have often invited friends and neighbors to join us for our novena, and most of them have other family obligations on Christmas Eve, we have sometimes started our novena on December 15 and ended it on the day before Christmas Eve. Again, we just do what works best for our family.

When we started doing the Christmas Novena, we were new to Los Angeles and to our parish, and we decided to use the novena as an opportunity to get to know some of our fellow parishioners better. I sent an e-mail to a few local families we already knew, inviting them to join us for as many of the nine nights as they were available, with kids in jammies, for prayer and a story and a snack. Then I reached out individually to a few people we didn't yet know well in the parish, whom we would see each morning at daily Mass, to ask if they would be available to join us for one of the nights.

It just so happened that the first few people I asked to join us were all international types, and it occurred to me that I could ask them to tell the children about Christmas traditions in their home countries. We could usually find two or three folks to join us each year and give the kids a casual little talk about their Christmas memories.

Christmas around the World

It became a wonderful experience over many years. It allowed us to get to know many people in our community whom we might not have otherwise known beyond a smile and a nod in the parking lot. And we got to learn about some amazing and very different regional Christmas traditions. It's how we learned that not all families and not all countries have traditions that include Christmas trees and Santa Claus.

Without looking further than our own parish and circle of friends, we were able to learn about Christmas traditions all over the world. One friend told us that growing up in Sri Lanka, where less than 10 percent of the population is Christian, they would bring large palm fronds into the house and decorate them as their Christmas tree. An Irish friend taught us that during Advent in Ireland, families leave a candle burning in the window to signify symbolic hospitality for Mary and Joseph. The candle is a way of saying there is room for Jesus' parents in this home, even if there was none in Bethlehem. On Christmas Eve, they set two extra places at their table, just in case the Holy Family stops by.

A Scottish friend who grew up without a religious tradition, but who is now a Benedictine monk (and the godfather of one of our daughters), told the kids a very moving story about one Christmas when he had wanted a shiny black bike with streamers on the handlebars, which he had admired in a shop window but knew his family couldn't afford. Then, a week before Christmas, his old bike was stolen! But, somehow, miraculously, when he woke up on Christmas morning, there was his own bike, back home—now shiny black and sporting a set of handlebar streamers.

We had friends from Argentina describe their summertime Christmas as an all-night beach party with barbecue and fireworks, and they even brought us homemade empanadas to try. Their Christmas presents are brought by the Three Kings on their camels on January 6. German friends told us that their presents were delivered on Christmas Eve by Christkind (the Christ Child) himself!

Mexican friends told us about Las Posadas, how the whole village would be involved for nine nights in reenacting the Holy Family's journey through Bethlehem. The children would knock on the doors of various homes and be told, "No room!", until they found the right house, where they would be welcomed inside for a party. They would find a different house with a different party each night, until finally, on Christmas Eve, the last house would have a big Nativity scene, and the children would put the baby Jesus in the manger before everyone went to Midnight Mass. Afterward, they went back to their homes for dinner and presents. On Christmas Day, everyone mostly just napped!

And, the most memorable of all—what my kids still talk about, years later—were the stories of a local parish priest from Uganda. His childhood Christmas memories included getting new clothes (but not necessarily shoes), all patients being released from the hospital for the day, and how, on Christmas Eve, the men of his village would slaughter the livestock just outside of town. The barefoot boys would bring the meat home to their families, using a stick to fight off wild dogs that were hoping to nab their own Christmas feast. Good times.

None of this really has anything to do with the novena itself, but if you can manage it, I can't recommend it enough!

The schedule that seems to work for us is to start the novena just after dinner, around six thirty or so. I have booklets printed up with all the prayers and readings, and we assign the roles and the readings to different people. The original novena calls for the readings to be done by the father and the eldest child, but we like to mix it up and let anyone who can read have a turn as one of the leaders over the nine nights.

We do the novena first, and, if we've got a special guest to give a talk, that comes next. Then, while Dad or a big kid reads a story aloud to the children, I, usually with the help of another mom or a big kid, set up a small snack for everyone. In theory, I stick to my rule about no Christmas treats before Christmas and serve things like cheese and crackers and fruit, but in practice, I sometimes find myself putting out homemade goodies that friends and neighbors have given us and that won't keep.

Whether it's with your whole parish, a few neighbors, or just your family, I really can't recommend the Christmas Novena enough.

Christmas Tree

Ah, the Christmas tree—can't have Christmas without it, can't put it up without worrying that you've done it all wrong somehow. When the husband and I were newly married, we did the what-everybody-else-is-doing thing and got our tree at the beginning of Advent. I had my third baby on December 2, and that year, I made sure we got our tree up and decorated the day after Thanksgiving.

But in all the sweet old-fashioned books and movies about Christmas that our family likes, getting the tree is something that happens on Christmas *Eve*. Elsa Chaney, in her 1955 book, *The Twelve Days of Christmas*, says, "Families living close to the spirit of the liturgical season do not, on any account, set up the tree and the other decorations ahead of time."[21] I can't help but imagine Ms. Chaney with a no-nonsense hairdo, but, also, I think she's got a point.

Now, I have to admit that sometimes the husband has to remind me that old-timey-ness is not, in itself, a virtue. I do think, however, that the shift in when we, as a society, have put up our Christmas trees is emblematic of the cultural shift away from observing Advent as a time of waiting and preparation. Longstanding Catholic tradition is to put up and decorate a Christmas tree after noon on Christmas Eve.

If we don't have a Christmas tree up, there's really no confusion in our home about whether it's Christmas yet. It definitely isn't.

What we like to do best is to go as a family and cut down our own tree on Christmas Eve or the day before. This avoids all the half-dead leftover trees at the Christmas-tree lots (although we have friends who regularly have gotten trees free or nearly free from a local lot on Christmas Eve). Full disclosure: most of the trees still at the cut-your-own place a day or two before Christmas are a bit wonky looking. But we don't mind having a tree with some character. We love it all the more because we choose it and cut it ourselves.

For the past couple of years, however, I've had to let go of the family trip to the Christmas tree farm, as fun as it was, because my oldest kids now attend a lovely Catholic school, and that lovely Catholic school has a yearly fundraiser that sells Christmas trees. So we buy our tree from them, in mid-December, and just keep it in a bucket of water on the side of the house until we're ready to put it up.

We have friends who do this differently. We know people who put up their tree at the beginning of Advent and use it in their Jesse

[21] Elsa Chaney and Jeanne Heiberg, *The Twelve Days of Christmas* (Collegeville, Minn.: Liturgical Press, 1955), Eternal Word Television Network, http://www.ewtn.com/library/family/12dayxma.txt.

Tree observation. We know people who put their tree up and wait until St. Lucy's Day to put on the lights, and until Christmas Eve to put on the ornaments. The Vatican tree has begun arriving in the square earlier over the years, but the lighting ceremony is left until a few days before Christmas. And the tree stays up until the feast of the Baptism of the Lord, which is after Epiphany.

I've said it before and I'll say it again: there is no section of canon law that tells us how we must observe feasts in our homes. There is no rule that says Catholics must have a Christmas tree at all, let alone anything that says when and for how long you must have it. But I would really, *really* encourage you to consider waiting to put up your tree, and even more importantly, if you choose to have one, to keep it up through Epiphany or the Baptism of the Lord. This was an adjustment for our family, and it felt like a big sacrifice for me at first. But in my case, it was a sacrifice that really bore fruit. It has made us more able to focus on the wait during Advent and more able really to celebrate Christmas. Just say no to sad, dried-out Christmas trees on the curb on December 26.

CHRISTMAS EVE AND THE FEAST OF SS. ADAM AND EVE: DECEMBER 24

The kids and I spend the days during the week before Christmas getting errands done and corners and counters decluttered. Any Christmas dinner preparations I can do ahead of time, I try to finish on the day before Christmas Eve. We usually have beef tenderloin, so I put that in a marinade and put it in the fridge. Au gratin potatoes and homemade cranberry jelly can be made ahead of time and put in the fridge. A birthday cake for baby Jesus can be baked, wrapped in plastic wrap, and put in the freezer, to be frosted and decorated on Christmas Day.

The morning of Christmas Eve we get the house tidied and ready for guests. According to an old Irish tradition, by Christmas Eve the house is to be thoroughly cleaned, all tasks finished or removed from sight, all borrowed items returned, and no task allowed to be begun that cannot be finished by nightfall. I love that. The idea is that we can't really focus on relaxing and celebrating if we can still see things that need doing. So, we get them done or we get them out of sight.

Half-done crafts and household projects are finished or stored in a cabinet. The kids' school books and bags are stashed in a closet. Out of sight, out of mind!

The Feast of SS. Adam and Eve

We all know that Adam and Eve were the first sinners. But did you know that they were also the first saints? It is the long tradition of the Church, both East and West, that Adam and Eve repented of their sin, worshipped God along with their children (Gen 4:26), were sanctified through hard work and suffering, which God had given to them as both a punishment and an opportunity (Gen 3:16–19), died, and entered into the limbo of the fathers. From there, along with all the holy men and women who died before Jesus, they were delivered by the Lord on Holy Saturday and now reside in heaven with him.

The feast of SS. Adam and Eve was an established tradition among Christians when Pope Gregory XIII commissioned the first official calendar of feast days, called the *Roman Martyrology*, in 1583. Focused on martyrs, that calendar included only a very few Old Testament figures, and Adam and Eve did not make the list. There's another possible reason Adam and Eve were excluded: apparently some of the medieval European celebrations for their feast day had gotten a bit out of hand and had to be suppressed by the local bishops.

The tradition for the day was to stage an elaborate Paradise Play, which acted out the Fall of Adam and Eve in the Garden of Eden. This play featured a tree decorated with red apples to represent the Tree of the Knowledge of Good and Evil, and a tree decorated with sweets or hosts (maybe *that's* what bothered the bishops) or both to represent the Tree of Life. They were called "paradise trees".

When the public performances were suppressed, people set up their own paradise trees at home on December 24. Our modern Christmas trees are likely descended from these paradise trees, and in Germany it was common up through the nineteenth century to place figures of Adam and Eve and the apple and the snake beneath or on the Christmas tree.

I think we can agree that it's good to have a day to remember the story and the lessons of Adam and Eve, but why December 24? It's a very mindful choice of the early Christians, because God's being born into the world is the beginning of God's answer to the Fall. As we hear in the Exsultet at the Easter Vigil Mass, "O happy fault that earned so great, so glorious a Redeemer!"[22]

The Story of Our First Parents

We've yet to put on a family Paradise Play. One of these years, perhaps we'll manage it. Until then, I use lunchtime to talk about the Fall. For lunch, each of us gets a shiny red apple and some peanut butter or cheese to go with it.[23] I read the kids the story of Adam and Eve from the Bible (Gen 2:4–3:24), and we talk about what went wrong there: listening to bad influences, not trusting God, not obeying rules, lying, blaming others for bad behavior. We do all this stuff too. There's nothing new under the sun, as they say. But also evident in this story is the great love God has for his creation, even in the face of baffling disobedience.

The story I tell the children goes like this. God gave Adam and Eve a paradise to live in, much as parents try to provide a happy and comfortable home for their children. He set up reasonable rules for Adam and Eve's safety and benefit. He explained the rules along with the consequences of breaking them—just as parents do. Eve allowed herself to be influenced by her curiosity and pride, and the lies of a flattering "friend" who never had her best interests at heart. Adam just went along with the crowd. He did it because everyone else was doing it (everyone else, at this point, being one other person).

Adam and Eve knew they had done wrong, but instead of trying to make it right, instead of seeking out God their Father, they hid from him. When they were caught red-handed (or leaf-skirted, as it

---

[22] "The Easter Vigil", *The Roman Missal*, English trans. according to the 3rd typical ed. by the International Commission on English in the Liturgy (Yonkers, N.Y.: Magnificat, 2011), 342.

[23] There is a long history in the Church of fasting before major feast days. In fact, until 1983, the Christmas Eve fast was still binding, which meant that on Christmas Eve Catholics would eat one regular meal and two small meals (technically, collations), all meat-free. It's no longer binding, but a simple, meat-free lunch and dinner is liturgically appropriate *and* practical.

were), neither took responsibility for his own wrongdoing. Adam said it was Eve's fault. Eve said it was the snake's fault. As a mother, hearing all of this seems *so very* familiar.

Then God, like a loving father, gave Adam and Eve punishments that could help them grow in virtue. He gave them their family relationships, telling Eve that it was through love for her husband that she would become a better person. He gave them physical suffering and told Eve that through the pain of childbirth she could become a better person. He gave them hard work and told Adam that the labor and the frustration of tilling the land would make him a better person.

Before the Fall, Adam and Eve could have lived in the garden forever, free from sickness, bodily infirmity, and death because of the Tree of Life. But after the Fall, God knew that they needed to die, so that eventually, after they were redeemed by Jesus' obedience and sacrifice, they could again live with God, this time in heaven. So he sent them away from the garden, away from the tree. But he gave them new clothes first. Pretty generous, all thing considered.

If you're really looking to tie everything together, this makes an excellent transition into making sure everyone's new Christmas clothes are clean and ironed and laid out for Mass!

Christmas Eve

In the afternoon, we hang the stockings and decorate the tree and the house for Christmas. We have ornaments that we've gathered over the years on our travels, or that have been passed down to us, or that commemorate births and deaths. It's a little walk down memory lane each year. Some ornaments have been given to a particular child. We set those ornaments apart, and the kids each get to put their own ornaments on the tree, plus some of the family ornaments. When our kids receive ornaments as gifts, I'm careful to write their names on them (inconspicuously) right away, because otherwise they get all mixed up with the others, and I want to be able to put together a starter set of ornaments to give each child when he has a Christmas tree of his own. We have a collection of unbreakable ornaments that are reserved for the bottom of the tree, at least as long as there are babies afoot.

For dinner, our tradition is to have a very international soup and salad. The Mexican *ensalada de Nochebuena* (Christmas Eve salad) is a festive mishmash of lettuces and fruits and veggies and seeds and nuts. And the German *spaetzle kartoffelsuppe* is a lovely potato, onion, and flour-dumpling soup from a recipe passed down by my great-great-grandparents. Serving such dishes is a way to observe the traditional Christmas Eve fasting and abstinence without guests even noticing!

After dinner, the kids put under the tree all the Christmas presents they've bought or made and wrapped. If there are any time-sensitive gifts from grandparents, we let the kids open those. One set of grandparents often gives them Christmas jammies, and the other often gives them Christmas ornaments, so those are best opened on Christmas Eve, in preparation for the big day.

Then it's on with the Christmas jammies and time to listen to stories. We read *'Twas the Night before Christmas* and the story of the birth of Jesus from the Bible (Lk 2:1–20). We say our evening prayers and get in those last few Christmas Anticipation Prayers. We award the last of the pieces of yarn for our Straw for Baby Jesus, for good deeds done during the day, and if there are still a few straws left, the kids run around trying to find more good deeds to do! It's super cute!

Then the baby Jesuses come out and are put into the Nativity scenes. Our life-size baby Jesus, who goes in the manger on the straw, is last. We all sing "Silent Night" and "Away in a Manger". The three Wise Men also come out, but they are put at a little distance from the rest of the figures, facing away from them (more on that later). We put out the milk and cookies for Santa, and some carrots and celery for the reindeer, and the little kids go off to bed. Then Santa's Helpers fill the stockings and assemble the some-assembly-requireds and eat the cookies. It's a lovely end to my favorite liturgical season!

To Sum Up

Advent is great. It's a beautiful time of year. It's the perfect time to start trying to add liturgical living traditions to your family life. But it can sometimes feel as if whatever we are doing is somehow not enough and too much, all at the same time. We all have different limitations in terms of time, talent, budget, and inclination. We face different expectations and challenges from extended family members.

The way we do it might not work for you. And that's okay. You have to do what works for you. But there are some points to keep in mind, I think, as you design your Advent plans.

1. Don't do Christmas yet.

This is the key. However you handle Advent in your home, it should feel different from Christmas.

2. Pray and prepare.

Advent is a great time for sprucing up the house. More importantly, it's a great time for focusing on adding a bit more prayer to your family's daily routine: the Christmas Anticipation Prayer, a Christmas novena, a family Rosary ... Or maybe you're just starting out with family prayer. Advent would be a great time just to try adding an Our Father to your bedtime routine. And maybe one Christmas Anticipation Prayer—that "in the piercing cold" part is so good.

3. Have a plan, and be flexible.

Real life very often gets in the way of liturgical living. And real life is particularly invasive around the holidays. Party invitations, extra work and school commitments, out-of-town visitors, or out-of-town visiting can all throw a wrench into our best intentions for a calm, recollected Advent.

If you're traveling and staying with family, and scheduling and traditions aren't yours to set, it might not be possible to avoid a full-on Christmas blitz before the big day arrives. And that's okay.

We have lots of family traditions and set plans for how we observe Advent. I know we won't always get to all of them every day or even every year, but they are still worth having and trying. Even a little Advent is better than none at all.

When we were a young family, we spent our Christmases visiting out-of-town family. It was great, but it meant we were pretty locked into the way our hosts wanted to celebrate. As our family grew, we made the decision to put down our own roots and establish our own traditions. We just announced one year that we were planning to stay put for Christmas, but that anyone who wanted to join us was welcome to do so!

We try to share joyfully our family traditions by welcoming people into our home throughout Advent, and all year long. I'm also happy to share ideas for how to observe the liturgical year with friends or family members who ask. But when we are in someone else's home, we just focus on being gracious guests. I'm pretty sure that's how Mary would handle it.

3

Christmas

That feeling of a child's Christmas morning: Who can forget it? There's no other morning like it. That's why, in our focus on religious traditions rather than secular, and on the true meaning of Christmas, I do want to leave room for *just* enough hedonism and excess to make the holiday memorable to my children in that visceral way I remember from my childhood—but without, you know, turning them into greedy, consumerist, secularists. It's a balancing act.

SOLEMNITY OF CHRISTMAS (HOLY DAY OF OBLIGATION): DECEMBER 25

Our Christmas morning begins at six thirty, which is the latest the kids can imagine waiting. We sing a couple of songs in the hall-way—"O Come, Little Children," and "Joy to the World" (the "Lord is come" one, not the bullfrog one)—and then the kids are released in a—mindful of little ones—frenzied mob to see what Santa has left for them in their stockings and around the fireplace.

Our younger kids usually receive a toy that they can play with, but the older kids often get tickets to a show or an amusement park that we can attend as a family—perhaps without the little kids—at a later date: not as fun to play with on Christmas morning, but in the long term, we have great memories and shared experiences on which we can look back together—and less stuff in the house. Santa is usually pretty good about putting a few little toys in the stockings of big kids, and maybe even the grown-ups, so we can shoot each other with little dart guns or race each other with little pull-back race cars.

And there are plenty of treats in there, plus a piece of fruit and ... a hard-boiled egg wearing a beard and a Santa hat, with a little drawn or painted face. The egg Santa hats were my grandmother's, and it's fun to keep an odd family tradition like that going for the third generation!

St. Nicholas always leaves our kids a handwritten letter, discussing the challenges and the triumphs of the year and singling out various kids for gentle praise or censure, as the year's naughtiness level has deserved. He always ends by encouraging all of us to be our very best in the coming year, to love God with all our hearts, and to emulate the saints in all we do.

After the Santa presents, we usually take a break for breakfast. I don't cook on Christmas morning, since there will be plenty of cooking to do for dinner. We just eat our candy and our fruit, our hard-boiled-egg Santa heads (trying not to think about it too much while we're cracking him open), and bagels or a loaf or two of the quick breads baked on Stir-Up Sunday and defrosted the night before.

Then we tackle the presents under the tree. Usually my parents spend the Christmas holiday with us, so on our most recent Christmas morning, there were thirteen of us around the tree. Despite my very concerted efforts to minimize the sheer volume of Christmas presents, with a present from Mom and Dad, and a present from each set of grandparents (although often the kids get a group gift from grandparents, which is great), and a present from Secret Santa, and homemade presents from kids to parents and grandparents and siblings, and an occasional grown-up-to-grown-up gift, that's still dozens of presents!

We could get through it quickly if we just all dove in there and started opening, but since we want our kids to focus on the joy of giving as much as, if not more than, receiving, we do our opening one gift at a time. That way there can be oohing and ahhing, and thank-yous.

We've got a Santa hat, and the youngest kid who can follow directions gets to put that on, go pick a present, and give it and the hat to the recipient of the gift. That person puts on the hat, opens the present, thanks whoever gave the present, and then picks the next present from under the tree to give to the next person, and so on and so on. When we get to a present with a tag from "Your Secret Santa", it's especially exciting, and there are especially big thanks, and the recipient makes a point of remembering aloud a few of the special good deeds done for him during Advent.

After the Gifts, Mass

On a regular Sunday, we usually prefer to go to a late-morning Mass. That time seems to work whether or not we have babies taking two naps and gives us time for a relaxing family Sunday morning. We stick with the usual on Christmas morning. Since we get such a very early start, we can usually be done with all the gifts in time to get chocolate wiped off faces and church clothes put on.

Speaking of chocolate, our standard thing to do with holiday candy is to transfer it from each kid's stocking or basket or pumpkin into a resealable plastic bag with his name on it. That keeps each person's candy his own and enables the owner to binge or save as he chooses, and to live with the consequences of that decision. But it also makes it easy for Mom and Dad to put the bags away in a high cabinet as circumstances warrant. We've found that little kids do better during Mass if they take a break from candy after breakfast until we get home from church. Then, if they want to eat the rest of their candy for lunch, so be it.

The kids are always excited to see their friends and the church all dressed up in Christmas finery. We try to arrive early enough to get seats up front—as is our goal every Sunday—so the kids can see what's going on. We use any time we have before Mass to look at the Christmas decorations and to say some prayers. Sometimes getting there early just doesn't happen. All we can do is our best. But it's good when we can manage it.

After Mass, as we always do, we stay in the pew until the end of the recessional hymn and then kneel to say some prayers of thanksgiving for three to five minutes or so. On a Sunday we would do this before the tabernacle, but on Christmas we go to the big Nativity scene and visit the Holy Family. The morning after a new baby is born in our family, the kids come to visit their new sibling in the hospital, so they have quite a bit of experience with newborns. As a result, more than one of my kids has wondered at the full, thick, wavy head of hair on the statue of the supposedly newborn baby Jesus. Then off they go to find their friends and share what they all got for Christmas and run around outside like a bunch of maniacs.

We get home from Mass around lunchtime, and we put out what my Mom calls "snack lunch". It's basically just an array of appetizers, to which folks can help themselves throughout the afternoon, if they're looking to supplement their candy. And it keeps foragers out of the kitchen, where the cooks are trying to prepare a fancy Christmas dinner.

In addition to the snacking, our Christmas afternoon consists of naps for little kids and pregnant ladies, board games, playing with new toys, and getting dinner on the table. We like to invite any extended family members we can get to come (unfortunately, we're pretty spread out across the country) and any single folks or young families we know who might not have family in town with whom to eat Christmas dinner. We've had years when we've had thirty or more around the table(s).

Christmas Dinner

I'm really not that creative when it comes to holiday cooking. We find a few things that seem to work, and then I just make them again every year. If we're having guests, I invite them to bring something to share if they would like. Normally, I make too much food anyway, so there's plenty for extra people.

Thanksgiving is turkey. Christmas is prime rib or beef tenderloin. Easter is ham. That way, over the course of the year, we've hit the main-course meat trifecta. I make a potato dish, and a vegetable side, and a salad, and bread. And then I really try to make myself stop. It's so easy to get carried away and want to make a ton of choices, but in my experience, that just makes more mess and too many leftovers.

I make an effort to choose dishes that can be prepared ahead of time and just popped into the oven that day, so my mom and I aren't hiding in the kitchen all afternoon while the rest of the family is visiting. I like to get in on the board-game action.

Birthday Cake for Baby Jesus

For dessert, we always have birthday cake. Sometimes it's fancy and seasonal, such as a yule-log cake or something peppermint flavored. Sometimes it's just a regular round, layered birthday cake. My favorite thing about this tradition is that it was started by the kids! When our oldest son was three and a half, he became indignant when he found out I was planning on making pies for dessert on Christmas, as I do for other big holiday dinners. We had been telling him that we were celebrating Jesus' birthday. So, Jack wanted to know, why didn't Jesus get a birthday cake? Well, I didn't have a good answer to that question. So that year, Jack helped with making Jesus a birthday cake *and* with blowing out the candles.

We've done a birthday cake for Jesus every year since. The children would really prefer that we put the correct number of candles on there. But a mom has to draw the line somewhere, so we do *not* do that.

I do as much as I can ahead of time. I bake the cake layers up to two weeks before Christmas, if I can, and wrap them in plastic wrap and freeze them. Then I pull them out of the freezer in the morning, unwrap them, and let them defrost. A yule-log cake can be baked, filled, rolled up, and then frozen. So all we have to do on Christmas Eve or Christmas Day is frost the cake and decorate it. I'm a bit of a stickler about the kids' birthday cakes. They get to pick the kind of cake and the theme they want, but then they have to let me alone to make it for them. That's the deal. But for Jesus' birthday cake, they get to help. It's usually a bit of a mess—made with love and all the birthday candles they can find in the house.

At Home Nativity Play

After all the Christmas dishes are washed comes the highlight of the evening: our At Home Nativity Play. It is so, so great. You're going to think it's crazy to try to put on a play in your house on Christmas. And then I'm going to spend many paragraphs trying to explain how simple it is, and you'll be more convinced than ever that this is complicated. But really, it does *not* have to be complicated at all. There's no memorizing required. The actors don't even have to be able to read. Usually, I'll read the part of the narrator, and for our littlest actors, I'll just feed them their lines in a low voice, one or two at a time, and they repeat them.

The first year we did the play, I spent some time during Advent creating and printing out the script, and making shepherd crooks and angel wings. Now we store those things in the garage, so we can reuse them each year. We throw up a very simple backdrop and gather some costumes and props made of household items. We can be ready to start the show in fifteen or twenty minutes. We enjoy the costumes and the stage direction, but you don't have to do even that much. There's no reason you can't just read the script together sitting around the table after dinner. But do consider trying to throw it together with all its big stick and T-shirt-turban glory. It really is a blast.

You can make a script yourself based on Luke 2:1–20 and Matthew 2:1–12, or use the *At Home Nativity Play* I put together. It's available online at CatholicCulture.org and as a booklet on my blog, *Catholic All Year*.

If you're worried about non-Catholic friends or extended family members getting weirded out by your foray into religious musical theater in the home, I understand. I've been there. But over the course of many years, we have done this little play with some of my family members who are agnostic and some who were raised Jehovah's Witnesses, and with the husband's not particularly religious coworkers, and in every case they were really good sports about it and participated and had a great time. And you just never know what's going to plant that seed that gets people thinking about their faith. Maybe it will be that time you invited them to be Wise Men.

The (How Many?) Days of Christmas

The days of Christmas used to be very simple and have become much less simple with modern changes to the liturgical calendar. I'll go ahead and explain it, because I am a person who likes knowing backstories, but the short version is that there can, technically, be up to twenty days of Christmas, and in the United States there can never be twelve. But as far as our family celebrations go, we just stick with the traditional twelve days.

From about the fourth century until 1970, the first day of Christmas began in the dark on Christmas Eve, and the twelfth day of Christmas ended on the evening of January 5, Twelfth Night, which is the eve of the solemnity of the Epiphany on January 6. (Our practice of beginning a holy day on the evening before comes from Jewish tradition and is the reason we have Midnight Mass, the Easter Vigil, and Halloween.)

In the current calendar, officially: "Christmas Time runs from First Vespers [Evening Prayer] of the Nativity of the Lord ... up to and including the Sunday after Epiphany or after January 6."[1] With the reforms of the liturgical year after Vatican II, in the United States, the celebration of the solemnity of Epiphany was transferred to the Sunday after Christmas. The Baptism of the Lord, which used to be celebrated on Epiphany, is now observed on the Sunday after that, *except* if Christmas falls on a Sunday, which means January 1 (the solemnity of Mary, Mother of God, and a holy day of obligation) is also a Sunday. In that case, Epiphany is moved to the next Sunday, and the Baptism of the Lord is observed on the next day, Monday. Officially, Christmastide ends and Ordinary Time begins the day after the Baptism of the Lord. So that means that Christmas ends as early as January 7 or as late as January 13, depending on the year, and can be between fourteen and twenty days long.

But there are no cute little songs about the "between fourteen and twenty days of Christmas, depending on the year". So, in our house, we just stick with celebrating the old-timey twelve days. The key thing to remember is that December 25, which starts the night before, is the beginning of Christmas, *not* the end.

We know families who spread out their Christmas gifts and open them for many days instead of just on the first day of Christmas. We know people who always spend the whole two weeks celebrating while visiting family or away on a vacation. It doesn't matter exactly what you do. What matters is that you manage Advent so that the days of Christmas are fun and exciting and feel like Christmas, with special foods and special music and special activities.

Our Twelve Days of Christmas

Our Advent wreath was a visible reminder that we were still waiting, so we like to replace it with a visible reminder that we are still

[1] *Universal Norms on the Liturgical Year and the General Roman Calendar*, no. 33, quoted in "Liturgical Notes for Christmas", United States Conference of Catholic Bishops, http://www.usccb.org/prayer-and-worship/liturgical-year/christmas/liturgical-notes-for-christmas.cfm.

celebrating! After dinner on Christmas Eve, we swap the pink and purple candles of the Advent wreath for a large white Christ candle in the middle. We light it for the first time at Christmas dinner and then use it as our centerpiece for as long as it lasts, at least through Epiphany, hopefully all the way through Candlemas (February 2).

Since we only just decorated for Christmas on Christmas Eve, all of it seems shiny and new. We've got the halls decked and the tree lit, and it looks and smells and feels like Christmas. For something a bit more interactive, I also get one of those little potted Christmas trees—you can usually get a really good deal on one if you wait until December 26!—and we put it somewhere very visible, such as on the kitchen table. Each morning, we sing that day's part of the "Twelve Days of Christmas" and add a matching ornament. With that, we are reminded for the day that it's still Christmas! When the kids were all little, and all early risers, it was easy enough to do as a family over breakfast. These days, with babies and toddlers up at dawn and teenagers using Christmas break to catch up on sleep, sometimes we don't do it until lunch, or even dinner. Sometimes we do it in two shifts. But it gets done!

We crank all of our Christmas tunes starting on Christmas morning and listen to them throughout the twelve days. It makes things such as doing the dishes after breakfast seem so much more festive. And it's not just music. The kids get to watch Christmas cartoons in the afternoons, even though it's not necessarily in our family routine these days to watch TV every afternoon. *Plus*, we all watch a Christmas movie together as a family in the evening, even though family movie night is usually a once-per-week phenomenon around here. We have a bunch of favorites that we plan to watch every year, and I try to find at least one or two new ones to mix in. But there's no leaving out an old favorite; they *will* remember.

Our older kids want to spend at least some of their school vacation time hanging out with friends, and that's fine. If they are invited to tag along on a friend's family's special event on a particular evening, it's okay with us if they miss one of our family movies. We're also happy to have their friends come over and join us for any or all of our movie nights. Especially in the teenage years, we've found that it's really a great idea to hang out with our kids' friends. Welcoming them into our family activities is an easy way to do that. All I have to do is be sure to have made plenty of treats.

We observe saints' and other feast days during Christmastide, but there's only one that has a specific dessert that I like to make for the day. Otherwise, it's time to pull all those cakes and cookies out of the freezer and give them away or eat them. If we start running low on treats, I can always make something new, but I can't remember ever having that problem. It's nice to enjoy the fruits of the work we did in the kitchen during Advent and to spend less time in there over the Christmas holidays.

Traveling Wise Men

On Christmas Eve, we added the baby Jesuses to the mangers of our Nativity sets. But *not* the Wise Men: those guys don't yet get to come to the party. Why? For accuracy in decorating, we think. The Bible gives us precious little in the way of specific information about the Wise Men. What we know comes only from the Gospel of Matthew and begins: "Now when Jesus was born in Bethlehem of Judea in the days of Herod the king, behold, Wise Men from the East came to Jerusalem, saying, 'Where is he who has been born king of the Jews? For we have seen his star in the East, and have come to worship him'" (Mt 2:1–2).

The Wise Men were magi. The exact meaning of the term is vague, but it seems clear that they were learned men and astrologers. The Bible doesn't say that they were kings or what countries they came from, nor does it say that there were three of them, just that they gave three gifts to the baby Jesus. In fact, there are early Christian paintings showing as few as two and as many as twelve Wise Men venerating Jesus. However, Catholic tradition has settled on three; has understood them to be kings from Asia, Europe, and Africa; and has called them SS. Caspar, Melchior, and Balthasar.

When the magi observed a new star at the time of Christ's birth, they interpreted it as a sign that a new king had been born and followed it. The Bible doesn't tell us exactly when they arrived in Bethlehem, but since the early centuries of Christianity, their visit to Jesus has been celebrated on January 6.

So, short story long, in the Catholic tradition, the Wise Men depart on their journey upon the rising of the Star of Bethlehem at the birth of Jesus. On Christmas Eve, when we put the baby Jesuses in the mangers of our Nativity sets, we put the Wise Men out a few feet away and facing in the opposite direction from the Holy Family. Each night, the Wise Men move—they're following the star, so they prefer to travel by night—until they've circled the house (or the yard) and come back to arrive at the Nativity set on the morning of Epiphany. Each day the kids get up and look for where the Wise Men have ended up.

Occasionally, the Wise Men will forget to move during the night. This can be very troubling to the children. It just means, however, that there must have been a sandstorm overnight, or one of the camels was sick, and usually they'll manage to make their move during the day, but always when no one is watching. Some years there are more sandstorms than others, but, somehow, the Wise Men always manage to reach their destination on time.

We have acquired quite a few Nativity sets over the years. We have one that goes on the mantle and a larger one that goes outside on the front porch, but we also have toy sets and a fancy crystal set, and a couple of the kids have their own sets that they received as gifts. Not *all* the Wise Men get to make the journey. In our house, only the mantle set and the outdoor set move. If the kids want to know why, I just tell them that ... I don't know why. But they are welcome to send their toy Wise Men on a journey if they would like. Sometimes they do.

So, regular Christmas tree, decorations, "Twelve Days of Christmas" tree, music, treats, movies, and looking for the Wise Men are the things that happen every day of the twelve days of Christmas for us. But there are also feast days! The saints whose feast days fall during Christmastide are referred to as the *Comites Christi*, or "Companions of Christ", and as such, they each have a place of particular honor. Let's take a look at them.

FEAST OF ST. STEPHEN—BOXING DAY: DECEMBER 26

On the day after Christmas, we celebrate St. Stephen, the first martyr. He was a deacon in the early Church who became the first Christian to be put to death because of his faith, three years after Jesus was crucified. After being accused of blasphemy, St. Stephen made the longest speech recorded in the Bible, in which he recounted the history of the Jewish patriarchs from Abraham to Moses, lobbed some well-timed insults at his accusers, and then was stoned to death. The whole episode was observed by Saul of Tarsus, a Pharisee who later had a rather spectacular conversion to Christianity and is now known as St. Paul. The story can be found in the Acts of the Apostles 6–8.

It seems counterintuitive to celebrate the death of a martyr the day after we celebrate the birth of the Savior. But, really, what we are celebrating on St. Stephen's Day is another kind of birth, the *dies natalis* (literally "day of birth" but meaning "birth into heaven") of the first Christian to follow Jesus' example of obedience even unto death (Phil 2:8).

St. Stephen's feast day, deliberately placed as it is on the Church calendar by the early Christians—as the Bible doesn't tell us the date of his execution—serves as a reminder to us that Jesus was born in order that he might die for our sins. St. Stephen, like Jesus, was wrongfully accused and wrongfully killed. And like Jesus, he died forgiving his executioners. In that way he is an example to us of living our lives in imitation of Christ. Although it is unlikely that most of us will be called to imitate Christ as literally as did St. Stephen, certainly we will have many opportunities in our lives to practice evangelization and forgiveness.

As St. Stephen was one of the first deacons of the Church, this has traditionally been a day on which to honor all deacons. If your parish is blessed with a deacon, this would be a good day to send him a card to tell him you appreciate the work he does!

Good King Wenceslas

Although his feast day is September 28, St. Wenceslas gets all tied up with St. Stephen on this day because of the popular Christmas carol written by John Mason Neale in 1853. St. Wenceslas was born in Bohemia in 903. His paternal grandparents had been converted to Christianity by SS. Cyril and Methodius, but his mother was a pagan. When Wenceslas was thirteen, his father, the duke of Bohemia died, and his mother became regent and began to persecute Christians within the realm. As soon as Wenceslas came of age, he restored and renewed Christianity in Bohemia. In his lifetime, he was just a duke, but the Holy Roman Emperor Otto I posthumously conferred upon Wenceslas the title of king, in honor of his wise leadership and heroic goodness.

In the Middle Ages, King Wenceslas became the ideal of the *rex justus*, or "righteous king", whose power comes from God and who is therefore a kingly model of piety, generosity, and courage. His care for the poor wasn't limited to December 26. In a biography written around 1119, it was said, "No one doubts that, rising every night from his noble bed, with bare feet and only one chamberlain, he went around to God's churches and gave alms generously to widows, orphans, those in prison and afflicted by every difficulty, so much so that he was considered, not a prince, but the father of all the wretched."[2]

The example of King Wenceslas is thought to be the origin of the European tradition of Boxing Day on December 26, when Christmas boxes of food, money, and gifts were given to servants and delivery workers. It all ties together quite nicely with St. Stephen, actually, as Stephen and six others were made deacons by the apostles specifically to address the corporal needs of the faithful, so that the apostles could focus on their spiritual needs.

We will have given gifts to the kids' teachers already, before Christmas vacation began, and we usually try to catch our mail carrier and all the package delivery guys with a gift of homemade treats during their very busy week before Christmas. On St. Stephen's Day, we like to make plates or boxes of treats for all our neighbors and go around and drop them off and wish them a very happy whatever it is they celebrate at this time of year. There is often enthusiastic, if not beautiful, singing of Christmas carols to go along with it.

Traditional St. Stephen's Day dinners are all about using up leftovers. You can find recipes for St. Stephen's Day pie and St. Stephen's Day stew, both of which are meant to be made with leftover meat and veggies from Christmas dinner. I have to admit, though, that I usually just reheat everything as is, and serve it again, rather than transforming it into pie or stew.

[2] Lisa Wolverton, *Hastening toward Prague: Power and Society in the Medieval Czech Lands* (Philadelphia: University of Pennsylvania Press, 2001), 150.

FEAST OF ST. JOHN: DECEMBER 27

St. John, apostle and evangelist, was born in Galilee six years after Jesus. He and his brother St. James were fishermen and disciples of St. John the Baptist. With St. Andrew and *his* brother St. Peter, they were called by Jesus to become his first apostles.

John, along with Peter, and sometimes James, was present at the most important moments of Jesus' ministry. He was there when Jesus raised the daughter of Jairus from the dead. He witnessed the Transfiguration and the Agony in the Garden. He traveled ahead to prepare the Last Supper, during which he leaned his head against Jesus and asked him who would betray him. He was the only one of Jesus' disciples who didn't cut and run during Jesus' Passion and Crucifixion. John was there at the foot of the cross with the Virgin Mary and the holy women. From the cross, Jesus gave Mary and John to each other, as mother and son. After the Resurrection, when Mary Magdalene discovered the empty tomb, John was the first apostle to get there to see it for himself, but he waited for Peter before he went in.

I love how the different apostles give us examples of different temperaments. Peter was loud and brash and impulsive, and a natural leader. Paul was exacting and studious.[3] John was quiet and contemplative and loyal. It's great when our kids can recognize some of their own personality traits in the saints.

John is the author of the Gospel of St. John, the three Letters of St. John (probably), and the book of Revelation. He doesn't mention himself by name in his Gospel, instead calling himself "the disciple whom Jesus loved".

He was the youngest of the apostles, and he lived to be the oldest, surviving his brother James by more than fifty years. He was almost a hundred years old when he died. By tradition, he is the only one of the twelve apostles to die of natural causes. But that's through no fault of his own. He survived being boiled in oil by the Roman emperor Domitian and drinking a cup of poisoned wine given to him by the same. His reward for having the gall to survive such attacks was to be exiled to the island of Patmos until the emperor's death. He spent many decades sharing the gospel and the love of Christ. St.

---

[3] St. Paul wasn't one of the original twelve but is still considered an apostle.

Jerome tells us that when St. John was a very old man and could no longer walk or speak in public, he would ask to be carried to visit the faithful, saying to them only, "My dear children, love one another."[4]

For dinner on the feast of St. John, we are often still working our way through Christmas leftovers, but if we're having guests, or if we've run out of leftovers, anything deep fried in oil always seems liturgically appropriate. You can even steal my son Bobby's joke for the day: "What's the difference between St. John and a chicken? A chicken cooks when you put it in boiling oil." Hilarious.

Blessing of Wine

More important than what one eats on the feast of St. John is what one drinks. St. John is often pictured holding a cup with a cute little dragon curled up inside, to symbolize the poisoned wine that didn't kill him. Because of the whole surviving-drinking-poisoned-wine thing, St. John's Day is traditionally the day to bring a bottle—or a few—of wine to church for your priest to bless after Mass. If that isn't done at your parish, you can always chase down Father after Mass and ask him to bless your wine for you. And while you've got Father's attention, give him a special thank-you, and perhaps a card or a gift, because, like deacons on St. Stephen's Day, priests are traditionally honored on the feast of St. John.

If you're not able to make it to Mass, or your wine isn't, you can ask God to bless the wine yourself, in your own home. Blessings are not just for priests. In our family, we always welcome the opportunity to have an ordained person perform a blessing for us, but we also take advantage of approved do-it-yourself blessings. The *Catechism of the Catholic Church* states, "Every baptized person is called to be a 'blessing,' and to bless.[5] Hence lay people may preside at certain blessings" (1669). As can be seen in Church law, however, certain blessings are reserved to the ordained ministry (bishops, priests, deacons).[6]

---

[4] Leopold Fonck, "St. John the Evangelist", *Catholic Encyclopedia*, vol. 8 (New York: Robert Appleton, 1910), New Advent, http://www.newadvent.org/cathen/08492a.htm.

[5] Cf. Gen 12:2; Lk 6:28; Rom 12:14; 1 Pet 3:9.

[6] *Code of Canon Law* (Vatican: Libreria Editrice Vaticana, 1983), cann.1168, http://www.vatican.va/archive/ENG1104/_INDEX.HTM.

Blessings are the most important of the sacramentals, which are special prayers, actions, or objects that, through the prayers of the Church, prepare a person to receive grace and to cooperate with it better. An example of a sacramental is blessing ourselves with holy water and the sign of the cross as we enter a church, to prepare ourselves to receive the graces of the Mass.

Some blessings, particularly those that dedicate or transform a person or a thing, are properly reserved for a bishop, priest, or deacon, as are any blessings performed within the context of a Mass or another formal religious ceremony. But anyone can perform "invocative" blessings, in which we ask God to bestow his blessing on a person or thing. Parents are encouraged to bless their children, we bless our food before we eat it, we bless people when we hear them sneeze. And on the feast of St. John, we bless our wine!

If we were able to get a priest's blessing earlier in the day, we skip right to the drinking part; if not, we use this prayer, and the head of the household blesses the wine:

Graciously bless and sanctify, O Lord God, this wine and this drink with Thy right hand, and grant that by the merits of St. John, Apostle and Evangelist, all who believe in thee and partake of this wine may be blessed and protected. And as St. John drank poison from a cup and was unharmed, so may all those who this day drink of this cup in honor of St. John be preserved from all poisoning and other harmful things, and as they offer themselves to thee in body and soul may they be free of all guilt. Through Christ our Lord.

ALL: Amen.

Bless, O Lord, this creature drink, which thou hast created, that it may be a salutary remedy for all who partake of it, and grant that all who taste of it may, by invoking thy holy name, receive health for body and soul. Through Christ our Lord.

ALL: Amen.

And may the blessing of Almighty God, of the Father, of the Son, and of the Holy Spirit, come down upon this wine and any other drink, and remain forever.

ALL: Amen.[7]

---

[7] "Blessing of Wine", Catholic Online, https://www.catholic.org/prayers/prayer.php?p =392.

Then, before we say the blessing for the food, we pour a glass of the wine. The husband, sitting at the head of the table, takes the glass and lifts it up to the person sitting to his right—that's usually me—and says, "I drink to you the love of St. John" and takes a sip. I answer, "I thank you for the love of St. John" and take the glass and take a sip. Then I turn to the person to my right, and we start over. Each person around the table, young and old, drinks from the cup (twice) and gives and receives the love of St. John. It's really quite lovely, and all the kids get a kick out of it, especially the ones who are yet too young to receive the Precious Blood at Mass.

If you're worried about allowing minors to drink wine, feel free to check the applicable laws in your state or country. However, most laws pertaining to minors and alcohol in the United States forbid the *sale* of it to minors or the *possession* of it by minors, neither of which would be applicable in this situation. In addition, most states specifically allow for the consumption of alcohol by minors in private spaces, under the supervision of their parents, and the First Amendment is understood to allow for the use of alcohol by minors in the context of a religious ceremony.

FEAST OF THE HOLY INNOCENTS—CHILDERMASS: DECEMBER 28

To discuss the Holy Innocents, we must return to the story of the Wise Men. We've already discussed how, in the Gospel of Matthew, magi from the East go to Judea in search of the newborn king of the Jews, "having seen his star" (Mt 2:2). King Herod directs them to Bethlehem and tells them to come back to let him know who this king is when they find him. They find the baby Jesus and honor him, but an angel tells them not to alert Herod, and they return home by another way.

St. Matthew continues:

Now when they had departed, behold, an angel of the Lord appeared to Joseph in a dream and said, "Rise, take the child and his mother, and flee to Egypt, and remain there till I tell you; for Herod is about to search for the child, to destroy him." And he rose and took the child and his mother by night, and departed to Egypt.... Then Herod, when he saw that he had been tricked by the Wise Men, was in a furious rage, and he sent and killed all the male children in Bethlehem and in all that region who were two years old or under, according to the time which he had ascertained from the Wise Men. Then was fulfilled what was spoken by the prophet Jeremiah: "A voice was heard in Ramah, wailing and loud lamentation, Rachel weeping for her children; she refused to be consoled, because they were no more." (Mt 2:13–14, 16–18)

These saints of Christmas week all gave their lives for Christ, but in different ways. St. Stephen is considered the first full martyr, being a martyr of will, love, and blood. St. John was not killed for Christ but still gave his life to Christ and to the gospel and is therefore considered a martyr of will and love. The Holy Innocents are the "first buds of the Church, killed by the frost of persecution",[8] and are considered to be martyrs of blood alone. They did not know Christ, they did not choose to die for him, and yet they did die for him, and what's more, they died *in his place*, which is an extraordinary honor.

In paintings of the event, it sometimes appears that the number of infants killed was in the hundreds or thousands. The population of Bethlehem at the time of Jesus' birth, however, is estimated to have been about three hundred,[9] so the number of male children under the age of two would have been perhaps six or seven.[10] Regardless, it's a very, very sad story. The haunting fifteenth-century Christmas song "Coventry Carol" isn't about the baby Jesus; it's a song sung by a mother to her baby, about to be murdered by Herod's men.

> Lully, lullay, thou little tiny child,
> By, by, lully, lullay.
>
> O sisters too, how may we do,
> For to preserve this day,
> This poor youngling for whom we sing,
> By, by lully lullay.

[8] Frederick Holweck, "Holy Innocents," *Catholic Encyclopedia*, vol. 7 (New York: Robert Appleton, 1910), New Advent, http://www.newadvent.org/cathen/07419a.htm.

[9] Gordon Franz, "The Slaughter of the Innocents: Historical Fact or Legendary Fiction?", Associates for Biblical Research, December 8, 2009, http://www.biblearchaeology.org/post/2009/12/08/The-Slaughter-of-the-Innocents-Historical-Fact-or-Legendary-Fiction.aspx.

[10] Ibid.

Herod the king in his raging,
Chargèd he hath this day,
His men of night, in his own sight,
All young children to slay.

Then woe is me, poor child, for thee!
And every morn and day,
For thy parting not say nor sing
By, by, lully lullay.

Lully, lullay, thou little tiny child,
By, by, lully lullay.

I have a hard time getting through this carol without getting sniffly. It would be easy to want to skip this story altogether and talk about Frosty the Snowman instead. You know your children best, and you're the one who can best decide when they can handle learning this truth about the story of the baby Jesus. But in our home, we do talk about it, with all the kids. We think it's okay for our kids to know sad stories, especially when we know that those stories have a triumphant happy ending.

We are sad for the cruelty and cowardice of King Herod. We are sad for the suffering of the families of those babies. But we rejoice for the Holy Innocents themselves, who were among the very first to enter heaven.

St. Augustine says:

And while [Herod] thus persecutes Christ, he furnished an army [of martyrs] clothed in white robes of the same age as the Lord. Behold how this unrighteous enemy never could have so much profited these infants by his love as he did by his hate; for as much as iniquity abounded against them, so much did the grace of blessing abound on them. O blessed infants! He only will doubt of your crown in this your passion for Christ, who doubts that the baptism of Christ has a benefit for infants. He who at his birth had angels to proclaim him, the heavens to testify, and magi to worship him, could surely have prevented that these should not have died for him, had he not known that they died not in that death, but rather lived in higher bliss.[11]

---

[11] Quoted in Thomas Aquinas, *Catena Aurea: Commentary on the Four Gospels, Collected Out of the Works of the Fathers* (Eugene, Ore.: Wipf and Stock, 2005), 82.

So, really, we are happy to see that the wicked Herod was tricked, first by the Wise Men and then by the babies themselves. Herod, who meant to harm Jesus and these children, instead gave crowns to the babies and saints to the Church. It's a chance to talk to our children about how God does not *will* bad things to happen, but he does allow them to happen, because of the free will of men. Through God's grace, we often see that good can come from something that seems nothing but terrible at the time.

There are some who use this feast day to draw attention to and pray for an end to the scourge of legal abortion all over the world. I can certainly see why, as those babies are innocent victims, as were the Holy Innocents. I think, however, that to do so takes away our focus from the most beautiful and meaningful part of the story of these children, which is that they were mistaken for Jesus and killed in his place. That is truly the glory of their story. We should all strive to live in such a way that we, too, might be mistaken for Christ. In the United States, we have a different day set aside by our bishops to pray for an end to abortion: January 22.

Childermass

Despite its heavy subject matter, because of the way King Herod was tricked, and because of the happy ending in which we trust for these children, the feast of the Holy Innocents, also known as Childermass, has traditionally been celebrated by Catholics with great silliness and frivolity.

In the Middle Ages, the day was marked by role reversals, in which children would be in charge of the home, and the youngest members of monasteries and convents would be prior or prioress for the day. There was even a tradition of having boy bishops in full regalia to preside over the day's Mass at the cathedral. But that one was met with disapproval and eventually suppressed by the powers that be.

These days, in many Spanish-speaking countries, *Día de los Santos Inocentes* is celebrated as their day for tricks and pranks, akin to America's April Fools' Day. Since the kids are off from school for Christmas break, it's a great time to play a little prank on them or to let them loose to play pranks on each other. It's a good chance for them to learn what kind of practical jokes are acceptable and how to trick someone without being unkind, destructive, gross, or too messy (in the house). You can find plenty of classic pranks online.

Part of the role-reversal tradition for the day was to serve "baby food" to everyone for dinner, which could be accomplished by serving the whole family a big pot of cream of wheat or oatmeal. For something a bit more substantial, but that still gets the idea across, I like to serve grits for dinner, with an array of toppings such as shrimp, bacon, cheese, sausage, and scallions. Or, since we aren't a family that ever makes a separate meal for little kids, and they're just stuck eating whatever the grown-ups are having, I might, just for Childermass, serve the whole family toddler favorites, such as chicken nuggets and applesauce.

As St. Stephen's Day is a day to honor deacons, and St. John's Day is one to honor priests, the feast of the Holy Innocents is traditionally the day to honor altar servers. If your children serve at Mass, or if you're involved with the altar-server program, this would be a great day to throw a party for all of them at your home or the parish. You could serve pizza or cream of wheat, your call, or you could take them to a bowling alley or a movie theater.

Finally, in the home, this is a day to bless your children. It's very quick and easy. Bring some holy water home from church in a jar or a bottle. Most churches have a holy-water dispenser set up somewhere for parishioners to access, or just ask a priest or someone in the parish office how to get some. If you don't have access to holy water, the blessing can be done without it.

The blessing should be performed by the head of the household, which would ordinarily be the father of the family, but whoever that is in your home can do it. Line the kids up and, one by one, dip your thumb into the holy water and trace the sign of the cross on the child's forehead, saying, "May almighty God, Father, Son, and Holy Spirit, bless you, my child, for time and eternity, and may this blessing remain forever with you." Any child old enough to play along can shout, "Amen!" in reply. Then move on to the next child. It's a beautiful family habit that can be done every night before the children go to bed, or once a week on Sundays, but it's especially appropriate on this day.

FEAST OF THE HOLY FAMILY

The feast of the Holy Family is celebrated on the Sunday between Christmas and New Year's Day. If Christmas and New Year's Day are both Sundays, the feast of the Holy Family is celebrated on December 30, a Friday (but it's not a solemnity).

Outwardly, the Holy Family wouldn't have looked like anything special: a mom, a dad, a kid; a modest, tidy home. But, of course, they were the most special family that ever lived. Jesus is the Word of God, who "became flesh and dwelt among us" (Jn 1:14). Mary was favored by God (Lk 1:30) and preserved from sin from her conception. Joseph was "a just man" (Mt 1:19) who got messages from God in his dreams. Let's be honest here: we are never going to reach their level of family perfection. But beyond the special graces given them by God, they also were holy in their *choices and actions and reactions.* And *that* we can emulate.

Mary and Joseph are models for all parents of piety, trust, and restraint. Mary submits to the will of the Father, which must have sounded pretty bonkers, when the angel Gabriel appears to her at the Annunciation. Joseph trusts God and marries Mary despite the unusual circumstances surrounding their betrothal. When a skyful of angels and various local shepherds and wandering kings show up to pay homage to her newborn baby, Mary doesn't flip out; she just reflects on these things in her heart (Lk 2:19). When an old man at the temple tells her that her cute little baby will mean a sword through her heart, she keeps her cool (kind of puts in perspective the "you've got your hands full" comment from strangers at the grocery store).

And this is the one that always gets me: when twelve-year-old Jesus goes missing for three days, and Mary thinks that somehow she has managed to lose not only her son but also the Chosen One of her people, she and Joseph frantically search for him. When they find Jesus in the temple among the teachers, Mary tells him that she has been worried. When Jesus replies, "How is it that you sought me? Did you not know that I must be in my Father's house?", Mary calmly accepts this answer and keeps it "in her heart" (Lk 2:41–51).

Jesus, though he is God, goes home with them and is "obedient to them" (Lk 2:51), not because they are smarter or more capable than he or because they are worthy in some way of his obedience, but just because children owe obedience to their parents. Love, understanding, obedience: in these ways, we, in our own families, can be more like the Holy Family.

The feast of the Holy Family is an opportunity to reflect for a moment on what it means to be a Catholic family. Every family, and each person in it, faces a unique set of hardships. But one of the most beautiful things about our Catholic faith, and one of the reasons I love learning about the saints and living the liturgical year in our home, is the wide and varied examples of holiness the communion of saints provides.

The feast of the Holy Family is a day to honor Jesus, Mary, and Joseph in our homes and in our hearts, and also to ask ourselves what more we can do to make our own families holy. It would be a perfect day to plan a special family outing or event or to invite other families over to celebrate with a potluck meal. Or, have an in-the-family potluck, in which each member of the family contributes one part of the meal.

Since the feast of the Holy Family usually falls on a Sunday, you can ask the priest after Mass to give a special blessing to your family. Or, at home, you can consecrate your family to the Holy Family. We are each already officially consecrated (meaning transformed by God and dedicated to him) by virtue of our baptism. As a pious practice, however, Catholics throughout history have chosen further to consecrate themselves to God through Mary or the Holy Family. Such a consecration gives us an extra inspiration and an extra example as we strive for holiness. A consecration can take place as part of a formal religious ceremony performed by a priest or can be done simply, at home, once or on a regular basis, with the head of the household reciting a prayer. In our experience, prayers and blessings are always improved by Dad's winging holy water around at everyone.

SOLEMNITY OF MARY, MOTHER OF GOD (HOLY DAY OF OBLIGATION): JANUARY 1

January 1 is the eighth day after the feast of the Nativity and ends the octave of Christmas. It commemorates the day when Jesus was circumcised and formally given his name according to Jewish tradition. The day is considered noteworthy in that it was the first time that

Jesus' blood was spilled, thus beginning the process of the redemption of mankind. It also is understood to be a demonstration of Jesus' humanity and of his submission to the Mosaic Law.

In the early days of Christianity, this eighth day, celebrated in honor of the motherhood of Mary, was the first Marian feast day to be officially observed. From the thirteenth or fourteenth century on, while continuing to honor Mary, the focus instead was on the circumcision and the naming of Jesus. But in the 1969 revision of the calendar, the Marian feast was restored and January 3 was made the feast of the Holy Name of Jesus.

While other Marian feasts celebrate events in the life of Mary, such as the Annunciation or the Assumption, or apparitions, such as Our Lady of Lourdes or Our Lady of Fatima, this feast celebrates Mary as the Mother of God. Pope Paul VI explained:

> This celebration, placed on January 1 in conformity with the ancient indication of the liturgy of the City of Rome, is meant to commemorate the part played by Mary in this mystery of salvation. It is meant also to exalt the singular dignity which this mystery brings to the "holy Mother...through whom we were found worthy to receive the Author of life"(*Roman Missal*, 1 January, Entry antiphon and Collect). It is likewise a fitting occasion for renewing adoration of the newborn Prince of Peace, for listening once more to the glad tidings of the angels (cf. Lk. 2:14), and for imploring from God, through the Queen of Peace, the supreme gift of peace.[12]

This solemnity is one of the six holy days of obligation observed each year in the United States. When January 1 falls on a Saturday or Monday, however, the obligation to attend Mass is normally abrogated.

We live in Los Angeles, and, as a family, we've always attended the Rose Parade on New Year's Day. But we find an early Mass that we can attend on the way to the parade. Even in years when attendance isn't mandatory, we always find a Mass to go to. It really does feel

---

[12] Paul VI, apostolic exhortation *Marialis cultus* (February 2, 1974), no. 5, http://w2.vatican .va/content/paul-vi/en/apost_exhortations/documents/hf_p-vi_exh_19740202_marialis -cultus.html.

fitting to start the new calendar year by going to Mass and honoring Our Lady. *Then* we have fun at the parade.

A plenary (or full) indulgence is available for anyone who sings or recites the hymn "Veni Creator Spiritus" ("Come, Holy Spirit, Creator Blest") on the first day of the year.[13] This hymn is traditionally sung for beginnings of things, calling on the Holy Spirit before endeavoring something new.

Apparently, in many European countries, the traditional dinner for the solemnity of Mary, Mother of God, was a whole suckling pig. To remind us of motherhood, I guess? That sounds very dramatic, and I'm sure it would make quite an impression on my kids if I were to pull one of those babies (literally) out of the oven while everyone is hanging out watching football. Maybe one of these years I'll give it a try. In the meantime, I think a corn dog is a reasonable approximation!

FEAST OF THE MOST HOLY NAME OF JESUS: JANUARY 3

The entire month of January is devoted to the Holy Name of Jesus. St. Paul tells us that because of Jesus' obedience to the will of the Father, "God has highly exalted him and bestowed on him the name which is above every name, that at the name of Jesus every knee should bow, in heaven and on earth and under the earth, and every tongue confess that Jesus Christ is Lord, to the glory of God the Father" (Phil 2:9–11). Appropriate for this feast is the Litany of the Holy Name. It's long, but there's a partial indulgence in it for you![14]

Something to consider doing for this feast—and from now on!—is to avoid taking the Lord's name in vain in all forms. In our house we don't say or type (right now excluded) "Oh God", "O my God", "Jesus", and so forth, unless it's part of a prayer. We also avoid cutesy alternates such as "Oh my gosh" and "jeez", since, really, those are just substitutes and mean the same thing. We don't use "OMG", even ironically. It took some getting used to, but now I don't even miss them, as it turns out there are plenty of other ways to express myself.

---

[13] See appendix B for more information on indulgences.
[14] See appendix B for more information on indulgences.

Once we had managed to stop using those expressions, we began the practice of saying a quick, quiet prayer of reparation whenever we hear or see someone taking the Lord's name in vain. The words of Jesus are good for this: "Father, forgive them; for they know not what they do" (Lk 23:34). Or the words of Job: "Blessed be the name of the LORD" (Job 1:21).

I like to serve alphabet soup for dinner. Around the table we talk about how special each of our names is, and how we got them, and see what names we can find in our soup. Full disclosure: it definitely involves some fingers in the soup.

FEAST OF ST. ELIZABETH ANN SETON: JANUARY 4

St. Elizabeth Ann Seton was born on the cusp of the American Revolution on August 28, 1774, in New York City. She was raised Episcopalian, married a businessman at age nineteen, and with him had five children. After the death of her father-in-law, she and her husband also became guardians of his six younger siblings, aged seven to seventeen.

At the age of twenty-nine, she became a widow—with eleven children—and started a boarding school for girls in order to support her family. About a year later, she converted to Catholicism, along with her children. As a result, most of the parents of her pupils withdrew them from her school. She was about to give up on teaching altogether when she met a priest who was the president of St. Mary's College and Seminary in Baltimore. He had for some time been envisioning a system of specifically Catholic education in the United States, and he encouraged Elizabeth to begin what became the first institution of the Catholic parochial school system in the United States. She also established a religious community in Emmitsburg, Maryland, the first order of sisters to be founded in the United States. She died in 1821, and by 1830, her congregation was running schools all over the country, as far west as Cincinnati and New Orleans. She is the first American-born canonized saint (not the earliest to live, just the first to be canonized).

A colonial recipe, such as brisket or quail or fish mousse or something, or some Maryland blue crabs, would be authentic for the day, but what *we* like to have is a New York feast of thin-crust pizza followed by cherry cheesecake. Another option for dessert is the black and white cookie, appropriate both for being a New York favorite and for being reminiscent of the habit of the Daughters of Charity. It's very likely that if Mother Seton had ever tried New York pizza or cheesecake or black and white cookies, she would have been a fan. And we pray for teachers, especially Catholic school teachers.

FEAST OF ST. JOHN NEUMANN: JANUARY 5

St. John Neumann (pronounced "*Noy*-mun"), bishop, whose feast day is the day after Mother Seton's, continued the work of Catholic education she began. He was born in 1811 in Bohemia. He studied for the priesthood, but his bishop would not ordain him because he thought there were enough priests in his country. So, in 1836, he emigrated to the United States and was ordained in New York. He later joined the Redemptorist Order. Eventually he became the fourth bishop of Philadelphia. As bishop, he lived frugally, supported the poor, and worked to combat anti-Catholic and anti-immigrant sentiment. He established the first diocesan Catholic school system. He died in 1860 and is the only male United States citizen to have been canonized (so far).

For dinner we like to have Philly cheesesteak sandwiches and, for dessert, leftover cheesecake from yesterday. We say a special prayer for school administrators and for our Catholic school.

SOLEMNITY OF THE EPIPHANY OF THE LORD: JANUARY 6 (OR THE SUNDAY AFTER JANUARY 1)

The traditional date of Epiphany is January 6, and the eve of Epiphany is the traditional end of the celebration of the twelve days of Christmas. Shakespeare's *Twelfth Night*, a comedy involving trickery and romance and mistaken identities, was written to celebrate the end of the twelve days of revelry of the Christmas season. Since the 1969 liturgical-calendar revision, however, in most countries the observance of this feast has been transferred to the Sunday after January 1.

The traditionalist in me wants to have an unambiguous twelve days of Christmas and an old-timey Twelfth Night, whenever it may fall. However, as I don't live and work in a feudal system in which the lord of the manor is bound to give us a holiday from Christmas

Eve through Plough Monday,[15] my more practical side appreciates having a weekend to throw a party for friends, a Saturday to take down Christmas decorations, and a Sunday with the family together to celebrate the feast of Epiphany and all the fun traditions that go along with it. And even though we talk a lot about the twelve days of Christmas in our house, to emphasize that it's a season, rather than just a day, no one ever complains if we add a couple more days of Christmas onto the end there.

In years when the new calendar moves Epiphany up (it can fall as early as January 2), we observe all of our Epiphany Day traditions on that day, but we wait to stop our Christmas festivities and put away our Christmas decorations until the next weekend, on which we celebrate the Baptism of the Lord, the liturgical end of the Christmas season.

As noted previously, between Christmas and Epiphany we sing "The Twelve Days of Christmas" and put the corresponding ornaments on our little tree. We listen to Christmas carols, watch Christmas movies, eat treats, and follow the Wise Men on their journey.

During these festive days, I try to cut the kids some slack on their chores. We can't dissolve into complete sloth and anarchy, but while I'm usually a stickler for getting dressed and making beds first thing in the morning, and never leaving toys out, over Christmastide I can live with some lounging in pajamas until midmorning, some unmade beds, and all the new Christmas toys still in the living room.

White Elephant Party

On or around Twelfth Night, we like to throw one last Christmas party and invite a few friends over to remind us all that it's still Christmas. It's fun to have it on Twelfth Night, and, if the kids are still out of school, that might work. But when that's not the case, and it's a weeknight, it's not usually convenient for people. So we're more likely to go with the new calendar and throw the party on Saturday night.

[15] The Monday after Twelfth Night and the traditional start of the English agricultural season.

We encourage people to wear their ugly—or not ugly; either is fine—Christmas sweaters, or novelty Christmas accessories for the occasion. Any type of party will do, but my favorite is a Twelfth Night(ish) International Potluck and White Elephant Party. Because the Wise Men are traditionally understood to have come from different continents—Europe (Melchior), Asia (Caspar), and Africa (Balthasar)—I like to ask guests to bring a favorite international food, be it eggrolls or empanadas or ravioli, so that our dinner spread is as universal as our Catholic faith.

The entertainment for the night is the white elephant gift exchange (also known as a Yankee swap). A "white elephant gift" is an extravagant but burdensome gift that's not easily disposed of, based on the story that the king of Siam was in the habit of giving courtiers who displeased him the gift of a rare white elephant, so that they would be ruined by the cost of the upkeep of the animal. But don't worry, the gifts at a white elephant party are rarely extravagant or burdensome.

The rules are the following:

1. Everyone who wants to play brings one wrapped gift to put under the tree. You can set a price range if you would like, but usually we just encourage people to bring the oddest or least-loved present they received for Christmas to foist on someone else.
2. When it's time to play, everyone draws a number from a hat to set the gift-picking order.
3. The person who goes first chooses a gift from under the tree and unwraps it.
4. The person who goes second can choose to steal the first person's gift or to unwrap a new gift. If the second person chooses to steal, the first person chooses a new gift to unwrap.
5. From the third person on, if your gift is stolen, you can choose to steal a gift yourself or choose a new gift from under the tree. But you can't steal back the gift that has just been stolen from you.
6. Once a gift has been stolen for the third time, it's "frozen" to the person and can't be stolen again.
7. Play continues until everyone has a gift.
8. At the end, the person who chose first can choose to steal an unfrozen present, and then the person he stole from can steal one, and so on, until someone chooses to stick with what he has, and the game is over.

The fun of the game is seeing which crazy presents are the most popular. One year, the most stolen gift at the party was a bucket of fried chicken!

Epiphany Presents

One thing we learned from inviting international-type friends over for our Christmas Novena (see the Advent chapter for the whole story) is that there are lots of gift-giving traditions all over the world. In some countries it's traditional to give gifts on St. Nicholas Day, in some on Christmas Eve, in some on Christmas Day, and in some on Epiphany. In our home, we decided to adopt *all* those traditions, but we try to keep it all as minimal as is practical.

The gifts on Epiphany are given by the Wise Men. We tell the children that ever since the night of Jesus' birth the three Wise Men have been following the star, seeking the newborn king. On the last day of their journey, they like to swing by the houses of the faithful with a little something for those who have been keeping Christmas in their hearts all through Christmastide. To get them to come to *your* house you must leave a shoe (or shoes) out by the front door, along with some hay (or grass or lettuce) and water for the camels, and you've got to have a king cake in the house: apparently the Wise Men are drawn to houses by the presence of a king cake.

King Cake

In the United States, we are mostly familiar with the New Orleans–style king cake, but king cakes are served all over the world and vary quite a bit by region. So you really can get away with serving just about anything as a king cake. In Spanish-speaking countries, it's the *rosca de reyes*, a sweet bread shaped into an oval ring, topped with dried fruits. In France, it's the *galette des rois*, a round cake made of puff pastry with fruit filling, often topped with a cardboard crown. In Switzerland, it's pull-apart sweet rolls. In Scotland, it's a fruitcake loaf. In England, it's a star-shaped jam tart.

The New Orleans king cake is a brioche shaped in a ring to look like a crown, covered with frosting and green, purple, and gold sprinkles. If those colors seem more appropriate to Mardi Gras than to Epiphany, that's because in New Orleans, king cakes are served throughout the season of Carnival—from the end of Christmas to the beginning of Lent—but that's it! In our house we always have one on Epiphany and another on Fat Tuesday, but we haven't yet made a habit of eating them in between.

Real New Orleans king cakes can be ordered online and delivered by Next Day Air! But I usually like to make one. My favorite "cheat" for king cakes is to use canned cinnamon-roll dough. For a cake that approximates the real New Orleans one, I layer two or three cans of cinnamon-roll dough in a Bundt cake pan. Once the cake has baked and cooled, I use the frosting that came with the cinnamon rolls to cover the top of the ring, and use green, purple, and gold sugar sprinkles to decorate it, in bands of color. Ideally, the cake is the right size to be completely consumed by the family at breakfast; otherwise you run the risk of no one finding the surprise inside.

As I said, it doesn't really matter what type of cake you use or what shape it is; the important thing is to hide a little something inside. We usually use a stainless-steel jewelry ring, which I tuck into the dough and bake right into the cake. In some countries, they use a dried bean. In New Orleans they poke a little plastic baby Jesus into the bottom of the already-cooked cake. Whatever the item, the person who finds it is the King (or Queen) of Epiphany.

When the kids wake up on Epiphany morning, they find that the Wise Men have finally arrived at the Nativity scenes and that their shoes are filled with a few treats: maybe chocolate coins, maybe some Smarties or Nerds candies (because they're *Wise* Men!) or some little Milky Way bars (because the Wise Men look at the stars). They also find that the camels have eaten most of the hay and left some camel spit in the bottom of the container. It's hilarious! (Camel spit looks an awful lot like an egg white that someone whipped up a bit.)

Then it's time to cut the king cake. The cake is cut into pieces of equal size, one for each person in the family. Then everyone covers his eyes. I ask, "Who shall have this one?" and the youngest kid gets to shout out a name. You can also send just the youngest, or all the kids, under the table so there's no peeking while the pieces are claimed. Once everyone has a piece, we start eating. Whoever finds the ring holds it up triumphantly and is crowned

King or Queen of Epiphany with a homemade paper crown or one from the dress-up box.

If a boy finds the ring, he chooses a queen consort from the family. If it's a girl, she chooses a king consort. If it's a toddler or a preschooler, we appoint a regent to help rule. Then, for the rest of the day, the king and the queen get to choose what we have for meals and where to sit and what we do for family entertainment. They get to assign their chores to others in the family. At meals, whenever the primary ruler picks up his glass, everyone stops and shouts, "The king is drinking, the king is drinking!" (or the queen, as the case may be), and then takes a drink from his own glass.

It's all in good fun, and the kids are required to stay within the bounds of reason: no ordering people to do things that are dangerous or destructive or gross or against our family rules; no bullying. The ruler gets to pick the meals, but usually it's from what we have on hand in the house. The ruler gets to pick an activity, but one that's doable and within the budget; and since we usually celebrate Epiphany on a Sunday, it has to work around Mass and our other usual activities for the day.

House Blessing

The feast of Epiphany is traditionally associated with house blessings. A house blessing is an invitation for Jesus to be a guest in our home and part of our daily lives within it. In some places, the local priests will use Epiphany week to visit the homes of parishioners and bless them. If that's not a tradition in your parish, you could always just invite your priest over for dinner and a house blessing sometime during the week. We did that when we first moved into our new house, and it was great. The priest put on his stole and read the official house blessing, and he went through every room of the house, sprinkling holy water, with all of us trailing behind him. But, for the yearly upkeep Epiphany blessing, we just make use of the do-it-yourself version, using blessed chalk, and prayers.

A traditional way of blessing your home for Epiphany is to use chalk to write above the home's entrance, for instance, "20 + C + M + B + 19". The numbers, combined, should be the current year.

The letters *C*, *M*, and *B* have two meanings. They are the initials of the traditional names of the three magi: Caspar, Melchior, and Balthasar. They are also the first letters of the Latin words *Christus mansionem benedicat*, "May Christ bless the house." The "+" signs represent the cross.

Many parishes have embraced the Epiphany house blessing and give pieces of blessed chalk to everyone after Mass. If your parish doesn't, you can bring your own chalk to Mass and ask Father to bless it, or the head of the household can do it at home using the following blessing:

V. Our help is the name of the Lord:
R. The maker of heaven and earth.
V. The Lord shall watch over your going out and your coming in:
R. From this time forth for evermore.
Let us pray.
Loving God, bless this chalk, which you have created, that it may be helpful to your people; and grant through the invocation of your most Holy Name that we, who use it in faith to write upon the door of our home the names of your holy ones Caspar, Melchior, and Balthasar, may receive health of body and protection of soul for all who dwell in or visit our home; through Jesus Christ our Lord. Amen.

Using the blessed chalk, you bless your house by marking the lintel of your front door with 20 + C + M + B + 19 (or whatever the current year) while saying:

The three Wise Men, Caspar, Melchior, and Balthasar, followed the star of God's Son, who became man two thousand nineteen years ago (or whatever the current year). May Christ bless our home and remain with us throughout the new year. Amen.

Visit, O blessed Lord, this home with the gladness of your presence. Bless all who live or visit here with the gift of your love; and grant that we may manifest your love to each other and to all whose lives we touch. May we grow in grace and in the knowledge and love of you; guide, comfort, and strengthen us in peace, O Jesus Christ, now and forever. Amen.[16]

---

[16] Daryl Moresco, "Chalking the Door: An Epiphany House Blessing 2016", January 1, 2016, Order of Carmelites, http://www.carmelites.net/news/chalking-door-epiphany-house -blessing-2015/.

Because the chalk is blessed, it shouldn't go back into the box with the rest of the regular old chalk. You can put it away to use again next year or bury it in the yard.

After we conclude our Christmas season celebrations, we put away the decorations. The Nativity sets, however, stay out until Candlemas on February 2. It's always a bittersweet day, but usually I'm glad by that point to get the house back in order and the toys out of the living room. The kids are less excited about helping to "undecorate" the house than they were to help decorate on Christmas Eve, but they have to do it anyway.

FEAST OF THE BAPTISM OF THE LORD
(SUNDAY OR MONDAY AFTER EPIPHANY)

We rejoice that Jesus is born, and then a few weeks later, we celebrate his baptism. Seems reasonable. Our kids are used to attending the baptism of a new baby brother or sister within a couple of weeks after the birth. But, of course, in Jesus' case, he wasn't baptized *quite* that quickly. Jesus was about thirty years old when he was baptized, at the beginning of his public ministry, by St. John the Baptist in the Jordan River. The event is recorded is the Gospels of Matthew, Mark, and Luke, and it's alluded to in the Gospel of John.

Jesus' baptism was originally celebrated on the same day as his birth and the arrival of the Wise Men. All three events in his life were considered one single manifestation of God's presence in the world. Then, for a while, his baptism was celebrated as the octave day of Epiphany, which was January 13. Today, in the United States, we celebrate the feast of the Baptism of the Lord on the Sunday after the observation of Epiphany, unless Epiphany falls on January 8, in which case the Baptism of the Lord is observed on Monday, January 9. On the day after the Baptism of the Lord, Christmastide is over and Ordinary Time begins.

Water Fun

Because the feast of Jesus' baptism was once part of Epiphany, Catholics in many Eastern European countries and in most Orthodox churches celebrate Epiphany with some pretty great water-related local customs. I love seeing the photos of Eastern European dudes jumping into icy rivers and seas to celebrate Jesus' baptism. Since we live in Southern California, it's not quite as manly an undertaking, but we do like heading out to the ocean for a winter beach day. Those are my favorite anyway: no crowds, no sunburn, and it's not as if *I* will be going into the water. But the kids usually do! Now that we have a pool, the kids can dare each other to jump in, but it's probably sixty-five degrees outside, so we're not likely to impress any Bulgarians. Maybe you're tough enough to do a *real* winter swim. Or maybe you can just hit an indoor pool for a swim day.

Baptismal Promises

Because the feast day is almost always on a Sunday, we like to try to invite our kids' godparents to join us for dinner. They are spread out all over the country (and there are a lot of them!), but it's worth a try. And, whether or not godparents can join you, what better way to celebrate St. John the Baptist's dunking Jesus in a river than by dunking bread in melted cheese? Right? *Right?* Baptism of the Lord fondue party!

We, as a family, renew our baptismal promises at dinner on the anniversary of each child's baptism. So, at this point, we're doing it *all the time*. But, really, you can't go wrong with enthusiastically rejecting Satan as often as possible. The feast of the Baptism of Jesus is another great time to do it. The head of the household does the call, and everyone enthusiastically responds, "I do!" And we all get sprinkled with holy water.

V. Do you reject Satan?

R. I do.

V. And all his works?

R. I do.

V. And all his empty promises?

R. I do.

V. Do you believe in God, the Father Almighty, Creator of heaven and earth?

R. I do.

V. Do you believe in Jesus Christ, his only Son, our Lord, who was born of the Virgin Mary was crucified, died, and was buried, rose from the dead, and is now seated at the right hand of the Father?

R. I do.

V. Do you believe in the Holy Spirit, the holy catholic Church, the communion of saints, the forgiveness of sins, the resurrection of the body, and life everlasting?

R. I do.

V. God, the all-powerful Father of our Lord Jesus Christ has given us a new birth by water and the Holy Spirit, and forgiven all our sins. May he also keep us faithful to our Lord Jesus Christ for ever and ever.

R. Amen.[17]

[17] "Renewal of Baptismal Promises", Catholic Online, https://www.catholic.org/prayers/prayer.php?p=1653.

4

Ordinary Time after the Baptism of the Lord

After the Baptism of the Lord comes the window of Ordinary Time between the joy of the Christmas season and the sobriety of Lent. There's plenty to keep us busy as we prepare our hearts and homes for the coming season. Since Easter is a movable feast, the beginning of Lent also moves. Ash Wednesday can occur as early as February 4, and Easter can occur as late as April 25. So, any feast here mentioned from St. Agatha to St. George might fall during Lent in a particular year. Feasts that occur between March 10 and 22, notably those of St. Patrick and St. Joseph, *always* fall during Lent.

If a feast that we usually observe as a family falls on a Friday during Lent, we can't eat meat as part as our celebration, unless the feast is a solemnity or we are given a dispensation by a priest or bishop. As I've mentioned before, however, our family abstains from meat on every Friday of the year, unless a solemnity falls on a Friday.

When a solemnity falls on a Friday, be it within Lent or without, we make a point of having meat and making it a big celebration. If a feast that isn't a solemnity falls on a Friday, we have two options during Lent, and three at other times.

1. We can celebrate the feast without meat. This is what we normally do. Since most of our food-related celebrations are just regional recipes, I can prepare a vegetable or fish dish from that region, rather than a meat dish. In a very few cases, however, such as serving lamb on the feast of St. Agnes, we might choose option 2.
2. We can move our family's observation of a feast to a non-Friday. With nine kids and a busy schedule of work, school, and sporting events, we don't have every evening available for the whole family to eat dinner together. So, whether it's a child's birthday

dinner or a favorite feast day, sometimes we move a celebration. If we want to include friends in our celebration, often a weekend works better. We don't usually move a feast day *just* so we can serve meat, but, really, I don't see any problem with doing so.

3. If it's not Lent, we can choose to eat meat and make an alternate sacrifice in its place. I have always struggled with this one. Usually, I try to do too much and end up doing too little. But it's an available option.

FEAST OF ST. SEBASTIAN: JANUARY 20

St. Sebastian was a third-century captain of the Praetorian Guard, an elite, hand-picked unit of Roman soldiers charged with the personal protection of the emperor. He was born into a Christian family in Milan. He converted fellow soldiers, local leaders, and Roman prisoners but kept his faith secret from his superiors in order to avoid persecution by Emperor Diocletian.

Eventually, however, he was discovered to be a Christian and sentenced to death by an archer firing squad. Riddled with arrows and left for dead, his body was recovered by his friend St. Irene (feast day: January 22), who discovered that he was still alive and nursed him back to health. Sebastian worried that he had let down the emperor he had promised to protect by never attempting to share the joy of Christianity with him. So, as soon as he was able, Sebastian sought out Emperor Diocletian and implored him to stop persecuting Christians.

The emperor was, understandably, surprised to be faced with public criticism from an inferior whom he had recently had executed. Rather than being persuaded, he chose to have Sebastian arrested and executed again, by bludgeoning. Sebastian's body, dead this time, was recovered by another holy woman, St. Lucina (feast day: June 30), who buried him in an abandoned mine underneath Rome. This became the Catacombs of San Sebastiano, a Christian burial ground that has been continually accessible to the faithful since that time. We've been there!

St. Sebastian is a patron saint of soldiers, archers, and athletes. So, feel free to shut the kids in the backyard or the basement with some sports equipment and call it liturgical living. Or plan a banquet for your club or school's athletes and coaches to coincide with the feast day.

For dinner, I like to give a nod to the holy cards of St. Sebastian tied to a tree and stuck full of arrows, by serving shish kebabs! You can skewer just about anything, but my favorite is marinated beef, with sliced red onions, red and yellow bell peppers, squash, and cherry tomatoes, grilled and served over rice. Letting the kids make their own skewers makes it also an activity for the day. They especially like it because it lets them leave out the squash.

FEAST OF ST. AGNES: JANUARY 21

St. Agnes was twelve years old when she was martyred by beheading for the crime of being a Christian. Most of the legend surrounding her martyrdom is similar to the stories told of other virgin martyrs, specifically St. Lucy and St. Agatha, but we really don't know for sure the historical details of any of their lives.

In any case, St. Agnes is remarkable for her faith and steadfastness, especially at such a young age, and that is why she has been held up to us as an example since the early days of the Church. St. Jerome writes: "All nations, especially their Christian communities, praise in word and writing the life of St. Agnes. She triumphed over her tender age as well as over the merciless tyrant. To the crown of spotless innocence she added the glory of martyrdom."[1] And St. Ambrose: "It is the heavenly birthday of St. Agnes, let men admire, let children take courage, let the married be astounded, let the unmarried take an example."[2]

St. Agnes is the patroness of engaged couples, chastity, and girls.

The thing I focus on when teaching my older children about the virgin martyrs is that the Church holds them up as examples because of the respect and regard with which they viewed their faith and their virginity. It is their *opinion* of their virginity that matters, not just the fact of their virginity—and certainly not because women who are unable to preserve their physical virginity miraculously under similar

---

[1] Pius Parsch, *The Church's Year of Grace*, vol. 1 (Collegeville, Minn.: Liturgical Press, 1953), 403.

[2] Ambrose, *Concerning Virginity* 1, 2, in *Nicene and Post-Nicene Fathers*, second series, vol. 10, ed. Philip Schaff and Henry Wace, trans. H. de Romestin, E. de Romestin, and H. T. F. Duckworth (Buffalo, N.Y.: Christian Literature, 1896), rev. and ed. for New Advent by Kevin Knight, http://www.newadvent.org/fathers/3407.htm.

circumstances are in any way guilty of sin. People who are the victims of crimes retain their spiritual innocence and virginity.

In fact, we read in *The Golden Legend* (a thirteenth-century collection of hagiographies by Bl. Fr. Jacobus de Voragine) these words from St. Lucy, another virgin martyr: " 'The body is not defiled,' Lucy responded, 'unless the mind consents. If you have me ravished against my will, my chastity will be doubled and the crown will be mine.' "[3]

It is my goal mindfully to instill in my children an understanding of and respect for virginity, which is sadly lacking in our culture, and to teach them that virginity is worth defending, while always avoiding placing any blame on victims of assault.

The word "Agnes" means "lamb" in Latin, so St. Agnes is usually pictured holding a lamb. I like to serve lamb for dinner, but if that weirds you out (it's not as if she *was* a lamb, though, right?) you could always go with a lamb cake (or a Rice Krispies Treat lamb; see "Holy Thursday" in chapter 6) instead. Or do both!

Because of the Agnes-lamb connection this is traditionally the day to have your lambs blessed, if you've got any of those ambling about. And then there's this. Once upon a time, a young lady who wished to know the identity of her future husband would go to bed on the eve of the feast day without supper and in the altogether, believing that she would be sure to dream of him (just FYI).

DAY OF PRAYER FOR THE LEGAL PROTECTION OF THE UNBORN: JANUARY 22

January 22 is the anniversary of the 1973 *Roe v. Wade* Supreme Court decision that struck down abortion restrictions in all fifty states. The *General Instruction of the Roman Missal* designates this anniversary as the Day of Prayer for the Legal Protection of Unborn Children: "In all the Dioceses of the United States of America, January 22 (or January 23, when January 22 falls on a Sunday) shall be observed as a particular day of prayer for the full restoration of the legal guarantee

---

[3] Jacobus de Voragine, *The Golden Legend: Readings on the Saints*, trans. William Granger Ryan (Princeton, N.J.: Princeton University Press, 2012), 4.

of the right to life and of penance for violations to the dignity of the human person committed through acts of abortion."[4] Our bishops call upon us to observe this day through the penitential practices of prayer, fasting, and giving alms. We are also encouraged to participate in the many public gatherings commemorating this tragic anniversary—for instance, one of the various marches or walks for life held across the country on or around January 22.

Before 1966, Catholics observed *fifty-six* days of required fasting (as in one regular meal and two smaller collations) each year: every day of Lent (excluding Sundays), four sets of three Ember Days, and the vigils of Christmas, Pentecost, Immaculate Conception, and All Saints' Day. Since 1966, only two are required—Ash Wednesday and Good Friday. I think we can probably handle the extra day of fasting being asked of us by our bishops.[5]

In our house, some members of the family fast, we all abstain from meat, sweets, and snacks, and those of us who can't fast do other types of penance. Since I've been pregnant or nursing or both for the past sixteen years, I fast from things such as sweets, TV, music, or social media.

Someday, I would love to go to the March for Life in Washington, D.C., or the West Coast Walk for Life in San Francisco. In the meantime, we have had a family tradition of attending Mass and praying the Rosary outside of an abortion clinic on January 22. It's a beautiful and meaningful family activity, but it raised some issues for us. Figuring out how much to share with the kids about what we were praying for took us many years.

Talking about Delicate Subjects

Preserving the innocence of my children is important to me, but it's also important to me that we be engaged in our culture and the world around us. We aren't hermits; we aren't cloistered religious; we live

---

[4] United States Conference of Catholic Bishops, *General Instruction of the Roman Missal* (Washington, D.C.: United States Conference of Catholic Bishops, 2010), no. 373, http://www.vatican.va/roman_curia/congregations/ccdds/documents/rc_con_ccdds_doc_20030317_ordinamento-messale_en.html#DECREE_OF_PUBLICATION.

[5] See appendix A for more information on fasting and abstinence.

in this world. And that means my children will be exposed to some concepts that I'd just as soon they never hear about at all, let alone hear about as children. Figuring out how to handle that fact has been a journey for me.

My oldest son was a very bright, observant little kid. He was always very aware of his surroundings, asking me about things he overheard in grown-up conversations, read on billboards, and heard about from kids in the neighborhood. My policy with him was almost always to tell him that the topic was for grown-ups and that we would discuss it when he was older. We prayed for an end to abortion without his understanding what that was. He didn't know that there was such a thing as divorce or out-of-wedlock births.

Eventually, I realized that I would have to talk to this kid about some stuff. For one, I wanted to take the kids to say the Rosary outside the abortion clinic. For another, we became close friends with a family in which one child has a different mom, having been born before our friends were married. I couldn't avoid these topics forever.

But by this point, since I had waited so long, it had to be a Big Important Conversation. I suppose there's a place in life for Big Important Conversations, but I don't remember with a particular fondness any of the ones I had with my parents, and I sure didn't like being on the giving end of one either.

So, I've totally changed how I approach touchy subjects with my kids. Here's what we do now:

I don't make a big deal out of big subjects.

I am not afraid anymore to name things for my kids. Instead of attempting to shield them as much as possible from any particular subject, I allow them to gain an awareness of it and an understanding of our family's position on the matter, but without a big to-do. This is especially true of subjects that are not moral matters, such as why the rooster jumps on the hens.

Then there are subjects that *are* moral issues. I would prefer that my children did not have to know about same-sex marriage, child abuse, divorce, and abortion, at all, ever. But they *will* have to learn of those things eventually, and I would rather that they did in a loving familial environment.

I have found that "little by little" is a much less traumatic way to gain information than "completely oblivious to Big Important Conversation". So, I am comfortable with my children understanding, at an age-appropriate level, that some men want to be married to other men or that sometimes people who aren't married do the "special kind of hug" that God wants only mommies and daddies to do together, and so sometimes babies are born without a whole family.

We discuss uncomfortable matters in the car.

Whenever possible, I would prefer that the information gathering be child led. I am guardedly open in my conversation and don't avoid controversial subjects entirely. I prefer that my children put together for themselves a general concept of something and come to me with a question, rather than to sit them down and give them a Big Talk that they might not be interested in.

Most often, our important conversations happen in the car. I'm a captive audience for my kids there, plus there's no eye contact required, so that tends to be where my kids ask me things. I wait until we've been driving a while to turn on the radio or even to start our Rosary. I want to give the kids a chance to bring up anything they've been wanting to talk about, controversial or mundane.

It is very, very important to me that my kids feel they can come to me to talk about anything. I want to foster an environment in which we can talk about even evil or immoral things, without feeling that having a conversation about such things is wrong. I think that my former policy of putting off almost all my son's questions didn't help with that.

When my kids ask questions, I answer them, but I start very, very small.

Often, that's enough. When my kids bring up a touchy subject, it can be tempting to launch into a detailed treatment of that and all related matters. But I have found out through experience that, sometimes, all my child wanted was a very small, specific answer. And my broad answer had kinda freaked him out. So now, I start with a small answer, and then, if the child has follow-up questions, I answer those.

I try to make these moments lessons in compassion rather than in horror.

When we have conversations about abortion or divorce or out-of-wedlock births, I try to emphasize how unfortunate the act is and how sad and complicated the effects of the act are. We do not discuss the state of the person committing the act, because only God knows that.

Abortion, for example, is a tragedy for every person involved, from the mother and the father and their extended families to the doctors and nurses and cleaning crews at the clinics. I want my children to pray for all those people. I want them to understand that many people who participate in an abortion feel as if they have no other options, or they wrongly feel as if they are helping a woman. Then we can pray that God will soften their hearts and heal them.

I present out-of-wedlock physical relations as just not God's plan for us, and not the way to feel happy and fulfilled and connected to God and our fellow man. I also let them know that inclinations aren't sinful, only actions.

Again, you know what's right for your child. For me, when my child prays for an end to abortion, it feels right that he understands what he's saying. It's not a conversation any parent *wants* to have, but, since we're supposed to be looking for opportunities for penance anyway, this might just be the day to start.

FEAST OF ST. VINCENT OF SARAGOSSA: JANUARY 23

In the United States, St. Vincent's feast day has been moved from January 22 to the 23, to accommodate the Day of Prayer for the Unborn.

Vincent was a third-century Spanish deacon, martyred, as were so many, by the Roman emperor Diocletian. Not much is known for certain about his life, and the legends associated with him are nearly identical to those told about another martyred deacon, St. Lawrence—barbecued on a grill and everything.

So, let's focus on a story that, though it may not be historically accurate, is unique to St. Vincent and helps to explain why he is the patron saint of winemakers. It is said that Vincent was friendly and talkative and often traveled from town to town through the countryside to tend to the faithful of Saragossa. One winter's day, he encountered some workers in a vineyard. As Vincent chatted with them, his donkey wandered off and began eating all the young shoots off a nearby grapevine, reducing the limbs to stubs. Later that year, at harvest, the workers noticed that the vine that had been nibbled by the donkey produced more and better fruit than the rest of the vineyard. And thus, they learned that grapevines should be pruned!

It just so happens that St. Vincent's feast day marks the point in the growing cycle when all pruning should be completed. That means that the feast of St. Vincent is a day for winemakers to relax and celebrate. And wine aficionados can join them. It's an excellent day to visit a vineyard, host a wine tasting for friends, or just kick back on the couch with a glass of sherry.

FEAST OF THE CONVERSION OF ST. PAUL: JANUARY 25

The conversion of St. Paul is, for me, among the most compelling stories in the Bible. St. Paul, one of the most important figures of the apostolic age and the author of fourteen of the twenty-seven books of the New Testament, not only wasn't one of the original twelve apostles, but he never even met Jesus (in the usual way). More than that, as Saul of Tarsus, the Jewish Pharisee and self-described zealot for ancestral traditions, he was an active enemy of the early Church: "I persecuted the church of God violently and tried to destroy it" (Gal 1:13). He was even a witness to the stoning of the first martyr, St. Stephen. And, as the faithful were burying Stephen's body, "Saul laid waste the church, and entering house after house, he dragged off men and women and committed them to prison" (Acts 8:3).

So, what changed?

The whole story is in Acts 9, but the short version is that, while Saul was on the road to Damascus with some companions, hurrying to arrest more Christians, Jesus appeared to him as a white light, flashing from the sky and knocking him to the ground. Jesus identified himself, told Saul to knock off the persecuting, blinded him, and ordered him to get going. Saul's companions helped him up and got him to Damascus.

Meanwhile, the Lord appeared in a vision to Ananias, a disciple living in the city, and told him to find Saul and to heal him. Ananias, knowing Saul by reputation, was understandably wary, but the Lord assured Ananias that he had everything under control. So, Ananias went and healed Saul, who had been blind for three days. Saul was then immediately baptized, and within days he was proclaiming Jesus in the synagogues, calling him the Son of God.

Unlike Peter, Paul didn't receive his new name from Jesus. As both a Jew and a Roman citizen, Paul had both a Jewish and a Roman name— "But Saul, who is also called Paul" (Acts 13: 9). After his missionary journey to Cyprus, Paul began using his Roman name exclusively.

We don't observe this feast day with any special foods or activities— just a normal dinner, a dessert to celebrate, and a conversation about how much we can change, if we are open to God's grace and the way he wants to use us, with all our flaws and imperfections. St. Paul's early persecution of the Church was a constant source of humility for him for the rest of his life, but his background as both a Jewish scholar and a respectable Roman citizen allowed him access to circles of people who weren't likely to be converted by a bunch of smelly fishermen from Galilee. Ananias, and all the other Christians in Damascus, were called upon to trust God and to forgive Paul for what he had done to them. It couldn't have been easy.

Without going into too much detail, or any detail at all actually, I want my kids to know that I did a *lot* of knuckleheaded stuff in my day. I may never have attended a stoning, but I was a party to plenty of other sinful things. Jesus called me too, not in quite as dramatic a fashion as what happened on the road to Damascus, but he reached out to me just the same. And because I was willing to correspond to the grace he offered me, Jesus has used me and my love of liturgical living. My life experience makes me a better fit for *that* than some smelly fishermen.

But now I feel as if I'd better give you *something* for the day. How about Middle Eastern food, such as hummus and falafel, and a rousing game of blind man's bluff?

FEAST OF ST. THOMAS AQUINAS: JANUARY 28

St. Thomas Aquinas was born into a noble family in Sicily in 1226. He had six older brothers, all of whom were tall and athletic and became soldiers. Thomas, on the other hand, was big and slow and clumsy, and his mom decided he had better become a bishop instead. Of course. He went off to school and enjoyed his studies, especially philosophy and theology. But he was quiet and kept to himself, so his classmates nicknamed him "the Dumb Ox".[6]

Some of his teachers were Dominican priests, and at the age of nineteen, Thomas decided he would prefer the life of monastic study and contemplation the Dominicans offered rather than the political power his mom had in mind for him as a bishop, so he secretly joined the order. He attempted to move to Rome to continue his studies with the Dominicans, but his mother wouldn't have any of that. She sent his brothers to kidnap him on the road and to bring him home to the family castle, where she imprisoned him for over a year in one of the towers.

The family tried every threat they could think of to get Thomas to renounce the Dominicans, even hiring a woman of ill repute to try to seduce him. He chased her off with a smoldering fireplace log, and that night, two angels appeared to him in a dream and gave him an invisible rope that he wore around his waist for the rest of his life as a reminder of his vow of chastity. Eventually, his mom realized he really meant it about becoming a Dominican, but rather than risk losing face among the kidnapping moms in the neighborhood by letting him go, she decided to let him escape out the window.

He devoted his life to God, to philosophy and theology, and to the use of reason to prove the existence of God. He composed dozens of treatises and hymns on various subjects. His biographers record that one day, near the end of his life, Jesus appeared to him in a vision. Thomas anxiously asked Jesus if what he had spent his life writing was correct. Jesus replied, "You have spoken well of me, Thomas. What is your reward to be?" And Thomas said: "Nothing but You, Lord!"[7]

After his death in 1274, he was named a saint and a Doctor of the Church. He is considered one of the greatest philosophers ever to have lived.

For the day, we could kick back and relax with the *Summa theologiae* (he intended it to be for beginners) or sing one of his hymns ("Pange Lingua Gloriosi", "Adoro Te Devote", or "Tantum Ergo"). For older kids, it might be a day to talk about chastity and how it

---

[6] "Dumb" in the older sense of "silent", rather than "stupid".

[7] Warren Carroll, "The Eucharistic Devotion of St. Thomas Aquinas", *Soul*, January-February 1996, Eternal Word TelevisionNetwork, https://www.ewtn.com/library/DOCTRINE/TAEUCHDV.TXT.

applies to every person, according to his state of life. Some teens choose to wear a special ring or cord to remind them of their responsibility to guard their chastity.

If you're looking for something a bit more lighthearted, the "Dumb Ox" nickname lends itself to any number of fun things to do, such as pin the tail on the ox or tic-tac-toe (think about it; you'll get it). And for dinner . . . oxtail soup! Really, I love it when I get to serve a saint-story-themed dinner to my children, the idea of which will be shocking and horrifying to them, but which is actually a totally normal dinner that they'll like eating. Oxtail soup is perfect. An ox is just a bull with a job (and some surgical modifications), so oxtail is just a cow's tail, which, once it's skinned and whatnot, is just a piece of beef with some bones in it. If you can't find an oxtail, you can make mock oxtail soup with beef stew meat (including some bones makes the soup thicker and richer). The important thing isn't that it's a tail but that your kids *think* it's a tail. That's what makes it memorable.

FEAST OF ST. BRIGID OF IRELAND: FEBRUARY 1

St. Brigid was born into the pagan druid religion in 452, during St. Patrick's ministry in Ireland (he died in 493). The stories say that her mother was a slave and that Brigid was born into slavery herself. She was named Brigid after a druid goddess of the same name. As a child she tended the cows on her father's land, milking them and churning butter, and often got herself into trouble by giving away butter to the poor.

One day, she returned to the kitchen with empty butter churns, having given away all the butter she had churned that day, and was about to be punished by the steward. She prayed to the one true God to help her, as, she had heard, St. Patrick taught people to do. When the steward looked into the butter churns, they were miraculously full. That day, Brigid decided to become a Christian and give her life to God. Eventually, she became a nun and, with seven followers, established the first order of nuns in Ireland. The sisters supported themselves by picking wild berries and making and selling jam.

Brigid established a convent in Kildare, on the grounds of a former pagan shrine to the goddess Brigid, where druid priestesses had formerly tended a naturally occurring eternal flame. Rather than stamp out the flame, Brigid and her nuns tended it themselves, in honor of

Christ. They led many pagan Irish to conversion by showing them how the druid worship of nature could find its full expression only in the leaving behind of their old gods and goddesses and the acceptance of Christianity.

Brigid died on February 1, so her feast is celebrated on that day. Providentially, in Ireland February 1 was originally the pagan festival Imbolc, honoring the goddess Brigid. The Irish customs and festivities that were formerly associated with the pagan deities came to be used to honor God through St. Brigid. So, St. Brigid, in her death, continued to lead her people away from pagan worship and toward Christianity.

The flame that Brigid and her sisters tended was kept burning in Kildare until the suppression of the monasteries in Ireland in the sixteenth century. It was rekindled in the twentieth century and still burns today, tended by the Brigidine Sisters.

Because of St. Brigid's association with butter and jam, Irish scones topped with both make a lovely and appropriate meal for the day. Butter is surprisingly easy to make at home, and my kids always get a kick out of it. There are online tutorials available, but the gist of it is this: Pour some heavy cream into a large mason jar with a lid, shake it for five minutes, and it's whipped cream. Shake it for five more minutes, *and it's butter*—delicious butter. Amazing! Add some salt if you like.

Very important aside: I happen to think that the existence of butter is an excellent proof of the existence of God. It doesn't do the cow any good for her milk to turn into butter when shaken. But it does do people quite a lot of good. Butter makes sense only as a gift to mankind from a benevolent Creator. Very important aside over.

St. Brigid is said to have woven rushes into a cross as she converted a pagan man on his deathbed. If you have access to rushes, you can weave a St. Brigid cross yourself. Or, if you're feeling less outdoorsy, you can make one with pipe cleaners.

FEAST OF THE PRESENTATION OF THE LORD, PURIFICATION OF THE BLESSED VIRGIN, MEETING OF THE LORD, CANDLEMAS: FEBRUARY 2

This feast commemorates three distinct but related historical events in the life of the Holy Family, plus a traditional yearly sacramental observance. It marks the day when Mary and Joseph brought the baby Jesus to the temple in Jerusalem for the first time. The Mosaic Law required them to consecrate their firstborn son to God. Additionally, it required Mary to submit to ritual purification forty days after childbirth, which involved making a sacrificial offering in the temple. Luke tells us that, as Mary and Joseph were poor, they took the option provided for those who could not afford a lamb, instead sacrificing "a pair of turtledoves, or two young pigeons" (Lk 2:24).

Of course, Mary was—at Jesus' birth and at every moment since her Immaculate Conception—perfectly pure. And Jesus, who *is* God, hardly needs to be consecrated to God. But Mary and Jesus give us here an example of obedience to God's law, respect for traditional practices, and an avoidance of creating the appearance of sin (we call that scandal).

This feast day also commemorates the encounter in the temple between the Holy Family and St. Simeon the prophet (this is also his feast day!) and St. Anna the prophetess (feast day: February 3), called the Meeting of the Lord. This is the third and final infancy epiphany of Jesus. The first epiphany was to the poor Hebrew shepherds, the second was to the foreign Gentile kings, and the third is to the righteous elders of the Israelites. The next epiphany will be to the public, at the Baptism of the Lord, and won't occur for thirty years.

Churching

In the current calendar, our focus is on the Presentation, but in previous eras the Church highlighted the Purification. From the observance of the Purification of Mary came the tradition of "churching" women. This was the blessing of a woman, forty days after childbirth (regardless of outcome), that reintroduced her to society after her period of recovery at home. There was never an implication within the Catholic tradition that a woman was made impure by childbirth. Instead, the tradition was an acknowledgment of the difficulty of childbirth and new motherhood, and an official Church mandate for women to rest for six weeks after giving birth. In fact, the period between birth and churching was called the "gander month" because men were expected to tend to domestic affairs during that time.

Churching has virtually disappeared as a custom, and now the blessing of the mother after childbirth is given as part of the baby's baptism ceremony. This makes sense, since it's now the norm to wait weeks for the baptism, and the mother always attends (which wasn't usually the case when baptisms took place within a day or two after birth).

I have, so far, always had a pretty easy time of it, physically and emotionally, after childbirth. I have, so far, always felt up to attending Sunday Mass right away. But I also have often overestimated what else I was up to doing, and done too much, and really wiped myself out. I think churching is something we Catholic mothers should remember. Our Church has specific, long-observed traditions in place to safeguard the time after birth as one of rest and recovery, and as a time humbly to allow others to help us. One of the most touching aspects of our local Catholic community is the custom of providing meals to families for the first few weeks after a baby is born. This is organized through our homeschool moms' group, but I also know of churches that provide this service as an official ministry. It really is beautiful to support women and families and our pro-life values in a tangible way. I can't recommend it enough.

In this time of easy transportation, many of us may well be up to attending Sunday Mass soon after childbirth, but that doesn't mean everyone is. It is not required of us. And, either way, we should make a point to view those first few weeks as set apart, as Mary did in the weeks between the Nativity and the Presentation.

The Blessing of Candles

Another name for this feast is Candlemas, because of the words of St. Simeon: "For my eyes have seen your salvation \ which you have prepared in the presence of all peoples, \ a light for revelation to the Gentiles, \ and for glory to your people Israel" (Lk 2:30–32). Jesus is the Light of the World, so this is the day when the Church blesses candles for use throughout the year. Traditionally, families would bring their own candles to church to be blessed on this day for use in their homes. We like to do this still.

Candles used in church for the liturgy must contain at least 51 percent beeswax. We are encouraged to use candles containing beeswax in our homes when they are used as sacramentals, but it is not required. I make an effort to buy candles with beeswax in them (they smell really good). Church supply stores often have them available in bulk, but if we end up with regular drugstore candles, that's okay too.

We like to light candles during our family dinners, so I purchase a large box of taper candles each year and bring them to Mass on Candlemas to be blessed. If the priest doesn't do the blessing for the congregation after Mass, we just track him down afterward and ask him to do it for us. Then, throughout the year, the blessed candles illuminate our family dinners and all our discussions of the lives of the saints that happen over meals.

Now, you are probably *not* wondering what to do with the stubs of blessed candles. But I did. Canon law requires us to treat all blessed objects with reverence. This is understood to prohibit throwing them away. If a blessed object becomes unusable, it must be returned to the ground by being dissolved (as we do with the Eucharist if it cannot be consumed), burned (as we do with palms or linens), or buried (as we do with broken rosaries or religious statues). If a blessed item has been already used up for its intended purpose, however, then its blessing is considered to be used up as well. So that means that unusable candle stubs *may* be thrown away.

But I tend to save them in a box and eventually melt them down to make new candles or wax-dipped pine-cone fire starters, either as a Candlemas project or on the feast of St. Ambrose during Advent. But you *don't* have to. You *can* toss them once they've been used up.

The kids' favorite Candlemas tradition is to spend the day without electric lights. We don't give up *all* electricity—we're not quite that crazy yet (maybe someday). But it is fun, one day per year, to try to do our schoolwork and chores and eat our meals by candlelight only. Especially since it's winter, it really does motivate one to get dinner ready early! I like us to have these little glimpses of what life would be like without (one of) all our modern conveniences.

We say our family Rosary by candlelight or by the light of the fireplace. It's an especially good day to say a family Rosary, as the Presentation in the Temple is one of the Joyful Mysteries.

In the old calendar, rather than a period of Ordinary Time between Christmas and Lent, there was Christmas, then "time after Epiphany", then "pre-Lent", then Lent. This time after Epiphany, while technically Ordinary Time, with green vestments, was considered to be part of the Christmas "cycle" before the Lent cycle began. Candlemas marked the transition between the two and meant that it was the really, no kidding, last day to take down your Christmas decorations and start your pregame for Lent. Today, some folks leave out just their Nativity sets, as a nod to the Christmas cycle of old, until Candlemas. That's what we like to do. (Some folks even leave up all their decorations until Candlemas; that's fine too, but after Candlemas, it's not really liturgically defensible to have them up.)

It might seem as if it would be a pain to have to revisit the hassle of putting away Christmas decorations three weeks after we did it the first time. But I end up appreciating it, since we invariably miss a few Christmas books or knickknacks the first time around, and this is the *only* way I would be motivated to put them away in a place where they may be found for another Christmas. We also have a set of wintry dishes that I received as a wedding gift. This is the day we switch back from using those to using our everyday dishes.

Groundhog Day and Crepe Day

While the Catholics are trying to juggle basically four feast days on February 2, the rest of America is watching to see whether a groundhog in Pennsylvania will notice his shadow. But, guess what? The whole American Groundhog Day thing is based on a Catholic Candlemas tradition that dates back to the Middle Ages: "If Candlemas Day is clear and bright, winter will have another bite. If Candlemas Day brings cloud and rain, winter is gone and will not come again." So, take *that*, Punxsutawney Phil! Just kidding; he's adorable.

In France, Candlemas is also known as "crepe day". For those unfamiliar with them, crepes are thin French pancakes, and February 2 is a perfect day to eat them. The beauty of crepes is that they are delicious whether sweet or savory. For dinner, I make savory crepes with whole wheat flour and fill them with ham and cheese, like yummy French burritos. For dessert, I make them with white flour, and we top them with fruit, chocolate, and whipped cream. If you're not feeling up to experimenting with a crepe recipe, regular American pancakes would work just fine or whole wheat "wrap" tortillas.

FEAST OF ST. BLAISE: FEBRUARY 3

St. Blaise was an early-fourth-century physician from Armenia. After the death of the local bishop, Blaise was chosen to succeed him. Rather than living in the mansion of a bishop, he chose instead to fulfill his duties from a hermitage in a cave. There, he tended to the spiritual needs of the faithful, and, because he was a physician, he tended to their physical needs as well. His cures became more and more miraculous, and the stories say he even healed injured wild animals who would show up at his cave, seeking his assistance.

In 316, the governor arrived at Blaise's cave and arrested him for being a Christian. While he was being escorted away, a distraught woman ran up to him, carrying her young son, who was choking on a fishbone. She laid the boy at the bishop's feet, and he was immediately healed. The governor, unmoved, beheaded St. Blaise. The martyr is one of the Fourteen Holy Helpers, the favorite saints of the late Middle Ages. St. Blaise's intercession is now invoked against choking and other ailments of the throat.

The Blessing of Throats

The Catholic traditional practice for this feast day is the blessing of throats. I find it interesting that this custom has persisted and is practiced at every parish our family has attended, when so many other Catholic customs have fallen by the wayside over the years. Not that I'm complaining about the blessing of throats—it's great!—but is choking really such a concern of parishioners? I guess so. After the homily or after Mass, everyone lines up and the priest, using two of the newly blessed candles from Candlemas, tied together in the middle to form a cross, blesses the faithful one by one, saying: "Through the intercession of Saint Blaise, bishop and martyr, may God deliver you from every disease of the throat and from every other illness: In the name of the Father, and of the Son, and of the Holy Spirit."[8] If you are not able to attend Mass, the blessing may be done at home by the head of the household.

And that night for dinner, just to show how efficacious I think the blessing is, I like to serve a whole fish! It's another one of those liturgical-living-plus-life-skills things. In the United States it seems as if eating fish with the bones in it is becoming very rare. But it's a skill that needs to be learned and practiced, if one ever wants to be able to eat fish that hasn't been filleted or sticked. The feast of St. Blaise is a good way to make sure we do it at least once a year.

FEAST OF ST. AGATHA: FEBRUARY 5

St. Agatha was a virgin martyr from Sicily, who is believed to have died in jail in 251 after suffering various torments at the hands of her captors during the persecution of Emperor Decius. Most notable among her tortures was having her breasts cut off. While in jail, St. Peter the apostle appeared to her and healed her wounds.

She has been honored by the Church for centuries as a martyr, as a virgin (for more on this topic, see the feast of St. Agnes), and as a courageous and eloquent defender of the faith. She is one of the Fourteen Holy Helpers and, along with SS. Lucy and Agnes, one of the fifteen martyrs mentioned by name in the Roman Canon of the Mass.

In art, she is often depicted holding a tray upon which are her breasts (like St. Lucy and her eyeballs). She has traditionally been invoked as the patroness of bell makers because of the, um, shape of bells, and of wet nurses. In recent years, she has been invoked as the patron saint against breast cancer.

My grandmother, mother, and father (not a typo) are all breast cancer survivors, and all had mastectomies. That perspective gives new depth to this responsory from Matins (the prayers traditionally said in monasteries during the final hours before daybreak) for the feast of St. Agatha:

---

[8] International Commission on English in the Liturgy, *Book of Blessings* (Collegeville, Minn.: Liturgical Press, 1989).

R. While the blessed Agatha was being grievously tortured in the breasts, she said to the judge: Thou foul, cruel, and bloody tyrant, art thou not ashamed to do this to me, having thyself sucked at a mother's breast?

V. I have breasts within, which have been the Lord's from my childhood, and them thou canst not mangle.[9]

The traditional food for the day in many countries is *minni di virgini*, or St. Agatha's Breasts. These are cream-filled pastries covered in white icing and topped with a candied cherry, and they look exactly as you're thinking they might look. You can find them in many Italian bakeries, although the folks working there might not realize what they're supposed to be. If you don't have access to an Italian bakery, and don't want to attempt a fussy, multistep pastry at home (it's on my list of things to try, though!), a frosted cupcake with a cherry on top would do the trick.

FEAST OF ST. PAUL MIKI AND COMPANIONS (THE JAPANESE MARTYRS): FEBRUARY 6

On February 5, 1597, Br. Paul Miki, a native Japanese Jesuit, and twenty-five companions were crucified on a hill overlooking Nagasaki. It was the middle of an amazing story of conversion and survival.

In 1549, St. Francis Xavier (feast day: December 3) and two fellow Jesuits arrived on the shores of Japan, eager to bring Christianity to a civilized people who knew nothing of Christ. Francis soon came to love the people and culture and customs of Japan. At that time, Japan was in the midst of a civil war, with control of the country split between dozens of feudal warlords who were eager to wrest power from each other and from the Buddhist religious leaders.

With the support of one of the main warlords, Francis made remarkable progress in evangelizing and converting individual feudal lords and their people, who were won over by his kindness and simplicity. By 1580, Francis and eighty-five Jesuits, sponsored by Portugal, were tending to two hundred churches and more

[9] "Saint Agatha, Virgin and Martyr", Divinum Officium Matutinum, http://divinum officium.com/cgi-bin/horas/Pofficium.pl?date1=2-5-2015&command=prayMatutinum &version=pre%20Trident%20Monastic&testmode=regular&lang2=English&votive=.

than one hundred fifty thousand Japanese Catholics. That number eventually doubled, and Portugal enjoyed a booming silk trade with Japan.

Things changed when Toyotomi Hideyoshi reunified Japan and the Spanish Franciscans showed up. Spain wanted in on the Japanese silk trade, and so, as was their custom, they sent their own missionaries to learn the culture of the country and to make converts. But a new set of Christians, at odds with the Jesuits on some points of doctrine and on how to respond to Japanese cultural practices, confused the Japanese people and made Hideyoshi suspicious to the point of ordering all Christians to leave Japan in 1587.

Both the Jesuits and the Franciscans quietly continued their work in the country, until a mouthy Spanish ship captain, trying to intimidate Hideyoshi, told him that the Spanish always sent in missionaries before their soldiers arrived to conquer a country. In response, Hideyoshi burned down one hundred thirty churches and crucified Paul Miki along with two other Japanese Jesuits, six Spanish Franciscans, and seventeen Japanese and Korean catechists. Among the group were three young altar servers. Persecution continued sporadically until September 10, 1632, when fifty-five more Christians were martyred in Nagasaki. Catholicism was formally outlawed in Japan, and all the European missionaries left.

Japan was closed to foreigners for nearly two hundred fifty years. When a French priest arrived in the country in the nineteenth century, he discovered that the Catholic faith had *not* died out in Japan when the Europeans left. Without bishops, the Japanese priests had been unable to ordain new priests, but laypeople had continued to baptize and share the Gospels from memory, passing verses from parent to child, and creating statues of Jesus, Mary, and the saints, disguised as pagan figures. When religious freedom was reestablished in Japan in 1873, more than thirty thousand underground Catholics came out of hiding.

The feast of the Japanese martyrs is observed on February 6 (because the fifth was already the feast of St. Agatha). It's a good day to talk to children about the blessing of religious freedom and about the persecution that Christians still face today, in many parts of the world. We say our Rosary for persecuted Christians and for missionaries all over the world.

It's also a good day to go out for (or order in) Japanese food, or to take a stab at a Japanese recipe at home. Homemade sushi can feel intimidating, but once you get everything prepped, it's really pretty foolproof, and a fun activity for kids. If you don't have access to (or an affinity for) raw fish, you can make sushi with cooked fish, shrimp, or even beef. And there are delicious Japanese curries that are easy to make from ingredients found in the international aisle of most grocery stores in the United States. Japanese Castella Cake, or Kasutera, is a popular Japanese honey spongecake which was originally introduced to the country by those sixteenth century Portuguese missionaries and merchants. It's made with just bread flour, eggs, sugar, and honey.

FEAST OF ST. JOSEPHINE BAKHITA: FEBRUARY 8

St. Josephine Bakhita was born in 1869 in Darfur, Sudan, into a large, happy family. Her uncle was the village chief, and she had three brothers and three sisters. When she was nine years old, she was kidnapped from her village by Arab slave traders. She was forced to walk barefoot for more than six hundred miles to the trading port. The trauma of her kidnapping caused her to forget her own name, so the slavers gave her the name Bakhita, which means "lucky" in Arabic. Little did they know.

Over the next twelve years she was sold five times and was subject to profound physical abuse. In one home, she was forced to undergo a painful process of decorative, permanent scarring covering her torso and right arm. Her 144 scars were meant to mark her as a slave for life.

In 1883, she was bought by the Catholic Italian vice-consul, who was living and working in Sudan. For the first time, Bakhita was enslaved in a home in which she did not suffer beatings. Two years later, when the vice-consul prepared to leave Sudan, Bakhita asked to go with him. In Italy, she was given as a gift to the Michieli family, Italians who owned hotels in the Sudan, and she became nanny to their daughter Alice.

When the Michielis needed to spend some time in Sudan on business, they left Alice, with Bakhita, in the care of the Canossian Sisters in Venice. It was at this convent that Bakhita, overhearing Alice's catechism lessons, first learned about Christ and the Catholic faith.

When Signora Michieli returned to collect Alice and Bakhita to take them with her to Sudan, Bakhita refused to leave. When Signora Michieli attempted to force her to come along, the Mother Superior of the sisters contacted the Italian authorities.

Bakhita's freedom became the subject of an Italian court case, and in 1889 a judge ruled that, since slavery was technically outlawed in Sudan since before Bakhita's birth, and was certainly illegal in Italy, she had never been a slave and was a freewoman according to the laws of Italy.

Bakhita, twenty years old and free to make her own decisions for the first time, chose to remain with the Canossian Sisters. The next year, she was baptized with the name Josephine Margaret Fortunata ("Fortunata" being the Latin translation of the Arabic name that her captors had given her). She was also confirmed, and she received her First Holy Communion from the future Pope Pius X. Ten years later, she made her final profession as a nun and remained with the Canossian Sisters in Italy for the rest of her life.

To be kidnapped as a child, sold into slavery, dehumanized and abused for years and years—it's terrible even to think of. And unlike some of the fanciful legends surrounding saints of the Middle Ages, Josephine Bakhita's story is raw and not in doubt. She is a modern saint; we have her autobiography and photographs of her. The horrors she endured are all true. But it's also true that she found peace and happiness for the last fifty years of her life, through God and forgiveness and service to others and her Catholic faith.

St. Josephine Bakhita teaches us that we don't have to be defined by the bad things that happen to us. She triumphed utterly over her abuse. She forgave her abusers and embraced God. A young student once asked her: "What would you do if you were to meet your captors?" Without hesitation she responded: "If I were to meet those who kidnapped me, and even those who tortured me, I would kneel and kiss their hands. For, if these things had not happened, I would not have been a Christian and a religious today."[10]

St. Josephine Bakhita is the patron saint of Sudan and against human trafficking. Her feast is a good day to pray for people all over the world, and even here in our own country, bound in slavery.

[10] Maria Luisa Dagnino, *Bakhita Tells Her Story* (Rome: General House, Canossian Daughters of Charity, 1993), 113.

There are Sudanese recipes available online. Or you can always just go with Italian food, as this saint lived in Venice for most of her life.

FEAST OF OUR LADY OF LOURDES: FEBRUARY 11

In February of 2006, the husband was diagnosed with stage 3 melanoma. Three days later, I discovered I was pregnant with baby number four. The husband's cancer began in a tumor associated with a mole on his shoulder and spread to his lymphatic system. He had multiple surgeries and started a year-long course of debilitating interferon injections. The survival rate for a cancer diagnosis like his are below 50 percent, but the surgeries had seemed successful and he had tolerated the interferon.

There was no way to know for sure, but things were looking up. We decided to cover all our bases by planning a pilgrimage to the shrine of Our Lady of Lourdes. Then, just weeks before we were set to depart for France, Jim's oncologist called to say that a routine check of the original tumor site had turned up evidence of cancer—again. Either they hadn't removed the entire tumor in the first two surgeries or the cancer had returned. It was bad news either way, because it meant that the year of misery on interferon had basically been for naught and that Jim was statistically back in the "unlikely to survive" camp.

We decided that, if possible, we would still go on our trip, and he was scheduled quickly for yet another surgery. We were sitting there in the hospital. I had a nursing baby. He had a terribly flattering hospital gown. We prayed the Rosary and specifically asked Our Lady of Lourdes for her intercession.

As soon as we finished, the surgeon walked in brusquely, holding some slides and some paperwork. The doctor announced that *he* didn't see any evidence of cancer in the tissue samples. He thought that the slides had just been misread and that the cancer was not, in fact, back or still there. He did another excision just to be sure, and that biopsy turned up clear, as he thought it would. All of a sudden, just like that, Jim was cancer-free again.

It wasn't what you would think a miracle would look like. But that was certainly what it felt like to us. A week later, the husband and I and baby Gus headed to Lourdes, where we all were dunked in the healing waters. For the next ten years or so, Jim's checkups showed no evidence of cancer, and during that time we were able to make two more trips to Lourdes, once with seven kids in tow.[11]

I love everything about Lourdes. I love that it's pretty and quiet and feels set apart. I love that it has beautiful buildings made by man and beautiful surroundings made by God. I love seeing all the pilgrims, but especially the sick ones. So often the weakest among us are unseen, hidden away in houses or facilities, but at Lourdes that's not the case. I love that everywhere you go, you must make way for sick pilgrims in their chairs, being pushed by attendants.

I love that it is a place of quiet reflection but also a place with so many rewarding Things to Do. Mostly, when we visit a religious site, this is the routine: wander into the church, have a look around, snap some pictures, kneel and say some prayers—that's pretty much it. But at Lourdes we can drink the water, go to Mass, go to confession, and get dunked in the baths. If we want more we can tour that basilica, and that one, and that other one over there. We can walk the Way of the Cross.

My favorite thing is the candlelight procession. "While walking" is my favorite way to pray. Add beautiful surroundings, candlelight, and thousands of other people praying alongside me, and, wow! It's really a thing to behold.

Act Locally

If you can hop on a plane to France and visit the shrine yourself, definitely do that. But if you can't, try making a pilgrimage to a shrine near you. There are at least dozens of replica grottos of Our Lady of Lourdes scattered through the United States, notably the National Shrine Grotto of Our Lady of Lourdes in Emmitsburg, Maryland, and the lovely grotto on the campus of the University of Notre Dame. We have been to both! Catholic parishes called Our Lady of Lourdes are sure to have a grotto of some sort, and sometimes Catholic parishes bearing other names have them too.

---

[11] Just as this book was going to the printer, cancer was discovered elsewhere in his body, and we are in need of another miracle. We are again asking for the special intercession of Our Lady of Lourdes.

Catholics are called to make pilgrimages. We've been doing it for thousands of years. The *Catechism of the Catholic Church* specifically recommends it: "Pilgrimages evoke our earthly journey toward heaven and are traditionally very special occasions for renewal in prayer" (2691).

If you have kids—especially little kids and especially lots of kids—making a pilgrimage of any sort, even to a parish across town, will feel like an undertaking, but that's all part of the pilgrimage experience. And, if we're being honest, packing a cooler and loading up the minivan isn't quite as arduous as the preferred pilgrimage method of the saints: point oneself in the direction of the Holy Land, and start walking.

When we make a family pilgrimage, we try to make sure it involves some praying and some walking and some inconvenience. Those are the ingredients—also some fun, ideally. Before we go, we gather prayer intentions from friends and family members. If our destination is a big shrine, or it's on a campus, we can count on having someplace to walk once we're there. If it's a neighborhood parish, we'll often park some distance away (a half mile to a mile or so) and walk that. Either way we pray a Rosary while walking.

Next we visit the grotto (or whatever is the special feature of our destination) and quietly pray there for as long as kids can handle it (perhaps only five minutes for little ones, up to thirty for older kids). If there is an associated church, we also make a visit to the Blessed Sacrament and attend Mass, if possible, and make our confession, if possible. All the while, we pray specifically for the intentions we gathered, and we always end our pilgrimage with an Our Father and a Hail Mary for the intentions of the pope. Somewhere in there, we also eat a picnic lunch: baguettes and cheese and *saucisson* (French for "salami") and fruit. It's easy *and* French.

FEAST OF STS. CYRIL AND METHODIUS (YES, YOU READ THAT RIGHT): FEBRUARY 14 (AND A SHOUT OUT TO ST. VALENTINE)

Before describing how our family celebrates St. Valentine's Day, I need to talk about the 1969 revision of the liturgical calendar. Again. But in my defense, it keeps being relevant. Church authorities added some modern saints, changed the way feast days are classified, moved some feasts around, and de-emphasized saints about whom there is little or no historical record. There are dozens of recognized saints, some of whom we've already discussed, whose existence, though it can't be *disproven*, can't be proven either. There are others whose existence we know for sure, because their names can be found on grave markers or in contemporary historical accounts, but we can't be certain of anything else about them.

The method for canonization in the early Church didn't have much oversight. If a cult grew up around the sanctity of a dead person, the process was just to wait and see if people's devotion stuck, and if it did, boom, he was a saint. Honestly, I don't have a problem with that. I don't have a problem with knowing something by its fruit.

St. Barbara (feast day: December 4), for example, appears nowhere in the historical record. She is said to have lived in the fourth century, but no mention is made of her in the early martyrologies. Her name doesn't appear anywhere until the seventh century. But then, for whatever reason, she became popular and widely venerated. People reported miracles due to her intercession. People reported visions that told her legend. Her story inspired Christians. There are countless souls in heaven, and we don't know the names of the vast majority of them. If, a couple of hundred years after she died, St. Barbara decided to reach out to the people of the Middle Ages, it's okay with me.

But ... there was also "St." Guinefort. Guinefort was a greyhound who belonged to a thirteenth-century French knight. The knight came home to find the nursery in chaos, his baby missing, and his dog with bloody jowls. In a rage, believing that the dog devoured his child, the knight slew it. Just then, he heard the baby cry and found him unharmed, under the upturned cradle, next to a dead, bloody viper. Realizing his mistake, the knight buried the dog in the yard and marked the grave. Townspeople, hearing of the dog's valor and tragic death, began to visit the grave. And then things got out of hand.

The grave became a makeshift shrine. The dog's intercession began to be invoked for the protection of infants. The shrine was dismantled and the cult officially suppressed in 1240 by a Dominican friar,

Stephen of Bourbon.[12] But the whole incident can teach us about the advisability of some top-down oversight (not to mention the general inadvisability of dog babysitters).

In a Church that takes pride in being both rational and spiritual, we want to make sure to avoid the confusion and the embarrassment of things like dog saints. And it's understandable that the Church would stop emphasizing saints with no historical footprint, when there are plenty of saints, even very ancient saints, about whom we do have verifiable information.

So, in the 1969 revision, all those undocumented saints (with a couple of exceptions) were removed from the universal liturgical calendar. They weren't "de-sainted". It's still permissible to ask for their intercession and to have a personal devotion to them and to celebrate their feast days. (Except for "St." Guinefort, of course; let's not go there.) But the Church stopped *promoting* them, as it were.

The Fate of St. Valentine

St. Valentine didn't make the cut. All we know for sure about St. Valentine is that he was martyred and buried in a cemetery in the north of Rome on February 14. According to legend he officiated at Christian marriages, at a time when young men being drafted into the military were forbidden to marry—hence his connection with young lovers. But we have no way of verifying this story.

We do, however, know quite a bit about St. Cyril and his brother St. Methodius. We know about their lives and their reputation for holiness. They created the Cyrillic alphabet and translated the Bible into it, which I'm sure the Slavs still appreciate. We also know that St. Cyril died on February 14, 869. His tomb is San Clemente Basilica in Rome. So he and St. Methodius are emphasized on the feast day. That said, we are still allowed to celebrate St. Valentine. Valentine's Day, as it's celebrated between sweethearts and schoolchildren, is a lovely tradition.

[12] Stephen of Bourbon, "On the Worship of the Dog Guinefort", *De Supersticione*, trans. Paul Hyams (?), Internet Medieval Source Book, Fordham University, https://sourcebooks.fordham.edu/source/guinefort.asp.

In our homeschool group, we have a kids' valentine exchange. Some kids bring store-bought cartoon-based valentines; some kids bring clever tidy homemade valentines that, if we're being honest, they probably lost interest in making and their moms finished for them. I like both. I'm pretty sure my kids don't know the difference. As for us, I just plunk our craft bin full of paper and markers and glue and pipe cleaners and googly eyes in the middle of the dining room table and let the kids make whatever they make. Kids' valentine exchanges feel pretty low-stakes to me, so it's not something I need to be particularly involved with.

The more important part of Valentine's Day for me is spending time with my love. These days, we have kids old enough to babysit, and a routine they can follow, and it's easy peasy for the husband and me to go out for a romantic dinner together (although I usually prefer not to go *on* February 14 because "it's a madhouse out there" and "kids these days" and other old-lady complaints).

But when we had a bunch of little kids, it was hard to go out to dinner. It's not easy to find a babysitter who thinks she can handle more than two kids and actually *can*. And do you leave the baby, or do you bring the baby? And do you stay for dessert if that means you'll be later than you told her you would be back? The whole thing adds a layer of stress and expense to the holiday. One year, we just decided it was too much trouble. So the husband invented "Tierney Bistro". And, honestly, it's my all-time favorite Valentine's memory. We've done it quite a few times since, for Valentine's Day and anniversaries and other occasions. Just thinking about it makes me want to organize a surprise "Tierney Bistro" for this weekend.

Here's how we do it:

- We set a festive table (kids can help with this, of course) and print out a menu for the evening, for added fanciness.
- A grown-up prepares the food for the grown-ups (but older kids could probably manage this part too). Fancy prepared finger foods from the grocery store, steaks on the grill, or ordered takeout—anything will do. The more small courses, the better. Plus, we make something quick and easy for the kids to eat.
- The kids eat first.

- We go outside and knock on the front door. The kids escort us in, seat us, and wait on us at dinner.
- We ring a little bell if we need service; otherwise they stay (somewhat) out of sight. But there is great ceremony as they bring out the courses and refill the drinks. Occasionally, there have even been dinner shows.

The kids love it because they like the pageantry and playacting. They wear aprons. We call them "miss" and "young man". They get to feel like responsible adults with real jobs. I love it because it really does allow the husband and me to have some quality time together, in the comfort of our own home. And it's really, really cute and affordable. There *are* dishes to do afterward, but other than that, it's perfect.

THE CHAIR OF ST. PETER: FEBRUARY 22

This feast celebrates both an actual, physical, very old chair housed at the back of St. Peter's Basilica *and* the spiritual authority that the chair represents, passed down through apostolic succession from St. Peter to our current Holy Father. Our family has been fortunate enough to travel to Rome twice. We have seen two popes and visited St. Peter's Basilica, where the famous chair is located on the back wall below the stained-glass dove. The visible chair is very fancy and baroque and was built around the original plain oak armchair. We know for sure that the inner chair is very old, but it's not certain that it dates to apostolic times or that St. Peter actually sat in it.

On this day, we talk to the kids about what it means to be the pope. It's an especially good time to explain to older children the concept of teaching *ex cathedra*, or "from the chair". When a pope speaks ex cathedra, defining morals or doctrines that have been handed down through the ages, he is preserved by the Holy Spirit from making errors. But at other times, a pope can make errors just like anyone else.

An activity we've adopted recently is to write a letter to the pope on this day. We've written to the pope to say thank you or just to assure him of our prayers for him, and we've written to ask respectfully for clarification on statements a pope has made that were confusing to us (when he was *not* speaking ex cathedra). As of this writing, the pope does not have an e-mail address, so you've got to go old school and put pen to paper. Another life skill to be learned!

His mailing address is:

His Holiness Pope [insert the name of the pope here]
Apostolic Palace
00120 Vatican City

The proper salutation for a Catholic writing to the pope is "Your Holiness" or "Most Holy Father". The proper closing for a Catholic writing to the pope is the following: "I have the honor to profess myself, with the most profound respect, your Holiness' most obedient and humble servant" or "I am, Your Holiness, most respectfully yours in Christ". I like the first one. When do we ever get to talk like that anymore?

As our treat for the feast day, I buy a small assortment of cookies and candies, and we use frosting to stick them together to make little chairs. We decorate them with whatever sprinkles I have in the cabinet. It's always fun to see how different they can turn out, even though all the kids start out with the same materials!

It's a little thing, but since this feast day usually falls within Lent, the kids are extra excited to have treats. We, as a family, don't eat treats during Lent. As we eased into that practice, we did have treats on any feast days we celebrated. Now that I'm more informed about historical Lenten practices, and now that we are more used to managing without sweets, I'm of the opinion that "best practice" is to break our voluntary Lenten disciplines only for Sundays and solemnities. However, we've been doing this candy chairs thing for ten years now. It was one of our first family liturgical-year traditions, and I think it's the first one I can take credit for inventing. I came up with it just rummaging around in the pantry, trying to figure out something fun and meaningful that we could do for the feast day without my having to go to the store. So, this isn't quite in keeping with my current Lenten mind-set, but in our house it's grandfathered in! And there's no requirement for Catholics to refrain from eating candy chairs during Lent. So, you're allowed to join us if you choose.

FEAST OF SS. PERPETUA AND FELICITY: MARCH 7

As we've discussed already, many early saints have a lot of great stories, but not much in the way of verifiable historical record. Also, most of them are priests or religious, and virgins or celibate. That's

great, but it's easy to start to wonder if marriage and motherhood
are at odds with sanctity. Furthermore, early saints are depicted in
art, pretty exclusively, as white. Enter SS. Perpetua and Felicity to
solve everything.

They were born in the late second century in the African province
of the Roman Empire, which is basically the part of Africa that the
boot of Italy would kick, if it could stretch out a bit. At the time of
their arrest, St. Perpetua was a twenty-two-year-old married noble-
woman and the nursing mother of a young son. St. Felicity was her
servant, also young and married, and eight months pregnant with her
first child. We can't know for sure what they looked like, as Romans
valued and recorded citizenship rather than race. But it's very likely
that they (like St. Augustine, who lived a couple of hundred years
later) were ethnically Berber and identified as African, but were culturally Roman and looked like a cross between the two.

We know their story because we have a record of Perpetua's diary,
written in 203 while she was in jail and edited by an unknown person
who witnessed her martyrdom and added that information to Perpetua's record. It is one of the oldest and most notable early Christian texts, survives in both Latin and Greek forms, and is believed by
scholars to be authentic. You can read the whole thing, called *The
Passion of Saints Perpetua and Felicity*,[13] in its original Latin, the early
Greek translation, or an English translation, all available online. It's
only a few pages long and is an amazing piece of history.

Perpetua and Felicity were catechumens (Christians who were
being instructed in the faith but were not yet baptized) who were arrested and imprisoned along with six other Christians. They refused
to renounce their faith, despite the pleading of Perpetua's father
and the fact that if they didn't, they were going to be thrown to the
wild beasts in the games celebrating the birthday of the emperor at
the stadium of Carthage. But they were steadfast. They were baptized
right there in jail, and at their trial they confessed their Christianity
publicly before the Roman governor.

Perpetua at first suffered terribly at being separated from her son.
But after bribing the guards, she was allowed to keep her baby with

her in prison and continue to nurse him, and "suddenly the prison was made a palace for me, so that I would sooner be there than anywhere else."[14] Felicity was to be spared the gruesome fate of her companions, as Roman law forbade the execution of a pregnant woman. She went into labor early, however, and gave birth in prison to a healthy baby girl, three days before the start of the games.

On the day of their execution, the women gave their babies over into the care of their families and were led with their companions into the arena.

> Now dawned the day of their victory, and they went forth from the prison into the amphitheatre as it were into heaven, cheerful and bright of countenance; if they trembled at all, it was for joy, not for fear. Perpetua followed behind, glorious of presence, as a true spouse of Christ and darling of God; at whose piercing look all cast down their eyes. Felicity likewise, rejoicing that she had borne a child in safety, that she might fight with the beasts, came now from blood to blood, from the midwife to the gladiator, to wash after her travail in a second baptism.[15]

They were set upon by a line of gladiators, then a boar, a bear, a leopard, and finally both women were gored by a "savage cow"— which sounds almost funny. But cows have horns and certainly can inflict great injury, and the intent was that a cow would mock the femininity and motherhood of the young women. But Perpetua's femininity would not be stopped. My favorite quote from the whole thing is this: "She likewise pinned up her disheveled hair; for it was not meet that a martyr should suffer with hair disheveled, lest she should seem to grieve in her glory."[16] I find that visual to be terribly motivational. Perpetua fixed her hair *while* she was being attacked by wild beasts in the arena. Kinda makes me feel as if I should do my hair this morning—make it more ... meet, ya know? If my martyrdom is all these kids, I would hate to be assumed to be grieving in my glory.

So our activity for the day is fancy hairdos for the girls. The boys are on their own for this one, as I don't have any beasts wilder than

---

[14] Ibid.
[15] Ibid.
[16] Ibid.

chickens to set upon them. A perfect meal, especially since it's usually Lent, is *stracciatella alla Romana*, Roman egg drop soup. It's quick and easy and has only a few ingredients. It's Roman, as were SS. Perpetua and Felicity. And the eggs highlight the motherhood of these martyrs. If you would prefer more of a revenge-type dish, you could always go with burgers. Who's laughing now, savage cow?

FEAST OF ST. FRANCES OF ROME: MARCH 9

Born to a wealthy family in the fourteenth century, Frances knew at the age of eleven that she wanted to become a nun. But—and stop me if you've heard this one before—her family wanted her to marry a rich nobleman instead. Unlike in so many of these stories, however, her betrothed was a good man who really loved her, and after much prayer and discernment, Frances consented to the will of her parents, marrying Lorenzo at the age of thirteen.

She was thrust into a world of parties, social customs, and household management that was unfamiliar to her and not at all to her liking. But she loved her husband and grew to love his family and to become an able mistress of her home. This quote of hers is one of my all-time-favorite saint quotes and is a frequent consolation to me as a homemaker: "Sometimes she must leave God at the altar to find him in her housekeeping."[17]

Frances had three children and was well known throughout Rome for her piety and charity. After almost forty years of happy marriage, her husband died. His last words to her were, "I feel as if my whole life has been one beautiful dream of purest happiness. God has given me so much in your love." At the age of fifty-two, her children grown and married, she became a professed Benedictine Oblate of Mary, realizing her childhood dream on God's time, not hers.

The Art of Homemaking

There are women who pursue excellence in homemaking to a truly staggering degree. Empires have been created around cooking and

[17] Rev. Alban Butler, *Lives of the Fathers, Martyrs, and Other Principal Saints*, ed. Rev. F.C. Husenbeth, vol. 1 (Great Falls, Mont.: St. Bonaventure Publications, 1997), 530.

decorating tips. There are magazines and television shows and blogs and social media accounts devoted to beautifully unrealistic visions of aspirational homemaking. That's not the kind of homemaking that St. Frances calls us to pursue. I'm not sure that's a temperate level of homemaking. At the same time, some women fear that to be a proficient homemaker somehow subjugates them. And others would like to be proficient homemakers but were never taught how and don't know where to begin.

For many, many years, I was in the third group. Domesticity doesn't come naturally to me, and I resisted all my mother's attempts to teach me any basic homemaking. I didn't know how to do the most rudimentary home-ec stuff until after I got married. Once I was out of the house and no longer had anyone looking after me, my lack of skill in this area became embarrassing, and probably a health hazard.

I want my daughters to learn homemaking skills precisely *because* they were not skills I valued as a young woman. It's exactly because I experienced what it's like that I'm not a member of the second group, and you will never convince me that withholding skills and information from girls is empowering, or that giving them skills and information is sexist.

Cooking, cleaning, laundry—these are *important life skills*. I hope my daughters will grow up to take pride in their careers (if they have them) and their children (if they have them). But I'm assuming they will also live somewhere, and wear clothing, and eat stuff. I hope that they can also take pride in their ability to manage those things well.

That's what I've learned to do. I've been able to find interesting challenges and unexpected joys in homemaking tasks. Sure, there's also drudgery. But some of that is good for me too. I don't expect my children to love every second of doing laundry. But maybe they also won't like driving. That doesn't mean I'm just going to let them be terrible at it.

Most "homemaking" skills, are really just "Catholic" skills, right out of the Corporal and Spiritual Works of Mercy. None of us is above learning those things, no matter how accomplished we are outside the home.

In our family, we require both the boys and the girls to do chores around the house. All our children, boys *and* girls, know how to cook, clean, take out the trash, make beds, and do laundry. For my boys, homemaking is a skill they should know so they won't die of self-neglect. For my girls, I hope homemaking is an art they can cultivate, whether or not they also have another career—but also so they won't die of self-neglect.

If you are where I was as a young adult, it is *not* too late for you to learn this stuff. Learning for my kids, and beside them, has definitely worked for me. I read books and blogs about basic homemaking skills and asked my mom to give me another chance to learn all that stuff she tried to teach me as a teenager. And my mother-in-law, who really loves to cook, gave me another perspective in the kitchen. I now consider myself an accomplished cook, baker, seamstress, interior decorator, and hostess, and a competent (if unenthusiastic) laundress and cleaner of houses. I remain a very lousy gardener. But you can't win them all. A willingness to try and fail is a big part of achieving success in homemaking, as in almost everything else in life. The first step is just taking that first step!

If you're new to the art of homemaking, this feast day is perfect for getting a little out of your comfort zone. I think the two things that make me feel the most like a "real" homemaker are homemade yeast bread and soup from scratch.

Especially for Lent, homemade pretzels are a great way to jump into bread baking. Pretzels are historically associated with Lent, as their traditional shape is meant to look like arms folded in prayer (with a twist!). Also, they can be made without sugar, eggs, or dairy, so they worked with historical Lenten food restrictions. There are easy recipes online for chewy homemade soft pretzels that don't even require a separate rising step. My kids love to help make Lenten pretzels, even if the ones they make don't necessarily end up looking exactly pretzel-like.

To make stock (also called soup base or bone broth) I save bones from meat meals and keep them in the freezer in separate bags for chicken, ham, lamb, and so forth. I also keep in the freezer a bag of carrot, pepper, celery, and squash peels and tops, celery and herb bottoms, onion and potato skins, various wilted veggies, and so forth. In the morning, I choose one type of bones, put them in a big pot with an equal amount of veggie parts, cover it all with water, bring it to a boil, reduce the heat to very low, and simmer it for six to eight hours, or until I'm ready to make dinner. This can also be done in a Crock Pot or a pressure cooker, for more or less time. Then I strain all the old bones and veggies out, and skim the fat off, if necessary, and it's an amazing hearty soup base—made from stuff I was going to throw away! All that's left is to add whatever new meat, lentils, beans, noodles and veggies I want, and it's ready for dinner.

FAT TUESDAY (MARDI GRAS, SHROVE TUESDAY, PANCAKE TUESDAY)

In amongst these saints' days, somewhere between St. Blaise and St. Frances of Rome, will fall Fat Tuesday—the last day before Lent begins. I would say that Fat Tuesday is—after Christmas and Easter— the most popular day of the year in our house. Big international Carnival celebrations all over the world have a deservedly dubious reputation. But the *idea* of fun and feasting and carrying on before buckling down for Lent is a very good and very Catholic one, and it's something I highly recommend for all families planning to get serious about Lent, come Ash Wednesday. Toplessness and drunkenness can be easily eschewed in one's own home.

The word "carnival" comes from the Latin *carne vale*, meaning "farewell to meat". (I like to imagine that waving Mardi Gras parade queens are waving good-bye to meat.) Carnival is an entire season, from Epiphany to Fat Tuesday, and in places such as Rio de Janeiro, Quebec City, and New Orleans it's one long party. But it all culminates on the last day, which is always a Tuesday, since Lent always begins on a Wednesday. Since Lent is observed all over the world, there are different Fat Tuesday traditions all over the world. Almost all involve costumes and festivities and eating all the sweet and fatty foods people will have to give up the next day.

In Poland, and in parts of the United States, such as Chicago, with a large Polish population, Fat Tuesday (and sometimes also the Thursday prior) is Paczki Day, and people eat sugar-covered, jelly-filled donut-type pastries called *paczki*, sometimes in a contest.

In England, it's Shrove Tuesday after another word for confession, and you're supposed to go to confession and eat pancakes, which both sound like really good ideas. Also, in some towns they have pancake races, in which participants must wear an apron and a head scarf and flip a pancake on a frying pan while running. I wholeheartedly support this tradition.

In Portugal and Hawaii, it's Malasada Day, after the Portuguese egg-size, sugar-sprinkled donuts traditionally eaten on the day. In Spain it's Día de la Tortilla (omelette day) and they eat omelettes, and in Finland it's Laskiainen and they eat pea soup, so, let's just agree to avoid Spain and Finland for Fat Tuesday, shall we?

In our house, we like to observe French-derived New Orleans Mardi Gras traditions (the French words *mardi gras* mean "fat Tuesday"). We start the day with a king cake and a crowning of the family king or queen of Mardi Gras (see the Epiphany section for all the details). My homeschooled kids do only a half day of school, and they get time to watch TV and play video games, because we don't do those things during Lent. Sometime during the day, we make Mardi Gras masks, using templates I find online and print on card stock, and the kids decorate their masks with paint, markers, feathers, and jewels. They make masks for the grown-ups too, and for any kids who have to be away at regular school during the day, and I help them cut them out and staple pieces of elastic to them. Then we wear the masks around the house while we get ready for dinner, and we pretend we can't recognize each other. It's pretty funny.

For dinner we have something Cajun, such as jambalaya or *étouffée*. And then, for dessert ... things get crazy. Our Fat Tuesday tradition is to eat up all the treats in the house. First, I separate out any hard candy we have, and we donate it to the troops through Operation Gratitude. Then we have a go at the rest of the leftover candy from Halloween and Christmas, the frozen cake scraps and ice cream from the five family birthdays we have in fall and winter, the various open bags of cookies—all of it. The kids make crazy ice cream sundaes, the details of which I will not share—because they are gross. Then (hopefully) before we're all sick, whatever we don't eat is fed to the chickens or tossed.

Usually, we end with a family movie night, which is unheard of on a weeknight around here, but Fat Tuesday is a crazy day. And with that, we are ready for Lent.

5

Lent

The liturgical year begins with Advent. But liturgical living often begins with Lent. There's just something about it that seems to call to us. Folks who may not even attend Mass with any regularity feel that pull to give up something for Lent. Ash Wednesday, while not a holy day of obligation, sees the third-highest Mass attendance of the year, behind only Christmas and Easter.[1] If you're just starting out on this journey, Lent just might be the push you need to begin living the liturgical year in the home.

As with so many other things in a Church two thousand years old, the season of Lent has changed over the centuries. Currently it begins on Ash Wednesday and ends before the Mass of the Last Supper on Holy Thursday. The three days of the Triduum are their own liturgical season. As far as what's specifically required of us during Lent, it's not much. We are bound to fast and to abstain from meat on Ash Wednesday, just as we are on Good Friday. We are also required to abstain from meat on Lenten Fridays (as we are on every Friday of the year, but during Lent we are not allowed to make a substitute penance).[2]

Lent is a period of preparation of our hearts and minds, observed before the joy of Easter. During this season we reflect upon, and participate in, the sufferings Christ endured for our salvation. We also recall the forty days Jesus spent in prayer and fasting in the desert before he began his public ministry. In one form or another, Lent has

---

[1] Mark Gray, "'Headless' Catholics, A Trick and My Treat", *Nineteen Sixty-four* (blog), October 31, 2013, http://nineteensixty-four.blogspot.com/2013_10_01_archive.html.

[2] See appendix A for more information on fasting and abstinence.

existed since the earliest days of the Church. By the fourth century, the season was meant to provide forty days of penance in the forms of prayer, fasting, and almsgiving.

Lenten Norms

In earlier centuries, Catholics abstained from meat, dairy, and eggs throughout Lent (except on Sundays). In the modern era, Catholics were required to fast throughout Lent (except on Sundays), eating one full meal and two smaller meals (collations) per day, but the non-Friday meals could contain meat. Beginning in 1966, the United States bishops amended the regulations to do away with the mandatory Lenten weekday fast, although they still recommend the practice. They retained the fasting requirement for Ash Wednesday and Good Friday. The bishops allowed for another form of penance to substitute for abstinence from flesh meat on all Fridays, but they kept mandatory abstinence for Ash Wednesday, Good Friday, and the Fridays of Lent.

Allowed on abstinence days are all salt and freshwater species of fish. Amphibians, reptiles, and shellfish are also permitted (and even mammals, such as beavers and capybaras, that spend the majority of their lives in the water!), as are animal-derived products, such as gelatin, butter, cheese, and eggs, which do not have any meat taste, and broths made from meat or bones, as long as they don't have pieces of meat in them.

Other Lenten observances recommended by the bishops are attendance at daily Mass, generosity to the needy, "spiritual studies, beginning with the Scriptures", and traditional Lenten devotions such as Stations of the Cross and the Rosary. They encourage Catholics to embrace "all the self-denial summed up in the Christian concept of 'mortification'".[3] The Christian concept of mortification is dying to self so that the life of Christ can grow in us. Among Catholics, the

---

[3] National Conference of Catholic Bishops, *Pastoral Statement on Penance and Abstinence* (November 18, 1966), no. 14, United States Conference of Catholic Bishops, http://www.usccb.org/prayer-and-worship/liturgical-year/lent/us-bishops-pastoral-statement-on-penance-and-abstinence.cfm.

most common voluntary practice of this self-denial is "giving something up" (or taking something up) for Lent.

Sundays Not Included

There is a long-standing tradition of suspending Lenten acts of self-denial on Sundays (and solemnities), even though Jesus did not come in from the desert on Sundays during his forty-day fast. When Jesus was in the desert, Sundays weren't Sundays yet. He had not yet begun his ministry, had not yet suffered his Passion, and had not yet died for our sins and risen again on the third day. But once that very first Easter happened, Sundays became something set apart, something special. Each and every one is a feast.

When you count up all the days from Ash Wednesday to Holy Thursday, you will notice that the season of Lent is more than forty days. Over time more days were added so Catholics could set aside Lenten disciplines on Sundays and still observe forty days of penance before Easter.

We're not required on Lenten Sundays to enjoy the things we have given up. But if the opportunity arises to partake in a licit pleasurable activity on a Sunday during Lent, we shouldn't refrain because of our Lenten disciplines. Every Sunday is a little Easter and should feel like a celebration, even in the midst of Lent.

If, however, we have given up a bad habit we are trying to conquer, continuing to abstain from that behavior on Sunday would certainly be a good idea. If we are trying to break a physical addiction to something such as alcohol or caffeine or nicotine, it might be detrimental to the cause to indulge in those things once a week. And any good habits we are trying to add to our lives during Lent shouldn't be abandoned on Sundays.

If you've chosen to give up for Lent something such as going to the movies, but you usually go to the movies only on Sundays, may I suggest that that's not a particularly good thing to give up for Lent?

Lent is not a time to punish oneself. It is a time to perfect oneself, with the help of grace. A perfect Christian life respects the rhythm of the Christian year and the rhythm of the week. Even within the season of Lent, there are days that are meant to be celebrated. We need not deny ourselves the joy those days can provide.

Prayer, Fasting, and Almsgiving

During Lent, the Church asks us to focus on prayer, fasting, and almsgiving rather than all the stuff we usually focus on. It seems straightforward enough, but I always do best when I have a plan.

I used to labor under what I think is a pretty common misconception about Lent: that we are supposed to be miserable for forty days. But, really, that's not the right way to look at it. Lent isn't a time to try to punish ourselves into being deserving of God's grace (especially since that's not possible, during Lent or any other time; grace is an unmerited gift). Lent is a time to grow closer to God: to take up new practices that lead us toward him and to leave behind practices that distract us from him.

The easiest way for me to understand it, and to be able to explain it to my kids, is by thinking about the concept of *attachment*. Jesus tells us, "For where your treasure is, there will your heart be also" (Mt 6:21). Our goal, as Christians, is to be attached to God and the things of heaven, and to be detached from sin and the things of the world. That doesn't mean we can't enjoy the things of the world, but we shouldn't feel as if we would not be able to survive without them. Things such as coffee, sweets, social media, phones, TV, and even our food and our homes and our cars aren't sinful in themselves, and it's perfectly acceptable to enjoy them. But once we start to see them as things we require, or things we deserve, rather than gifts from God to be used in service of him, we've formed an attachment. The season of Lent is a perfect time to detach ourselves.

In our house, we now view Lent as a time to try adding things to or taking things away from our personal and family lives to see if we become better versions of ourselves. We make it a time not of suffering for its own sake but of increased focus on God and others and decreased focus on self and personal comfort. I have found that I can take up or give up just about anything, no matter how big or small, and use it as a reminder to pray more and to love more.

The stereotypical thing is to give up chocolate, right? And perhaps, for a particular person in a particular year, that would an efficacious choice. But if you're looking for something outside the box, here are sixty-six ideas for things to consider giving up or taking up, at beginning, intermediate, and advanced levels, for beginning, intermediate, and advanced Lents.

1. Don't take the best spot available in the parking lot.
2. Take the worst parking spot you can find.
3. Don't drive: walk or take public transportation.

1. Make your bed every day.
2. Make your bed every day before you leave your bedroom.
3. Make other people's beds too.

1. Go to daily Mass once per week in addition to Sunday Mass.
2. Go to daily Mass two or three times per week.
3. Go to daily Mass every day.

1. Don't leave dishes in the sink overnight.
2. Do the cooking dishes before dinner and the dinner dishes immediately after dinner.
3. Don't use the dishwasher.

1. Buy only things written on your shopping list.
2. Keep a shopping list and shop only once per week.
3. Don't buy anything during Lent (except maybe food).

1. Don't eat out at restaurants.
2. Make all your food from scratch.
3. Grow or raise all your own food.

1. Don't watch TV or movies alone.
2. Watch TV or movies only as a whole-family activity.
3. Don't watch TV or movies.

1. Give up one social media platform.
2. Check social media just once per day.
3. Remove all social media apps from your devices.

1. Say a family Rosary once a week.
2. Say one decade of the Rosary as a family each day.
3. Say a family Rosary every day.

THE CATHOLIC ALL YEAR COMPENDIUM

1. Listen only to audiobooks or classical music in the car.
2. Turn off the radio in the car.
3. Say a Rosary in the car or listen to a spiritual audiobook.

1. Be in bed for a set amount of time each night.
2. Go to bed and get up at specific times each day.
3. And don't bring your phone with you (get an alarm clock).

1. Get dressed before 8 A.M.
2. Don't wear workout clothes (unless you're working out).
3. Wear clothes that make you feel put together every day.

1. Have dinner as a family.
2. Have a family game night.
3. Read a book aloud as a family.

1. Make regular social phone calls to friends or relatives.
2. Write regular letters to friends or relatives.
3. Make regular visits to friends or relatives.

1. Know what you're going to make for dinner by 10 A.M.
2. Start a meal-planning system.
3. Teach your kids to plan meals and cook.

1. Have the house clean before Sunday each week.
2. Have the house clean before bed each night.
3. Have the house clean before dinner each evening.

1. Eat up the food that's in the back of your pantry and freezer.
2. Eat only soup for dinner.
3. Observe the voluntary recommended weekday Lenten fast.

1. Give up one type of treat.
2. Eat desserts only in company.
3. Give up all sweets.

1. Switch from coffee to tea or vice versa.
2. Limit yourself to one cup of coffee or tea per day.
3. Give up caffeine.

1. Turn the lights off in empty rooms.
2. Have lights turned on in only one room at a time.
3. Don't use electricity.

1. Say the Morning Offering when you wake up.
2. And say the Angelus at noon.
3. And do an examination of conscience and say the Act of Contrition at night.

1. Read the Sunday readings before Mass.
2. Read the Bible each day.
3. And read the *Catechism* each day.

1. If you like TV, read a novel instead.
2. If you like novels, read a classic.
3. If you like the classics, read great Catholic nonfiction.

Our family has voluntary Lenten disciplines that we do together in community, and we also each choose one or two specific things to take up individually, and one or two specific things to give up individually. We give the kids the freedom to choose their individual Lenten disciplines, but no smart-alecky ones, such as "I'm giving up vegetables."

Sometimes they give up expected stuff, such as breakfast cereal or a particular type of toy, but sometimes they get creative. One year, my oldest daughter, Betty, decided she wanted to walk to morning Mass for Lent. Since the baby had started sleeping through the night in her crib, I figured I would go with her. So, as *his* Lenten discipline, my son Bobby offered to sleep in the baby's room and get up with her and get her something to eat on days when she woke up before we got back at 7:30 or so. Seemed like a good plan.

Fast-forward to the next morning: 3:20 A.M.

Bobby (opens the door to our bedroom): Dad? Are you awake? I fed her some applesauce, but she's still sad.

Me: Bobby, it's three in the morning.

Bobby: Oh. There's not a clock in there.

Sometime the Lenten sacrifices just find *you*.

Lent is when we have adopted many of our best practices, such as saying a family Rosary, and mostly we've been able to keep up those good practices after Lent is over. But each Lent is its own work in progress. I learned the hard way not to try to do food-related mortifications when I'm pregnant. I've been pretty sick with a few of my pregnancies, and I felt like a huge failure when the only things I could imagine eating were on my banned list. Then my spiritual director told me I needed to forget the food stuff and get more creative in the active mortifications I decide to do, and to embrace more joyfully the passive mortifications that find me. So that's what I do.

Some things that we give up now took a few years of false starts to gain traction. TV was one of those things. The first time I tried giving it up was the second winter we lived in Chicago. I had kids ages three, two, and two months and a very tiny house. And, for me, it just wasn't the time to give it up. I needed the kids to be able to stop making messes and to watch a show so I could make dinner.

But it still felt like something I wanted to be able to detach from, so I kept trying, for two more years, until it finally took. Now, it's a completely different story. My current little kids watch very little TV because they have plenty of brothers and sisters to play with and because having the TV on would be disruptive to my big kids' finishing schoolwork or practicing piano or reading or doing a craft or blinking. So we just don't usually turn it on anyway. It's not that the kids don't notice or don't ever ask to watch (they still do), but these days, not watching TV doesn't make our lives miserable. We can manage it.

Even the little kids "get" how we do Lent. For instance, I overheard Anita (six) and Frankie (four), discussing a wedding invitation that came in the mail:

Anita: It's a wedding! We get to go to a wedding!

Frankie: And there will be *cake*!... Wait. Oh no, it's Lent.

Anita: The wedding isn't in Lent. You can't get married during Lent. Because of cake, I guess.[4]

---

[4] Despite what my kids think, Catholics *are* allowed to get married during Lent, or on any day of the year except for Good Friday and Holy Saturday, according to the *Circular Letter Concerning the Preparation and Celebration of the Easter Feasts*, distributed by the Congregation for Divine Worship in 1988. The reason many dioceses and parishes discourage or prohibit weddings during Lent is that if you have one, it's supposed to be "somber" so that "the penitential character of the season be preserved", and who wants that? The issue of cake is *not* specifically addressed.

Lent in the Home

I try to create a general atmosphere in our home that makes Lent feel *different* from other times of the year. On the morning of Ash Wednesday, after we get back from Mass, we decorate our house for Lent. We put burlap and little cacti and rocks on the mantle above our fireplace and as the centerpiece of our dinner and school tables. On Passion Sunday, we drape our crucifixes and our little altar table with purple cloth. Since we spend so much time at home, it's nice for our house to reflect the season. We see Lent all around us.

We keep track of all the good deeds the kids do and all the small sacrifices they make during Lent with our Lenten sacrifice beans. I put out a tin of dried purple kidney beans next to an empty jar. Each time one of the children does some small thing in a perfect way, such as coming quickly when Mom calls or not fighting over who gets to spit first while brushing teeth, he gets to put a bean in. When they make small sacrifices, such as wiping up a spill or letting someone else have the last bit of something, they get to put in a bean. When the Easter Bunny comes, he changes all the sacrifice beans that we've put in the jar into jelly beans. Then, we keep up our good deeds and sacrifices during the Easter season. But instead of putting a sacrifice bean in, they get to take a jelly bean out and eat it.

I really try to be wildly generous with the bean jar—which is hard for a picky mama. But God can never be outdone in generosity, right? So, pretty much anything they do—picking up the baby's spoon, clearing their own socks out of the living room, putting up the kneeler quietly—if they do it for love of God or love of beans, they get a bean. They get a bean anytime they say, "Okay, Mama", *except* when they say it in response to *my* response to their question. For instance, "Can I have a cookie?"

"No. It's Lent."

"Okay, Mama. Can I put in a bean?"

"No. That was me answering *your* question. No bean."

But otherwise, I'm very freewheeling with them. The good part is that they're two for one. The kids have to do another good deed to take a jelly bean out during Eastertide.

Lent is *long*. It is hard for kids to remember how much time is left until Easter. I do not enjoy answering the same question more than fifteen or twenty times, so we have a Lent calendar that I can point to if the kids ask how many more days until Easter. For our simple calendar, I print out a Lent-related clip-art image (such as a desert, or nails, or a cross) for each of the forty days of Lent, plus a cheery image (such as a baby chick or a flower) for each of the six Sundays. (You could also use forty pieces of purple paper or sticky notes, and six pieces of white or light yellow.) Then I cut out the images and tape them to our kitchen door around a printout of our family Lent disciplines, in case the kids have a hard time remembering that we're really, really *not* going to have sweets or watch TV or play video games until Easter. Each day we take one picture off, until Lent is over. I've also seen families make a paper chain and take off a link each day.

At our house we observe the required days of fasting and abstinence, of course, but we also make a point of using up all the perfectly good food that has been hanging out in the back of the pantry or the freezer because it's not our absolute favorite. I try to limit my grocery spending to perishables, such as dairy and fruits and vegetables, until we've gone through what we've got in the house. During Lent we try to live simply and to eat simply. I make soups often and try to go through all the meat bones and vegetable scraps I've been saving in the freezer by making homemade broth.

The thing we do as a family that is probably most meaningful to our littlest members is counting before we begin meals. Once we all have our food in front of us and are seated at the table, we say Grace and then count to forty out loud before we start to eat. It helps us remember that Lent is a time of waiting and preparation (side bonus: it teaches our little kids to count).

Soup and Stations

But the most popular thing we do during Lent is Soup and Stations. The Stations of the Cross are a devotion dating back to the late Middle Ages, in which pilgrims to the Holy Land would follow the Way of the Cross in Jerusalem, tracing Jesus' actual path to Mount Calvary. Eventually, the Franciscans in Europe began to build replica paths with varying numbers of stations along the roads to churches. In the eighteenth century, Pope Clement XII fixed the number of stations at fourteen and gave permission for them to be installed within churches. The traditional fourteen stations are these:

1. Pilate condemns Jesus to die.
2. Jesus accepts his cross.
3. Jesus falls the first time.
4. Jesus meets his Mother, Mary.
5. Simon helps carry the cross.
6. Veronica wipes the face of Jesus.
7. Jesus falls the second time.
8. Jesus meets the women of Jerusalem.
9. Jesus falls the third time.
10. Jesus is stripped of his clothes.
11. Jesus is nailed to the cross.
12. Jesus dies on the cross.
13. Jesus is taken down from the cross.
14. Jesus is placed in the tomb.

Many parishes offer Stations of the Cross on Friday evenings in Lent, and some offer a soup or fish dinner as well. It's a great way to build community at a parish, and if you can make it to one in your area, that's great! However, I've never seen one that didn't start right when my little kids go to bed. And at some, silence and stillness are given priority over family friendliness. It can be stressful. At first, we just figured this wasn't the time in our lives to be able to do the Stations of the Cross.

But then we realized that there was no reason we couldn't do the Stations of the Cross in our own home, at a time that works for us. *Then* we realized that many of our friends were in the same boat, so we started inviting them to join us. Now, each Friday of Lent we host Soup and Stations at our house. We enjoy a simple meat-free soup and some bread, and have water to drink. I'll provide the soup for a couple of Fridays, and usually friends will offer for the other weeks. We use paper bowls and disposable cups and spoons so there aren't dishes to do. On Good Friday, my mom, a Memphis native, does up a simple Southern catfish fry for everyone!

My oldest son made our stations from a kit, and we hang them outside on the trees in our backyard. All that's required for "legitimately erected" Stations of the Cross is fourteen crosses. The images are nice, but not necessary.[5]

After dinner, as soon as the sun has gone down, we pass out fourteen lighted taper candles with drip protectors. The drip protectors are very important for little hands. You can find plastic or paper ones online or at church supply stores, or you can do what we do: cut a small X in the bottom of a disposable cup and slide the candle up through it. If the weather is uncooperative, we set the stations up in one room of the house (a room without carpet because of the candles). We choose one person to move from one station to the next with a candle, to illuminate that station, and everyone else stays put. Our preference, however, is to set the stations up outside in the yard, where there is more room, and the entire group can walk from one station to the next.

As you'll recall from Advent, real candles and real fire are a big draw for kids. They are an important part of many timeless Catholic traditions. With close supervision, we let even our preschoolers hold candles. We teach them how to hold the candles so they won't hurt themselves or burn the place down.

There's no one required formula for doing the Stations. We have a few copies of the kid-friendly (but still orthodox) booklet *Stations of the Cross for Children* that takes less than thirty minutes to do.[6] The Society of the Little Flower offers a lovely version online with short Scripture reading and prayers, appropriate for all ages.[7] Someone reads the meditation at each station, and then one candle gets blown out. Preschoolers get called on to blow their candles out earliest. As we walk to the next station, we sing the first verse of the "Stabat Mater", usually going back and forth between the Latin and English versions. The hymn has enough verses to do a different verse at each station, but this way everyone can sing from memory, which is helpful because as the candles are blown out, it starts getting dark.

The people with the final candles read the final meditations, because they're the ones with the light. When we get to the last station, we

[5] United States Conference of Catholic Bishops, *Manual of Indulgences: Norms and Grants* (Washington, D.C.: United States Conference of Catholic Bishops, 2006), no. 13.

[6] Julianne M. Will and Patricia Mattozzi, *Stations of the Cross for Children* (Huntington, Ind.: Our Sunday Visitor, 2005).

[7] "Carmelite Stations of the Cross", Society of the Little Flower, https://blog.littleflower.org/category/prayers/carmelite-stations-of-the-cross/.

blow out the last candle and stand in the darkness for a moment. It is a powerful and wonderful experience for kids and grown-ups alike.

It can be troubling for a parent to introduce the subject of suffering, and particularly the suffering of Jesus, to young children. But we do it. If a child is sad about the Crucifixion, that probably isn't something that needs to be fixed. True sorrow over Jesus' Passion and death is a gift from the Holy Spirit. In our home, we focus on age-appropriate facts, and, of course, we know that this story has a happy ending, but we avoid the newfangled fifteenth station and other things that attempt to speed kids (and grown-ups) past the sorrow of what Jesus went through for us.

Some things are sad. It's okay for kids to know and understand that. It's something we should all let ourselves stew in a bit during Lent. The joy of Easter is coming, but true sorrow at Jesus' death, tears over the Crucifixion, is a gift that not all people are given. (Of course, sometimes it does go too far, and this means that the child doesn't understand the whole story or is being self-indulgent, or something else is going on. Trust your mama gut.) We comfort our kids if they are sad. But we don't withhold the truth. At each Friday Stations of the Cross, we allow our kids and all of our guests to leave with that fourteenth station, "Jesus is laid in the tomb", fresh in our minds.

Finally, because it is our goal to live out our wonderful Catholic faith in a perfect way during Lent, we keep the fasts *and* the feasts. Our Holy Mother Church has seen fit to give us days of great joy in the midst of our sorrows. And so we celebrate the feasts that fall within Lent. They vary each year but always include St. Patrick's Day (I know it's just an optional memorial in the United States, but don't try to tell that to my Chicago Irish relations), the solemnity of St. Joseph, and the solemnity of the Annunciation, and we celebrate each Sunday as the feast day that it is. And because it's Lent we try to celebrate as perfectly as we can!

ASH WEDNESDAY

On Ash Wednesday everyone in our family gets marked with ashes, even babies. Ashes aren't a sign of our sin, but rather of our mortality. Infants and children under the age of reason, the mentally disabled, and non-Catholics are all welcome to get ashes. Ashes are a sacramental, not a sacrament.

When the priest makes the cross on our foreheads, he says, "Remember, man, you are dust, and unto dust you shall return." Ash Wednesday is when we remember that, because of the first sin Adam and Eve committed in the Garden of Eden, we are mortal. We will die. The only way I'm going to avoid death is if Jesus' Second Coming beats my natural death, or maybe if God decides to send the prophet Elijah's chariot of fire for me. Otherwise, I, and everyone I've ever known are all going to die. It's not something that's necessarily pleasant to think about, but it's just the right motivation to get our acts together as we head into Lent.

During the Middle Ages, clocks, paintings, sculptures, and tombs featured skulls (called *memento mori*, Latin for "remember that you have to die") to remind the living that time is short. I recently asked for, and received, a golden skull that sits on my desk to remind me that someday I will die and that I should live accordingly. It helps keep the trials of daily life in perspective!

Ash Wednesday is a day of fasting and abstinence, which for a Catholic means one full meat-free meal, and two smaller meat-free meals that together add up to less than the full meal. No snacking is permitted during the day, but liquids can be taken between meals (just not things such as milkshakes and smoothies, which are more like food and less like drinks). Fasting is required for Catholics from age eighteen through fifty-nine who are not ill, pregnant, or nursing. People whose jobs require intense physical labor may also be exempt. When in doubt, consult a trusted priest.

We observe the fast as a family, as each is able. Though children aren't bound by the fast, our school-aged kids can manage going without snacks for the day.[8]

Most churches have a day on which you can bring back your blessed palms from Palm Sunday of the previous year, so they can be burned and distributed on Ash Wednesday. But I never can seem to remember to bring them. Instead, I let the kids take them out in the yard and burn the palms in an old metal can; then they sprinkle the ashes in our garden.

---

[8] See appendix A for more information on fasting and abstinence, and specifically on fasting as a pregnant or nursing mother.

As something the kids can *see* and *do*, we like to bury the Alleluia. Since, in the Western Church, we discontinue the use of that most joyful exclamation, "Alleluia", during Lent, there is an ancient tradition of actually burying it and digging it up again on Easter. The kids write and decorate the word "Alleluia", either on paper (which will be placed in a plastic bag to protect it), wood, or rock, and then bury it in the garden, with much singing and pomp and circumstance, to await Easter morning. (Make sure to mark where you buried it.)

As I said before, we like to have visible reminders of the season in our home, so we decorate with rocks and little cacti and burlap and purple cloth, and we cut out the forty-six little pictures for our Lent calendar and tape them to the kitchen door, around our family's Lent reminder. It says:

IT IS LENT

I SHOULD NOT
Watch TV
Play Video Games
Eat Treats

I SHOULD
Make Sacrifices
Pray Often
Come When I am Called
Be Nice
Be Polite
Let Others Go First
Do for Others
Wait to Eat
Behave Mannerly at Table

IF I AM BORED I CAN
Clean my Room
Clean Someone Else's Room
Say the Rosary
Draw a Picture
Read or Look at a Book
Go Outside

Over dinner we discuss what each person would like to give up and take up for Lent. We encourage everyone to make his voluntary Lenten disciplines public, because peer pressure is good for accountability. If someone particularly wants to keep a discipline private, however, that's allowed. We each write our disciplines on a piece of paper, using this format:

THIS LENT I WILL STRIVE EACH DAY
To do LESS _____
To do MORE _____
NEVER to _____
ALWAYS to _____

Throughout Lent, we keep the papers folded up in a small basket on our altar table. Some years it feels right to attempt something hard. Other years aren't right for that. As an example, one year mine was: "This Lent I will strive each day: To do LESS yelling; to do MORE going for morning runs; NEVER to say no if the kids ask me to do something with them; ALWAYS to make all our food from scratch." Another year, when I was pregnant, it was: "This Lent I will strive each day: To do LESS yelling (again); to do MORE reading; NEVER to stay up past 11 P.M.; ALWAYS to say the Angelus." We try to give the kids a lot of leeway to choose their own disciplines, but we do give them guidance if we think they've missed the mark in either direction. We want their choices to be challenging but doable.

FEAST OF ST. PATRICK: MARCH 17

St. Patrick was born into a Catholic family in Roman Britain in the fifth century and is known as the Apostle to Ireland. The historical details we know of his life come from two documents, written in Latin by St. Patrick himself.

At the age of sixteen, he was minding his own business when he was kidnapped by a group of pagan Irish pirates and enslaved as a shepherd in Ireland for six years. Then God spoke to Patrick in a dream and told him that a ship awaited him. He fled from his master, traveled to a port two hundred miles away, and jumped aboard the ship that was indeed waiting there.

Back home with his family, he had a dream in which the people of Ireland called him to return and to teach them about Christ: "And thus did they cry out as with one mouth: 'We ask you, boy, come and walk among us once more.' "[9] Convinced, Patrick was ordained a priest, then confirmed a bishop, before receiving permission to return to the land of his captivity.

He loved the people of Ireland and had extraordinary success in evangelizing them. In his lifetime he baptized thousands of people, ordained priests, and established religious communities. He converted men and women, rich and poor, slaves and sons of kings. The prayer he composed known as "St. Patrick's Breastplate" makes an excellent start to the day.

Alongside the historical record of St. Patrick have grown up many traditions and stories. He is said to have taught the pagan Irish, who practiced a nature-centric druidical religion, about the Holy Trinity, using the three-leaf clover, or shamrock, as a symbol of the three Persons in one God. He is also said to have driven the snakes out of Ireland, using his bishop's crozier as Moses used his staff in the Old Testament. And there are, in fact, no wild snakes in Ireland. But some folks say there never were, even before St. Patrick.

St. Patrick's Day is a solemnity and a holy day of obligation in Ireland, but not in the universal Church. In the United States it's just an optional memorial, but if you were raised Irish on the South Side of Chicago, as was my husband, there is *no* not celebrating St. Patrick's Day. St. Patrick's Day is our *biggest* liturgical celebration of the year, though, of course, not the most important. We host a huge backyard hooley with corned beef sandwiches, cabbage, potatoes, whiskey, beer, and lots of treats. There is singing and dancing and carrying on and the wearing o' the green.

Because it's not a solemnity, the feast day doesn't exempt us from our voluntary Lenten disciplines, and, if it falls on a Friday, we are still bound to abstain from meat. The bishops of many dioceses routinely give an abrogation of the Friday abstinence, however, in honor of St. Patrick's Day. In some places, the day of abstinence is moved to another day. Check with your diocese to find out. To avoid

[9] *The Confession of St. Patrick*, Eternal Word Television Network, http://www.ewtn.com /library/MARY/PATCONF.htm.

interfering with the voluntary Lenten disciplines of our friends, who have often given up sweets or alcohol, or both, we have the hooley on the Sunday closest to St. Patrick's Day.

It's possible that you don't want to serve whiskey and corned beef to the multitudes. If not, a simpler celebration will certainly do. For a small group of moms and kids, we've had fun hosting a St. Patrick's tea party, with tea, little sandwiches, and a rainbow of fruits, with a pot of Goldfish crackers at the end. Cutting shamrocks out of paper and labeling each leaf with symbols of the Father, the Son, and the Holy Spirit is an easy craft for the day. Just make sure you're making a shamrock, which has three leaves, rather than a four-leaf clover.

For a family dinner, corned beef is traditional in the United States, although not in Ireland. There they would more likely opt for lamb. Shepherd's pie would be fitting for a saint who spent six years as a shepherd. If the feast day falls on a Friday, and you aren't excused from abstinence from meat by your bishop, there are many traditional Irish fish recipes from which to choose, such as fish chowder or fish and chips. Beer, of course, is 100 percent meat-free.

SOLEMNITY OF ST. JOSEPH: MARCH 19

St. Joseph is the husband of the Virgin Mary and the father of Jesus on earth. He is mentioned in the Gospels of Matthew, Luke, and John. We know he worked as a carpenter and taught his trade to Jesus. The last mention of Joseph in the Gospels is the finding of the twelve-year-old Jesus in the temple. Joseph is understood to have died, in the company of Jesus and Mary, sometime before Jesus' public ministry began at the wedding feast at Cana. Because of this, he is the patron saint of a happy death.

St. Joseph is also invoked as the patron saint of workers and a model for fathers and was declared by Pope Pius IX to be both the patron and the protector of the universal Catholic Church. In many European countries, St. Joseph's Day is celebrated as Father's Day. In California, it is the day when the swallows return to Mission San Juan Capistrano after having flown south for the winter.

If St. Joseph's Day falls on a Friday, the solemnity trumps our Friday abstinence from meat, as well as abrogating our voluntary Lenten disciplines. If it falls on a Sunday, the feast day is observed on the following Monday, and it's still a solemnity. If it falls during Holy Week, it's transferred to the closest possible day before March 19, usually the Saturday before Palm Sunday. I'm not sure how they let the swallows know.

In 1955, Pope Pius XII established a second day to honor St. Joseph, under the title of St. Joseph the Worker, celebrated on May 1, in order to remind communists and socialists celebrating May Day of St. Joseph's status as the "patron of workers" and "model of workers".

The traditional practice in preparation for St. Joseph's Day is the Seven Sundays of St. Joseph. Beginning at the end of January, on each of the seven Sundays preceding the feast of St. Joseph, we receive Communion in his honor and remember one of the seven joys and sorrows of St. Joseph, found in the Bible. We also pray the Litany of St. Joseph, in which he is remembered as the "Terror of Demons", amongst other things. Pretty awesome.

Here are the Seven Sorrows and Joys of St. Joseph:

First Sorrow – Joseph Resolves to Leave Mary (Mt 1:18–19)
First Joy – The Annunciation to St. Joseph (Mt 1:20–21)
Second Sorrow – The Poverty of Jesus' Birth (Lk 2:6–7)
Second Joy – The Birth of the Savior of Mankind (Lk 2:10–19)
Third Sorrow – The Circumcision of Christ (Lk 2:21)
Third Joy – The Holy Name of Jesus (Mt 1:24–25)
Fourth Sorrow – Simeon's Prophecy (Lk 2:34–35)
Fourth Joy – The Salvation of Mankind (Lk 2:29–33)
Fifth Sorrow – The Flight into Egypt (Mt 2:13–14)
Fifth Joy – The Toppling of the Idols (Is 19:1)
Sixth Sorrow – The Perilous Return from Exile (Mt 2:19–22)
Sixth Joy – Family Life at Nazareth (Lk 2:39–40)
Seventh Sorrow – The Loss of Jesus in Jerusalem (Lk 2:42–45)
Seventh Joy – The Finding of Jesus in the Temple (Lk 2:46–52)

Prayers and meditations for each of the sorrows and joys can be found online and in various prayer books.

It is hard to remember to start praying the Seven Sundays of St. Joseph before Lent has even begun. You can't even put a recurring reminder on your phone calendar, because the dates of the Sundays involved will change each year. I try just to be generally aware that it's going to start sometime near the end of January. Then we do the readings and say the prayers right after dinner, or in conjunction with bedtime prayers.

The *real* thing to do for St. Joseph's Day is a St. Joseph's Table. This is a stair-step multilevel table, covered in breads baked in the shape of tools, various pastries in liturgical shapes, multiple pasta and vegetables dishes (all sprinkled with bread crumbs to remind us of the sawdust in St. Joseph's workshop), lots of fava beans, twelve whole fish, and so forth. St. Joseph's cream puffs (*sfinge*) are a must. Also, you're supposed to wear red. It sounds amazing. And if you're planning to put one together, please invite me ... because I am *not* going to put one together. I think I would need a whole army of Italian grandmas to manage that.

But the day must be celebrated, and our family meal, while much less traditional than the above is also very memorable. One of the best parts of my high school career was eating at the home of a friend who came from an Italian-American family. Every meal his mom cooked was amazing, but the most fun were the days when they would invite big groups of kids for what we called Pasta un Gobola Tabola, which doesn't translate into anything, but *means* "Pasta on the Table". They would set a large, sanded, oiled sheet of plywood on sawhorses in the front yard. Entire high school sports teams or our whole three-parish youth group would gather hungrily around, and Mrs. Vitale would dump pots of pasta with butter and parmesan cheese in the middle of the "table". Then we would all eat it ... with our hands. It was the *best*.

It's perfect for the feast of St. Joseph. As a carpenter, Joseph worked with his hands. In honor of his day, we eat with our hands! I can boil noodles, and I'm not averse to giving the table a good scouring every once in a while. For our St. Joseph's Day celebration, we gather around the table and eat spaghetti with our hands. We sprinkle it with parmesan cheese and canned Italian bread crumbs to look like the sawdust from St. Joseph's workshop. *And* there are cream puffs. I can manage cream puffs too. Some years they're homemade; some years they're from the frozen-dessert section of the grocery store.

Since it's a solemnity, I usually add some fancy sides, such as caprese salad, meatballs on toothpicks, and cantaloupe with prosciutto. We have wine and Italian soda for the kids. Of course, St. Joseph wasn't Italian; he was a Galilean. But neither was St. Patrick Irish. Anyway, the Italians have officially claimed him, so we just go with that.

For dinner conversation, we talk about St. Joseph. You often hear St. Joseph referred to as the "guardian" or "foster father" of Jesus. But I think that's more confusing and not as accurate as calling him Jesus' adoptive father, also known as *his father*. Jesus is of the line of David, a lineage he gets from being Joseph's son. Joseph isn't just playing a role; he isn't just looking after Jesus like a bodyguard. He is Jesus' actual, no-kidding father, just as much as any other adoptive father would be—that is to say, completely.

God (in the Person of the Holy Spirit) is, of course, Jesus' biological father. But since delving into what it means to be a biological father is probably not great dinner-table conversation, we take this opportunity to explain what adoption is. We explain that, when a baby's parents are not able to care for him and take care of his daily needs (often because they have died, but sometimes for other reasons), another mother and father can take care of him and be his mom and dad. We know that God is Jesus' father, but God the Father and God the Holy Spirit are not human beings. We know that God loves each one of us and cares for us, but we don't see him and we can't touch him.

Jesus is completely God *and* completely human, and his human nature needed a father on earth who could feed him and rock him to sleep and teach him to fish. Jesus was, from the moment of his conception, fully God and fully man. From the moment of his conception, he, as God, knew *all things*, past, present, and future. But, as man, he "increased in wisdom and in stature" (Lk 2:52). He needed someone on earth, with a body, who could help him do that.

A guy like that deserves to be remembered with cream puffs.

FEAST OF ST. CATHERINE OF SWEDEN: MARCH 24

St. Catherine lived in the fourteenth century and was the daughter of St. Bridget of Sweden. She was married at a young age, but she and her husband chose to live as brother and sister, until his death, when she became a nun alongside her mother. Through their work with the poor throughout Europe, they often counseled women who suffered from difficult pregnancies or miscarriages, and St. Catherine has long been invoked as the patron saint against miscarriage.

So far, I have had nine pregnancies and no losses. The majority of my friends, however, have experienced miscarriage. Parents of a miscarried child can often feel alone in their grief. I find it comforting to know that the Catholic Church has long recognized the need for an intercessor in heaven against, and after, miscarriage.

In addition to St. Catherine of Sweden, we have St. Gerard Majella, an eighteenth-century Italian lay brother of the Redemptorist Order. He is often invoked by expectant mothers and by those having difficulty conceiving. His feast day is October 16.

Limbo

The Catholic Church does not have an official teaching on what happens to babies who die before they can be baptized. There has been speculation of a "limbo of infants", which would be a place of natural happiness apart from the Beatific Vision, to which unbaptized babies—free of actual sin, but not cleansed of original sin—would go. But that was never more than one possible theory, and there have always been saints and theologians who believed differently.

The *Catechism of the Catholic Church* (*CCC*) tells us:

> As regards children who have died without Baptism, the Church can only entrust them to the mercy of God, as she does in her funeral rites for them. Indeed, the great mercy of God who desires that all men should be saved, and Jesus' tenderness toward children which caused him to say: "Let the children come to me, do not hinder them" (Mk 10:14; cf. 1 Tim 2:4), allow us to hope that there is a way of salvation for children who have died without Baptism. All the more urgent is the Church's call not to prevent little children coming to Christ through the gift of holy Baptism. (1261)

This, however, applies to children who were born and could have been baptized, but for some reason were not. That isn't the case for miscarried or stillborn babies.

A mother whose child died in her womb certainly did nothing to "prevent" the baptism. In fact, in the case of expectant parents who desired the baptism of their child, and *would* have baptized their child if they had had the opportunity, it seems to me that the Church's position on catechumens would be more applicable: "For catechumens who die before their Baptism, their explicit desire to receive it, together with repentance for their sins, and charity, assures them the salvation that they were not able to receive through the sacrament" (*CCC* 1259). But this passage specifically refers to adults, not the unborn.

I take comfort in the long-standing Church tradition that St. John the Baptist was sanctified and filled with the Holy Spirit and cleansed of original sin within his mother's womb,[10] because of what his *mother* heard and believed: "And when Elizabeth heard the greeting of Mary, the child leaped in her womb; and Elizabeth was filled with the Holy Spirit and she exclaimed with a loud cry, 'Blessed are you among women, and blessed is the fruit of your womb! And why is this granted me, that the mother of my Lord should come to me? For behold, when the voice of your greeting came to my ears, the child in my womb leaped for joy'" (Lk 1:41–44). It is my conviction that babies who die before they could be baptized are similarly sanctified by the belief and desire of their mothers.

But, again, unless and until the Church gives us an official teaching on this, we can't know for sure, and it's an issue upon which good Catholics may disagree. The best advice is probably both to pray for the repose of their souls *and* to ask for their intercession; that way, all bases are covered.

I love that St. Bridget and St. Catherine are venerated as saints together, as mother and daughter. That's the goal, right? We want to become saints, and we also want to inspire our children to sanctity. Other examples of this ideal are SS. Louis and Zélie Martin, the parents of St. Saint Thérèse of Lisieux; SS. Anne and Joachim, the parents of Mary; St. Monica, the mother of St. Augustine; and St. Elizabeth, the mother of St. John the Baptist. The faith of these parents set the ultimate good example for their children.

See the feast of St. Bridget of Sweden on July 23 for some ideas for Swedish foods that would be appropriate for a family meal for the day, but I often prefer to observe the day with some low-key

---

[10] For more on this see the Solemnity of the Nativity of St. John the Baptist in chapter 8.

one-on-one time with one of my older kids. I can usually find time on this day, or sometime during the week, to have lunch or dinner out together, or to go for a walk. Especially in a large family, time alone with older kids is at a premium, but it's something I make sure to accomplish at least every now and then. Attaching it to a feast day is a good way to remember!

SOLEMNITY OF THE ANNUNCIATION OF THE LORD (LADY DAY): MARCH 25

March 25 is the most important date in human history. It has also been a very busy day in Christendom. You know it's the solemnity of the Annunciation, also known as Lady Day (for Our Lady), because it says so right up there. But did you know that March 25 is also understood by Christians to be the date on which God created man, the date on which Adam and Eve fell, the date on which Our Lord was crucified, *and* the date on which Frodo Baggins cast the one ring into the fiery depths of Mount Doom in J. R. R. Tolkien's *Lord of the Rings* trilogy?

And did you know that they're all connected?

The sixth-century *Martyrologium Hieronymianum* (the earliest surviving list of Christian martyrdoms and other important dates worth remembering) lists all those events, except the Frodo one, of course. It also lists the parting of the Red Sea and the final test of Abraham as being commemorated by the earliest Christians on March 25. Obviously, these guys weren't in possession of Moses' datebook—or God's. But they believed these important events must share a common date because of the way they complement and illuminate and fulfill each other. Each was a beginning or an ending that forever affected mankind.

Jesus Christ died on 15 Nisan of the Jewish calendar, which is March 25 on the Roman calendar. Jewish tradition held that a great man would die on the same day as his conception, so the early Christians determined that the date of Jesus' conception must have also been March 25. From the conception date came the date on which we celebrate Christmas, as December 25 is nine months after the Annunciation. So, when devout lifelong Catholic J. R. R. Tolkien was writing a story in which a humble hero triumphs over temptation and suffering and saves the world from the forces of evil, well, it *had* to happen on March 25.

That considered, it's an odd twist that because of the new ranking of feast days since the 1969 revision of the liturgical calendar, the feast of the Annunciation can no longer fall on Good Friday, when we remember the Crucifixion. Then again, it's good to have two different days to commemorate these two great events in salvation history. When the Annunciation falls on a Sunday in Lent before Palm Sunday, it is transferred to the following Monday. If it falls on Palm Sunday or on any day in Holy Week or Easter Week, it is transferred to Low Monday, the Monday after the Sunday after Easter. When it's not during Lent, it is somehow not *quite* as sweet.

We've been celebrating feast days for more than ten years now, and heaven help me if I try to mix things up too much. The kids love how the days come back around again the same way each year. Tierneys have waffles for dinner on the Annunciation. You can count on it. They started off as toaster waffles. Now they are usually homemade waffles. One year they were waffles from the International House of Pancakes across from Los Angeles International Airport. One way or another, there must be waffles for dinner for the Annunciation.

Apparently, the tradition is a result of the fact that in Swedish the words for "Lady Day" sound an awful lot like "Waffle Day". Somewhere along the line someone mentioned to me that folks were supposed to eat waffles on the Annunciation and call it *Våffeldagen*, and really, that was all I needed. My children are *very* excited about the idea of breakfast for dinner. I get excited about their excitement.

That's really what I'm trying to do with all of this. I'm trying to make the liturgical year fun and memorable for my kids. I want them to call me from college and ask me for my waffle recipe because they cannot imagine *not* eating waffles for dinner on the Annunciation. Because *that* will mean that they know when the Annunciation is, and hopefully they'll have gone to Mass. Hopefully they'll also know *what* the Annunciation is, because along with the waffles we always read (or perform) the story of the Annunciation in St. Luke's Gospel (Lk 1:26-38). It's my sincere hope that weaving our faith into our family culture and traditions will help my kids stay Catholic, forever and ever.

Since the angel Gabriel's message to Mary included the fact that she would give birth to a son, we like to decorate for the Annunciation with "It's a boy!" party supplies, as if we're throwing Our Lady a little baby shower. Blue balloons, paper bunting, crepe paper centerpieces, baby shower paper plates: it's all easy to find online or at a local party store and makes a really fun theme for the party. It can be confusing to our guests, as I am, as often as not, expecting a baby myself during our parties. But, unlike Mary, *we* don't find out what we're having ahead of time. Everyone assumes for a moment that I am making an announcement for myself, but *then* they get it.

For the entertainment, the kids will often put on an Annunciation puppet show. Any type of puppets will do. We use stick puppets that I created by printing out a fine-art version of the Annunciation on card stock, carefully cutting out each figure, and hot-gluing it onto a dowel. There are only three parts: the Virgin Mary, the angel Gabriel, and the narrator. Since the performers can't be seen by the audience, they don't need to memorize their parts; they can read their parts from the script. For nonreading kids, I sit just to the side of the stage and feed them their lines in a low voice.

At noon or at six, or both, we stand in front of the painting *The Annunciation* by H. O. Tanner that hangs in our living room and say the Angelus prayer, repeating the conversation between Mary and the angel Gabriel. The Angelus is a prayer that dates back to at least the thirteenth century. Traditionally the prayer was repeated at six in the morning, noon, and six in the evening, and church bells reminded the faithful to stop and pray.

If the Angelus isn't a usual part of your routine, this would be an excellent day to give it a whirl. It is our goal to say the Angelus every day, but we do it just once, at noon. Without the pealing of the church bells, I find it nearly impossible to notice when it's noon unless I set a reminder alarm on my phone. But if I hear the alarm, we always stop what we're doing, like the people of old, and pray. If you've got a church bells setting on your phone alarm, it makes it even better.

LAETARE SUNDAY: THE FOURTH SUNDAY OF LENT

Laetare Sunday occurs just after the midpoint of Lent, which means we're over the hump and on the downhill coast to Easter. This Sunday gets its name from the first few words of the Latin entrance antiphon for the Mass of the day: "Laetare Jerusalem" (Rejoice, Jerusalem), which comes from Isaiah 66:10.

Traditionally, this is a day of rejoicing that we've made it this far, and it is a little break from the somber tone of Lent. You might notice the priest wearing rose-colored vestments on Laetare Sunday, one of only two days of the year when those vestments may be worn, the other being Gaudete Sunday during Advent. (It's not required that priests wear them on either day, just permitted.) If you're as much of a liturgical-year nerd as I am, you might wear pink to Mass as well.

Unlike the rest of Lent, on Laetare Sunday—and also on some feast days—flowers are allowed on the altar, and instrumental music can be played (at other times instruments are allowed only to support the singing).[11] Because of this, weddings were often celebrated on Laetare Sunday, but not during the rest of Lent. It was also traditional on this day to make a pilgrimage to the church in which you were baptized, which would be your "mother church", or to the nearest cathedral. Today, in many places in Europe, Laetare Sunday is observed as their Mother's Day.

Medium-rare steaks (still a bit pink inside) are our favorite way to observe both the color and the specialness of the day. And I like to make a pink cake. Any type of cake will do for the inside. For the frosting, I make a standard powdered-sugar buttercream frosting recipe minus any liquid it calls for, and then dump a cup or so of (defrosted) frozen raspberries in there. It makes for a lovely pink frosting. A can of pink frosting would work too.

PASSION SUNDAY: THE FIFTH SUNDAY OF LENT

Traditionally, the fifth Sunday of Lent was Passion Sunday, and it marked the beginning of Passiontide, when the focus shifted away from Jesus' prayerful preparation in the desert to his suffering and death on the cross. Today the *title* of Passion Sunday has been suppressed, and instead the following Sunday is known as Palm Sunday of the Passion of Christ. But the beautiful customs associated with Passiontide are still allowed to be practiced in churches and in our homes.

---

[11] United States Conference of Catholic Bishops, *General Instruction of the Roman Missal* (Washington, D.C.: United States Conference of Catholic Bishops, 2010), nos. 305 and 313. http://www.vatican.va/roman_curia/congregations/ccdds/documents/rc_con_ccdds_doc _20030317_ordinamento-messale_en.html#DECREE_OF_PUBLICATION.

Veiling of Statues

The traditional Gospel reading for Passion Sunday concludes: "So they took up stones to throw at him; but Jesus hid himself, and went out of the temple" (Jn 8:59). From these lines, from Jesus hiding himself from the crowd that rejects him, comes the tradition of veiling statues and crucifixes in churches and in homes on the fifth Sunday of Lent. During the preceding weeks of Lent, we try to focus on the ways we can better love and serve God and our neighbor. Finally, in these last two weeks, we have the opportunity to recognize and humbly admit our weakness and sin, and all the ways that we reject Jesus.

As Catholics, we know the power of sacred images, and especially the crucifix, to draw us toward Jesus. For fifty weeks of the year, the many crucifixes in my home recall my thoughts to Jesus and his great love for me. For two weeks of the year, they are hidden beneath a veil of purple cloth. Covered, they become an even more visible reminder to pray and to recollect my thoughts to Christ and his Passion. If you don't have a crucifix in your home, Passiontide would be a great time to get one. Then consider getting some inexpensive purple cloth from the fabric store and veiling it, along with other prominent religious images you might have in your home. In this way you can enter into the spirit of admitting faults and preparing for the sorrow of Holy Week and the joy of the Resurrection.

Just a note: the veiling of statues is a tradition that seems to be making a comeback in Catholic churches over the past few years. It's a great tradition. It's not a requirement, and a parish can choose to participate or not. But if they do, it should happen on the fifth Sunday of Lent, not at the beginning of Lent.

Also, some of us own *many* religious statues and images. In our home, we have a crucifix in each room, and we have paintings of Our Lady and the saints, and we have many various small statues and plaques and knickknacks collected on our travels over the years. It isn't practical to try to cover them all. Instead, I choose to cover the most visible pieces, especially the crucifixes. That's enough to set the tone in our home.

Sometimes kids, used to seeing their favorite statues of Jesus and Mary and the saints at church, can be troubled or upset or downright

furious at finding them covered. This is just another example of kids
setting an example for us grown-ups. That's exactly how we are all
supposed to feel about it. That's the whole reason it has been done
for centuries. To avoid possible meltdowns during Mass, however,
it might be a good idea to get to church early on the fifth Sunday of
Lent, to have a chance to talk about what's going on, and why Jesus
and his friends are hiding from us.

Surrounded by our purple statues, it seems appropriate to have a
purple dinner. I like to serve chicken or pork with red cabbage, and,
if I can find them, purple potatoes. For dessert, a berry pie makes a
nice purple mess.

Confession

There are seven precepts of the Church, seven rules understood as
the bare minimum for active participation in the Catholic Church.
Five are listed together in the *Catechism of the Catholic Church* (2041–
43), and the other two are found elsewhere in the *Catechism* (1631,
905). The seven precepts don't address all the things we may *not* do,
just the bare minimum of what we *must* do to be a Catholic in good
standing. They are the following:

1. Attend Mass on Sundays and holy days of obligation, and rest on
   those days from our usual work.
2. Confess our sins to a priest at least once a year.
3. Receive Our Lord Jesus Christ in the Holy Eucharist at least
   once a year, during the Easter season.
4. Observe the days of abstinence and fasting.
5. Contribute to the support of the Church.
6. Obey the laws of the Church concerning matrimony.
7. Participate in the Church's mission of evangelization of souls.

Probably we're not looking to be "bare minimum" Catholics. But
sometimes it's helpful to know what that bare minimum is. The one
that specifically concerns us this week is number 2, confession at
least once a year. Hopefully we are confessing our sins regularly.
We needn't have committed a mortal sin in order to benefit from

confession. The regular confessing of venial sins helps us to grow in grace and in the strength to avoid those sins in the future.

That said, sometimes the days and weeks get away from us, and we realize it has been quite a while since our last confession. In our family, our goal is to get to confession once a month, usually after First Friday Mass. But we make a special point of going to confession as a family during Advent and Lent, and as part of our January 1, Sacred Heart, and All Souls' Day plenary indulgences. The adults and older kids each make an annual retreat, during which they receive the sacrament of confession, and our parish priest is great about staying after daily Mass if one of the kids (or grown-ups) needs to get something off his chest.

It's a good practice to make sure to have those regular times of confession so that we don't inadvertently go more than a year without receiving the sacrament. Lent, and particularly this week before Holy Week, is a great time to fit in that yearly bare minimum. I don't personally prefer reconciliation services, where the whole congregation lines up at stations throughout the church and we all make our confessions as if at the drive-through. The absolution is valid (as long as each person confesses individually to a priest) and it answers the precept, but it doesn't have the same personal feel as individual confession. We go during our parish's regular confession times, or we make an appointment with the priest, usually during this week, to avoid burdening an already very busy priest during Holy Week.

PALM SUNDAY: THE SIXTH SUNDAY OF LENT

The sixth and final Sunday of Lent is Palm Sunday, on which we commemorate Jesus' triumphal entry into Jerusalem. Blessed palm fronds are distributed at Mass, for better and for worse. The palms are sacramentals, material objects that can help dispose us to receive the grace available in the sacraments—which is lovely. These sacramentals seem an awful lot like swords or lightsabers, though, which can make getting through the Mass that day a challenge for parents— especially since it's a long Mass (we hear the entire Passion of Our Lord from one of the Gospels).

Because the palms are blessed, they may not be thrown away. For that reason, we don't let our kids use them as weapons. But we do let them bring home as many as they've collected. There, they can do their best to fold them into crosses and flowers and curlicues. We put the whole bunch in a vase on our home altar table, where it stays until I realize on Ash Wednesday that I forgot to bring them back to church—again. So, we burn them ourselves and scatter the ashes in the garden.

The priest's vestments on Palm Sunday are red. Red vestments are worn to celebrate feasts of the Holy Spirit and feasts of martyrs. The red symbolizes the shedding of the blood of the martyrs, and it symbolizes the fire of the Holy Spirit when it's worn on the feast of Pentecost and for confirmation Masses. On Palm Sunday it reminds us of Jesus' suffering.

In our family, we like to wear red to Mass also. We wave our palms and shout, "Hosanna!" just as the people lining the streets of Jerusalem did. But then, moments later during the Gospel, we shout "Crucify him!" just as the people of Jerusalem turned on Jesus a few days later and demanded that he be crucified.

It makes me cringe to hear my voice and the voices of my parents, husband, children, friends and neighbors all shouting together, "Crucify him!" And yet it's true: it is for us he was crucified—for our sins. Not for the sins of some unruly mob two thousand years ago, but for my sins and for yours. We shout, "Crucify him!", every day in the secrecy of our hearts, and then, once a year, we shout it out loud for everyone to hear. It's a humbling thing, but I'm grateful for it, nonetheless—for this opportunity to enter into the Gospel, to enter into the story of the Passion.

For dinner on Palm Sunday, I like to serve Middle Eastern food, such as falafel and hummus and flatbread. And I make a hearts of palm salad to go with it. You can find hearts of palm in the canned-vegetable section of the grocery store.

HOLY WEEK: MONDAY AND TUESDAY

I like to spend (hmm, I guess "like" might be too strong a word, but either way, I *do* spend) the first three days of Holy Week cleaning. The idea of "spring cleaning" is just too vague ever to happen around here. But a set three days of the year, during Holy Week? *That* I can remember and do. And the kids are expecting it, so there is less drama. I get significantly less pushback on things like this when they know it's coming. It becomes just another family-culture thing. They know that for Tierneys, Holy Week is a working week. I think it's an appropriate time for us to run ourselves a bit ragged and then enjoy Easter and eight days of celebration all the more.

I make a giant pot of soup, and we eat that for dinner for the three days of cleaning. It's not everyone's favorite thing to eat the same dinner three days in a row, but ... it's Lent, right? And this way, I don't have to worry about cooking each night and am more available to work on projects around the house.

The Gospel for the Monday of Holy Week is the Anointing at Bethany (Jn 12:1–8), when Mary, the sister of Martha and Lazarus, anointed the feet of Jesus with expensive perfumed oil and wiped them with her hair. The "waste" *really* bugged Judas. Other events remembered on Holy Monday include Jesus cursing the fig tree for failing to give fruit and Jesus cleansing the temple, when he overturned tables and chased out the money changers with a whip made of cords.

It really puts one in the mood to get things done, I tell ya.

So, on Monday, we clean out the playroom and schoolroom and living room. That means overturning the toy bins, and broken or little-used toys are tossed or donated. We sort books, music, and movies. We get rid of the things we don't use and love. We organize the remaining media, toys, books, and craft supplies. Usually, it doesn't require whips, but I'm not ruling them out.

Tuesday of Holy Week is remembered as the day on which Jesus predicted his coming death: "The hour has come for the Son of man to be glorified. Truly, truly, I say to you, unless a grain of wheat falls into the earth and dies, it remains alone; but if it dies, it bears much fruit. He who loves his life loses it, and he who hates his life in this world will keep it for eternal life" (Jn 12:23–25).

On Tuesday, we clean bedrooms. Stained, worn out, ill-fitting, or unloved clothing comes out of closets and is tossed or donated. We go through all the treasures that have been squirreled away in there over the past year. If it's not loved, if it's not in good shape, or if it doesn't have a place, it's gone. I try to sell the kids on how, just like the wheat, if their old clothes stay in the closet, they remain just old clothes, but if they fall to the ground and are put in bags and trucked out of here, we can get new Easter clothes. It's a bit of a stretch, I know.

Also on Tuesday, I finalize my guest lists for dinners for the rest of the week, make sure I know what I'm making, and write out my shopping lists.

SPY WEDNESDAY

On Wednesday, the kitchen gets deep cleaned, including the inside of the fridge and the insides of cabinets and drawers. Once the kitchen is ready to go, I do the grocery shopping for the rest of the week. Then, that evening, our Holy Week activities begin.

This is the day we remember Judas betraying Jesus, telling the high priest when Jesus would be in a place where he could be more conveniently arrested, in exchange for thirty pieces of silver. It's traditionally called *Spy* Wednesday, because of Judas' sneakiness.

At home, we read the parts of the Gospels that tell the story. In Matthew: "Then one of the Twelve, who was called Judas Iscariot, went to the chief priests and said, 'What will you give me if I deliver him to you?' And they paid him thirty pieces of silver. And from that moment he sought an opportunity to betray him" (26:14–16). And in Luke: "Then Satan entered into Judas called Iscariot, who was of the number of the Twelve; he went away and conferred with the chief priests and captains how he might betray him to them. And they were glad, and engaged to give him money. So he agreed, and sought an opportunity to betray him to them in the absence of the multitude" (22:3–6).

Then I hide our own thirty pieces of silver (quarters) in one area of the house for the kids to find. It usually turns into an interesting social experiment. My (mostly) kind and pleasant children tend to turn into a bunch of Judases themselves. They push past each other and grab quarters that other kids had spotted first but couldn't reach, and the baby usually gets knocked over—all over thirty pieces of silver.

We talk about it. We talk about how dangerous greed can be, and how easy it is to make bad decisions where money and power are concerned. It's too easy just to write Judas off as a "bad guy". Judas knew Jesus. He had been with Jesus for three years, listening to him talk, watching him pray, seeing him perform countless miracles. It's reasonable to think Judas "believed" in Jesus but had come to expect that he would rise up and overthrow the Roman occupiers of Jerusalem. After all, God had given this land to the Jews, but now they were subject to pagan rulers. Judas may have been waiting for Jesus to establish his kingdom on earth, in the tradition of the great Old Testament warrior kings, such as David.

In betraying Jesus to the chief priests, Judas might well have thought he was a patriot spurring Jesus into action. The problem with that is it shows a grievous lack of both trust and humility, for him to think that he knew better than God what the plan should be and when it should be carried out.

When Luke says about Judas that "Satan entered him", this shouldn't be understood to be something that happened to Judas passively. Satan is able to enter a person only if the person opens himself up to Satan in some way. Judas had been thinking about betraying Jesus. When he finally made his decision, at that point he was resolved that he would do this evil thing: betray his friend and turn over a man he knew to be innocent to be tried and punished. *That* is when he gave Satan permission to enter his soul.

In the same way, the fact that Jesus foretells Judas' betrayal at the Last Supper and even tells him to get on with it (Jn 13:21–30) shouldn't be understood to be a command to betray him or support of the betrayal. All it means is that Jesus, as God, can see that Judas' free decision has been made. Judas could have chosen differently.

Judas and Peter

It interesting to note the similarities between Judas and Peter. After all, Jesus predicts the disloyalty of both men. Each protests that he never would turn against Jesus, but in the end, both do. On the night of Holy Thursday, after the Last Supper, Judas betrays Jesus with a kiss, indicating to the guards whom they should arrest. Just a few hours later, outside the house of the high priest, Peter denies Jesus three times.

Both men repent almost immediately. Matthew tells us: "When Judas, his betrayer, saw that he was condemned, he repented and brought back the thirty pieces of silver to the chief priests and the elders, saying, 'I have sinned in betraying innocent blood'" (27:3–4). And Luke writes about Peter: "And immediately, while he was still speaking, the cock crowed. And the Lord turned and looked at Peter.

And Peter remembered the word of the Lord, how he had said to him, 'Before the cock crows today, you will deny me three times.' And he went out and wept bitterly" (22:60–62).

So how does Peter end up the leader of the early Church, the first pope, and a saint, while Judas is the great villain of Christianity? What's the difference between the hero and the zero?

Humility.

Faced with what he had done, Judas "went and hanged himself" (Mt 27:5). In Judas' case, this is the ultimate act of pride. He sees his sins as so great that even God couldn't forgive them. He despairs and takes matters into his own hands. Judas' refusal to trust in God's mercy and seek forgiveness is his true sin.

None of us is in a position to judge the eternal state of another's soul. It's possible that Judas repented again, of this last great sin, before he died. We can't know. But it is likely that Judas did not repent and is in hell. After all, Jesus said it would have been better for Judas if he had never been born (Mt 26:24).

Peter, on the other hand, waits. And for a guy prone to rash acts such as jumping out of boats and cutting off people's ears, that can't have been easy. He has the courage and the humility to face his friends, none of whom but John can be very proud of how they behaved that night. After the Resurrection, Jesus appears to the disciples while they are fishing. Peter had denied Jesus three times. Now Jesus asks Peter three times, "Do you love me?" And three times Peter gets to reply yes (Jn 21:15–17). His reward is a beautiful reconciliation, a life lived for Christ, and a martyr's crown.

After a discussion like that, my kids' better natures can be prevailed upon to pool their quarters and put them in the poor box on our church visits the next day.

Tenebrae

An ancient tradition for the night before any of the three days of the Triduum is Tenebrae (Latin for "shadows" or "darkness"). In this service, all of the candles on the altar are gradually extinguished until the church is in complete darkness. At the moment of darkness, a loud clash occurs, symbolizing the *strepitus*, the earthquake that followed Jesus' death: "And behold, the curtain of the temple was torn in two, from top to bottom; and the earth shook, and the rocks were split" (Mt 27:51).

We can recreate this feeling at home. All it takes is a candlelight dinner and your utensils. After everyone has finished eating (the third day of the soup at our house), the plates are cleared but not the silverware. Any lights in the house visible from the table are turned off, leaving just the light of the candles. One person is chosen to hold the candle snuffer, and everyone else holds his fork and spoon. The snuffer person puts out the candles, slowly, one by one. When the last candle is extinguished, the snuffer whispers, "One ... two ... three." On "three" everyone bangs his fork and spoon on the table *once*: *Boom!* (This might not work for you if you have a glass table.)

With that, the liturgical season of Lent has ended, and the Triduum begins.

6

The Triduum

As the end of Lent comes into sight, one of my favorite things is saying the word "Triduum" (pronounced *trij*-oo-um). Seriously, how great is that word? It's right up there with "trousers", "gubernatorial", and "ladle".

But the Triduum is more than just fun to say; it's also fun to do. It is only three days long, from the evening of Holy Thursday to the evening of Easter Sunday, but those three days pack a lot of punch. Even though Lent officially ends before the evening Mass of the Lord's Supper on Holy Thursday, at which time the Easter Triduum begins, Catholics do not abandon their Lenten disciplines until the celebration of Easter begins, either after the Easter Vigil or on Easter morning.

Entering the Silence

After the Gloria at the Mass of the Lord's Supper, the organ is not used and all church bells are silenced until the Easter Vigil on Saturday night. In earlier eras, church bells would ring throughout the day to alert the townspeople to the time and to recollect them to prayer. The silence was a very noticeable change, and the Triduum was referred to as "the still days".

It's a good chance to think about how we can find a little of that stillness in our own lives. To a mom, that can feel impossible. And, as a person who is about to launch into a description of the approximately six thousand things our family does over the Triduum, I recognize the irony of even attempting to advocate for silence. But bear with me.

For me, what it comes down to is figuring out what fills me up, as a mom and as a Christian, and what drains me or just takes up time. Over the course of these three days, I usually do a lot of activities with the children, from-scratch cooking, and entertaining. Largely, those are things that fill me up. Teaching my kids and spending time on adventures with them are things I really enjoy. I also enjoy occasionally making a challenging dinner, and I enjoy sharing those dinners with friends. The work involved is a sacrifice I can make for others, and the result is something I can feel proud of (or something that can help me grow in humility, if it's one of *those* days).

On the other hand, I try to get rid of stuff that doesn't help. I like having things tidy, but I don't find cleaning and laundry particularly fulfilling, so I try to get ahead of that stuff at the beginning of the week. I like social media overall, but I have to admit that on a day-to-day basis, it's a time suck and can be a distraction from my prayer, my family, and my daily responsibilities. So, for these three days, I'll usually share a message for the day in the morning and then stay away from it completely for the rest of the day. If I'm feeling tempted to spend time on my phone, I'll just delete the tempting apps and put them back on after Easter. As busy as we are with Masses and visits and special meals, just cutting out that one thing means that I find myself with moments in which I have nothing to do. I can't just grab my phone and busy myself with that. I'm forced to take the advice of Psalm 46: "Be still, and know that I am God" (v. 10).

Your pluses and minuses might be different from mine, and it might take some trial and error to figure them out. But it is worth the effort to find a bit of stillness in the chaos of Catholic family life during these few days.

HOLY THURSDAY (MAUNDY THURSDAY)

The evening of Holy Thursday begins the Triduum. We focus on the Last Supper, when Jesus observed the Jewish feast of Passover with his apostles, washed their feet, and instituted the Eucharist and the sacramental priesthood. On this night Jesus said to his followers, "A new commandment I give to you, that you love one another; even as I have loved you, that you also love one another" (Jn 13:34). This verse is the reason Holy Thursday is also called Maundy Thursday; the word "maundy" comes from the Latin word *mandatum*, which means "commandment". Sadly, on the very night that Jesus tells his followers to imitate his love for them, Judas betrays him and Peter denies him three times.

A Chrism Mass is held in the cathedral of each diocese during Holy Week, often on the morning of Holy Thursday. The holy oils needed for sacraments during the year, such as baptisms and confirmations, are blessed and distributed. The clergy gather from all the parishes in the diocese to receive the oils and to celebrate the institution of the priesthood at the Last Supper, when Jesus said, "Do this in remembrance of me" (Lk 22:19).

Apart from the Chrism Mass, no morning Masses are celebrated. Instead, the Mass of the Lord's Supper is offered in the evening. During this Mass, enough hosts are consecrated to fulfill the needs of the parish for Viaticum (Communion for the gravely sick) and for services offered on Good Friday because no Masses are celebrated until the Easter Vigil and no new hosts may be consecrated.

It seems a bit counterintuitive, doesn't it? On Good Friday, the anniversary of the day on which Jesus' actual sacrifice took place, we don't celebrate the Holy Sacrifice of the Mass. St. Thomas Aquinas tells us that the Mass "is a figure and a representation of our Lord's Passion. ... And therefore on the day on which our Lord's Passion is recalled as it was really accomplished, this sacrament is not consecrated."[1]

Following the Holy Thursday Mass, the Blessed Sacrament is removed from the tabernacle in the church, which is left open and empty. The Blessed Sacrament, in a temporary tabernacle or a pyx, is placed on an Altar of Repose in a different location in the church, an adjacent chapel, or another room on the parish grounds. It is traditional to chant or to recite the "Tantum Ergo" as the Blessed Sacrament is moved to the Altar of Repose. Afterward people can pray before the Blessed Sacrament until late at night, in imitation of the apostles who were with the Lord in the Garden of Gethsemane.

---

[1] Thomas Aquinas, *Summa theologica* III, q. 83, art. 2, ad. 2, trans. Fathers of the English Dominican Province (New York, N.Y.: Benziger Bros.,1947), Christian Classics Ethereal Library, http://www.ccel.org/a/aquinas/summa/cache/summa.pdf.

Seven Churches Visitation

From this practice arose the tradition of visiting several churches to pray before the Blessed Sacrament in each one. It began with St. Philip Neri (feast day: May 26), who would organize his sixteenth-century buddies on a walking tour of Rome to visit the city's seven basilicas on the night of Holy Thursday.

I love the concept of the Seven Churches Visitation, walking in the dark (maybe with St. Philip Neri), praying at the Altars of Repose in the grandest churches in the world. But I don't love the idea of keeping my little kids up so late at the beginning of a big weekend. And nobody walks in Los Angeles. And most of our churches were built in the sixties, so they're not, um, *grand*. But even in the face of all that, after I heard about this tradition I knew I wanted to adopt it in some way. And so, during the day on Holy Thursday, I spend a few hours driving around the city visiting seven churches with the kids.

Since we've been doing this, we've visited many churches of different Catholic rites, such as Byzantine, Coptic, Armenian Catholic, Syro-Malabar, and Chaldean. It's a very cool chance to teach the kids about our brothers and sisters of the Eastern churches, our Church's "other lung", who are in full communion with Rome but have a very different look and feel to their celebrations and spaces.

At each church, we play "find the tabernacle" and then kneel and say a quick hello to Jesus. Next we do two stations from the Stations of the Cross. We find the devotional candles or the poor box and put in some of the change we've been saving throughout Lent and the quarters from Spy Wednesday, and we pray for our intentions and the intentions of friends and family. Then it's back to the car and on to the next stop. In the car, between churches, we listen to the sections covering Holy Week in a dramatized audio version of the Bible.[2]

Unfortunately, many churches are locked up tight during the day. That is a huge bummer in and of itself, but especially so if we are trying to visit the Blessed Sacrament in each one. If a church is locked, we just point ourselves in what we hope is the direction of

[2] *The Story of the Bible*, vol. 2, *The New Testament*, dramatized audiobook (Charlotte, N.C.: Saint Benedict Press, 2015).

the tabernacle and say a quick prayer and two more stations out there on the front steps. It's still fun to see the outside of a church.

We try to mix it up each year and visit churches we've never seen before, which is possible for us, because there are 287 parishes in the Archdiocese of Los Angeles. But you've got to make do with what you've got. An elderly gentleman at our parish, when we told him we were planning to do the Seven Churches Visitation, told us that when he was growing up, his town had only one church. So his family would go in and out of the church seven times!

Our Own Last Supper

Holy Thursday is a bit of a paradox. We commemorate the institution of the Eucharist and the priesthood, truly something to celebrate. But we also remember that it was on this day that Our Lord was betrayed by a friend and arrested. So, it's happy *and* sad. Our family observation focuses mostly on creating our own Last Supper.

For dinner we do a modified seder meal, without attempting to copy the Jewish ceremony. We are not obliged to celebrate Passover, because Jesus' sacrifice ushered in the New Covenant. I don't even think it's appropriate to attempt the religious rituals of another faith. But I still think it's fun to approximate what Jesus and his friends ate that night. I serve roasted lamb, applesauce (I tried making charoset one year, and my kids didn't like it, so we just have applesauce), some sort of potato dish—knish or kugel or latke—unleavened bread, a salad of bitter herbs, wine, and grape juice.

We also have a lamb cake. Lamb cakes really teeter on that edge between adorable and terrifying (do a web search of lamb cakes if you want to have nightmares), so I just mold one out of Rice Krispies Treats. I make a batch of treats, dump the mixture on wax paper, and let it cool until I can comfortably touch it. Or, I get impatient and just power through the molten marshmallows and figure my fingerprints will grow back. With well-buttered hands, I look at a picture of a lamb cake and just mold the mixture into that shape. The whole process takes about twenty minutes. I might slave for hours on a "real" lamb cake and still end up with something that's just going to freak everyone out, so I don't. For the last couple of years, our junior chef Bobby has taken over lamb-molding duties. Having big kids is awesome.

Either we attend the Mass of Our Lord's Supper, or we do the readings at home at the table after dinner. Then we pick names from a hat and wash each other's feet. It's such a little thing, but it really is meaningful to do it within a family. I find it so much more profound than the slightly awkward washing of feet that sometimes happens at Mass on Holy Thursday. At home, where we all know each other, it's not awkward. But it is very humbling to kneel down as Jesus did and wash the feet of one of your parents or siblings. Jesus told us, "If I then, your Lord and Teacher, have washed your feet, you also ought to wash one another's feet. For I have given you an example, that you also should do as I have done to you" (Jn 13:14–15).

We like to recite the hymn traditionally associated with the day, "Tantum Ergo", composed by St. Thomas Aquinas.[3] If we have time, we often watch the animated movie *The Prince of Egypt*.[4] It covers the Passover, which is what Jesus and his disciples were commemorating at the Last Supper, so it's especially appropriate for the day. It is a wonderful movie.

GOOD FRIDAY

Good Friday is a day of fasting and abstinence from meat.[5] We eat certain traditional foods associated with the day, but we eat them in small quantities.

For breakfast, I make hot cross buns. I was pretty excited to learn that there was, in fact, a traditional pastry meant to be eaten on Good Friday, and it was considered so Catholic that its sale was forbidden by decree of Elizabeth I (not a fan of Catholics). When I looked up the recipe, they seemed awfully sweet and tasty for such a somber day. My love of tradition won out, however, and now I think their deliciousness adds to the mortification of having them for a collation. We *want* to eat ten of them, but we eat only two (and they're small).

---

[3] See appendix B for more on this and other indulgences.

[4] *The Prince of Egypt*, directed by Brenda Chapman, Steve Hickner, and Simon Wells (Universal City, Cal.: DreamWorks Pictures, 1998); rated PG.

[5] See appendix A for more information on fasting.

Most years, I can manage to make them from scratch, but if that's not possible, canned biscuits or cinnamon rolls will work. The important thing is that they are marked with a cross on the top. You kiss the cross before eating the bun, as a sign of reverence for the cross of Jesus. For the rest of the fasting day, we avoid snacks, eat a half lunch, and save our one full meat-free meal for dinnertime.

A Somber Day

If your kids don't have the day off from school, you might want to consider keeping them home for the day. Adults who work might consider taking a personal day or a half day. It can be really powerful to spend this day focused on Jesus' suffering and death. We dress in black, or in dark colors if I don't have anything black for little kids. As with mourning dress of previous eras, looking around and seeing everyone in the house in dark colors reminds us that it's a somber day.

Good Friday is meant to be a solemn and somber day. But little kids are *not* meant to be solemn and somber. So, what to do? Well, as with all things combining Catholicism and little kids, we get creative and stay flexible. Good Friday really is the *one* day of the year when I try all day—but most especially from noon to three—to keep my children from running around. And that takes some planning. I try to keep the kids busy and separated to maintain a silence in the house, as much as possible. That could mean individual chores or a quiet craft project, such as coloring pictures of the Stations of the Cross.

How much of Jesus' suffering and death to share with little ones is a question many parents struggle with. It can be overwhelming to feel as if you have to introduce so many facts and concepts and characters all at once, especially if your kids are perhaps more concerned with how close they are to getting to eat treats again than with the details of Jesus' Passion. How to handle it in your own family will depend, of course, on your kids, but here's how we do it in our family.

We give them the facts. Over the course of Holy Week each year, I read my kids the story of Jesus' Passion and death from the Bible. They've heard it in the Mass, but especially the little ones are probably not paying much attention there. Reading it at home allows them really to hear it. There are differences in what parts of the story are included in each Gospel account. Any one you choose would be great, since they're all the Bible. But I like to read from our children's Bible,[6] which compiles all the events from each of the Gospels into one narrative. It's also illustrated, which I find really helps to keep the children's attention and assists with their reading comprehension.

I read some each day, focusing on the part of the story that happened on that particular day of the week. I don't leave out any parts or soften anything, even for very little kids. I just read it to them as is, and we look at the pictures. Even though a two-year-old isn't ready to understand everything that happens in the story, and he's certainly not ready to grasp the horrors of Jesus' suffering, I do think he is ready to hear about it. I tell all the kids that we're going to read the story first, with no interruptions, then talk about it afterward.

Once the story is read, I let the children lead the conversation. Some kids will listen and then just want to move on. That's fine. Especially for toddlers, my desire is just that they listen. Hearing it in its entirety will plant the seeds for deeper reflection and understanding later. My toddlers have never been upset by hearing the story. For my preschoolers and younger grade school kids, I want to make sure they understand the basics of what happened.

This is what I would like them to know:

- The Mass of the Lord's Supper on Holy Thursday commemorates the evening on which Jesus celebrated the Passover with his friends, the disciples. Passover is the day the Jewish people remember when God saved them from slavery in Egypt.
- Jesus' disciple Judas left the supper and betrayed Jesus by telling the temple officials where Jesus would be so they could arrest him. The high priest, Caiaphas, wanted to get rid of Jesus because he could see how much the people liked Jesus, and Caiaphas worried that the people wouldn't listen to him anymore and would listen to Jesus instead.

[6] Golden Books, *The Children's Bible* (New York: Golden Inspirational, 1999).

- Later that night, Jesus prayed in the Garden of Gethsemane. He was very worried about all the terrible things he knew were about to come, but he was willing to do what God wanted him to do.
- Judas came with soldiers and found Jesus in the garden. Jesus was arrested.
- Peter followed behind Jesus to see what would happen to him. When people asked him if he knew Jesus, he got scared and lied and said he didn't know Jesus at all.
- The next morning, on Good Friday, the high priest turned Jesus over to the governor, Pontius Pilate. Pontius Pilate knew Jesus hadn't done anything wrong. But Pontius Pilate worked for Rome, and it was his job to make sure the people didn't make trouble. He wanted to let Jesus go, but all the people kept shouting, "Crucify him!" He had Jesus whipped to see if that would make the people happy, but they kept shouting, "Crucify him!" Pontius Pilate was a weak man, so even though he knew it was not right, he ordered his soldiers to crucify Jesus.
- Jesus had to carry his heavy cross out of the city of Jerusalem, up the hill to Golgotha. It was very hard to do. He fell down many times. The soldiers thought Jesus might not make it up the hill at all, so they made a man in the crowd named Simon of Cyrene help him.
- Jesus' hands and feet were nailed to the cross, and he was left to die there, between two criminals who were also being crucified that day as a punishment for their crimes.
- The people in the crowd made fun of Jesus. The soldiers mocked him and took his clothing. Only Jesus' mother, Mary, three other women, and John, the beloved disciple, stayed with Jesus while he was dying. All his other friends and followers ran away.
- Jesus was on the cross for three hours, from noon to three o'clock. Then he died.
- The soldiers took his body down from the cross and gave him to his mother, Mary.
- A rich man named Joseph of Arimathea came and took Jesus' body and laid it in his own tomb and covered the entrance with a stone.

If they have questions, I answer them. If they don't have questions, that's fine. I want my older kids to learn more details of the story and have a deeper understanding of the people involved and their motivations, but that comes with time and multiple exposures to the story.

If my kids ask me, "Why? Why did Judas do that? Why did Pontius Pilate do that? Why did the people do that? Why did God want it? Why did Jesus let them?" I try to answer with truth and compassion but not too many details. Judas and Peter and Caiaphas and Pontius Pilate and Herod and the good and bad thieves and the crowd are all weak in different ways. They are all sinners like us. They hurt Jesus. But so do we hurt Jesus when we sin. The thing that makes them different from one another is whether they trusted God and asked for forgiveness after they sinned. The same is true of us.

It is because of our lack of love that God sent Jesus to suffer and die for us. Jesus came to make up in a big way for all our sins, big and little—from the sin committed by Adam and Eve all the way to the sins that people are committing today, even the sins we ourselves commit. Jesus loves God so much and loves us so much, that he willingly went through all that suffering. Jesus loves *you* so much that he died for *you*, even though he was God and could have stopped all of it at any time.

Even though Jesus suffered so much, this is a story with a happy ending. We just have to make it through Holy Saturday, our day of waiting and preparing, to find the joy of Easter morning, when Jesus comes back to life and triumphs over death and saves us all.

That's what I tell them. Even though this is my little kids' first (and mostly only) exposure to heavy concepts such as betrayal and suicide and torture and death, I have found that they have always been able to see through all of that and understand that Jesus' Passion is a story of love. It is a story of God's Divine Mercy. I think even the littlest kids deserve to hear it.

Good Friday Devotions

Speaking of Divine Mercy, Good Friday comes nine days before the vigil of Divine Mercy Sunday. So, the Novena of Divine Mercy, given to St. Faustina by Jesus, begins on this day and continues through the rest of the Triduum and all of Easter week. In her diary, St. Faustina wrote: "The Lord told me to say this chaplet for nine days before the Feast of Mercy. It is to begin on Good Friday. By this novena, I will grant every possible grace to souls."[7]

The novena consists of a different short prayer offered each day for a different intention. It's a good way for kids to feel that they can actively do something to help Jesus and their fellow man.

At noon, we stop all chores and projects and stories and go for a walk to our closest parish. It's about a mile away, so I bring a stroller or a wagon for the littlest kids. We'll usually say a Rosary on the way. At the church, I have the children spread out into individual pews, and we sit there quietly, for as long as we can manage. Because we still have lots of little kids, it is never longer than fifteen minutes or so; some years it's more like five. We used to attend a parish that had services during that whole period, from noon to three, to commemorate when Jesus was hanging on the cross. I don't expect my kids to be able to handle three hours' worth of church services, but we would stay there for as much of it as we could manage.

One of the most moving things we do on Good Friday is to venerate the cross. Sometimes we've done it as part of the Good Friday services at church; other times we do it ourselves, either at church or when we get home. There's very little to it. All that's required is to kneel reverently before a cross and kiss it. Even the littlest kids can do it, but it feels weighty somehow, and it's officially recommended for the day.[8]

After our church visit, we walk back home and put the little kids down for naps. That allows grown-ups and big kids to spend the last hour recalling the Crucifixion at home, quietly. I encourage the kids (and myself) to avoid anything that would keep us busy or occupied, and instead just to sit quietly, or to walk quietly, until three o'clock.

[7] *Diary of Saint Maria Faustina Kowalska: Divine Mercy in My Soul*, trans. Richard J. Drabik, M.I.C. (Stockbridge, Mass.: Marian Press, 2005), 203.

[8] "The Roman Missal and the Celebration of the Lord's Passion on Good Friday", United States Conference of Catholic Bishops, http://www.usccb.org/prayer-and-worship/liturgical-year/triduum/roman-missal-and-the-good-friday-liturgy.cfm. For more on veneration of the cross, see the feast of the Exaltation of the Holy Cross on September 14.

After three o'clock, once the little ones are awake, I often put on a movie about the life of Jesus for the kids. There are a few good choices, but I think my favorite is a Claymation movie called *The Miracle Maker: The Story of Jesus*.[9]

Then it's time for our last Stations of the Cross of the year. Instead of our usual Soup and Stations, my mom (who grew up in Memphis, Tennessee) cooks up a real Southern catfish fry. We keep it simple, in keeping with the tone of the day: just fish, coleslaw, and cornbread, and water to drink. But you can't help but enjoy it *a lot* after a day of fasting, and I like that it seems different from the Fridays of Lent, because it *is* different. Every couple of years we'll watch *The Passion of the Christ*[10] once the younger kids go to bed. We are comfortable with our kids twelve and older watching it. But it is very violent and bloody, and some parents might decide to wait longer to show it to their kids. It's hard to watch, but good to understand.

HOLY SATURDAY

Holy Saturday is our Church's day of great silence. No bells, no sacraments.[11] An ancient homily for Holy Saturday says this: "What is happening? Today there is a great silence over the earth, a great silence, and stillness, a great silence because the King sleeps; the earth was in terror and was still, because God slept in the flesh and raised up those who were sleeping from the ages. God has died in the flesh, and the underworld has trembled."[12]

A great silence: That's what Holy Saturday is—a day of preparation and longing.

The United States bishops recommend a voluntary continuation of the Good Friday fast: "If possible, the fast on Good Friday is continued until the Easter Vigil (on Holy Saturday night) as the 'paschal fast' to honor the suffering and death of the Lord Jesus, and to

[9] *The Miracle Maker: The Story of Jesus*, directed by Derek W. Hayes and Stanislav Sokolov (Santa Monica, Cal.: Lionsgate, 2000); rated G.

[10] *The Passion of the Christ*, directed by Mel Gibson (Los Angeles: Icon Productions, 2004); rated R.

[11] Except in case of danger of death.

[12] Pontifical University of Saint Thomas Aquinas, "The Lord's Descent into Hell", http://www.vatican.va/spirit/documents/spirit_20010414_omelia-sabato-santo_en.html.

prepare ourselves to share more fully and to celebrate more readily his Resurrection."[13]

The Descent into Hell

On the first Holy Saturday Jesus' body rested in the tomb. His soul went to the limbo of the fathers to release all the holy men and women who had come before him and to welcome them to heaven. Adam and Eve, Moses, David, St. John the Baptist, St. Joseph ... It must have been a very happy day and a happy reunion for those folks. This event is also known as the "Harrowing of Hell", which sounds rather terrifying but just means the reaping, as it were, of what *we* call the limbo of the fathers, but earlier Christians understood to be a separate, nonsuffering section of hell in which the just waited for Jesus' redemption of mankind. We can see this use of the word "hell" in the Apostles' Creed when we say that Jesus "descended into hell".

Meanwhile, back on earth, Jesus' disciples were lost, confused, heartbroken, and could do nothing much about it because it was the Sabbath. Except for Mary. We know that Mary understood Jesus' mission and plan in a way that no one else among his followers did. I like to imagine her waking up that first Holy Saturday morning, after having gone through the worst day any mother could suffer, and immediately setting about her usual routine. She must have known, she must have trusted, that Jesus would conquer death.

A Day of Preparation

For us Holy Saturday is a day of preparation. We take down Lent decorations and put up Easter decorations, we prepare food for tomorrow's feast, and we dye Easter eggs. I make sure everyone's new Easter clothes still fit and are clean and ironed. It's a fun, quiet,

---

[13] "Fast and Abstinence", United States Conference of Catholic Bishops, http://www.usccb.org/prayer-and-worship/liturgical-year/lent/catholic-information-on-lenten-fast-and-abstinence.cfm.

mellow, anticipatory day, which is welcome after the rush of sorrow and activities of the last two days.

We managed to maintain that focus and that tradition in our family for many years. Then we had big kids. Last year, for the first time, we were faced with the dilemma of whether to participate in an all-day track meet scheduled for Holy Saturday. I have to say, I had a bit of a liturgical-living crisis of conscience when I found out about it. "We don't do stuff on Holy Saturday!" I may have shouted. But the husband and I talked it through. A track meet isn't an early celebration of the Easter feast. We aren't obligated to observe Holy Saturday in one particular way; this is just our preference. This track meet was important to attend, for a variety of reasons, so we decided to attend as a family and let the kids participate. Then, when we got home, we quickly decorated our Easter eggs before dinner, and those same big kids who kept us out all day helped to decorate the house and fill the Easter baskets. It wasn't my ideal Holy Saturday, but it worked out in the end. (Faced with a similar decision for Good Friday or Easter Sunday, I think we would have declined to participate.)

We make a point of avoiding Easter egg hunts on Holy Saturday. Many families are faced with the difficult decision of whether to attend Easter celebrations hosted by extended family on Holy Saturday. There are many of us who have converted or reverted to our Catholic faith from nonpracticing, non-Catholic, or non-anything families. Grandparents want to see their grandchildren on holidays. In some cases, Catholic parents might feel it's preferable to get a secular eggs-and-bunnies-and-candy-only Easter celebration out of the way on Saturday, so that they can focus on Mass and the Resurrection and their own family traditions on Easter Sunday.

I haven't faced this issue in my family, and I don't believe that there is an easy solution or a mandatory one. You have to make the call in your circumstances. One family I know attends a big extended-family Easter celebration on Holy Saturday, and the parents allow their kids to collect their Easter baskets from their grandparents and their eggs in the Easter egg hunt but have them wait until Sunday to eat any of the treats. That has always seemed like a reasonable compromise to me. It is a challenge for the kids, especially little ones, I'm sure. But it's an example of charity, sacrifice, and faith.

Good Friday and Holy Saturday are the only two days of the whole year when it's forbidden to celebrate marriages and baptisms except in danger of death. We don't even celebrate the Mass or consecrate the Eucharist. If hosts are distributed on those days, they were consecrated on Holy Thursday. Church bells do not ring. Altars are bare.

Paschales Solemnitatis, the main document governing the celebration of Easter, tells us, "On Holy Saturday the Church is, as it were, at the Lord's tomb, meditating on his passion and death, and on his descent into hell, and awaiting his resurrection with prayer and fasting."[14]

The waiting is almost over.

[14] Congregation for Divine Worship, *Paschales Solemnitatis: The Preparation and Celebration of the Easter Feasts* (January 16, 1988), nos. 73–74, Eternal Word Television Network, https://www.ewtn.com/library/CURIA/CDWEASTR.HTM.

7

Easter

Easter is the summit of the liturgical year. St. Paul told the early Christians, "And we bring you the good news that what God promised to the fathers, this he has fulfilled to us their children by raising Jesus" (Acts 13:32–33). The *Catechism of the Catholic Church* (*CCC*) tells us, "The Resurrection of Jesus is the crowning truth of our faith in Christ, a faith believed and lived as the central truth by the first Christian community; handed on as fundamental by Tradition; established by the documents of the New Testament; and preached as an essential part of the Paschal mystery along with the cross: 'Christ is risen from the dead! / Dying, he conquered death; / To the dead, he has given life' "[1] (638).

Calculating Easter

In A.D. 325, the Council of Nicaea set the date of Easter as the Sunday following the paschal full moon, which is the full moon that falls on or after the vernal (spring) equinox. In practice, that means that Easter is always the first Sunday after the first full moon that falls on or after March 21. Easter can occur as early as March 22 and as late as April 25, depending on when the paschal full moon occurs. Traditionally, the date of Easter for the upcoming year is proclaimed on the feast of Epiphany.

EASTER SUNDAY (SOLEMNITY OF THE LORD'S RESURRECTION)

On the evening of Holy Saturday, we often attend the Easter Vigil Mass, especially if we are fortunate enough to know one of the

---

[1] Byzantine Liturgy, Troparion of Easter.

candidates or catechumens being welcomed into the Church or into full communion with the Church. The big kids love to come along—first, because who doesn't love getting to stay out late when your little brothers and sisters have to go to bed, and second, because it means they get an Easter-treat-eating head start of many hours on those same sleeping siblings. Also because they are very devout. Probably.

In perhaps my all-time favorite rubric turn of phrase, the *Missale Romanum* calls it the "mother of all vigils" and also the "greatest and most noble of all solemnities".[2] If you've never participated in an Easter Vigil, it is worth making a point to attend it, at least once in your life. There's really nothing like it. Often it begins outside, in the dark, with a holy Easter fire, from which the faithful light candles and head into the dark church. Then there are readings that trace salvation history through the Old Testament. Still in the dark. Then: *boom*, the paschal candle is lit, the lights come on, the bells ring, the Alleluia is sung, and Jesus is risen!

The liturgy continues with readings from the New Testament, the baptisms and confirmations, various blessings and litanies, and the Eucharist. It's very long, but unique and beautiful.

Easter Morning

At dawn on Easter morning, Mary Magdalene and the other holy women went to Jesus' tomb to anoint his body with spices. They found that the large stone in front of the entrance had been rolled away, and Jesus' body was not there. An angel appeared to the women, telling them, "He is not here; for he has risen, as he said" (Mt 28:6). The women rushed off in wonder to tell the eleven apostles, "but these words seemed to them an idle tale, and they did not believe them" (Lk 24:11). How annoying would *that* have been? Finally, curiosity got the better of Peter and John, and they ran for the tomb. John got there first but couldn't bring himself to go inside, so Peter was the first one inside; then John followed, and they "saw

---

[2] "The Roman Missal and the Easter Vigil", United States Conference of Catholic Bishops, http://www.usccb.org/prayer-and-worship/liturgical-year/triduum/roman-missal-and-the-easter-vigil.cfm.

and believed" (John 20:8) ... Mary Magdalene. But did they believe in the Resurrection? Not quite yet, "for as yet they did not know the Scripture, that he must rise from the dead" (Jn 20:9).

I just love that visual of the women slowly approaching the tomb at dawn, concerned that the body of the Lord has been stolen, then rushing off in excitement after hearing the message of the angel. Mary Magdalene is called "the Apostle to the Apostles" because it was she who brought them the good news of the Resurrection. Peter and John, who were probably the oldest and the youngest disciples, end up in a footrace to the tomb, where they see, but hardly know what to think. Then Jesus appears to Mary Magdalene, but she thinks he's the gardener, and when she realizes it's Jesus, she's so excited that he has to ask her to unhand him (Jn 20:17). It might sound like a slapstick comedy if it weren't "the crowning truth of our faith in Christ" (CCC 638).

Early on Easter morning—but not before sunrise, please—the kids come and wake us up. First thing, we've got to dig up the Alleluia we buried in the yard! Next, we use it, singing "O Filii et Filiae" ("Ye Sons and Daughters") and "Jesus Christ Is Risen Today" as we walk from the Alleluia burial spot back into the house. We head for the living room, where we find that the Easter Bunny has made a visit, changing our Lenten sacrifice beans into jelly beans and leaving baskets with Easter treats, new bathing suits, and a few outdoor toys to enjoy for the summer.

Easter breakfast for us is usually candy and hard-boiled eggs. One of these years I'm going to manage a braided Easter bread, with the eggs right in there. They look so cool!

Easter Bunnies

Speaking of the Easter Bunny, the whole thing seems ... odd, right? At least Santa Claus is a saint. And he has a magic sleigh and flying reindeer. How is a bunny even supposed to make this happen? When I was a child, no one ever explained this to my satisfaction. Even as an adult, I have remained rather troubled by all the unanswered questions. A bunny delivering baskets of candy just doesn't seem to go with the Resurrection, *at all*.

Then a friend told me that her grandmother used to say that when Jesus walked out of the tomb on Easter morning, the first creature he saw was a rabbit. This was a great honor for rabbits, of course. So, in gratitude, every Easter, every rabbit in the world brings one Easter basket to one child. Suddenly, it all made sense to me. Obviously, a bunny *would* be honored to be the first creature to see the Risen Lord. And I can see a bunny managing *one* basket, for *one* child, if it were *really* important to him. He could drag it with his teeth, right? So, now I tell my kids that that's what *I* heard about the Easter Bunny. And we all get excited if we see a bunny in the yard, wondering whose bunny it might be.

We enjoy the baskets the bunnies bring, and we look for the plastic eggs they hide in the yard, and we usually do it all before morning Mass, because we get such an early start.

Even if some of us attended the Easter Vigil the night before, we all attend Mass together on Easter to remind us what the day is about. Our night Mass starts outside and can be chilly, so we save our new Easter clothes for the morning Mass.

Easter Dinner

At the Last Supper on Holy Thursday, Jesus established the New Covenant, which was sealed with his blood in the Crucifixion. Christians are therefore no longer bound by the laws of the Old Covenant, which God made with the Jews. For Easter dinner, I like to give a little wink and a nod to that by serving foods that weren't allowed under the Old Covenant. So our usual menu includes shrimp cocktail, ham, au gratin potatoes for the milk that wasn't supposed to go with the meat, and a selection of insects. Just kidding. We skip the insects. (Catfish, which we usually eat on Good Friday, was also on the banned list.) We also have dessert, usually pies, sometimes homemade, sometime store-bought. A family favorite is to use two sticks of butter to create a very cute butter lamb to go with our rolls. It's really adorable, and you can find online instructions on how to make it.[3]

---

[3] "Recipe: Create a Butter Lamb for Easter Brunch", *Faith and Fabric*, https://faithand fabricdesign.com/2013/03/recipe-create-butter-lamb-for-easter.html.

As on Christmas, we always try to include extra guests at our table, especially folks who otherwise wouldn't have anyone with whom to spend the holiday.

EASTER WEEK

When Easter Sunday is over, we still have something to look forward to: *seven more Easters!* That's right. The entire week, the octave from Sunday to Sunday is eight solemnities, each of which is another Easter Day. The Easter season is fifty days long, from the first Sunday of Easter to Pentecost Sunday. To keep the celebration going, we spend Easter week focusing on fun family outings and activities, and having dessert every night.

The third precept of the Church[4] is to receive the Eucharist at least once a year, if possible during the Easter season. Unlike in earlier eras of the Church, regular reception of the Eucharist is the norm these days. Assuming we don't have any mortal sins on our consciences, we expect to receive Holy Communion every week, if not every day.

But in the spirit of the historical focus on the Eucharist as part of the celebration of Eastertide, if you are not in the habit of attending daily Mass, more frequent attendance at daily Mass during Easter week or the whole Easter season would be very appropriate.

Throughout the fifty days of Eastertide, there are four things we do as a family to help us remember the joy of the season.

1. Paschal Greeting

In the churches of both the East and the West, there is a traditional Paschal Greeting. During the Easter season, instead of saying "Hello" you say, "He is risen", and the other person responds, "He is risen, indeed!" I love it. It's like a secret password for getting into a speakeasy or something. We incorporate it into our family life by adding it to the end of our Grace before Meals throughout Eastertide. It's especially meaningful since we spent all of Lent counting to forty after Grace. We all say Grace together and say amen. Then

---

[4] See Passion Sunday in chapter 5 for more on the precepts of the Church.

one person says, "He is risen." And everyone else responds, "He is risen, indeed!"

2. *Good behavior jelly beans*

We reward good behavior and sacrifices with jelly beans from the jar of (formerly) sacrifice beans. It keeps the kids in the habit of looking for opportunities for good deeds, but now with an immediate reward of a treat.

3. *Easter decorations*

We keep the Easter decorations out and the plastic Easter eggs available. We made it look like Lent in our home throughout Lent, and now I want to make sure it looks like Easter in our home throughout Easter. We have an Alleluia bunting that hangs across the fireplace, and various seasonal egg and chick and bunny decorations around the common areas of the house. It is always my goal to keep our potted Easter lilies alive for the whole fifty days, but I don't think I've ever managed it. (My gardening skills are better suited to the Lenten cacti.) The kids get to keep playing with the plastic Easter eggs for the whole Easter season. They refill them with candy from their baskets, and when that's out, they start filling them with small snacks or toys. They can be hidden again and again, and if they are lost or destroyed, it's not a big deal. I can supplement with new ones next year.

4. *Regina Caeli*

We replace the noon Angelus with the Regina Caeli. This is a traditional practice within the Church, and I love it because it really makes this season feel different from the rest of the year. Unlike the Angelus, however, I don't have the Regina Caeli memorized and must learn it again every year! It is quicker than the Angelus, though.

EASTER MONDAY (WET MONDAY)

In most historically Catholic countries, Easter Monday is a public holiday. Unfortunately, that description doesn't fit the United States, and most working folks in this country have to return to work on

Monday. Even public schools often don't have the week off, since "spring" break doesn't necessarily coincide with Easter. Fortunately, our Catholic school and our homeschool do have Easter week off, and we can therefore observe the very important Polish tradition of Śmigus-dyngus (Polish for "Wet Monday"). Folks in the United States just call it Dyngus Day.

Apparently, since the fourteenth century, Easter Monday has been one big national water fight in Poland, and—more recently—in some Polish neighborhoods of the United States, people are awakened by having buckets of water dumped on their heads (I can't support that), and spend the rest of the day chasing each other around with more buckets of water (if it's outside, I'm okay with it).

We've become aware of this tradition only recently, and the kids really loved having a big water fight with each other in the backyard last year. But I think it could only be improved by the addition of more kids, so I plan to let the kids invite some friends and their buckets over to participate next year—while the moms watch from the safety of the house, eating donuts.

EASTER FRIDAY (MEAT FRIDAY)

Easter Friday is one of two solemnities that fall on a Friday each year (the other being the feast of the Sacred Heart of Jesus). A Friday solemnity trumps the required weekly Friday penance (usually abstinence from meat),[5] so we always make a big to-do of it when we have a Meat Friday! Steaks on the grill, hot dogs cooked over a bonfire, panfried pork chops, pepperoni pizza: it doesn't matter what it is; it just matters that we make a big deal of it and really enjoy it.

DIVINE MERCY SUNDAY (SECOND SUNDAY OF EASTER)

In the early twentieth century, St. Faustina Kowalska, a Polish nun, received visits from Jesus and had conversations with him. He appeared to her as "the King of Mercy", wearing a white garment with red and pale blue rays emanating from his heart.[6] He asked her

---

[5] See appendix A for more information on fasting and abstinence.

[6] Faustina Kowalska, *Diary of Saint Maria Faustina Kowalska: Divine Mercy in My Soul*, trans. Richard J. Drabik, M.I.C. (Stockbridge, MA: Marian Press, 2005), 44.

to have this image made into a painting with the words "Jesus, I trust in You" (in Polish, *Jezu, ufam Tobie*) at the bottom, that the faithful might venerate it. He also specifically asked for a feast of Divine Mercy to be established on the first Sunday after Easter.

Pope St. John Paul II, also Polish, had a great devotion to the Sacred Heart of Jesus. In 2000 he canonized St. Faustina (feast day: October 5) and officially designated the second Sunday of Easter as Divine Mercy Sunday. In 2002 he also established a plenary indulgence for the day, in keeping with the promises that Jesus made to St. Faustina about this devotion.

> A plenary indulgence, granted under the usual conditions (sacramental confession, Eucharistic communion and prayer for the intentions of Supreme Pontiff) to the faithful who, on the Second Sunday of Easter or Divine Mercy Sunday, in any church or chapel, in a spirit that is completely detached from the affection for a sin, even a venial sin, take part in the prayers and devotions held in honour of Divine Mercy, or who, in the presence of the Blessed Sacrament exposed or reserved in the tabernacle, recite the Our Father and the Creed, adding a devout prayer to the merciful Lord Jesus (e.g., Merciful Jesus, I trust in you!).[7]

This indulgence is especially easy to obtain, as we all go to Mass and receive Communion on a Sunday anyway, so all we have to do is add a couple of prayers before the Blessed Sacrament after Mass and get to confession sometime within twenty-one days of the feast day. We always stay after Mass to say a few prayers anyway. *Plus*, if you took the family for a Lenten confession during Passion week (the fifth week of Lent), that's within the three weeks, so you're all set. It really is an amazing freebie. Don't miss it!

A perfect prayer for this feast is the Chaplet of Divine Mercy, especially if you made it through all nine days of the Divine Mercy Novena and don't want to lose the good habit of a quick afternoon prayer break. It is said using a normal rosary, but with different prayers. It is traditionally said at three o'clock in the afternoon and can be completed in about ten minutes.

[7] Apostolic Penitentiary, *Decree: Indulgences Attached to Devotions in Honour of Divine Mercy* (June 29, 2002), http://www.vatican.va/roman_curia/tribunals/apost_penit/documents/rc_trib_appen_doc_20020629_decree-ii_en.html. For more on indulgences, see appendix B.

There are lots of cute food-related ways to observe the day. Heart-shaped waffles (or regular ones) with whipped cream and rays of red and blue berries on top, make an excellent Sunday breakfast. A Polish beet borscht soup is a lovely red color that would be perfect for the day. But my favorite thing to serve is Divine Mercy *sundaes*. Any type of ice cream you like (I prefer vanilla, but I'm boring like that) topped with frozen berries and a big dollop of whipped cream, with rays of red and blue sprinkles on top. Easy, tasty, funny. What more could you want?

Saints' Days That (Might) Fall during Eastertide

The date of Easter can vary by more than a month, from March 22 to April 25. That means the saints' days that fall within the fifty days of Eastertide will vary from year to year. But I'll just go ahead and share the saints' days we observe in April and May. Any saint's day that falls during the Easter octave gets officially bumped for that year, as do any saints' days that fall on a Sunday. If one of those feasts is one to which your family has a particular devotion, however, there's nothing wrong with moving the day of your observance (that's what the Church does with important universal feast days) or just having your traditional special dinner in honor of the Resurrection *and* the saint. After all, Jesus likes all those guys, right?

FEAST OF ST. GEORGE: APRIL 23

St. George is another of the Fourteen Holy Helpers and another saint whose existence is supported by the historical record, but whose life story may have been rather misunderstood over the years. We know that he was a third-century Roman soldier of Greek descent. We know he was martyred in the persecution of Emperor Diocletian in 303, along with many other soldiers.

But then comes the fun stuff. The legends about St. George date back to the fifth century, and the one with the dragon dates back to a thirteenth-century collection of especially fanciful saint stories called *The Golden Legend*.[8]

---

[8] Jacobus de Voragine, *The Golden Legend: Readings on the Saints*, trans. William Granger Ryan (Princeton, N.J.: Princeton University Press, 2012), 58.

St. George and the Dragon

The story goes that there once was a pagan city called Silene. Silene had a lake. The lake had a dragon, a terrible, venomous dragon that plagued the land and the people with its dragony fire breath. The only thing that kept it from destroying everything in sight was to keep it well fed. So, the citizens fed it two sheep a day until they were out of sheep. Then they instituted a lottery, and whosever number came up had to feed one of their children to the dragon. One day, the king's number was drawn. The brave princess of Silene dressed herself in her most beautiful gown, and with bitter regret her father kissed her goodbye and sent her to the edge of the lake.

Just then, the noble knight St. George happened by the lake, upon his white horse. He asked the young lady what made her weep, but she, fearing that he too would be devoured by the dragon, insisted that he leave at once. St. George would do no such thing, vowing to save her in the name of Jesus Christ. When the dragon dared to show its head above the surface of the lake, St. George made the sign of the cross and smote the dragon with his spear, Ascalon, and threw the dragon to the ground.

George called to the princess to throw him her sash, which she did, and when he tied it around the dragon's neck, the dragon became as meek as a lamb, and they led it on its leash back to the castle, where the knight dispatched it in front of the king and his people. The king and the citizens were so grateful to God and to St. George that they all immediately asked to be baptized, fifteen thousand in all. The king offered the knight great rewards, but St. George refused them all, telling the king instead to give the money to the poor. And he went upon his way.

So, does the Catholic Church teach that dragons are real and that St. George smote one? No, she doesn't. Do *I* teach my kids that dragons are real and that St. George smote one? Maybe. A little. I do love a good dragon story.

But seriously, the dragon in St. George's story has always stood for something else, something that the people of the Middle Ages who were enjoying these stories would have understood was even more important. The citizens of the (fictional) city of Silene didn't love Jesus Christ. Their souls and the souls of their children were in danger because they weren't baptized. St. George brought Christianity to them, and baptized them, thus saving them from the threat of their pagan beliefs (like human sacrifice). Understood in this light, St. George is as much a missionary as a warrior.

It is not quite as fun to play missionary as it is to play knight, however, so on the feast of St. George the kids get out their swords and shields, or make new ones out of duct tape and old cardboard boxes, and have battles with imaginary dragons (and each other, of course).

Although St. George was Greek and Roman, he is best-known in the English-speaking world as the patron saint of Merrie England. For dinner we enjoy some traditional British fare, such as bangers and mash (white sausages and mashed potatoes), and for dessert a fruit crumble with a red St. George's Cross made of strawberries on the top.

FEAST OF ST. MARK THE EVANGELIST: APRIL 25

St. Mark: scribe, evangelist, naked guy in the Bible.

Wait. What?

It's true. St. Mark's Gospel features the description of a young man who, after Jesus' arrest in the Garden of Gethsemane, ended up fleeing the scene in his altogether. "And Jesus said to them, 'Have you come out as against a robber, with swords and clubs to capture me? Day after day I was with you in the temple teaching, and you did not seize me. But let the Scriptures be fulfilled.' And they all deserted him, and fled. And a young man followed him, with nothing but a linen cloth about his body; and they seized him, but he left the linen cloth and ran away naked" (Mk 14:48–52).

He's known as "the naked fugitive" (don't google that) and is considered by Bible historians to be the evangelist himself. Mark the evangelist is also known as John Mark in the Bible, and, in addition to the naked-in-the-garden episode, he's mentioned in Acts as an assistant accompanying SS. Paul and Barnabas on their missionary journeys.

Each of the four Gospel writers is traditionally associated with a symbolic winged creature. St. Matthew is represented as an angel. St. Mark is a lion. St. Luke is an ox. St. John is an eagle. St. Mark is the patron saint of Venice, and the winged lion is ubiquitous in the city.

We have been fortunate enough to visit Venice and see the stunning St. Mark's Basilica. Built over the entire tenth century, it's known for its Italo-Byzantine-style opulence and especially its gold mosaics. Various mosaics illustrate the life of Christ and the life of the Virgin and saints and angels and Church Fathers. They are lovely. But the mosaic we found to be the *most* interesting depicts the story of how, in 828, two Venetian merchants liberated the body of St. Mark from the city of Alexandria, which had been captured in a Muslim conquest. In order to smuggle St. Mark out of the city, the merchants ordered their sailors to load the relics into a basket and cover them with cabbage leaves and pork, so that the Muslim guards inspecting the ship's cargo wouldn't be able to touch the barrel and discover the saint. It's a great story, and a true story, and it's even better in a larger-than-life mosaic on the outside of a giant basilica. The sailors seem to be saying, "Sure, absolutely, come have a look." And the guards are cringing in horror at the sight of the pork. Amazing.

So, pork-stuffed cabbage rolls would be quite appropriate for the day. But if that doesn't sound like something your kids would be super jazzed about, you can always go with homemade pizza and arrange the toppings to look like the head of a lion.

FEAST OF ST. GIANNA MOLLA: APRIL 28

St. Gianna Molla was born in Italy in 1922. Her joyful Catholic faith infused every part of her life. She was a loving wife and mother of three, as well as a devoted pediatrician, working outside the home. In 1961, she became pregnant with her fourth child. Early on, it was discovered that she had a dangerous fibroma on her uterus. Her doctors gave her three options: an abortion and removal of the fibroma, a hysterectomy, or removal of the fibroma only.

Direct abortion is always forbidden by the Catholic Church, but the philosophical principle of double effect allows for a medically necessary hysterectomy, the unintended secondary consequence of which would be the death of the unborn child. Gianna chose instead to have only the fibroma removed, hoping to save her baby. On April 21, 1962, she gave birth, via cesarean section, to a healthy baby girl, whom she and her husband named Gianna Emanuela. Despite the efforts of her doctors, St. Gianna Molla died of septic peritonitis seven days after giving birth.

She was canonized in 2004 at a ceremony attended by her husband and four children, including Gianna Emanuela, who is a practicing doctor of geriatrics.

St. Gianna Molla's story is often presented in such a way as to indicate that she chose to give her life for her unborn child. That would certainly be a noble thing to do. As Jesus tells us, "Greater love has no man than this, that a man lay down his life for his friends" (Jn 15:13). In this case, however, it's clear that was *not* the intention of St. Gianna. She did not intend to *die* for her child. Rather, she intended for her child to *live*. She also hoped to live herself and to raise that child and her other children alongside her husband. She, a doctor herself, chose to have the fibroma removed, as opposed to her whole uterus, in the hope that it would allow both her *and* her unborn child to live. She was *willing* to die for her baby, but that's not the same thing as choosing it.

St. Gianna Molla is not to be understood as a martyr for childbirth and motherhood. She has been singled out by the Church as an example to us not because of how she died but because of how she lived. Her devout Catholic faith was a profound part of her marriage, her motherhood, and her professional life. She is an example to wives and mothers and working professionals, and especially to mothers who work outside the home.

This feast would be a good day to bridge the gap between moms who stay at home and moms who work outside the home and all the moms somewhere in between. Many mothers' groups meet during the day when working mothers can't attend. But I have a friend who organizes a mom's night out every couple of months for dinner and drinks after the kids are in bed. It's an opportunity for working moms and stay-at-home moms to hang out, sans mommy wars. After all, we crazy Catholic moms have much in common that outranks modifiers such as "working" or "stay at home". We had better stick together.

FEAST OF ST. CATHERINE OF SIENA: APRIL 29

St. Catherine of Siena is one of my very favorite saints. She reminds us that the passive martyr isn't the only path to sanctity.

222 THE CATHOLIC ALL YEAR COMPENDIUM

St. Catherine was the twenty-second of twenty-five children, born to a middle-class Italian family. She received no formal education, and remained a layperson her whole life (she was a third order Dominican, which is why she's usually depicted wearing a habit) but became one of the most respected figures of the fourteenth century and was an adviser to religious leaders, emperors, and kings all over Europe. She persuaded the Italian authorities to oust an anti-pope and then persuaded Pope Gregory XI to return to Rome from his hidey-hole in Avignon. All with the power of feistiness, and sanctity of course.

Looking for an activity for the day? If I really want to open a can of worms, I'll let the kids have an Airing of Grievances at dinner and we can discuss things that they think need improvement around here. It's a good chance to discuss how to approach authority figures respectfully and how to effect change positively. It's also pretty hilarious when attempted by grade-schoolers.

St. Catherine is one of thirty-six Doctors of the Church: saints recognized as having been of particular importance regarding their contribution to theology or doctrine. Along with St. Francis of Assisi, she is the patron saint of Italy, so we have Italian food for dinner. And for dessert: tiramisu. It's Italian, caffeinated, and full of lady fingers pointing things out. I think St. Catherine would love it.

A MAY CROWNING

The entire month of May always falls within the liturgical season of Easter, and the month is dedicated to the Blessed Virgin Mary, as the "Queen of May".

It's traditional to honor Mary in a special way this month, and the *most* traditional way to do that is with a May Crowning. This can take place at your parish or school or at your home. All it takes is a statue of Mary and a crown to place on her head. Usually the crown is made of flowers, which makes it pretty easy to make yourself.

We do a May Crowning at home each year, usually the Saturday before Mother's Day, in conjunction with a tea party that we host for all the moms and daughters in our Catholic girls' club. We also help organize a much larger May Crowning hosted by our homeschool group at the park, which includes both boys and girls. But there's no reason it couldn't be done with just one family. There are no official rules or guidelines, but here is how I plan a May Crowning.

1. Get a statue of Mary.

It can be large or small, permanently installed or portable. Ideally, it should be large enough to be the focal point of the event but small enough for the head to be easily reached. Otherwise, you'll also need a step stool.

2. Make a crown for the statue.

Using floral wire, or some other flexible wire, measure the circumference of the head of the statue. Clip enough wire to go around the head three times, with some overlap to spare. Loosely twist the wire around itself to make a form for the crown, leaving openings to weave flowers in between the wires. Choose any flowers you like to weave into the crown, tucking the stems behind the flowers. It is best to add flowers to the crown just before the crowning to avoid wilting. Bonus points if you have a little cushion on which the crown can be carried.

3. Encourage kids to dress up for the occasion.

At our tea party, First Communicants wear their First Communion dresses, and everyone else wears their Easter dresses. At our homeschool park day, boys and girls who made their First Communion this year come in their First Communion attire, but everyone else is just in play clothes.

4. Choose your May Queen.

We choose one of the First Communion girls to be the May Queen and to crown Mary. If we don't have a girl who celebrated her First Communion, we choose the oldest girl.

5. Get some blossoms and decorations.

A May Crowning needs flowers, so we ask people to bring some with them, either from their gardens or from the store. Any kind, any color will do. We set up a vase or vases at Mary's feet to hold the flowers. At our larger-group May Crowning, the children make banners with Marian slogans and symbols to hold or hang, and the boys bring swords to hold aloft to make a pathway to Mary.

6. Choose the music.

Recorded Marian hymns can be played, or folks who play an instrument can play, but we usually just sing a cappella. Some appropriate hymns are "Immaculate Mary", "Hail Mary, Gentle Woman", "Hail, Holy Queen", "Ave Maria", and, my favorite for the occasion, "Bring Flowers of the Rarest".

7. Do it.

A large group can be organized with sword and banner holders making a path to the statue. The others hold flowers and line up behind the Queen of May and the rest of the First Communicants, or just the queen's one attendant, who holds the cushion holding the crown. In a smaller group, everyone will process behind the queen. The group begins to sing, and all walk behind the queen as she slowly approaches the statue and places the crown on Mary's head. Everyone who follows behind places his flower in one of the vases at Mary's feet. Once all the flowers have been placed and the song or songs are finished, everyone prays the Hail Mary together, and the ceremony is finished!

Another appropriate activity for the month is to decorate your home altar with an image of Mary and keep fresh flowers for her there all month.

Or, follow in the footsteps of St. Fiacre (feast day: August 30), Irish patron saint of gardening and seventh-century founder of the Mary Garden, and plant one for yourself. A Mary Garden can be a raised bed or just a patch of earth, featuring an outdoor statue of Mary with flowers or herbs or both, planted around her. It can be as simple or as grand as your time, talent, and treasure allow.

Finally, it's traditional to make a Marian pilgrimage sometime during the month of May. This could be to an apparition site, any church named in honor of Mary, a Marian shrine or grotto, or a statue or painting of Mary. See the feast of Our Lady of Lourdes in chapter 4 for more on how we make a family pilgrimage.

FEAST OF ST. JOSEPH THE WORKER: MAY 1

The Feast of St. Joseph the Worker was established by Pope Pius XII in 1955 to remind everyone that the dignity of work and of the laborer is a very Christian tradition, with its roots in the Garden of Eden, despite what the communists were trying to tell everyone. This feast would be a good day to tackle a hands-on project, to pray for laborers, and to pray for the conversion of communist nations. (For a fun hands-on dinner, see the solemnity of St. Joseph in the Lent chapter. But in our family, we do it just once per year.)

FEAST OF OUR LADY OF FATIMA: MAY 13

In 1917 Our Lady of Fatima appeared to three peasant children in Portugal: Lucia dos Santos and Francisco and Jacinta Marto. One hundred years later, Pope Francis canonized Francisco and Jacinta, who died during the Spanish flu epidemic. Lucia, who survived and became a Carmelite nun, died in 2005 at the age of ninety-seven. Her cause for canonization is being investigated, and she is currently considered a Servant of God.

The three children were first visited by an angel, who taught them to pray and to make sacrifices. Beginning on May 13, Our Lady appeared to the children once each month through October 13. Our Lady of Fatima's messages emphasized prayer and making sacrifices for sinners, a devotion to the Immaculate Heart, and saying a daily Rosary. Our Lady gave the children a vision of hell and related prophecies to them about the end of World War I and the beginning of World War II, and about their own deaths. In her July 13 visit, Our Lady asked the children to add this prayer to the end of each decade of the Rosary: "O my Jesus, forgive us our sins, save us from the fires of hell, lead all souls to heaven, especially those most in need of thy mercy. Amen." So, in our house, we do!

The early twentieth century saw the advent of photojournalism, and newspaper coverage of the children made them national celebrities and a nuisance to the local authorities. They were arrested and were threatened with being boiled in oil if they did not recant their stories about the Lady. The children did not recant.

On the final visit to the three children in October, Our Lady promised to give them a sign that could be seen by others. Contemporary newspaper reports put the crowd of onlookers in the tens of thousands. Witnesses reported that after a period of rain, the sun broke through the clouds and began to dance across the sky, zigzagging toward earth, before returning to its position in the heavens.

To commemorate the day, we go to Mass and say a family Rosary. I might attempt Portuguese food for dinner. Portuguese-style mussels are amazing and are surprisingly quick and easy to prepare. Candy corn arranged around a cupcake makes for a fun dancing-sun dessert.

FEAST OF THE MEXICAN MARTYRS: MAY 21

We often think of gruesome martyrdoms as something that happened only in ancient Rome, under ancient emperors. The story of the Mexican martyrs is astonishing, perhaps most of all because it took place in North America in the twentieth century in a Catholic country! The 1917 Mexican constitution gave control of Catholic churches and ownership of their property to the state and outlawed religious schools, religious orders, and foreign-born priests. Mexican priests were prohibited from celebrating the sacraments, wearing clerical garb outside of a church, and voting, holding public office, or commenting on public policy. Priests accused of any offense had no right to a trial. Military leaders appropriated churches, soldiers desecrated altars, and government officials killed hundreds of priests. Many were hanged from telegraph poles and left there, as a warning to other Catholics.

Between 1926 and 1929 the Catholics of Mexico rose up against the Freemason government in what is known as the Cristero War. Their battle cry was ¡Viva Cristo Rey! (Long live Christ the King!). The war was halted, unresolved, due to diplomatic pressure from the United States, and it took decades before religious freedom was restored to Mexico. It wasn't until 1992 that the anticlerical provisions were removed from the Mexican constitution.

The feast of the Mexican Martyrs remembers twenty-five saints who arose from the Cristero War. The vast majority were Catholic priests, executed for continuing to minister to the faithful in violation of the new constitution (none of the canonized priests took up arms). All but two were martyrs.

We avoid the crowds at Mexican restaurants on Cinco de Mayo (which has problematic associations with the anti-Catholic Freemasons) and celebrate Mexican culture and its beautiful and storied Catholic history with a pitcher of margaritas on May 21 instead! Or, we celebrate at home with carne asada tacos and Mexican Cokes in glass bottles and tres leches cake—and a piñata. Cool side note about piñatas: you wouldn't guess it from the selection at the party store these days, but piñatas have a Catholic backstory. In Mexico, piñatas traditionally have seven points, to represent the seven deadly sins. A person whacks at the seven deadly sins with a stick while blindfolded, to represent having blind faith. If he triumphs over sin, he gets the sweet reward of heaven (represented by candy).

FEAST OF ST. RITA OF CASCIA: MAY 22

St. Rita of Cascia was a fifteenth-century Italian wife, mother, nun, and stigmatist. Married at a young age, she was dismayed to find that her husband, Paolo, was an abusive mobster embroiled in a public feud with another powerful family. After years of Rita's prayer, good example, and sacrifice, her husband was converted, renounced the feud, and became a better man. They had two sons together. (Just for the record: the Catholic Church does not condone spousal abuse, nor does it recommend living with an abusive spouse.)

As time went by, Paolo remained a changed man, but the feud worsened. Eventually he was betrayed by his allies and was violently stabbed to death by a member of the other family. St. Rita publicly forgave her husband's murderers, but her sons came under the influence of her husband's brother, and she soon began to fear that they would seek to avenge their father's death. She worked tirelessly to persuade them against retaliation, and, in the end, her sons died of an illness, without having committed mortal sin.

After the deaths of her husband and sons, Rita reconciled the two warring families and then became an Augustinian nun. At the age of sixty, she received a partial stigmata: one of Christ's wounds from the crown of thorns appeared on her forehead and remained there the rest of her life.

St. Rita is officially the patroness of impossible causes and is often invoked by those in difficult marriages. Because of a miracle associated with her intercession, featured in the 2002 movie *The Rookie*, she's unofficially the patron saint of baseball! Hot dogs and margaritas aren't Italian, but they work anyway for the patron saint of baseball.

FEAST OF ST. JOAN OF ARC: MAY 30

We're probably all familiar with the bare bones of the story of St. Joan of Arc: God tells girl to lead French army to victory over England. Girl does. Girl gets burned at stake. Or, as fifteen-year-old Jane Austen wrote in her (hilarious) *History of England*: "It was in this reign that Joan of Arc lived & made such a row among the English. They should not have burnt her—but they did."[9]

It would be understandable if we wrote off St. Joan's story as another St. George–type legend. But it's true.

St. Joan of Arc was born on January 6, 1412, in a small village in France, the youngest of five children. At the time, England and France were more than seventy years into the Hundred Years' War, fought over the English claim to the French throne. At the age of thirteen, Joan began to see visions of St. Michael, St. Catherine of Alexandria, and St. Margaret of Antioch, who told her to drive the English out of France and to bring the dauphin Charles VII to be crowned king.

Eventually, she met the dauphin, convinced him she wasn't a witch, and was outfitted with armor, horse, sword, and banner and sent to the front lines in Orléans. There she commanded the French forces, sustained multiple wounds in battle, drove the English out, and had the dauphin crowned king of France. Mission accomplished.

Then she was captured and turned over to England.

England and France were both Catholic countries in the fifteenth century, and the fact that Joan claimed that God was for the French and against the English in this war was a big problem for the English. The whole trial was a real soup sandwich. But more than once, the court was astounded by the simple wisdom of her replies to sophisticated questions meant to entrap her.

She was charged with heresy (never witchcraft), but that wasn't a capital crime for a first offense, so the crime for which she was

---

[9]Jane Austen, "Henry the Sixth", *The History of England* (1791), University of Chicago, http://penelope.uchicago.edu/austen/austen.html.

convicted and put to death was multiple counts of . . . having dressed like a man.[10]

She was executed on May 30, 1431, at the age of nineteen, by burning at the stake. She asked a priest to hold a crucifix up where she could see it as the flames were lit around her. After her death, her body was burned twice more, and the ashes dumped into the river, to prevent any collection of relics.

In 1455 she was declared by Pope Callixtus III to have been innocent and the victim of a secular vendetta. She was canonized in 1920 and is a patron saint of France and soldiers.

So, aside from the obvious things, such as wearing pants, or extricating one's country from English rule (America already did that), or maybe having a bonfire, what is one to do on the feast of St. Joan of Arc? Well, she was my confirmation saint and is one of my all-time favorite saints—if God ever needs me to save the world from hostile invaders, I'm on it. But we never really had any particular family traditions associated with the day.

Then, just last year, I didn't realize until four in the afternoon that it was St. Joan's feast day. I poked around in the kitchen a bit and found that we had bread, Swiss cheese, Parmesan cheese, ham, eggs, and butter—just what I needed to make our favorite sandwich from our pilgrimage to Lourdes a few years back: the croque madame. (It's a French grilled ham and cheese sandwich with a fried egg on top. Sounds odd, but it's *so* good.) *Then* I realized that the name of the sandwich basically translates to "crispy lady", and I knew it was meant to be. It's lovely with a flame-torched crème brûlée for dessert.

FEAST OF THE VISITATION OF THE BLESSED VIRGIN MARY: MAY 31

The feast of the Visitation, also known as pregnant ladies helping pregnant ladies, celebrates Mary's visit to her cousin Elizabeth.

At the Annunciation, Mary agreed to become the mother of Jesus and learned that her cousin Elizabeth was six months along in

[10] She was convicted based on Deuteronomy 22:5: "A woman shall not wear anything that pertains to a man, nor shall a man put on a woman's garment; for whoever does these things is an abomination to the LORD your God." Her posthumous retrial, however, determined that Catholic doctrine did, in fact, allow for her to dress as she had.

her own surprising pregnancy. St. Luke tells us that after the angel departed from her, "Mary arose and went with haste into the hill country, to a city of Judah" (Lk 1:39). This was likely a journey of a hundred miles.

When Mary arrived, little unborn John the Baptist recognized the unborn Jesus as God and jumped for joy in Elizabeth's womb. Elizabeth's greeting to Mary makes up part of the Hail Mary: "Blessed are you among women, and blessed is the fruit of your womb" (Lk 1:42). Mary's reply to her is known as the Magnificat (Lk 1:46–55). This feast would be an excellent day to recite it.

I always try to take this day to prepare a meal or two for friends who are pregnant or have a new baby. I make a casserole-type dish in a foil pan and freeze it; then the recipient can heat it up in the oven whenever she likes. It's not exactly the same as walking a hundred miles and staying for three months to help. But it's always well received.

SOLEMNITY OF THE ASCENSION OF OUR LORD (HOLY DAY OF OBLIGATION)

We know from the Acts of the Apostles that, after the Resurrection, Jesus spent forty days instructing his followers: "To them he presented himself alive after his passion by many proofs, appearing to them during forty days, and speaking of the kingdom of God" (Acts 1:3). Since Easter is always on a Sunday, and May always has thirty-one days, forty days later is always a Thursday. St. Augustine, writing in the fifth century, indicates that it was the apostles themselves who began celebrating the feast of the Ascension.[11] Whether celebrated on Thursday or the following Sunday, it is one of the feasts of the universal Church, celebrated everywhere in the world, and is a holy day of obligation.

Apostolic Learning Curve

I have to admit to enjoying the sheer muttonheadedness of the apostles in the Gospels. They spend years sitting at the feet of the Master,

[11] Augustine to Januarius, Letter 54 (A.D. 400), no. 118, New Advent, http://www.newadvent.org/fathers/1102054.htm.

listening to him teach, day in and day out, walking with him, eating with him—and they *just don't get it.*

Jesus teaches them in parables, using imagery from their daily lives to make his lessons easier to grasp, and when they are still totally lost, he has to spell it out for them in plain English (or plain Aramaic, I guess). He sets a constant example of humility and service to others but finds them arguing over who should get the best seat in heaven. They watch him feed five thousand with five loaves and two fishes, and when Jesus is surrounded by four thousand hungry followers, they still ask him, "How can one feed these men with bread here in the desert?" (Mk 8:4). They are confident and brash one moment, and petty and cowardly the next. Ten of the remaining eleven flee in fear and desert Our Lord as he suffers and dies on the cross.

And yet the men in the Acts of the Apostles are wise and noble. They are bold and fearless. They tirelessly work to advance the Church that Jesus founded. One after another they valiantly face gruesome martyrdoms rather than deny the divinity of Christ. What happened? The Holy Spirit happened. And that changed *everything.*

Before the Crucifixion, Jesus tells the apostles why he must leave them:

I did not say these things to you from the beginning, because I was with you. But now I am going to him who sent me; yet none of you asks me, "Where are you going?" But because I have said these things to you, sorrow has filled your hearts. Nevertheless I tell you the truth: it is to your advantage that I go away, for if I do not go away, the Counselor will not come to you; but if I go, I will send him to you. (Jn 16:4–7)

He explains it to them, but since the receiving-the-Holy-Spirit part hasn't happened yet, the disciples are probably pretty confused.

After his Resurrection, on the evening of Easter Sunday, Jesus appears to the apostles and gives them their first dose of the Holy Spirit: "Jesus said to them again, 'Peace be with you. As the Father has sent me, even so I send you.' And when he had said this, he breathed on them, and said to them, 'Receive the Holy Spirit'" (Jn 20:21–22).

In the days between the Resurrection and the Ascension, Jesus prepares the apostles for their missions of evangelization and, for all but one, martyrdom. It's easy to see the difference the Holy Spirit makes. Whereas the disciples were once anxious and filled with grief at the thought of Jesus' departure, immediately after his Ascension they "returned to Jerusalem with great joy, and were continually in the temple blessing God" (Lk 24:52–53).

Ten days later, on Pentecost, the Holy Spirit comes down and fills completely the hearts of Mary and the apostles, and what was impossible becomes possible. It happens for us too, in confirmation: the sacrament in which the Holy Spirit is given to those already baptized in order to make them strong and perfect Christians and soldiers of Jesus Christ. Strong and perfect soldiers: that's us. Muttonheads no more. So, while we might think of the feast of the Ascension as something sad, as Jesus leaving his friends behind, they didn't see it like that. They were ready for him to go, eager to prepare to be "clothed with power from on high" (Lk 24:49).

Novena to the Holy Spirit

And how did they prepare for that? With the very first novena. That's right, at Jesus' direction, after the Ascension, Mary, the apostles, the holy women, and some of the other disciples went back to Jerusalem and for nine days they "with one accord devoted themselves to prayer" (Acts 1:14).

We can imitate them, in a somewhat abbreviated fashion, with a Novena to the Holy Spirit, prayed from the Friday after the Ascension through the Saturday before Pentecost. It was instituted by Jesus, practiced by Mary and the apostles, and officially "decreed and commanded ... throughout the whole Catholic Church" by Pope Leo XIII in 1897.[12] So, maybe give it a go?

There are many versions of the Novena to the Holy Spirit available. We use one from the website Pray More Novenas. It takes only

---

[12] See Leo XIII, encyclical *Divinum Illud Munus* (May 9, 1897), no. 13, http://w2.vatican.va/content/leo-xiii/en/encyclicals/documents/hf_l-xiii_enc_09051897_divinum-illud-munus.html.

a couple of minutes each day. You can sign up online to receive daily e-mail reminders, including the prayers for this and other novenas. It's a huge help in remembering to say it each day!

Because Jesus ascended into heaven from "the mount called Olivet" (Acts 1:12), the feast of the Ascension is a traditional day to climb a mountain and have a picnic. If you don't have a mountain handy, a backyard, a porch, or a balcony will do.

Our special food for the day is popovers. They are simple to make with just milk, eggs, flour, butter, and salt, and they rise in the oven to triple their original height, making them perfect for the Ascension. The kids love watching them rise through the oven window. They are delicious with butter and jam, at home or on a mountaintop.

Although the Ascension is a feast of the universal Church, celebrated on a Thursday, canon law allows episcopal conferences, with prior Vatican approval, to abolish various holy days or to transfer their observance to a Sunday. Since 1999, most dioceses in the United States (and in some other countries) have transferred the observance of the feast day, along with the obligation to attend Mass, to the seventh Sunday of Easter. But even if the observation of the Ascension is moved to Sunday, the Pentecost novena starts on Friday.

SOLEMNITY OF PENTECOST

Pentecost is the end of the Easter season. But Pentecost (known in some parts of the world as Whitsunday) isn't just the end of something. It's the beginning of something and a big deal in its own right.

As discussed in the previous section about the Ascension, Mary and the apostles were praying together in Jerusalem while awaiting the Holy Spirit. On the Jewish feast of Pentecost, which celebrates when Moses received the Ten Commandments from God, "suddenly a sound came from heaven like the rush of a mighty wind, and it filled all the house where they were sitting. And there appeared to them tongues as of fire, distributed and resting on each one of them. And they were all filled with the Holy Spirit and began to speak in other tongues, as the Spirit gave them utterance" (Acts 2:1–4).

A crowd gathered around them, Jews from all over the region who had come to Jerusalem for the Jewish feast day, and each could understand the apostles in his native tongue. Some folks were astounded; some folks thought the apostles had been hitting the bottle. Peter assured the crowd, "These men are not drunk, as you suppose, since it is only the third hour of the day", that is, nine o'clock in the morning (Acts 2:15). Then he explained to them all about Jesus. To every last one of them he said, "Repent, and be baptized every one of you in the name of Jesus Christ for the forgiveness of your sins; and you shall receive the gift of the Holy Spirit" (Acts 2:38).

For the first time, the apostles announced salvation in Christ, risen from the dead, to those beyond their circle, and three thousand people were baptized. It was the beginning of the mission to spread the gospel throughout the world, and that is why Pentecost is considered the birthday of the Church.

The traditional symbols of the Holy Spirit are water, fire, wind, and a dove. And the traditional color associated with the Holy Spirit, and specifically with Pentecost, is red.

It feels as if we Christians don't do a great job of observing this feast. I would wager it's because there aren't secular traditions like bunnies and reindeer that go with it. And no presents. What if we all built Pentecost ... towers? I'm imagining they would include a fan or a pinwheel or something for the wind, and a burning fire, and a bucket of water, and a live dove. It could be very spectacular. And on Pentecost Eve all the children could put out their Pentecost Pails at the foot of the tower, and the Pentecost Dove would fly down from heaven and leave them flamin' hot candy and squirt guns and kites.

Too much? Perhaps. But we really should all do *something* to recognize the day.

At Mass on Pentecost, the priest wears red vestments. We like to join him and wear red for Pentecost too. Usual post-Mass donuts are especially appropriate today, since regular donuts are hole-y, and jelly donuts are filled—with the Holy Spirit! A birthday cake would also be great. In our family, we have a yearly tradition of a Pentecost bonfire. We cook hot dogs over the open fire and make s'mores. One year we played a game of Pin the Tongues of Fire on the Apostles. And we pray the Come, Holy Spirit prayer. We like to invite friends to join us and try to make it feel like the important feast that it is.

THE FEAST OF MARY, MOTHER OF THE CHURCH: MONDAY AFTER PENTECOST

In March 2018, Pope Francis, through a decree by the Congregation for Divine Worship and the Sacraments, established a new feast day on the universal calendar to honor Mary as Mother of the Church.

> Having attentively considered how greatly the promotion of this devotion might encourage the growth of the maternal sense of the Church in the pastors, religious and faithful, as well as a growth of genuine Marian piety, Pope Francis has decreed that the Memorial of the Blessed Virgin Mary, Mother of the Church, should be inscribed in the Roman Calendar on the Monday after Pentecost and be now celebrated every year.
>
> This celebration will help us to remember that growth in the Christian life must be anchored to the Mystery of the Cross, to the oblation of Christ in the Eucharistic Banquet and to the Mother of the Redeemer and Mother of the Redeemed, the Virgin who makes her offering to God.[13]

The timing of the feast highlights the fact that Mary was praying with the disciples on Pentecost—the birthday of the Church—as the Holy Spirit descended upon them. As the decree notes, veneration of Mary as the Mother of the Church has its roots in the New Testament and in the teachings of early theologians like St. Augustine and St. Leo the Great.

In more recent times, at the close of the Second Vatican Council, Blessed Pope Paul VI declared Mary as the "Mother of the Church" and invited Christians to invoke Mary's help under that title. The Vatican established a special votive Mass for Blessed Mary, Mother of the Church, in 1975 and subsequently gave permission for a feast in her honor to be observed on the Monday after Pentecost in Poland, Argentina, St. Peter's Basilica, and some religious orders. But now, the feast has been given a place on the universal calendar of the Roman Catholic Church.

---

[13] Congregation for Divine Worship and the Discipline of the Sacraments, Decree on the Celebration of the Blessed Virgin Mary Mother of the Church in the General Roman Calendar (February 11, 2018), http://www.vatican.va/roman_curia/congregations/ccdds /documents/rc_con_ccdds_doc_20180211_decreto-mater-ecclesiae_en.html.

Since this feast is brand spankin' new, its traditions are yet to be established. My vote is that we celebrate with Mass and the Rosary, the Litany of Loreto, and some traditional mom-style cooking, like meatloaf and apple pie!

Some people might wonder why the Catholic Church creates new feast days, when there are already so many! But as Pope Pius XI explained in his encyclical *Quas primas*, the Church establishes new feast days in order to promote devotions that will benefit the faithful in light of the particular struggles of their times. Feasts, he wrote, have a greater impact on people than official Church pronouncements:

> Such pronouncements usually reach only a few and the more learned among the faithful; feasts reach them all; the former speak but once, the latter speak every year—in fact, forever. The church's teaching affects the mind primarily; her feasts affect both mind and heart, and have a salutary effect upon the whole of man's nature. Man is composed of body and soul, and he needs these external festivities so that the sacred rites, in all their beauty and variety, may stimulate him to drink more deeply of the fountain of God's teaching, that he may make it a part of himself, and use it with profit for his spiritual life.[14]

The pope especially noted the role Marian feasts have played in keeping the Catholic faith alive:

> As a result of these men grew not only in their devotion to the Mother of God as an ever-present advocate, but also in their love of her as a mother bequeathed to them by their Redeemer. Not least among the blessings which have resulted from the public and legitimate honor paid to the Blessed Virgin and the saints is the perfect and perpetual immunity of the Church from error and heresy.[15]

[14] Pius IX, encyclical letter *Quas Primas* (December 11, 1925), no. 21, http://w2.vatican.va/content/pius-xi/en/encyclicals/documents/hf_p-xi_enc_11121925_quas-primas.html.
[15] Ibid., no. 22.

8

Ordinary Time after Pentecost

There are two seasons of Ordinary Time each year, from the end of the Christmas season until the beginning of Lent and from the end of the Easter season until the beginning of Advent.

During these seasons, we as a Church aren't focused on penitential preparation or joyful celebration, but that doesn't mean they don't have some great feast days. But, really, you can consider most of these feasts as extra credit.

Summer and fall make up the much longer of the two seasons of Ordinary Time and cover basically half the liturgical year. The end of the school year, summer vacation with its activities and travels, and school starting up again in the fall can nudge us out of the swing of liturgical living. But on the other hand, maybe we have some extra downtime during the summer, with all the kids at home, and we are going to eat dinner anyway, right? Summer is a good time to find feast days that match with various activities we want to do anyway, such as hiking, camping, bonfires, and going to the beach, which makes me less likely to blow them off and just stay inside, where the air conditioning is.

The first three solemnities we'll discuss are movable feasts, observed on the two Sundays that follow Pentecost, in late May or in June, and then the next Friday. After that we'll look at saints' days and feasts of Our Lady that fall from June through the feast of Christ the King in November.

SOLEMNITY OF THE MOST HOLY TRINITY: SUNDAY AFTER PENTECOST

The Trinity is *the* fundamental dogma of the Catholic Church. The *Catechism of the Catholic Church* (*CCC*) tell us, "The mystery of the

Most Holy Trinity is the central mystery of Christian faith and life. It is the mystery of God in himself. It is therefore the source of all the other mysteries of faith, the light that enlightens them. It is the most fundamental and essential teaching" (234). We believe in one God in three Persons: God the Father, God the Son, and God the Holy Spirit. They are each God; they are not each other. It's one of those Big Theological Concepts that some people find fascinating and want to delve deeply into, and that other folks would rather just accept and move on with their lives. I think either approach is perfectly fine.

Introducing the Holy Trinity to kiddos, especially the kind of kiddos who ask a lot of questions, can be a particular challenge. (For my all-time favorite story about the Trinity, see the feast of St. Augustine on August 28). With my kids, I've found it has worked well to introduce the Trinity not as a Big Complicated Mystery, but just as something that *is*, and then focus our discussion on *symbols* of the Trinity.

Symbols of the Trinity

The Shield of the Trinity is a cool traditional symbol that visually describes the relationships between the three Persons of God. In nature we find the pansy and the shamrock, which have reminded Christians of the Trinity for thousands of years. On the back of a United States dollar bill, you'll see the triangular Eye of Providence, surrounded by rays of glory. It is often misunderstood to be a symbol of Freemasonry, but it wasn't adopted by Freemasons until many years after its incorporation by Christians into the Great Seal of the United States.[1] The eye is historically a symbol of the all-seeing God and when enclosed in a triangle is a symbol of the Holy Trinity.

We focus on symbols of the Trinity, because it's pretty much impossible to use analogies to describe the Trinity without falling into one ancient heresy or another. We can't say that the Trinity is

---

[1] Freemasonry is officially considered incompatible with our Catholic faith, and membership in a Masonic lodge is grounds for automatic excommunication. An explanation of this can be found in "Reflections a Year after Declaration of Congregation for the Doctrine of the Faith", *L'Osservatore Romano*, March 11, 1985, http://www.vatican.va/roman_curia/congregations/cfaith/documents/rc_con_cfaith_doc_19850223_declaration-masonic_articolo_en.html.

like water, which is liquid, solid, and gas, because that would be the heresy of Modalism, which claims that the Father, Son, and Holy Spirit are just the three forms of God. We can't say that the Trinity is like the sun (star, light, and heat), because that would be the heresy of Arianism, which claims that the Son and the Holy Spirit are creations of the Father, as the light and the heat are created by the star. We can't say that the Trinity is like a shamrock, because that would be the heresy of Partialism, which claims that the Father, the Son, and the Holy Spirit are just different parts of God.

And, for the record, St. Patrick never said that the Trinity is like a shamrock in any of his writings. He never said anything about shamrocks at all. The shamrock is an excellent *symbol* of the Trinity, but the Trinity is not *like* a shamrock. The problem with trying to explain the Trinity as like anything else is that it isn't like anything else. So it's best not to try.

Celebrating the Trinity

We are more familiar with the Nicene Creed (which we say in the Mass) and the Apostles' Creed (which is a part of the Rosary), but there is also the Athanasian Creed. Historically (but probably inaccurately) attributed to St. Athanasius (feast day: May 2), its focus is on the Holy Trinity, and it is sometimes used in the Mass on this solemnity. The Lesser Doxology, also known as the Glory Be (Gloria Patri) is also a great (and much, *much* shorter) prayer for the day:

> Glory be to the Father, and to the Son, and to the Holy Spirit. As it was in the beginning, is now, and ever shall be, world without end. Amen.

Or try it in Latin:

> Gloria Patri, et Filio, et Spiritui Sancto. Sicut erat in principio, et nunc, et semper, et in saecula saeculorum. Amen.

I have a liturgical-living bucket list of crazy foods I would like to serve for feast days. They haven't happened yet because they are difficult to obtain or to prepare, or are prohibitively expensive. At the very top that list was my dream food for the solemnity of the Holy Trinity: Turducken. It's a chicken stuffed into a duck, stuffed into a turkey (all deboned and sewn back together with various stuffings in there too). Three birds in one meat. The chicken is meat. The duck is meat. The turkey is meat. The chicken is *not* the duck. The duck is *not* the turkey. The turkey is *not* the chicken. How perfect would that be?

I spent two years mulling it. Occasionally I would watch a video of a fancy-schmancy butcher making one or look up how much it would cost to order one, and decide it was still out of my league. But then, I saw another video, of a very easy-going barbecue expert. He made a Mini Turducken by butterflying a turkey breast and layering stuffing, chicken breast, more stuffing, and duck breast in there, then rolling the whole thing up and wrapping it in bacon.[2] It looked amazing and, more importantly, maybe doable for me! So, I put on my big girl pants and gave it a try.

The kids helped, and it was hilarious and fun. The stuffing kept wanting to fall out of the ends, and when we finally got them (we made two) cooking in the oven, one burst back open! But I tied it together with string, and it cooked up just fine. I was going to cut it up anyway, right? It was a great reminder that the experience of cooking is often as important as the meal—for the memories anyway—and it doesn't have to be perfect to be fun.

If you're still in the mulling stage, you might want to go with our old stand-by: three-meat chili and cloverleaf rolls. The rolls are easy to make and fun for kids to help with. You can use any bread or pizza dough, homemade or from the store. Just spray the inside of unlined muffin tins with cooking spray, divide the dough into pieces, roll them into one-inch balls, dip each ball into melted butter, and drop three of them into each muffin cup. And then bake! For dessert, if you're feeling sophisticated, you might like to know that crème brûlée is called trinity cream in England. You're welcome. Or if you're just trying to impress the kids, Neapolitan ice cream!

---

[2] Malcom Reed, "Mini Turducken", *How to BBQ Right*, http://howtobbqright.com /2017/11/16/mini-turducken-recipe/.

SOLEMNITY OF THE MOST HOLY BODY AND
BLOOD OF CHRIST (CORPUS CHRISTI,
SECOND SUNDAY AFTER PENTECOST)

We remember the Institution of the Eucharist on Holy Thursday, but
we also commemorate so many other events on that day and over
the course of the Triduum, that, starting in the thirteenth century, the
Church instituted the feast of Corpus Christi as a separate feast day,
observed after Pentecost. Traditionally, this was another Thursday
feast and a holy day of obligation, observed sixty days after Easter. It
is still a public holiday in some countries. In the United States and
most of the world, however, the celebration has been moved to the
following Sunday.

Without being tied up in the sorrows of Christ's Passion and death,
on the feast of Corpus Christi we can better rejoice in the extraordinary gift of the Eucharist. Jesus is truly with us and truly present in
every tabernacle in every Catholic church in the world. Christ has
given us his Body to eat and his Blood to drink. It's humbling and ...
unsettling, right? Jesus' followers thought the same thing.

> The Jews then disputed among themselves, saying, "How can this man
> give us his flesh to eat?" So Jesus said to them, "Truly, truly, I say to you,
> unless you eat the flesh of the Son of man and drink his blood, you have
> no life in you; he who eats my flesh and drinks my blood has eternal life,
> and I will raise him up at the last day. For my flesh is food indeed, and my
> blood is drink indeed. He who eats my flesh and drinks my blood abides
> in me, and I in him. As the living Father sent me, and I live because of
> the Father, so he who eats me will live because of me. This is the bread
> which came down from heaven, not such as the fathers ate and died; he
> who eats this bread will live for ever." This he said in the synagogue, as
> he taught at Capernaum.
>
> Many of his disciples, when they heard it, said, "This is a hard saying;
> who can listen to it?" (Jn 6:52–60)

Unfortunately, the saying hasn't gotten any easier to accept over
the last two thousand years. And now, belief in the Real Presence
of Christ in the Eucharist is something that divides Catholics and
Orthodox Christians from some Protestant denominations.

According to the *Catechism of the Catholic Church*, Catholics believe
in transubstantiation, that though the bread and the wine continue to

have all the *appearances* of bread and wine (color, shape, taste, calories, gluten, etc.) at the Consecration their *substance* is changed completely into Christ's Body and Blood. The *Catechism* quotes from the Council of Trent, which formulated this explanation of the Eucharist in 1551:

> Because Christ our Redeemer said that it was truly his body that he was offering under the species of bread, it has always been the conviction of the Church of God, and this holy Council now declares again, that by the consecration of the bread and wine there takes place a change of the whole substance of the bread into the substance of the body of Christ our Lord and of the whole substance of the wine into the substance of his blood. This change the holy Catholic Church has fittingly and properly called transubstantiation.[3] (1376)

I love that many parishes have brought back the traditional practice of ringing bells at the Consecration. It calls our attention, kids and grown-ups alike, to the moment of that real, no-kidding miracle. My three-year-old gasps and whispers, "It just *happened!*"

Eucharistic Procession

The traditional thing to do for this feast day is to have a eucharistic procession. Pope St. John Paul II encouraged the practice because "our faith in the God who took flesh in order to become our companion along the way needs to be everywhere proclaimed, especially in our streets and homes, as an expression of our grateful love and as an inexhaustible source of blessings."[4] If your parish has a procession, lucky you!—because, unfortunately, this isn't an observance that has an easy do-it-yourself version. A eucharistic procession isn't as fun without the Eucharist.

Going to Mass, however, and staying afterward to spend some time visiting Jesus in the tabernacle is also pretty good. If your church

---

[3] Cf. Mt 26:26ff.; Mk 14:22ff.; Lk 22:19ff.; 1 Cor 11:24ff.

[4] John Paul II, apostolic letter *Mane nobiscum Domine* (October 7, 2004), no. 18, https://w2.vatican.va/content/john-paul-ii/en/apost_letters/2004/documents/hf_jp-ii_apl_20041008_mane-nobiscum-domine.html.

has an adoration chapel, this would be a very good day to start—or to continue—a family tradition of staying after Mass for a quick visit there. We are fortunate enough to attend a church that our friends and our kids' friends also attend, and we are all in a hurry to socialize after Mass. But there is *nothing* we can do to make the Real Presence more real to our kids than to teach them to interact with Jesus in the monstrance and in the tabernacle—to sit with him, to talk with him. We model this ourselves, and we make sure the kids spend a few moments with Jesus before running out the door.

Another simple habit that acknowledges the divinity of the Most Holy Body and Blood of Christ is to make and say the sign of the cross whenever we walk or drive past a Catholic church. If we have time, we might stop inside for a visit, but even if we don't, making the sign of the cross as we go past reminds us that Jesus is truly there.

Some days, while out running errands or between dropping off kids and picking them up, we are able to stop at a church and make a visit to the Blessed Sacrament. Any—seriously, *any*—amount of time is great, even if we just pop in, genuflect (if the Blessed Sacrament is in the tabernacle), or kneel on two knees (if the Blessed Sacrament is exposed in a monstrance), tell Jesus we love him, and leave. The recommended best practice is to spend half an hour.[5] When I have little kids with me, I have been known to divide that amount of time by the size of our group: thirty minutes ÷ (me + four kids) = six minutes of adoration. But that's not *officially* authorized.

In those brief moments, on days when we are not able to receive Communion, we can make an Act of Spiritual Communion. This is a prayer that says, basically, that we *wish* we could receive Communion. I use one recommended by St. Josemaría Escrivá that's short and sweet: "I wish, Lord, to receive you with the purity, humility, and devotion with which your most holy Mother received you, with the spirit and fervor of the saints."

On Corpus Christi, we like to recite the prayer traditionally associated with this feast: "Tantum Ergo". It's the last two stanzas from a eucharistic hymn composed by St. Thomas Aquinas. Because of the relation of this feast to Holy Thursday, similar foods would be appropriate on this day.

[5] For information on this and other indulgences, see appendix B.

SOLEMNITY OF THE MOST SACRED HEART OF JESUS:
FRIDAY AFTER CORPUS CHRISTI

The month of June is dedicated to the Sacred Heart of Jesus. The solemnity of the Sacred Heart is celebrated on the Friday after Corpus Christi. And you know what that means: Meat Friday! A solemnity on a Friday means there is no obligation to observe a Friday penance. So, today, bring on the meat!

The Sacred Heart of Jesus is depicted as a flaming heart, usually surrounded by a crown of thorns, with a cross on the top, and it is often bleeding from a wound in the side. Some Church authorities prefer it be shown on Jesus' body, but there are popular images of it alone. It is often displayed together with the Immaculate Heart of Mary, which is traditionally also on fire, surrounded by a crown of flowers rather than thorns, and is usually shown pierced by a sword. (The feast of the Immaculate Heart of Mary is celebrated tomorrow.) While a devotion to the Sacred Heart of Jesus is one of gratitude for Jesus' love for us, a devotion to the Immaculate Heart of Mary indicates a desire to emulate the way in which Mary loves Jesus.

In 1673, Jesus began appearing to St. Margaret Mary Alacoque (feast day: October 16), a French nun. He told her that he wished to be honored in eucharistic adoration during a holy hour on Thursdays, that he desired a feast day devoted to his Sacred Heart, and that he wanted to encourage the faithful to receive Communion on the first Friday of each month.

It took a couple of hundred years, but eventually devotion to the Sacred Heart, and the recommended observances, spread throughout the world. The Church established the universal feast of the Sacred Heart in 1856.

A plenary indulgence is available for the day, under the usual conditions, for the recitation of the Act of Reparation to the Sacred Heart of Jesus. *The Manual of Indulgences* specifies that it must be a "public recitation",[6] meaning that it must be recited in a church, a religious community, or a family, rather than by oneself.

For dinner, we do meat. Any kind will do, but since the weather is usually nice, it's a great day to grill steaks on the barbecue, preferably

---

[6] A private recitation will get you a partial indulgence. See appendix B for more information on indulgences.

with friends. One year, a friend brought over the most amazing hors d'oeuvre platters. There was an Immaculate Heart made of fruit, and a Sacred Heart made of veggies. So cool. I've also seen lovely cakes and cookies decorated as the two hearts. But, as you may recall from the very beginning of this book, *my* go-to dessert for this feast day is a slightly weepy red Jell-O heart. It hasn't always looked beautiful (making it more of a finger-Jell-O consistency alleviates the weeping), but it tastes good, and the kids love it!

FEAST OF ST. ANTHONY OF PADUA: JUNE 13

St. Mary Magdalene is "the Apostle to the Apostles", St. Thomas Aquinas is "the Dumb Ox", St. Joan of Arc is "the Maid of Orléans", St. Thérèse is "the Little Flower". But maybe my favorite of all the saint nicknames is St. Anthony's. He is known as "the Hammer of Heretics". You don't want to mess around with that guy.

St. Anthony was born in Lisbon, Portugal, and died in Padua, Italy. (On our trip to Portugal we found that the folks there *insist* he's supposed to be called St. Anthony of Lisbon.) His wealthy family supported his desire to become a priest, and he entered the Augustinian Canons at the age of fifteen. After his ordination, he was inspired to join the newly founded Franciscan Order, and he eventually received permission to do so. This was during St. Francis' lifetime, and the two saints knew each other!

In his day Anthony was revered for his masterful preaching, knowledge of Scripture, and love of the poor. But he is best known, and most often invoked, as a finder of lost items. I have found myself, many a time, hunting around for lost keys or shoes or phone while saying, "Tony, Tony, look around; something's lost and can't be found!"

The association comes from the story that when St. Anthony was teaching at a seminary, one of the novices decided to quit and to take with him a very valuable book of psalms. When every book had to be copied by hand, each one was very valuable, but this one was especially important, as St. Anthony used it to teach his students. Rather than attempt to contact the novice's family or the authorities, St. Anthony decided just to pray that the book would be returned to him. And it *was*—along with one very penitential novice, who requested to rejoin the community!

St. Anthony Box

As a riff on the devotion to St. Anthony as the finder of lost items, and as a reminder to my kids that just because it's summer doesn't mean they can lose their minds and leave everything they own all over the house, I like to keep a St. Anthony box on a top shelf in a closet. Sometime near the end of the school year, when the kids' housekeeping habits start to get lax, I begin to gather the things they leave out (the stuff they *like*, not the trash, clothes, and junk) and I put them in the St. Anthony box. Mostly they know what I'm up to now, but if they ask whether I've seen their Nerf gun or their dress-up shoes, I can just say, "Hmmmm, have you asked St. Anthony?"

Then, on the morning of St. Anthony's Day, there on the kitchen table, miraculously, is all their stuff, sometimes with a little note from St. Anthony reminding them to take better care of their things. Usually I use the St. Anthony box for just a couple of weeks, but I reserve the right to break it out as the mess requires.

St. Anthony died at the age of thirty-five, after becoming sick with ergotism, the result of long-term exposure to grains (in his case, rye) contaminated with a fungus. The condition is sometimes called St. Anthony's fire. He was canonized less than a year later. As ergotism has been eradicated in the developed world, I boldly serve grilled pastrami and provolone sandwiches, on Italian rye bread.

One last thing: St. Anthony was born about twelve hundred years after Christ. So why is he so often depicted in art holding the baby Jesus? Well, it's a good question. Sometimes people say that the infant Jesus appeared to St. Anthony toward the end of his life. That story, however, didn't begin appearing until well after the depictions of St. Anthony holding Jesus began appearing, in the seventeenth century.

The more likely explanation is that it's a visualization of the love St. Anthony had for Scripture, remarkable for his time and well-known during his life. St. Anthony holds the Child Jesus in his arms, because he held the words of the Bible in his heart. As St. John tells us, Jesus *is* the Word of God: "In the beginning was the Word, and the Word was with God, and the Word was God" (Jn 1:1). I love the idea that St. Anthony would have looked at a Bible with the same tenderness with which one would look at a little child.

FEAST OF SS. JOHN FISHER AND THOMAS MORE: JUNE 22

SS. John Fisher and Thomas More are martyrs of the very complicated events surrounding King Henry VIII and the unfortunate English split from the Catholic Church in the sixteenth century that keeps us separated from our Anglican brothers and sisters.

St. John Fisher was an English Catholic cardinal, who, as a young priest, had been tutor to the boy Henry VIII. When Henry first made known his desire to divorce his wife Catherine, St. John Fisher was a staunch supporter of the queen and of the indissolubility of marriage. In this way, he was like St. John the Baptist, who was imprisoned for refusing to recognize the marriage of King Herod Antipas to Herodias, the wife of his still living brother. Like St. John the Baptist, St. John Fisher refused to back down and was imprisoned and beheaded. King Henry VIII inadvertently created an even greater connection between the two when he had St. John Fisher beheaded on the day before the still widely celebrated vigil of the feast of the Nativity of St. John the Baptist.

St. Thomas More was a lawyer and a statesman as well as a husband and father. He had four children with his first wife. After she died he remarried and gained a stepdaughter. He also raised two foster children. Unusual for his time, Thomas More educated his daughters as well as his sons, teaching them Greek, Latin, literature, debate, theology, and mathematics. He was secretary and personal adviser to King Henry VIII and was made lord chancellor in the midst of the national upheaval surrounding the king's second marriage. Like St. John Fisher, Thomas refused to sign a letter to the pope in support of the king's annulment and steadfastly refused to take the oath of supremacy of the Crown in the Church in England. He was eventually imprisoned in the Tower of London and was also executed by beheading.

SS. John Fisher and Thomas More were beatified along with fifty-two other English martyrs. They were eventually canonized in 1935 and given a shared feast day.

If you're planning a bonfire for the vigil of the Nativity of St. John the Baptist (see the next section), you could always include some St. John Fisher foil fish packets and St. Thomas s'Mores. That's *three* saints with one stone.

SOLEMNITY OF THE NATIVITY OF ST. JOHN THE BAPTIST: JUNE 24

St. John the Baptist is one of only a few saints who still have more than one feast day on the universal calendar since the 1969 revision. St. Joseph has two. SS. Peter and Paul each have one and share two. And Mary, the mother of Jesus, has many feast days.

We celebrate the feast of the Beheading of St. John the Baptist on August 29. The day of a saint's death (a.k.a. his birth into heaven), is the day on which we usually celebrate a saint. But on June 24 we celebrate John's birth. On the entire liturgical calendar only Jesus, Mary, and John the Baptist get feasts for their birthdays. Why? Because only those three people were born without original sin. It is the long tradition of the Church that John the Baptist was conceived in the usual way and therefore inherited original sin. But *then*, before his birth, he leapt with joy when he recognized the Savior in the womb of Mary (Lk 1:41). This was the moment that John was filled with the Holy Spirit, in fulfillment of the prophecy of the angel to Zechariah, "He will be filled with the Holy Spirit, even from his mother's womb" (Lk 1:15). His mission of preparing the way of the Lord had already begun, so he must have received in utero something like baptism, which cleansed him of sin and filled him with the grace of God.

The date of the Nativity of St. John the Baptist is significant. The Church chose June 24 because it is six months before Christmas and Elizabeth was six months pregnant when Mary visited her (Lk 1:36).

The date also reflects John's mission as the forerunner of the Messiah. John shows that he understands his role when he says, "This joy of mine is now full. [Jesus] must increase, but I must decrease" (Jn 3:29–30). After John's birthday his words are echoed as the length of each day decreases until, you guessed it, December. After Christmas the daylight increases each day until June.

Isn't it lovely?

Locusts and Wild Honey

I don't need to tell you what to eat for John the Baptist's birthday. It says it right in the Bible: "His food was locusts and wild honey" (Mt 3:4). As I've mentioned previously, I love "dare-able" foods for feast days. It makes for a hilarious family (and friends) bonding activity and makes our celebration totally memorable. This is one we do pretty much every year.

Locusts are just fancy, swarming grasshoppers. Grasshoppers are widely consumed all over the world and have similar nutritional value to more, um, traditional meats. If you have access to wild grasshoppers or crickets, you can prepare them for eating yourself. There are instructions available online. There are also already prepared edible grasshoppers and crickets available, however, and that's the route I prefer.

The first place I ever saw edible insects was at a giant gas station and novelty candy shop. They had little boxes of dried crickets in various chip-type flavors, such as sour cream and onion. I knew I had to buy them and save them for St. John the Baptist. Online, you can search for "chapulines", which is what they call dried grasshoppers in Mexico, or "edible insects", and plenty of choices come up. I also get honey sticks online; they are much less messy than just letting the kids have at a jar of honey.

In our family, the deal is, you don't have to eat a locust (although we *will* pressure you and chant your name), but if you don't eat one, you don't get any wild honey. My kids always end up doing it. You can certainly celebrate John the Baptist without daring your kids to eat bugs, but I'm going to be a *little* disappointed if you don't.

If, perhaps, you think your family might not want to consume enough locusts to count as dinner, you can also serve burgers or fish or something. And for dessert, of course, there's always grasshopper pie.

In Europe there is a long tradition of celebrating the eve of this feast day with great fanfare. It has traditionally been celebrated as the summer Christmas and is observed with vigil-night bonfires and big neighborhood parties.

FEAST OF ST. JOSEMARÍA ESCRIVÁ: JUNE 26

St. Josemaría Escrivá was born in Spain in 1902 and was ordained a priest in 1925. A few years later, he had a vision for an organization that he would call Opus Dei (Work of God) that would encourage all Catholics, especially laypeople, to sanctify their daily work. He is one of the saints of what we now call the universal call to holiness (others include St. Francis de Sales and Pope St. John Paul II), based on the words of Jesus on the Sermon on the Mount: "You, therefore, must be perfect, as your heavenly Father is perfect" (Mt 5:48).

As St. Josemaría told us, "Not all of us can be rich, wise, famous, but all of us—all of us—are called to be saints."[7] Yes, even moms. Even moms with crazy little kids or teenagers or both. *Our* holiness in daily life will look a lot different from a parish priest's or a cloistered nun's, but that doesn't mean that it doesn't exist, or can't exist. We just have to work with what we've got.

An excellent thing to do for this day is to examine our daily lives and see where we could add in prayer or pious practices. Perhaps last year or last month we really couldn't get to daily Mass in the morning. But what about now? Would our work or school or kids' schedules allow us to add in some time for daily reading of the Bible or mental prayer or both? Are the kids ready to start a family Rosary or to learn the Morning Offering? Do we have a friend or a co-worker we've been meaning to invite to Mass or confession or a retreat?

As a meal for the day, I like to make a Spanish tortilla, which is basically an omelette, to which can be added any meat or veggies we happen to have on hand. It's tasty as is or served on French bread as a sandwich. Or, if I'm feeling more adventurous, I'll make Spanish paella. For dessert: flan or deep-fried churros.

SOLEMNITY OF SS. PETER AND PAUL: JUNE 29

We observe a feast day for the Conversion of St. Paul on January 25, and a feast day for the Chair of St. Peter, celebrating the first pope and the papacy itself, on February 22. But these two apostles get to share two other feast days, an optional memorial on November 18 for the founding of the basilicas that bear their names in Rome, and June 29, a solemnity remembering their martyrdoms (a holy day of obligation in many parts of the world, but not in the United States or Canada).

[7] Josemaría Escrivá de Balaguer, *Furrow* (New York: Scepter, 1987), no. 125.

It's rather amusing that these two are sharing feast days until the end of the age, given their rather rocky history together on earth. St. Peter was an uneducated fisherman, bold and impulsive. St. Paul was a scholarly Pharisee, who taught himself tent making so as not to be a financial burden on the Church after his (rather spectacular) conversion to Christianity.

Peter was a natural leader, and despite his shortcomings—or because of them—he was selected by Jesus to be the first visible head of the Church. Paul didn't know Jesus during his time on earth, but the Risen Jesus appeared to him and inspired his conversion. Paul was "the Apostle to the Gentiles", traveling the known world by land and sea to make converts.

Incident at Antioch

A dispute between Peter and Paul, called the Incident at Antioch (I love that events in the history of Christianity have official names), centered on the Gentiles. At first, the Christians of Jewish and Gentile descent were coexisting nicely, worshipping together and eating together. St. Paul strongly supported this. But some, headed by St. James the Less, believed that anyone who wanted to become a Christian needed first to become a Jew through circumcision and acceptance of the Mosaic Law. They thought it was wrong for Jewish Christians to eat with Gentiles who didn't comply with their dietary restrictions.

St. Peter was being a flip-flopper on the issue. At first he agreed with St. Paul and ate with the Gentiles; he even had a vision in which God told him that all foods were clean and fit to eat (Acts 10:9–16). But then representatives from St. James the Less convinced him that it would cause scandal among Jews, and he stopped. They even per-suaded St. Barnabas, traveling companion of St. Paul, to stop eating with Gentile converts, which *really* frustrated St. Paul.

It was a huge issue, and it threatened the very existence of the young Church. But instead of giving up on the whole thing, instead of each disciple just starting his own little church in which he could have his own way, the apostles met in Antioch to work out their differences face-to-face (Gal 2:11–21; Acts 15:1–31). The good news is, SS. Peter, Paul, *and* James the Less all agreed that non-Jewish

Christians would not have to observe the Mosaic Law. St. James himself said, "Therefore my judgment is that we should not trouble those of the Gentiles who turn to God" (Acts 15:19). It really is an inspiring example of working through important disagreements in a charitable and productive way.

Foundational Leaders

Peter and Paul are now remembered together as the foundation of the Catholic Church. Tradition holds that they were both martyred in Rome on June 29—St. Peter in the year 64 by being crucified upside down; St. Paul by beheading three years later.

I keep wanting to plan a group camping trip with a couple of other families in honor of this feast day, so we could fish like St. Peter, sleep in tents (probably not homemade, but still ...) in honor of St. Paul, and have disagreements and resolve them. It would be perfect.

In the meantime, however, we content ourselves with snacks or desserts of little tents made out of cookies or graham crackers (they can be just balanced or can be held together with melted chocolate, frosting, peanut butter, or cream cheese) with Goldfish crackers or fish-shaped gummy candies on the side.

There are a number of indulgences associated with the day. If you are fortunate enough to have an article of devotion (a rosary, crucifix, cross, scapular, or medal) that has been blessed by the pope or by any bishop, this feast is the day to use it! Making a profession of faith by reciting the Apostles' or Nicene Creed with your blessed article is good for a plenary indulgence (per the usual conditions). An article blessed by a priest or a deacon can get you a partial indulgence. The Church also encourages a visit to a sacred place on this feast day. There is a plenary indulgence granted to the faithful who visit a basilica or a cathedral on the feast of SS. Peter and Paul, and there recite an Our Father and the Creed.

There is a partial indulgence for reciting this prayer: "Holy Apostles Peter and Paul, intercede for us. Guard your people, who rely on the patronage of your apostles Peter and Paul, O Lord, and keep them under your continual protection. Through Christ our Lord. Amen."[8]

---

[8] See appendix B for more on indulgences.

FEAST OF ST. KATERI TEKAKWITHA: JULY 14

St. Kateri was born in the seventeenth century in a Mohawk village in what is now New York State. She was the daughter of a Mohawk chief and a captured Christian Algonquin woman who became his wife. When Kateri was four years old she lost both of her parents and her little brother to smallpox. She survived, but the disease damaged her eyesight and left her with scars on her face. She went to live with an aunt whose husband was the chief of a different Mohawk clan.

The French Jesuits, after the gruesome martyrdoms of St. Isaac Jogues, St. Jean dé Brebeuf, and six others at the hands of Native Americans, continued their missionary work. Kateri had regular contact with Christian missionaries, and by the time she was a teenager she was determined to forgo marriage and to devote herself to Christ. She was baptized on Easter Sunday in 1676, at the age of nineteen. Her piety was known and admired by the Jesuits, but her faith made her a subject of suspicion and derision among the people of her village.

Four years later, her health began to fail, and she died at the age of twenty-four. The priest who attended her reported that about fifteen minutes after her death, her face began to glow, and her smallpox scars disappeared. She was canonized in 2012 and is known as "the Lily of the Mohawks".

Making authentic Native American food can be a challenge. First, it varies widely between different peoples in different parts of North America. Second, even once we've narrowed it down to the northeast, if we want to be authentically seventeenth-century Mohawk, we would need to make stuff like dried deer meat, pemmican (cakes made of dried berries and dried meat), and acorn mash that needs to be boiled and rinsed twenty-six times; if you do it only twenty-five times, it will make you sick.

So, I tend to favor going for more modern Native American cuisine, such as three sisters stew, featuring the three staples of the traditional Native American diet: corn, squash, and beans (I like to add some meat). It's delicious with fry bread, which can be made in a skillet or, if you're feeling daring, hung over an open fire! (Store-bought naan is an easy substitute.)

For dessert, it's fun and simple to make snow maple taffy. We don't have snow at our house, ever. So we might as well make this treat in the summer. All you have to do is bring 100 percent pure maple syrup to a boil and then pour it over "snow" (we make our own by chopping up ice cubes in the blender). The syrup cools to a sticky maple taffy that can be rolled up onto a stick.

FEAST OF OUR LADY OF MOUNT CARMEL: JULY 16

Our Lady of Mount Carmel is the title given to Mary in her role as patroness of the Carmelite Order of friars, nuns, sisters, and laypeople. She is usually depicted wearing a golden crown, with a circle of stars around her head, holding the infant Jesus and the Brown Scapular.

For folks who wear a religious habit, a scapular is like an apron that hangs down in the front and back and is the top layer of the habit. In its much smaller version, modified for laypeople, the Brown Scapular is two small pieces of brown woolen cloth, connected by strings and worn around the neck, under the clothes. Tradition holds that in the thirteenth century an English Carmelite prior, St. Simon Stock (feast day: May 16), had a vision of Our Lady of Mount Carmel, in which she gave him the Brown Scapular and encouraged devotion to it.

A description from the fourteenth century reads, "St. Simon was an Englishman, a man of great holiness and devotion, who always in his prayers asked the Virgin to favor his Order with some singular privilege. The Virgin appeared to him holding the Scapular in her hand saying, 'This is for you and yours a privilege; the one who dies in it will be saved.' "[9] Originally the promise was understood to apply to Carmelites who stayed faithful and didn't remove their habits (i.e., leave the order). Eventually the devotion spread to third order Carmelites and then to the masses.

The Brown Scapular is a sacramental. It is a way to focus our attention on our faith and our love for God and Our Lady. It shouldn't be viewed in a superstitious way or understood to guarantee our entry into heaven. The *Catechism of the Catholic Church* states that sacramentals such as the Brown Scapular "do not confer the grace of the Holy Spirit in the way that the sacraments do, but by the Church's

---

[9] Eamon R. Carroll, "The Marian Spirituality of the Medieval Religious Orders: Medieval Devotion to Mary among the Carmelites", *Marian Studies* 52 (2001), http://ecommons .udayton.edu/marian_studies/vol52/iss1/11.

prayer, they prepare us to receive grace and dispose us to cooperate with it" (1670).

We have a special love for Our Lady of Mount Carmel in our house, as the husband went to Our Lady of Mount Carmel High School in Chicago, and his mother taught there alongside the Carmelites for many, many years. The husband has been wearing the Brown Scapular for thirty years now. Our kids have been enrolled, and they wear it very enthusiastically for a while until they lose it and forget about it and then remember it and ask for another.

Any Catholic priest can invest any baptized Catholic in the Brown Scapular, using a prayer from the *Book of Blessings*. A Carmelite priest at a Carmelite parish would be especially happy to do it for you. Once you are enrolled, you can replace your scapular as needed.

For the day, we like to have Our Lady of Mount Carmel caramel brownie sundaes for dessert.

FEAST OF ST. MARY MAGDALENE: JULY 22

There has been a good deal of confusion about St. Mary Magdalene. Medieval Church tradition conflated her with Mary of Bethany—the sister of Martha and Lazarus—and the unnamed "sinful woman" who anoints Jesus's feet (Lk 7:36–50). Modern Scripture scholars, however, believe them to be three different women.

We know from the Gospels that Mary Magdalene was a companion of Jesus, traveled with him as he preached the good news, and—along with other women—provided the financial support for the group. We also know that Jesus exorcised seven demons from her (Luke 8:1–3). Mary's epithet "Magdalene" likely indicates that she was from the village of Magdala in Galilee and was used by the writers of the Gospels to distinguish her from other Marys who also followed Jesus.[10]

Mary Magdalene was a witness to Jesus' Crucifixion and burial on Good Friday, staying when so many others had fled in fear. Just after sunrise on Easter Sunday, Mary Magdalene went to the tomb,

---

[10] There are six New Testament women called Mary: Mary, the mother of Jesus; Mary Magdalene; Mary, the mother of James the Less and Joses; Mary Salome, wife of Zebedee and mother of James the great and John; Mary the wife of Clopas; and Mary of Bethany, sister of Martha and Lazarus.

carrying spices with which to embalm Jesus' body. There she saw the empty tomb, heard the angel proclaim Jesus' Resurrection, encountered the Risen Lord, and spoke to him (Mt 28:1–10).

Pope St. John Paul II wrote that "Mary Magdalene was the first eyewitness of the Risen Christ, and for this reason she was also *the first to bear witness to him before the Apostles.* This event, in a sense, crowns all that has been said previously about Christ entrusting divine truths to women as well as men."[11] In recognition of this fact, in 2016 the Church elevated the commemoration of St. Mary Magdalene from a memorial to a feast, like those celebrating the apostles (except SS. Peter and Paul, whose feast day is a solemnity).

An old story says that after Jesus' Resurrection, Mary Magdalene was invited to a banquet given by the Roman emperor Tiberius. It being the Easter season and all, she arrived carrying a plain white egg in her hand and announcing, "He is Risen!" The emperor scoffed, saying that Christ having risen from the dead was as likely as that egg she held turning red in her hand. At that very moment the egg turned red, and Mary proclaimed the gospel to all in the house.

So, even though the Easter season is behind us, we like to dye some eggs red for the occasion, either with food coloring or, if I'm feeling old-timey, onion skins. Then we use them for an egg tapping game, which is pretty much exactly what it sounds like. Two people face off, each holding one hard-boiled red egg, and tap them together once. The goal is to break the other person's egg without breaking your own. The winner of the pair moves on to face another winner until only one unbroken egg remains, and that person is the champion.

Because Mary Magdalene brought spices to the tomb of Jesus, I like to serve curry or another spice-heavy meal for dinner and to make spice cake for dessert. To drink, 7 Up reminds us of the seven demons from which she was delivered.

FEAST OF ST. BRIDGET OF SWEDEN: JULY 23

St. Bridget was born to an affluent family in Sweden in the fourteenth century. She was a mystic, and, beginning in her childhood, she

---

[11] John Paul II, apostolic letter *Mulieris dignitatem* (August 15, 1988), no. 16 (emphasis in the original), https://w2.vatican.va/content/john-paul-ii/en/apost_letters/1988/documents/hf _jp-ii_apl_19880815_mulieris-dignitatem.html.

experienced visions of moments in the life of Christ, from his Nativity to his Crucifixion. She loved to read and kept diaries throughout her life.

Bridget married young and gave birth to eight children, four boys and four girls. Six of her children survived to adulthood, including her second daughter, St. Catherine of Sweden. Bridget had a special devotion to unwed mothers and their children, establishing charity houses to clothe and feed them.

After twenty years of marriage she became a widow and decided to found a religious order dedicated to the poor. Men and women lived in joint community, but in separate cloisters. Upon joining the order, they would relinquish all their worldly goods, except their books. They could have as many books as they liked. Bridget died while on a pilgrimage to Rome and was canonized just a few years later.

Living near an IKEA has made preparing for this feast day very easy. They have an amazing selection of Swedish foods that are inexpensive and very easy to prepare. I can also pick up a new dresser or a couch while I'm there—so convenient. There are also plenty of choices at a regular grocery store to make a fun Swedish meal, such as meatballs with a cream sauce served over egg noodles, bread with lingonberry jam, or Swedish Fish candy.

FEAST OF SS. JOACHIM AND ANNE: JULY 26

The Virgin Mary's parents are not mentioned by name in the Gospels, but ancient tradition has called them Anne and Joachim. It was their love and faith that prepared their daughter, Mary, to give her *fiat* (let it be) to the angel Gabriel when he asked if she would bear the Son of God.

Because Anne and Joachim are the grandparents of Jesus, we invite our grandparents over and let the kids help make a special dinner for them. For our out-of-town grandparents, we have to plan ahead and make cards and get them in the mail. If your children don't have local or living grandparents, it would be a beautiful tradition for the day to visit a nursing home or visit elderly neighbors.

In France, the traditional meal for the day is lobster. That's not always in the budget, but our local grocery store carries live lobsters in a tank, and they are sometimes pretty affordable. They'll even steam them for me, so I don't have to kill dinner myself (a plus in my book). A few lobsters sitting there on a platter, looking at you, makes for a very memorable dinner! If lobster isn't an option, I'll make another shellfish dish, such as shrimp scampi. St. Anne is a patron saint of lace makers, so Florentine lace cookies, either store-bought or homemade, are a great dessert for the day.

FEAST OF OUR LADY, QUEEN OF ANGELS: AUGUST 2

Pull up a chair, kids; it's time for a quick lesson on the history of Los Angeles, the more broadly applicable parts of which will become clear, eventually.

In 1771, Franciscan friar St. Junípero Serra (feast day: July 1) authorized the foundation of Mission San Gabriel Arcángel, the fourth of twenty-one Catholic missions in California. Ten years later, a group of forty-four settlers founded a town they called *El Pueblo de Nuestra Señora la Reina de los Ángeles de Porciúncula*, which means, "the Town of Our Lady the Queen of the Angels of Portiuncula". One imagines that in the interest of saving time, it eventually became known as just "Los Angeles".

"Queen of the Angels" is a fairly well-known Marian title. But what's the Portiuncula? It's the tiny chapel within the Basilica of St. Mary of the Angels in Assisi, Italy. In the early thirteenth century it was a tumbledown chapel outside of town. St. Francis restored it and built a hut beside it. With the followers who joined him there he founded the Franciscan Order. St. Francis died in his cell, adjacent to the Portiuncula, in 1226.

Tradition tells us that in 1221, Jesus, Mary, and a host of angels appeared to St. Francis inside the Portiuncula. Jesus asked St. Francis what favor he would ask of him, and St. Francis requested a plenary indulgence—for *everyone*. He asked Jesus to grant that anyone who visited the chapel on the feast day of Our Lady Queen of the Angels, confessed his sins with a contrite heart, received Holy Communion, and prayed for the intentions of the Holy Father would be as pure as he was immediately after baptism. Our Lord agreed to Francis' bold request, and so, eventually, did Pope Honorius III, but he took more convincing.

Plenary indulgences had existed before, but this was the first that was accessible to everyday folks, and was so for quite some time. It was so significant, that 560 years later and 6,268 miles away, a group of settlers named a town after it. By that time the indulgence had been extended to any Franciscan church, which would include the California missions. In 1910, it was extended to include any church, anywhere.

So, on August 2, or the Sunday after, if the church isn't open on weekdays (as is the case with some rural churches), a plenary indulgence is available to anyone who visits any church and fulfills the usual conditions.[12] We like to visit a Franciscan church for the day, whenever possible.

FEAST OF THE TRANSFIGURATION: AUGUST 6

The Transfiguration is one of the major events in the earthly life of Jesus. It is recorded in the three synoptic Gospels: Matthew, Mark, and Luke. In all three versions, Jesus brings Peter, James, and John up a high mountain. The mountain isn't named, but tradition holds that it is Mount Tabor. Once there, Jesus' clothing and body become transfigured: "His face shone like the sun, and his garments became white as light" (Mt 17:2).

Next, Moses and Elijah show up and start having a chat with the glowing Jesus. It's all too much for Peter to handle in silence. He's got to do *something*, so he offers to put up some tents for Jesus and his friends. While he was still speaking, "behold, a bright cloud overshadowed them, and a voice from the cloud said, 'This is my beloved Son, with whom I am well pleased; listen to him.'" (Mt 17:5). Something similar happens when Jesus is baptized: "And behold, a voice from heaven, saying, 'This is my beloved Son, with whom I am well pleased'" (Mt 3:17).

After the Old Testament figures have disappeared, the four make their way down the mountain, and Jesus instructs the disciples not to tell anyone about what happened "until the Son of man is raised from the dead" (Mt 17:9). And (as usual) the disciples have no idea what he's talking about.

---

[12] United States Conference of Catholic Bishops, *Manual of Indulgences: Norms and Grants* (Washington, D.C.: United States Conference of Catholic Bishops, 2006), no. 33. See appendix B for more on indulgences.

This episode is a glimpse of Christ's Resurrection. It is also a reminder to us that our own physical bodies will one day be resurrected, glorified, and raised to heaven. An easy twist for dinner is to "transfigure" some leftovers into a new meal. Homemade whipped cream is great as an activity and an addition to a dessert. All it takes is heavy whipping cream, sugar, and an electric mixer of some sort—or a whisk and a lot of elbow grease. Just start whipping, and the cream transforms into something even better than it was before.

Talking about Heaven

Up there on the mountaintop, Peter, James, and John see not only Jesus, lifted up and shining in his glory, but also two of their beloved childhood heroes: Moses and Elijah, just hanging out there, having a conversation with the boss. This is a great day to talk to kids about whom we hope to meet in heaven. If we make it there, we can be assured of seeing Jesus, Mary, and all our favorite saints.

We can't know for sure who else will or won't have made it, but it's good to hope and pray. We like to talk about deceased relatives whom the kids knew, or whom they never got to meet on earth, or whom a child knows only from a photo of that relative holding him when he was a baby. We talk about famous figures from history or athletes or actors whom we hope to meet in heaven. One favorite around here is actor John Wayne, who converted to Catholicism on his deathbed, according to his grandson who is a Catholic priest!

Another fun food and activity for the day is making toad in the hole. We read the story of the Transfiguration from one of the Gospels[13] (it's really short) while heating a griddle on the stove over medium heat. Using a large, round cookie cutter or a wide glass, I cut a circular "cloud" out of the center of a piece of sandwich bread, spray the griddle well with cooking spray, and put both the piece of bread and the cloud on the griddle, separately. Then I crack an egg into the hole in the bread and we watch as the egg becomes dazzling white, just like Jesus! Well, not *just* like Jesus. But it's still fun.

---

[13] Mt 17:1–8; Mk 9:2–8; Lk 9:28–36.

It's ready to eat once the white of the egg is white, or you can flip the bread over and cook it on the other side as well. Then we serve it alongside the cloud, and maybe some bacon, because feast days deserve bacon.

FEAST OF ST. LAWRENCE: AUGUST 10

St. Lawrence of Rome was born in the third century in Spain. He accompanied the soon-to-be Pope St. Sixtus II to Rome and there was named the youngest of the city's seven deacons. St. Ambrose of Milan tells us that, as a deacon, Lawrence was in charge of the material goods of the Church and the distribution of alms to the poor. During the persecution of Christians ordered by the Roman emperor Valerian, Pope Sixtus II was executed along with many other priests and deacons.

The local prefect offered to spare the life of St. Lawrence if he would turn over to him the treasures of the Church. Lawrence asked him for three days to gather the treasures, and the prefect agreed. The deacon spent the days distributing the wealth of the Church to the poor of the city, and entrusting important books and documents to their care, asking only that they would agree to meet him outside the home of the prefect on the morning of the third day.

When the prefect came out, expecting gold and jewels, he was presented with a motley crew of widows and orphans, the poor, the crippled, and the blind. St. Lawrence declared that *these* were the true treasures of the Church. And he was promptly arrested.

The prefect was so angry that, rather than behead Lawrence, as he had the other Christians, he had a large gridiron prepared, with red hot coals beneath it. He had St. Lawrence placed upon the gridiron to suffer, but Lawrence, in the midst of his physical agony, just before his death, cheerfully declared, "You had better turn me over. I'm done on this side!"[14]

He is a patron saint of librarians and archivists, for the care he took to preserve the books and the documents of the Church. He is a patron saint of cooks, for the fact that he was cooked. And he is

---

[14]Jacobus de Voragine, *The Golden Legend: Readings on the Saints*, trans. William Granger Ryan (Princeton, N.J.: Princeton University Press, 2012), no. 117

the patron saint of comedians, for the excellent sense of humor he displayed about the whole ordeal.

Clearly, this guy was fun. And I really can't think of any better way to honor him than with a barbecue night and a comedy showcase. With either a big crowd or just our family, we cook meat and veggies on the grill, and everyone comes prepared with a couple of their favorite jokes to share. There really is nothing funnier than little kids badly telling jokes. One of my little guys got up and said, "Wanna hear a joke? ... Hop on the bus!" I have no idea why it was supposed to be funny, but it still cracks us up, years later.

FEAST OF ST. CLARE: AUGUST 11

St. Clare was born in Assisi at the end of the twelfth century, the eldest daughter of wealthy noble parents. At the age of eighteen, while attending Mass at the church of San Giorgio in Assisi, she heard St. Francis preach a sermon. She knew immediately that what he had, she wanted.

Her father wished her to marry, but she was able to persuade her mother and aunt to support her desire to devote her life to Jesus. So, on the evening of Palm Sunday in 1212, her aunt accompanied her to the small chapel of the Portiuncula to meet St. Francis. There St. Clare had her hair cut off and exchanged her fine gown for a simple robe and veil. She was soon joined by her sister, then by other women, and became the abbess of the Poor Ladies of San Damiano, now better known as the Poor Clares. They lived a simple life of work, prayer, poverty, chastity, austerity, vegetarianism, near silence, and seclusion from the world, according to a set of rules provided by St. Francis.

When Assisi came under attack by the army of Frederick II, Clare left the cloister to face them down. She was alone, armed with the Blessed Sacrament in a monstrance. When the soldiers saw the lone nun, they were seized by an inexplicable fear and fled Assisi as quickly as they could, leaving the town unharmed.

Clare and Francis remained close friends for the remainder of his life, and she cared for him in his final illness until his death in 1226. She was often unwell herself. She reported that, when she was unable to attend Mass due to illness, she could hear and see on the wall of her room a vision of the Mass as it took place. Pope Pius XII must have had a good sense of humor, because he designated St. Clare the patron saint of television in 1958.

It's a perfect day to enjoy a family movie on TV and have some veggie pizza for dinner and éclairs for dessert.

SOLEMNITY OF THE ASSUMPTION OF THE BLESSED VIRGIN (HOLY DAY OF OBLIGATION): AUGUST 15

Have you been paying attention to the Nicene Creed that we say at Mass each Sunday? If so, you'll have noticed the part at the very end that says, "I look forward to the resurrection of the dead and the life of the world to come." This means we believe that everyone who is now, or will ever be, in heaven will receive back his own body, glorified, at the Second Coming of Jesus. The *Catechism of the Catholic Church* says, " 'We believe in the true resurrection of this flesh that we now possess' (Council of Lyons II). We sow a corruptible body in the tomb, but he raises up an incorruptible body, a 'spiritual body' " (cf. 1 Cor 15:42–44) (1017).

But guess what? A very select few folks are already sporting their bodies in heaven. The Old Testament tells us that the prophet Elijah's departure from this earth in a chariot of fire was far from typical: "And Elijah went up by a whirlwind into heaven. And Elisha saw it and he cried, 'My father, my father! the chariots of Israel and its horsemen!' And he saw him no more" (2 Kings 2:11–12). Genesis says that "God took" Noah's great-grandfather Enoch (5:24), and the Letter to the Hebrews confirms this: "By faith Enoch was taken up so that he should not see death; and he was not found, because God had taken him" (Heb 11:5). Jesus, of course, ascended bodily into heaven by his own power at the Ascension. Finally, we come to the Blessed Virgin Mary.

Dogma of the Assumption

That Mary was assumed bodily, by God's power, into heaven is not up for debate. The Assumption is not in the Bible, but it is considered to be such an important part of the tradition of the Church that in

1950 Pope Pius XII, speaking ex cathedra, declared, "By the authority of our Lord Jesus Christ, of the Blessed Apostles Peter and Paul, and by our own authority, we pronounce, declare, and define it to be a divinely revealed dogma: that the Immaculate Mother of God, the ever Virgin Mary, having completed the course of her earthly life, was assumed body and soul into heavenly glory."[15]

The pope purposely left open the question of whether Mary died before being assumed into heaven. Catholic tradition in both the East and the West has been that she did die first, but we are not obligated to believe that, since that part isn't dogmatically defined in the Western Church.

The day is a solemnity, a feast of the universal Church, and a holy day of obligation, so get thee to church.

The fleur-de-lis is a symbol of the Virgin Mary, but specifically of her Assumption. My grandmother's wedding china, which I was honored to inherit, is decorated with fleurs-de-lis, so we make a point of using it for dinner on this feast. You can often find paper plates with fleurs-de-lis on them around Mardi Gras. I like to stock up on them and use them on Marian feast days if we're having a larger or more casual get-together.

The traditional practice for this feast day is the Blessing of Herbs. You've got to go to Mass anyway, so bring some store-bought or homegrown herbs with you and ask the priest to bless them for you after Mass. They can then be used to make sachets to put in drawers, dried for decorative use or for later cooking, or used to make dinner. I like to make an herb-heavy meal, such as herb roast, herb salad, and, for dessert, a blackberry basil tart.

FEAST OF THE QUEENSHIP OF MARY: AUGUST 22

The Virgin Mary's arrival in heaven was celebrated a week before this feast. On the octave of her Assumption, it's time to celebrate her coronation and queenship.

On January 1, we recognize Mary as *Theotokos* (literally "God-bearer", hence also "Mother of God"). As her Son Jesus is the King

[15] Pope Pius XII, apostolic constitution *Munificentissimus Deus* (November 1, 1950), no. 44, http://w2.vatican.va/content/pius-xii/en/apost_constitutions/documents/hf_p-xii _apc_19501101_munificentissimus-deus.html.

of the Universe (feast day: the last Sunday in Ordinary Time), biblical and popular traditions make her queen. Mary's queenship is a share in Christ's kingship. Jesus is King of all creation through divine right and right of conquest, meaning that he won back mankind for God through his victory over sin and death. Mary is queen through Jesus and subordinate to him. She shares in the struggle for souls because God willed her to have an exceptional role in the work of salvation.

The belief in Mary as Queen of Heaven obtained the sanction of Pope Pius XII in his 1954 encyclical *Ad Caeli Reginam*, but Mary has been invoked under this title by Church Fathers and the faithful since the earliest centuries of the Church. There is a rich history of art featuring depictions of Mary's coronation, usually by the Holy Trinity, and images and statues of Mary often show her wearing a crown. The Crowning of Mary as Queen of Heaven is the fifth Glorious Mystery of the Rosary.

Crownings and Processions

It is traditional for Catholic churches, schools, and homes to celebrate a May Crowning. May crowns are usually made of flowers, so they don't last very long. This feast is a good day to give the family's statue of Mary a slightly more durable crown.

There are many beautiful hymns and prayers to Mary as queen, such as the Regina Caeli and the Salve Regina. The Litany of Loreto, also known as the Litany of the Blessed Virgin Mary, was composed in the Middle Ages and allows us to invoke Mary under all her titles, including the many that call her queen.

This feast is traditionally celebrated with a Marian procession through the streets. The city of Los Angeles held one each year for the first hundred years after its founding, to honor Mary as Our Lady of the Angels, Queen of Heaven, and Empress the Americas. Fortunately, our archbishop has recently revived the tradition, and for the past few years there has yet again been a procession through downtown Los Angeles, beginning at the cathedral, to honor Our Lady.

If you don't have the option of a public procession, this would be another great day to have a do-it-yourself procession through your home, yard, or neighborhood, in which the kids get to hold posters, banners, images, or little statues of Our Lady and march along, singing "Ave Maria" and "Hail, Holy Queen" at the tops of their little lungs.

For food, I like to borrow traditions from our friends across the Atlantic. The Brits know how to honor a queen with food. Queen cakes are lemon–flavored cakes with currants (or raisins), baked in muffin tins or shaped mini–cake pans. The cakes are complemented by tea and finger sandwiches, such as cream cheese and cucumber, and, of course, coronation chicken salad (which is like regular chicken salad but with mango chutney and curry powder). Fancy dresses and crowns for everyone would be appropriate.

FEAST OF ST. BARTHOLOMEW: AUGUST 24

In our family, we had never heard of St. Bartholomew until our first pilgrimage to Rome. We were touring the Archbasilica of St. John Lateran, admiring all the larger-than-life white marble statues, when we came across one that really caught our attention. It was a muscled middle-aged man with impressive, wild (marble) ringlets of hair, draped in (marble) fabric, and holding a knife. Oh yeah, and he was also holding his own skin, with visibly deflated face and hands. It made quite an impression. We were inspired to find out more about him. Since then we've found a few other statues of flayed St. Bartholomew, and he's a favorite of our boys. Jack even dressed up as St. Bartholomew holding his own skin for our school saint pageant one year!

St. Bartholomew, one of the twelve apostles, is mentioned in the three synoptic Gospels and in Acts, always in the company of St. Philip. He is understood to be the same guy as Nathanael of John's Gospel, of whom Jesus said, "Behold, an Israelite indeed, in whom is no guile!" (Jn 1:47). Seems like a pretty good endorsement.

After the Ascension, Bartholomew preached the gospel in India and Armenia. It was in Armenia that he is believed to have suffered one of the more spectacular martyrdoms in history, at least as far as visual representations go: he was skinned alive.

Catholics have always had a bit of a sense of humor as far as assigning patron saints to professions (see St. Agatha and bell makers, and St. Lawrence and cooks), so it should come as no surprise that St. Bartholomew is the patron saint of various professions that skin animals or use animal skins, such as trappers, tanners, bookbinders, and shoemakers.

We don't skin many animals around here. (If you do, by all means, do it on this feast day!) But we do have an apple tree. It just so happens that the apples ripen in late August, and the feast of St. Bartholomew is always the inspiration we need to pick and ... *skin* all those apples. We make them into applesauce and apple butter and apple pies. Turning the crank on the apple peeler is a completely different experience when you have St. Bartholomew on your mind.

Of course, if you don't have an apple tree of your own, they do have apples at the store. And peeling a few apples, talking about St. Bartholomew (and maybe looking up a picture of his statue), and enjoying some homemade applesauce makes for a very memorable feast day.

There are many options for a "skinned" dinner: peeled potatoes and carrots go nicely alongside skinless chicken breasts with barbecue sauce. It seems to be quite a regular dinner, until everyone realizes it's not!

FEAST OF ST. MONICA: AUGUST 27; FEAST OF ST. AUGUSTINE: AUGUST 28

We celebrate the feast of St. Monica on the day before we celebrate the feast of her son St. Augustine, which is fitting. She not only bore him and raised him, but she spent decades in tearful prayer for his return to the faith, while he lived a life of heresy and hedonism. Eventually her prayers were answered. As St. Ambrose, a friend to both, foretold: "A child of so many tears cannot be lost."[16]

St. Monica and St. Augustine were both native to North Africa, ethnically Berber, but culturally Roman. St. Monica was a Christian and instructed her child in the faith, but her husband was a pagan, who would not allow his son to be baptized as a child. Augustine left the faith entirely as a young man when he fell in with a group of intellectual bon vivants who valued debate, rhetoric, and the pursuit of pleasure above all things. He took a mistress and had a son out of wedlock.

---

[16] Hermann Wedewer and Joseph McSorley, *A Short History of the Catholic Church* (St. Louis, Mo.: B. Herder, 1918), 63.

He describes in his autobiography, *Confessions*, that in the year 386, at the age of thirty-one, he heard a childlike voice telling him, "Take up and read; take up and read."[17] He began to read the Bible and to study the faith. A year later he and his son, Adeodatus, were baptized by St. Ambrose, to the great delight of St. Monica.

Augustine's mother and his son both passed away within a few years. He gave away the family fortune to the poor and converted the family home into a monastic residence. Augustine was ordained a priest and in 395 became bishop of Hippo. He spent the rest of his life in service and study, writing more than one hundred works of theology, apologetics, and philosophy. He died of an illness at the age of seventy-five, as the Visigoths were sacking Hippo. He was venerated as a saint immediately and was recognized as a Doctor of the Church in 1298.

Our family tradition for the day is inspired by my favorite story about St. Augustine and about the Trinity. One day, Augustine was walking along the beach in North Africa, pondering the mystery of the Holy Trinity and trying desperately to understand once and for all how there could be three persons in one God. He was distracted from his thoughts by the sight of a boy who had dug a hole in the sand and was running back and forth from the ocean, dumping bucketful after bucketful of water into the hole. Finally, Augustine's curiosity got the best of him, and he asked the boy, "What are you doing?" The boy replied, "I'm emptying the ocean into this hole." The man, amused, said, "Why, you can't empty the ocean into a hole!" The boy looked into his eyes and said, "Neither can you understand the mystery of the Holy Trinity." And then the boy was gone.

That vision did *not* stop St. Augustine from thinking about the Trinity. He pondered and wrote about that mystery of the faith, among others, for the rest of his life. But it's a good reminder that a complete understanding of some parts of our faith won't come in this life.

And the feast of St. Augustine is a good day to go to the beach and dig a hole and recite his Holy Spirit Prayer:

---

[17] *The Confessions of St. Augustine*, trans. E. B. Pusey (Oxford: John Henry Parker, 1840), 153.

Breathe in me, O Holy Spirit,
That my thoughts may all be holy.
Act in me, O Holy Spirit,
That my work, too, may be holy.
Draw my heart, O Holy Spirit,
That I love but what is holy.
Strengthen me, O Holy Spirit,
To defend all that is holy.
Guard me, then, O Holy Spirit,
That I always may be holy.[18]

We have a Gus, named for St. Augustine, who gets to choose what we have for dinner on his feast day. Dishes from the Berber region of North Africa include couscous, *pastilla* (meat pie), and slow-cooked savory tagine. St. Augustine is a patron saint of brewers, so be sure to have beer alongside it—or maybe root beer. For dessert, salted caramel anything is a reminder of the tears St. Monica shed for her son.

THE PASSION OF ST. JOHN THE BAPTIST: AUGUST 29

We celebrated the birth of St. John the Baptist on June 24. This feast celebrates his martyrdom. His life was a witness to the coming of the Truth and the Life; his death was a witness to the truth of marriage.

St. John was something of a counselor to King Herod Antipas. King Herod was hardly devout, but he recognized the goodness he heard when St. John the Baptist spoke, and he liked to listen to him. But John refused to accept Herod's marriage to Herodias, whose still-living first husband was ... Herod's brother. John spoke out against the validity of the marriage, and Herodias conspired to have him executed for it.

When Herodias' daughter performed a dance at King Herod's birthday party, he liked it so much that he promised her anything her heart desired. Herodias told her daughter to ask for the head of St. John the Baptist on a platter. She must have been a real piece of work.

King Herod was horrified, but like Pontius Pilate about a year later, he was a weak man. He cared more about not losing face in

[18] "St. Augustine's Prayer to the Holy Spirit", Catholic Online, https://www.catholic.org/prayers/prayer.php?p=81.

front of his party guests than about doing the right thing. So, he had an innocent man executed (see Mk 6:14–29; Mt 14:3–13).

The tradition of some Eastern Catholics is to eschew platters, knives, and round foods on this day, which sounds funny *and* challenging. But I only just found out about that. Our family tradition has been to serve lettuce wraps, with a head—of lettuce—on a platter.

FEAST OF ST. TERESA OF CALCUTTA: SEPTEMBER 5

The Catholic Church holds up all these saints we've been talking about in all these pages expressly to give us examples of how to live a faithful Catholic life, whatever our personal circumstances. It's wonderful, really.

But one challenging thing is that so many of the most familiar saints are so old-timey! It's easy to slip into thinking, well, *I* could face down the wild beasts or dedicate my life to the poor or renounce my fortune and join a monastery, if only I had lived back then. But things are different now!

Not so fast, my friend. While we've yet to have our first canonized saint of the social media age (will it be *you*?), there are saints and blesseds who lived lives of great holiness in our modern era. They lived, as we do, with the modern blessings and curses of photography, television, phones, cars, airplanes, and air conditioning.

A Modern Saint

Mother Teresa is a modern saint. She was born Anjezë (Agnes) Bojaxhiu in Albania in 1910. She left home at the age of eighteen to join the Sisters of Loreto in Ireland so she could learn English and become a missionary. She arrived in India the next year, learning Bengali and teaching in the convent school. She made her first religious vows in 1931 and chose the name Teresa, the Spanish spelling of the name of St. Thérèse of Lisieux.

In 1946, while on her way to her annual retreat, Teresa felt a call to leave the protection of her convent and serve the poor while living among them. Two years later, with the permission of her superiors, she replaced her traditional habit with a white sari trimmed with blue and began her missionary work among the poorest of the poor. In 1950, she obtained the permission of the Vatican to found her own religious order, the Missionaries of Charity, with thirteen fellow sisters.

At the time of her death from heart failure in 1997, her ministry had grown to 610 missions in 123 countries, including orphanages, schools, hospices, and charity centers for people of all faiths, and had the help of over 300 brothers and 4,000 sisters worldwide. Those numbers have continued to grow. There are now more than 800 missions and 5,000 sisters!

Teresa lived and worked quietly with some of the world's most forgotten people, but she was also an international celebrity. She disliked having her picture taken, but she appeared all over the world on television and in film documentaries, in newspapers and magazines. She gave hundreds of speeches that were heard by millions of people, upholding Catholic teaching about controversial subjects such as war and abortion. She was honored with countless awards and honorary degrees, including the 1979 Nobel Peace Prize. She was lauded as a saint and a hero well before her death. She also endured slander from the media and anonymous threats from strangers. Hers was a life of heroic virtue lived in a very modern world.

St. Mother Teresa's canonization process was begun by her friend Pope St. John Paul II immediately upon her death. She was named a saint by Pope Francis in 2015, in a ceremony conducted in St. Peter's Square and live-streamed on the Internet to every corner of the world.

Admiration through Imitation

So, what to do for her feast day? Well, starting an orphanage or holding a dying person would probably be best. But, I have to admit to never having done either. We have, however, been fortunate enough to visit, on a couple occasions, a day-care home run by the Missionaries of Charity in Tijuana, Mexico. The joy of the sisters and the love they have for the children in their care is a thing of beauty.

My kids were curious and asked the sisters lots of question. In response to the question, "Where do you keep your stuff?" one of the sisters replied that she had just packed up all her worldly goods because she was being transferred to another city that very afternoon, and would the kids like to see all her stuff? Enthusiastically, they said they would. The sister disappeared for a moment and returned with a pail and a piece of fabric. In the pail were some letters and a couple of small books and photographs and keepsake items. The fabric was her spare sari. And that was it. The kids were floored, especially considering we had driven to Mexico with two vans full of extra toys, clothes, and furniture we didn't need—to donate to the home. What a blessing to peek into that way of life.

If you are able to visit a Missionaries of Charity center, I would highly recommend it. Making a donation to their work is also a wonderful way to celebrate Mother Teresa's life. It takes a bit of legwork though: you have to find the address of a specific center and mail them your donation. As of this writing, they don't have any sort of central donation system—keeping that overhead low.

For dinner we like to have Indian food. Whether in a restaurant, as takeout, from the grocery store, or homemade, it's all good. And if you don't like spicy, it doesn't have to be spicy.

Just because I happened to have some in the pantry one year, it has also become our family tradition to have blue Jell-O on the feast of St. Teresa, for the blue stripes on her sari. It's easy and cute. Last year, however, I leveled up and made a Bundt-pan mold of white Jell-O with three blue stripes, like Mother Teresa's sari, using a recipe I found online for red, white, and blue finger Jell-O.[19] It was a big hit! It's time-consuming, but not hard, and if you have the kind of family or friends who appreciate Jell-O molds that look like religious habits, they'll be very impressed.

FEAST OF THE NATIVITY OF MARY: SEPTEMBER 8

As we discussed in the section on St. John the Baptist, Mary's is one of only three birthdays on the liturgical calendar each year (the third being Jesus', of course).

Kids love a birthday party, and this is a perfect day to let them head up the decoration committee and create drawings and random paper cutouts that they claim are flowers. In the garage, we have a shelf of

---

[19] "Red, White, and Blue Layered Finger Jello", *Browneyed Baker*, https://www.brown eyedbaker.com/red-white-blue-finger-jello/.

birthday-party leftovers, such as plates and streamers and balloons, and they get to use those too. So the party becomes quite a mishmash of decorations, the kind of thing I could never let go enough to allow at the birthday parties of my kids. As I said, they love it.

At the birthday party, I try to serve blue food, as blue is Mary's color. Of course, there aren't many blue foods, so the menu gets a bit odd, but that's part of the fun. Blue-corn-chip nachos and blueberry cornbread are my go-to. Blue crabs and blue cheese are fancier, but not actually blue. For dessert, there are plenty of blueberry-based desserts, but we like to go with a birthday cake, decorated in blue with love and messiness by the kids.

Finally, you know that on your mother's birthday, you definitely have to call her. For our Mother Mary, that means saying the Rosary!

FEAST OF THE EXALTATION OF THE HOLY CROSS: SEPTEMBER 14; FEAST OF OUR LADY OF SORROWS: SEPTEMBER 15

And now, to get serious for a moment, we have the mid-September feast days of the Exaltation of the Holy Cross and of Our Lady of Sorrows. Most feasts on the Church calendar, even when they commemorate things such as your dad chopping your head off (St. Barbara, December 4) or your intestines being wound up on a winch (St. Erasmus, June 2), we Catholics still manage to make a party of it. But these two days, like a mini–Holy Week, don't have that same whimsical feel to them.

The True Cross

The Exaltation of the Holy Cross commemorates the finding of the True Cross by St. Helena in 326. On this day we focus on the cross itself. We focus on how Jesus Christ transformed an instrument of torture and humiliation into a symbol of triumph and salvation. As St. Paul says, "We preach Christ crucified, a stumbling block to Jews and folly to Gentiles, but to those who are called, both Jews and Greeks, Christ the power of God and the wisdom of God. For the foolishness of God is wiser than men, and the weakness of God is stronger than men" (1 Cor 1:23–25).

Veneration of the cross is an ancient tradition, powerful for grown-ups and kids alike but easy to manage. If it's not offered at your parish, you can do it at home using any large-ish crucifix or even just two pieces of wood nailed together to form a cross.

The cross should be placed so that the head is higher than the foot, perhaps resting on the bottom stair or on a few books. Everyone in the family lines up behind the head of the household. He turns to the next person in line and says, "Behold the wood of the Cross." That person kneels. Placing his forehead on the wood and then his lips, he kisses the cross. Then he says, "I adore you, O Christ, and I praise you, because by your Holy Cross, you have redeemed the world." He stands and turns to the next person in line and says, "Behold the wood of the Cross." And so on, until the last person in line says, "Behold the wood of the Cross" to the head of the household, who kisses the cross. And you're all done.

The Sorrowing Mother

The next day, for Our Lady of Sorrows, I have a challenge activity I like to do with the kids. The Seven Sorrows of Mary are a devotion given to us by St. Bridget of Sweden, based on seven sad events that occurred in the life of Our Lady and are recorded in the Bible.

1. The Prophecy of Simeon (Lk 2:25–35)
2. The Flight into Egypt (Mt 2:13–15)
3. The Loss of the Child Jesus in the Temple of Jerusalem (Lk 2:41–51)
4. The Meeting of Jesus and Mary on the Way of the Cross (Lk 23:26–31)[20]
5. The Crucifixion (Jn 19:17–18, 25–30)
6. The Removal of Jesus' Body from the Cross (Mk 15:43–47)
7. The Burial of Jesus (Jn 19:39–42)

---

[20] The meeting of Jesus and Mary comes to us from tradition even though it is not mentioned in Scripture. The listed verses recount the meeting of Jesus with the women of Jerusalem. The two events are remembered in two different Stations of the Cross: Mary in the fourth, the women of Jerusalem in the eighth. Although she isn't named, it's possible that Our Lady was also among the women of Jerusalem.

All you need for the activity is a Bible and seven pieces of something sour for each person participating. It can be lemon slices, sour candies, whatever you've got. The sourer, the better. Chewy candies are better than hard candies, since the latter take so long to eat. We look up the events in the Bible, one at a time, and read the passages aloud. For children who can read, this is a great opportunity to teach them how to look things up in a Bible, since that's not exactly intuitive. ("Matthew, Mark, Luke, and John, you saddle the horse and I'll jump on.")

After we read each of the sorrows, I hand out a sour something to each kid. Then we recite a Hail Mary while meditating on the sorrow and eating the sour thing. The challenge is to think about how Mary would have felt during that experience, and be eating the sour thing, and *not* make a sour face. Because, as we know, *she* did not make faces: "Mary kept all these things, pondering them in her heart" (Lk 2:19). It manages to be somber and slightly hilarious at the same time.

The feast of Our Lady of Sorrows is a good day to remember that Jesus, just as in the country song, never promised us a rose garden. His mother was spared original sin, but not suffering. The greatest saints have had great sorrows. Our devotion to God and our faithfulness to the Catholic Church doesn't promise us material wealth or physical health. It promises us true joy and meaning in our lives on this earth, despite our hardships (and even because of them), and eternal happiness with God in heaven when this life is over.

There is a tradition that basil grew up around the foot of the cross, where Jesus' blood and Mary's tears hit the ground. St. Helena is said to have found the True Cross hidden beneath an overgrowth of basil. So, for dinner on the feast of the Holy Cross, I like a basil-heavy meal such as caprese salad, pesto pasta with shrimp, and strawberry-basil lemonade to drink. On Our Lady of Sorrows, I like to recall the bitter sweetness of Our Lady's life with a sweet-and-sour dish. We drink 7 Up in memory of her seven sorrows.

FEAST OF ST. MATTHEW: SEPTEMBER 21

St. Matthew was one of the twelve apostles and also one of the four evangelists, credited with writing the first of the four Gospels. His symbol as an evangelist is an angel, and he is often depicted in art as copying down the Gospel as an angel dictates the words to him.

He is called Matthew in the Gospel of Matthew but is understood to be the same person as Levi in the Gospels of Mark and Luke. Though he was a Jew, he was considered a traitor to his people because he worked as a tax collector for the Roman government. The Romans were an occupying force, resented by the people of Israel, and tax collectors were reviled for collaborating with them and for the common practice of overcharging their neighbors in order to line their own pockets.

Matthew's answer to Jesus' call is impressive, to say the least: "As Jesus passed on from there, he saw a man called Matthew sitting at the tax office; and he said to him, 'Follow me.' And he rose and followed him" (Mt 9:9). Two words, and Matthew gets up, leaving a pile of silver coins on the table, and follows Jesus. He was there with the other apostles throughout Jesus' public ministry. After Pentecost, tradition holds that he preached the gospel in Egypt and Ethiopia until he was martyred in his nineties.

To celebrate the feast, we like to remember Matthew's counting table and have silver dollar pancakes for dinner. My son Bobby is our official family chief officer in charge of pancake making. With some scrambled eggs and bacon, it's a totally real dinner.

FEAST OF THE ARCHANGELS (MICHAELMAS): SEPTEMBER 29

Michaelmas was the first Ordinary Time feast we started celebrating as a family. I was familiar with it, as a name, because Michaelmas (pronounced mickle-mus) is always coming up in classic British literature and BBC miniseries. It's one of the four "quarter days", on which rent comes due for old-timey British heroines. There is usually goose. I was intrigued.

It turns out that it's the day on which we celebrate the victory of the archangel Michael over Satan in the war of heaven. It's the day on which Satan was cast into hell, by way of some blackberry bushes (more on that in a sec), and the day on which, in the fifth century, a basilica near Rome was dedicated in honor of St. Michael. In a house with many little boys, I knew we could have fun with this one.

Since the 1969 revision of the liturgical calendar, we honor the archangels Gabriel and Raphael on this day as well. Previously, each had his own feast day. But since being the leader of God's armies is, in general, more compelling to kids than announcing or healing, we go ahead and focus our celebration on St. Michael.

The Fall of the Angels

We don't know for sure why Lucifer (a.k.a. Satan or the devil) led one-third of the angels in a rebellion against God. It seems impossible that angels, endowed with supernatural gifts and knowing God in an intimate, face-to-face way, would choose to rebel against him, yet some of them did. The same thing could be said of Adam and Eve: they knew God and saw God and spoke to God. They had supernatural gifts. And yet they rebelled against him too. Both angels and men have free will and can choose evil.

Tradition holds that when God revealed to the angels his plan to create mankind and to become a man, as Jesus, Lucifer and his followers refused to accept it. In their pride they would not serve a flesh-and-blood being they considered inferior to themselves.

Unlike Adam and Eve, who were tempted by the deceit of the devil, the fallen angels said *non serviam* (Latin for "I will not serve") with full understanding of their choice and its consequences. They are therefore incapable of remorse. Since an angel cannot change his mind or repent, the rebellion of Satan and his followers, once decided upon, was forever.

The war in heaven is described in Revelation, the last book of the Bible, in symbolic and allegorical language: "Now war arose in heaven, Michael and his angels fighting against the dragon; and the dragon and his angels fought, but they were defeated and there was no longer any place for them in heaven. And the great dragon was thrown down, that ancient serpent, who is called the Devil and Satan, the deceiver of the whole world—he was thrown down to the earth, and his angels were thrown down with him" (Rev 12:7–9).

The Taste of Victory

It makes for a great party. It's a good feast day for including Protestant friends and relations, since the story is biblical, and kicking the devil's keister is something upon which we can all agree.

The kids' favorite part each year is the devil piñata. Now, devil piñatas are not widely available for purchase. But I have seen them in stores occasionally. There are plenty of dragon piñatas, and one of those would work just fine, especially considering the words of Revelation. But there's something really satisfying about beating a devil-looking devil with wooden swords for the feast of St. Michael. So, we made our own reusable devil piñata out of cardboard boxes, tape, and red spray paint.

Each year, we repair any damage from his last beating and make a new pouch of candy in a plastic bag with newspaper or packing paper folded around it. This gets taped to his belly and painted red and he's good to go for another year. He's about four feet long and hangs from a tall tree in the yard, suspended over the party until it's time for the beatings to commence. It really makes a statement.

Now, you're supposed to eat goose for Michaelmas. I keep hoping that someday my family will let me cook a goose. But so far they have been steadfastly against it. The first year we threw the party I special ordered one from our grocery butcher. I guess they thought I was joking because it never came in, and I had to make chicken, to great rejoicing in the Tierney house.

My compromise has been to make cornish game hens. They're a bit more exotic than chicken somehow. And it feels old-fashioned to have a whole bird (or half of one anyway) sitting on your plate. But they are easy to find at the grocery store and don't need to be special ordered. Since I don't want to be stuck in the kitchen the whole time our guests are here, I usually just roast potatoes and onions underneath the hens, and make a green salad with goat cheese (for the devil's goat feet) and blackberries (explanation coming) and asparagus spears! That's the whole feast.

But the fun part is the appetizers and desserts and drinks. Usually I ask our guests to bring something to share, and we always get great stuff, such as deviled eggs, angel food cake, devil's food cake, and so forth. I also like to put out a bowl of Flamin' Hot Cheetos and watch the kids dare each other to eat them. Hilarious.

I recently discovered a couple of nineteenth-century appetizers that I couldn't resist making for our Michaelmas feast. "Angels on horseback" are scallops wrapped in bacon and skewered, then fried, baked, or broiled. "Devils on horseback" are prunes given the same treatment. They are quite good! And not difficult to prepare, especially if you use prepared scallops, though all that bacon-wrapping is time-consuming. It makes a good kitchen job for kids.

The husband is in charge of the adult drinks. With dinner we have wine, but as the guests are arriving we like to go old school and offer folks a cocktail. The husband made up this recipe in five minutes one Michaelmas and calls it the Battle of Heaven:

> Muddle two lime wedges and three or four small or medium mint leaves in an eight-ounce jelly jar (or other extremely classy cocktail glassware).
> Fill the glass two-thirds full with ice cubes.
> Add one shot (one and a half ounces) of blackberry brandy (we have used Hiram Walker's).
> Fill the remainder of the glass with chilled club soda.
> Stir, garnish with one or two fresh blackberries, and serve.
> Enjoy and repeat.

For the kids, I make a blackberry fizzy punch with blackberry juice, Sprite, berry sorbet, mint sprigs, and fresh blackberries for garnish.

Why all the blackberries? you ask. Well, according to legend, blackberries should not be picked after this date. This is because, as Satan was thrown down from heaven, he fell into a blackberry bush and spat on the blackberries. Nobody wants to eat devil spit ... or *do* they? Maybe that's what I should call the kids' drink from now on! Yep. I just decided. I'm doing that.

We all recite the St. Michael Prayer before dinner. We also read aloud one of my all-time favorite picture books, *The Bearskinner: A Tale of the Brothers Grimm.*[21] It's not about St. Michael, but it is about the power of prayer and beating the devil at his own game. (It's also about making deals with the devil, so we are sure to point out that that's not a good idea.) Finally, we let the kids whack the devil until he is vanquished, and we take our reward, and a good time is had by all.

---

[21] Laura Amy Schlitz, *The Bearskinner: A Tale of the Brothers Grimm* (Somerville, Mass.: Candlewick Press, 2007).

One more thing: a couple of years back, a friend pointed out that in all paintings of St. Michael, he is wearing crazy leggings. So now we like to wear crazy leggings for Michaelmas.

FEAST OF ST. THÉRÈSE OF LISIEUX OF THE CHILD JESUS: OCTOBER 1

If you haven't read the autobiography of St. Thérèse of Lisieux, *The Story of a Soul*, you *really* should. The simplicity of her approach to faith and the relatability of her everyday struggles make it easy to see why she has become one of the most beloved saints in the history of the Church.

St. Thérèse was born in France in 1873, into a very devout upper-middle-class Catholic family. Her parents, Louis and Zélie Martin, are both canonized saints (feast day: July 12). Louis owned a watch-making shop, and Zélie was a lace maker. Together they had nine children. Five daughters survived childhood, and *all* became nuns. St. Thérèse was the youngest. Her mother died of breast cancer when Thérèse was just four years old.

In her autobiography, written at the request of her prioress, who was her older sister, St. Thérèse describes herself as a difficult and willful child, prone to tantrums. She slowly learned to direct her strong will and abundant energy toward God, and she spent her life fighting against her tendency toward selfishness and trying to honor God each day with small sacrifices and small acts of will. She chose to eat foods she didn't enjoy. She sought out the company of the nuns whose personalities she liked the least. She used her perceived faults, her weakness and pettiness and littleness, to give herself more fully to God. In a year full of saints whose stories are often fantastical, St. Thérèse's is accessible in a way that is inspiring and challenging at the same time.

Thérèse died of tuberculosis at the age of twenty-four, having lived a life of quiet obscurity. However, after the publication of her autobiography, along with photographs of her taken by her sister and fellow Carmelite Céline, her "little way" became so popular that Pope Benedict XV dispensed with the usual fifty-year delay required between death and beatification. Thérèse was canonized in 1925, only twenty-eight years after her death. Because of the way her philosophy of littleness helps to explain the message of the gospel, Pope St. John Paul II declared her a Doctor of the Church in 1997.

St. Thérèse's nickname is "the Little Flower", and in art, she is depicted holding a crucifix and roses. On her deathbed she said, "After my death, I will let fall a shower of roses. I will spend my heaven doing good upon earth. I will raise up a mighty host of little saints. My mission is to make God loved."[22]

The Little Way

To celebrate her feast day, we like to focus on making small sacrifices, as she did. As a child she kept in her pocket a string of ten beads and used them to keep track of the ten sacrifices she hoped to make each day. St. Thérèse sacrifice beads are easy to make—even little kids can string them themselves—and they're very motivational to kids (and grown-ups like me) who like to have a little something to show for their selfless sacrificing. Instructions for making them at home are available online.

If you've got a bit of time on your hands, there are some really beautiful recipes for foods that looks like roses. My absolute favorite thing to make for the day is a vegetable rose tart: I roll up long, thin slices of cooked purple, yellow, and orange carrots and green zucchini to look like roses and set them atop a ricotta tart. It's *beautiful* but maybe best appreciated by grown-ups. Our children *do* like French onion soup, though, and puff-pastry apple roses. An easy, no-cook rose treat can be made by making small slices into a strawberry, bending the slices outward a bit, and dipping the strawberry in sugar. It makes a very convincing and tasty rose.

FEAST OF THE GUARDIAN ANGELS: OCTOBER 2

Once, while sitting in a doctor's waiting room with Lulu when she was three, we were looking at a poster of an illustrated underwater

---

[22] *Story of a Soul: The Autobiography of St. Thérèse of Lisieux*, ed. Rev. T. N. Taylor, 8th ed. (London: Burns, Oates and Washbourne, 1922), Project Gutenberg, https://www.gutenberg .org/files/16772/16772-8.txt.

scene, and I asked her which creatures she thought were real and which were pretend. She was pretty confident that crabs and jellyfish were pretend, but she knew *for sure* that mermaids were real.

This is why it's important to talk to kids about their guardian angels.

I'm a big fan of fantasy tales and fairy stories, and imagination in general. My kids will tell you I'm not one to rule out the possibility of even the most unlikely creatures. I've never seen a unicorn in real life, but I've never seen a narwhal either.

I do, however, make a point in all the fun to make sure my kids know that angels are 100 percent real and not to be confused with banshees and elves and Loch Ness monsters, for whom there is very little scientific evidence and about whom no mention is made in the Bible.

As Catholics, we believe in angels: "With the clear and sober language of catechesis, the Church teaches that the existence of the spiritual, non-corporeal beings that Sacred Scripture usually calls 'angels' is a truth of faith. The witness of Scripture is as clear as the unanimity of Tradition."[23]

The archangels Gabriel, Raphael, and Michael appear by name in the Bible. There are many angels in the New Testament. For instance, at the birth of Jesus, an angel of the Lord appears to shepherds followed by "a multitude of the heavenly host" (Lk 2:13). Jesus speaks specifically about our guardian angels: "See that you do not despise one of these little ones; for I tell you that in heaven their angels always behold the face of my Father who is in heaven" (Mt 18:10).

A Powerful Friend

It's important that my kids understand that each has such a powerful intercessor, all to himself, looking after him on earth and advocating

---

[23] Congregation for Divine Worship and the Discipline of the Sacraments, *Directory on Popular Piety and the Liturgy: Principles and Guidelines* (December 2001), no. 213, http://www.vatican.va/roman_curia/congregations/ccdds/documents/rc_con_ccdds_doc_20020513_vers-direttorio_en.html.

for him to the Father. We make a point of remembering and honoring our guardian angels each day. Our homeschool days begin with morning prayers. Each day we say a Morning Offering and a Guardian Angel Prayer. This is the traditional one, recommend in the *Manual of Indulgences*:[24]

> Angel of God, my guardian dear, to whom God's love commits me here, ever this day be at my side, to light and guard, to rule and guide. Amen.

After the prayer I announce, "Say good morning to your guardian angel." And everyone replies, "Good morning, guardian angel!" Then, "Say good morning to someone else's guardian angel." And everyone runs around hugging each other and saying, "Good morning, Gus' angel!", "Good morning, Anita's angel!", and so forth. It's pretty cute. At the parochial school my mother-in-law attended, they used to have the kids scooch over a bit on their chairs to leave room for their angels. So sweet.

But the point is for my kids to know that each has a guardian angel, that he is real, and that he is there with us, even though we can't see him. St. Josemaría Escrivá used to ask his guardian angel to wake him up in the morning and to talk to another person's guardian angel before he had an important meeting with that person. St. Padre Pio was known to chat with his guardian angel and to receive prayer requests from the guardian angels of other people. Pope Francis said in a homily for this feast day that we should all be like children and should listen to the nudges of our guardian angels, who are the voices of our consciences.

I have heard, occasionally, of people naming their guardian angels or believing that their guardian angel has revealed his name to them. Certainly, for faithful Catholics, this is done in all innocence. However, because of some occult practices that attempt to harness the power of the angels by naming them, and because the angels are above us, and so we do not have the authority to name them,

---

[24] United States Conference of Catholic Bishops, *Manual of Indulgences: Norms and Grants* (Washington, D.C.: United States Conference of Catholic Bishops, 2006), no. 18. See appendix B for more information on indulgences.

this practice is officially frowned upon by the Catholic Church: "The practice of assigning names to the Holy Angels should be discouraged, except in the cases of Gabriel, Raphael and Michael whose names are contained in Holy Scripture."[25] Similarly, we should be careful not to fall into the flawed thinking that all aspects of everyday life, good and bad, are a product of the work of angels and devils in our lives. We have free will, and so does everyone around us.

Another commonly held error in regard to angels is that people, when they die, become angels. One of my all-time favorite movies, *It's a Wonderful Life*, promotes this mistaken belief. Christian teaching, however, is absolutely clear on the fact that angels and men are different types of creature. Angels are spirit only. Men are spirit and body. When men die, hopefully, they become saints. Men don't die and become angels any more than bees die and become giraffes.

On their special feast day, we make sure to say thank you to our guardian angels. For dinner, we have angel hair pasta, and for dessert, we have an angel food cake. We sing "For He's a Jolly Good Fellow" to all the guardian angels celebrating invisibly above us over the dining room table.

FEAST OF ST. FRANCIS OF ASSISI: OCTOBER 4

St. Francis of Assisi is one of the most well-known saints in history, to people and birds alike. He was born in Assisi, Italy, in 1182, to wealthy Catholic parents. His father was a silk merchant, and Francis lived a life of leisure and comfort. As a young man he was a soldier and fought in a battle between Assisi and the city of Perugia. When he returned home he had trouble readjusting to his life of luxury and began to spend more time in prayer and service to the poor. While praying at an old country chapel in San Damiano, he heard the icon of Christ Crucified speak to him, saying, "Francis, Francis, go and repair my house which, as you can see, is falling into ruins."[26]

---

[25] Congregation for Divine Worship and the Discipline of the Sacraments, *Directory on Popular Piety and the Liturgy*, no. 217, http://www.vatican.va/roman_curia/congregations/ccdds/documents/rc_con_ccdds_doc_20020513_vers-direttorio_en.html.

[26] Voragine, *The Golden Legend*, no. 149.

Francis figured Jesus meant that he should fix up the chapel, so he took some cloth from his father's shop, sold it, and used the money to begin repairs. His father was not pleased when he found out. And, in all fairness, Francis *had* stolen from him. So, Francis decided once and for all to renounce the wealth of his family. He returned the money he had taken from his father, along with everything his parents had given to him, including the clothes right off his back, and he strode off through the town square in his birthday suit.

He spent the next few years rebuilding ruined churches in the area (including the Portiuncula Chapel) with the help of donations. He felt more and more called to embrace a life of complete poverty. Eventually he gained some followers and received permission from the pope to begin his order of brothers. This was followed by an order of sisters, under the supervision of his friend St. Clare of Assisi. Francis never became a priest, but his love of poverty and his joyful preaching converted people everywhere he went.

During the Crusades he walked from Italy to Egypt with his follower Br. Elias, hoping to convert the sultan. Some stories say that the sultan secretly converted after speaking with Francis. We know for sure that when the rest of the Christians were driven from the Holy Land, Br. Elias and the Franciscans were allowed to stay.

St. Francis had a great love for all of God's creatures and was known to practice his preaching by giving talks to the birds. It's said that he was so compelling that the birds would fly down from the trees and perch on his shoulders to be able to hear him better. "Canticle of the Sun", composed by St. Francis to praise God though his creatures, is an excellent prayer for the day.

Back in Italy, hoping to inspire people with the beauty and the humility of the first Christmas, St. Francis created the first Nativity scene, complete with living animals!

Another story says that there was a wolf terrorizing the town of Gubbio. Francis agreed to speak to the wolf and brokered a peace between it and the town. In exchange for being given food, the wolf agreed to leave the town's flocks and children alone.

At the age of forty-two, while in prayer at a mountaintop retreat with his brothers, St. Francis had a vision of an angel and received the stigmata (the five wounds of Christ Crucified) in his hands, feet, and side. Since then, a few other saints have also received this rare gift, but St. Francis was the first. He had the wounds for the rest of his life. He died two years later and was canonized by popular demand two years after that.

Blessing the Animals

Many parishes offer a blessing of pets in honor of this feast day. Our former parish did, and it was always a fun occasion for the kids. Everyone else would be out there after Mass with their dogs and cats and rabbits, and there were my kids ... holding chickens. If your parish doesn't offer the blessing, you can do it yourself at home.

It's a great day for making bird feeders, visiting the zoo, or taking a nature walk. Any animal-theme snack would be very appropriate: ants on a log, animal crackers, and so forth. For dinner, I like to make gnocchi, Italian dumplings. They can be made from scratch or found at the grocery store. For dessert, bird's nest cookies or bear claw cookies are fun. I like to call the latter Gubbio wolf paws.

FEAST OF OUR LADY OF THE ROSARY: OCTOBER 7

October is dedicated to the Rosary. If you're already saying a family Rosary, awesome! Keep it up. If you're not, or if you were before but you're not now, this is the month to do it.

It's impossible to overstate the beauty and the power of a daily family Rosary. Pope St. John Paul II tells us, "The Holy Rosary, by age-old tradition, has shown itself particularly effective as a prayer which brings the family together.... The family that recites the Rosary together reproduces something of the atmosphere of the household of Nazareth: its members place Jesus at the centre, they share his joys and sorrows, they place their needs and their plans in his hands, they draw from him the hope and the strength to go on."[27]

In the car is a great place to start a family Rosary, since everyone is all strapped in anyway. It's a regular habit for us now. Any car

---

[27]John Paul II, apostolic letter *Rosarium Virginis Mariae* (October 16, 2002), no. 41, https://w2.vatican.va/content/john-paul-ii/en/apost_letters/2002/documents/hf_jp-ii _apl_20021016_rosarium-virginis-mariae.html.

ride longer than fifteen minutes means a Rosary. Sometimes we'll stay after daily Mass, to say our Rosary with the old ladies there. On busy days we'll put a Rosary podcast on over a speaker while we tidy up the house or do the dishes. But my favorite is when we're all able to sit down in the living room together, rosaries in hands, and give twenty minutes to Our Lady and to each other, to say a family Rosary.

We have a few rules, just to keep things from getting away from us.

1. School-aged kids must stay seated, pay attention, and participate. Younger children must stay in the general area and may be only somewhat disruptive.
2. Kids may sit anywhere they like but must not change seats once the prayers begin.
3. Rosaries are for hands only, not feet, not knees, not whipping upside the head of a sibling.
4. Everyone must speak up. Praying in community means we must be able to hear each other.

Children don't have to love it, nor do grown-ups, but if our family is saying the Rosary, we all have to do it and be respectful. It's easy to think that our innocent children should naturally want to pray, go to Mass, and so forth, and that if they don't, it is somehow wrong to require it of them. But in my experience, kids rarely want what's good for them. It's my job as a parent not only to set a good example, but to use our family rules and family culture to create good habits in our kids. Complaining about or misbehaving during prayers earns the same types of consequences as complaining or misbehaving at other times. It's really not a piety thing; it's just a parenting thing.

Edible Rosary

To celebrate the feast day, we like to make an edible rosary! This can be accomplished with just about anything: mini muffins or cereal pieces at breakfast time, nuts or Goldfish crackers or dried fruit at snack time, cupcakes or candies for dessert. You just need fifty-three of one thing for the Ave (Hail Mary) beads and six of another thing for the Pater (Our Father) beads, plus about six of something to make the cross.

With our homeschool group, we like to make rosaries out of marshmallow breakfast cereal. In our family, we always make a chocolate chip rosary. I (or the big kids) can put these together pretty easily, one for each person. We use chocolate chips for the Aves and the cross, and M&M's for the Paters. Then we sit around the table and say the Rosary. We let the kids eat each "bead" as we go along (this is why we don't make the rosary out of chewy or hard candy; the chocolate chips can be eaten quickly) or they can move them to the side and save them for later. Everyone really looks forward to it each year!

FEAST OF ST. LUKE: OCTOBER 18

St. Luke the evangelist is believed to have been from a Greek, non-Jewish family. He was an early convert to Christianity after the death of Jesus, a disciple of St. Paul, and the author of the Gospel of St. Luke and the Acts of the Apostles. He is the only Gentile author of the Bible. His symbol as an evangelist is a winged ox. He was a physician and an artist, and tradition says he was the first painter of icons, and, specifically, that he was the painter of the very first icon, one of Our Lady.

In England, what we in America call Indian Summer is known as St. Luke's Little Summer. It just sounds so cute. If your weather happens to cooperate, it's a great time to get outdoors for a beach day or a picnic before the chill settles in. In my neck of the woods, that won't happen until January—but still, any excuse to hit the beach. If the weather doesn't cooperate, a day at an art museum would be very appropriate.

It's also a good day to read the Gospel of St. Luke or to pray one of the three beautiful canticles he preserved for us: the Magnificat (said by Our Lady at the Visitation), the Benedictus (said by Zechariah at the Nativity of John the Baptist), and the Nunc Dimittis (said by Simeon at the Presentation). St. Luke is the patron saint of physicians and surgeons, so hug or pray for a doctor today!

Because of the ox thing, St. Luke is also the patron saint of butchers, so you can't go wrong with grilling burgers or steaks, or getting bold and serving oxtail soup. In England, Banbury cakes and tarts were traditionally eaten for the feast of St. Luke. These are pastries with a fig and orange filling, and recipes are available online. Or just grab a package of Fig Newtons—because that's what Fig Newtons are too—and *call* them Banbury tarts.

FEAST OF POPE ST. JOHN PAUL II THE GREAT: OCTOBER 22

Pope St. John Paul II, affectionately known as JPII, was born in Poland in 1920. His name was Karol Józef (Charles Joseph) Wojtyła, and he enjoyed school, sports, the outdoors, and the theater. He had great sorrows as a child, losing his older sister, his mother, his older brother, and his father all before he turned twenty. It was a difficult time for the country as well. In 1939 Nazi German and Stalinist Russian forces invaded and occupied Poland, and Karol was forced to leave his studies at the university and work as a laborer in a limestone quarry.

He began to consider the priesthood and was accepted into the secret underground seminary, run by the archbishop of Kraków. He was active in helping the city's suffering population, especially the Jews, during the occupation, which ended in 1945. The next year, Karol was ordained a priest, and at thirty-eight he became the youngest bishop in Poland. He participated in the Second Vatican Council. In 1967 he was promoted to cardinal.

In 1978, Pope Paul VI died, and Cardinal Wojtyła voted in the papal conclave, which elected Pope John Paul I. Apparently God had other plans, and John Paul I died after only thirty-three days as pope. In the next conclave, Cardinal Wojtyła was elected, and he took the name John Paul II to honor his predecessor. In contrast to JPI, JPII served for twenty-six years and became the third-longest-serving pope in history, after St. Peter and Bl. Pius IX. (There are *ten* popes who served *shorter* terms than John Paul I!)

The focus of John Paul II's pontificate was the universal call to holiness, and a (related) surge in beatifications and canonizations, as he sought to provide role models for Catholics in all walks of life. His papacy was marked by his unprecedented accessibility at public events at the Vatican and all over the world, where he spoke to millions. He had friendly relationships with world leaders, reached out to non-Catholic religious leaders, and had a gift for connecting with young Catholics. He is remembered for his affirmation and clarification of traditional teaching on Catholic social issues, especially human sexuality, abortion, and birth control, and his firm stance against communism.

As a priest, and even as pope, he never lost his love for sports and the outdoors, continuing to run, swim, lift weights, hike, and ski. He survived two assassination attempts. In 2001 he was diagnosed with Parkinson's disease. Four years later, he died of complications from the disease at the age of eighty-four and was buried beneath St. Peter's Basilica in "bare earth", per his request, rather than in a tomb. His successor and friend, Pope Benedict XVI, waived the usual five-year waiting period and opened his cause for canonization a month after his death. John Paul II was beatified in 2011 and canonized in 2014. His feast is celebrated on the day of his installation as pope rather than of his death because April 2 would often fall during Holy Week. Pope Francis added his feast to the universal calendar.

In recognition of his love for the outdoors, our family tradition for the day is always a walk of some sort. Sometimes it's a real hike in the mountains, sometimes it's a stroll down the hill to the ice cream shop on the corner, but there is always walking, saying the Rosary, and striving for holiness.

When I was expecting our first baby in 2002, I remarked to the husband that it would be nice if the pope died so that we could name the baby after him. The husband looked at me askance and pointed out that we could name the baby after the pope even if he wasn't dead. So we did. That means Jack gets to pick what we have for dinner, but I can usually talk him into Polish sausage and pierogies and sauerkraut.

Because John Paul II is such a new saint, we can see recordings of him and hear his voice, which always gives me chills. We love to watch videos of him online. He wrote many, many beautiful prayers and letters, any of which would be great for the day. A favorite of mine is the moving "Act of Entrustment to Mary", part of which reads,

> Today we wish to entrust to you the future that awaits us,
> and we ask you to be with us on our way.
> We are the men and women of an extraordinary time,

exhilarating yet full of contradictions.
Humanity now has instruments of unprecedented power:
we can turn this world into a garden,
or reduce it to a pile of rubble.
We have devised the astounding capacity
to intervene in the very well-springs of life:
man can use this power for good, within the bounds of
    the moral law,
or he can succumb to the short-sighted pride
of a science which accepts no limits,
but tramples on the respect due to every human being.
Today as never before in the past,
humanity stands at a crossroads.
And once again, O Virgin Most Holy,
salvation lies fully and uniquely in Jesus, your Son.[28]

We also know what this saint's favorite dessert was! It's a Polish pastry similar to a French napoléon now known as *kremówka papieska*, or "papal cream cake", and it's not too tough to put together. It's a layer of pastry cream between two layers of puff pastry, with powdered sugar on top. You can use frozen puff-pastry sheets from the grocery store, and, if you don't mind a messier result, you can substitute vanilla pudding mix for the pastry cream.

ALL HALLOWS' EVE: OCTOBER 31

I have occasionally heard from Catholics who wonder if Catholics should participate in Halloween festivities, to which I usually reply: Well, no festivities of any kind are mandatory, so participation is up to you. But Catholics invented Halloween, so if it's appropriate for *anyone*, it's appropriate for us.

In fact, virtually all historical attacks on the celebration of Halloween have come about specifically because it was *too* Catholic. Halloween is All Hallows' Eve, the vigil of All Saints' Day, which was instituted as a feast by Pope Gregory III in the eighth century. Going door to door, collecting treats, and carving veggies into lanterns

---

[28] John Paul II, "Act of Entrustment to Mary" (October 8, 2000), no. 3, https://w2.vatican .va/content/john-paul-ii/en/speeches/2000/oct-dec/documents/hf_jp-ii_spe_20001008 _act-entrustment-mary.html.

were all ancient Celtic traditions associated with the harvest, but the spookier side of Halloween was never occult or even pagan; it was all Catholic.

All Saints' and All Souls' Days commemorate the dead, in heaven and in purgatory respectively. When Catholics celebrating the feasts of All Saints and All Souls talked about ghosts, they didn't mean monsters; they meant the souls of persons who had died and gone to heaven, purgatory, or hell. The word "ghost" is of Germanic origin and comes from the Old English *gast*, meaning "soul", "life", "breath", "good or bad spirit", "angel", or "demon". Christian texts in Old English use *gast* to translate the Latin *spiritus*, which is why we used to refer to the third Person of the Holy Trinity as "the Holy Ghost", until the general usage of the word had shifted enough to make that confusing to people, and now we say "Holy Spirit" instead.

For medieval Catholics, skulls and skeletons were popular year-round motifs; they were called *memento mori* and were meant to remind us of our mortality and to inspire us to live our lives well. Some of the ideas at the heart of the best-known monster stories are rooted in Catholic beliefs. Vampires drink human blood to live forever. We drink the Precious Blood to have eternal life. Zombies' human bodies rise from the dead. We hope to rise again too, at the Second Coming. It's right there in the Apostles' Creed.

When Halloween celebrations were banned in Puritan New England, it wasn't because of concerns about witches; it was because of concerns about Catholics and their insistence on praying for the souls—or ghosts—of the dead. (The Puritans also canceled Christmas.) Anti-Halloween sentiments in America continued into the late nineteenth century, at which point the fun, secular, candy-and-costumes aspects of Halloween were able to outdo the anti-Catholic, anti-Irish beliefs that had shut out Halloween for so long.

Halloween Misinformation

Today's familiar attacks on Halloween, the ones that call it a vestige of the pagan festival Samhain or the devil's night or Satan's birthday are a direct result of a campaign by a fundamentalist Protestant and vehement anti-Catholic named Jack Chick. He distributed nearly a billion fundamentalist tracts beginning in 1960, and hundreds of thousands of specifically anti-Catholic and anti-Halloween tracts beginning in 1980.

The claims that Halloween is for witches and Satanists started with him. The idea that evil neighbors might be poisoning candy started with him. He believed that Catholicism is (and always has been) a hidden form of pagan worship. He claimed that the Christ of Catholicism is the reincarnation of the Babylonian deity Nimrod and that it wasn't until the Protestants split from Catholicism in the sixteenth century that anyone actually started worshipping the true Christ. It would be funny if it weren't so sad.

Without even knowing where these ideas came from, some mainstream Protestants, and even some Catholics, have come to believe that they are true. As a result, they have distanced themselves and their children from traditional Halloween observances, such as trick-or-treating and carving jack-o'-lanterns.

I'm not here to advocate for all the ways Halloween is currently celebrated by the masses in the United States. Horror movies have changed the way we see Halloween (and our neighbors). There are skimpy costumes. There are decorations that are gory and tasteless, if not downright demonic. The very small number of people who do practice witchcraft and Satanism and paganism have claimed the day as their own.

But, frankly, I'm not willing to let them have it. Even in its twentieth-century incarnation as a day for costumes and candy, it was innocent fun with Catholic roots. That's how my family, and how our neighbors and friends celebrate it today. Ecumenical harvest festivals and Catholic All Saints' Day parties *in lieu* of Halloween parties, in my mind, solve a problem that isn't there. They are caving in to the anti-Catholic terrorist tactics of one crazy dude with a printing empire.

Have an All Saints' Day party, *for sure*. We do every year. Have a harvest festival if you wish—although if anything *does* have pagan ancestry, it's a harvest festival, right? But I don't think those things need to be done instead of Halloween—not for Catholics, anyway.

Happy Halloween

For Halloween, we put up a few spooky decorations, we carve pumpkins, the children dress up, and we go out into the neighborhood and trick-or-treat. We hand out candy (and *never* toothbrushes or fundamentalist tracts) at our house. We don't make a huge deal out of it in our home, but we're certainly not going to be bullied into skipping it.

We aren't afraid to be Catholic on Halloween, either. In the next section, I'll share lots of All Saints' Day costume ideas that we've used over the years. Sometimes those costumes can be easily adapted into a secular Halloween costume. Sometimes the kids wear them for just All Saints' Day and find some dress-up clothes to wear on Halloween. But other times our kids go trick-or-treating dressed as a saint. One year, when my three oldest were little, they went trick-or-treating as St. George, the Silene princess, and the dragon (in a wagon). Jack was not shy about correcting neighbors who suggested that he was "just" a knight. It was a very Catholic Halloween.

All Hallows' Eve, as the vigil of the important solemnity of All Saints, was historically a day of required fasting and abstinence. Since 1962, fasting and abstinence are recommended but no longer required. Our family tradition for those under eighteen is to fast from TV, computer, and phone screens (but not treats) and to abstain from meat for the day. Fortunately, Halloween candy is 100 percent meat-free. I usually make "spooky" baked macaroni and cheese. The spookiness comes from cutting a ghost shape out of cheese slices and laying it on top of the macaroni and cheese as soon as it comes out of the oven. Very scary—and meat-free.

SOLEMNITY OF ALL SAINTS (HOLY DAY OF OBLIGATION): NOVEMBER 1

All Saints' Day is a solemnity and a holy day of obligation. We need to attend Mass and to refrain from our usual labors as much as we are able. If it falls on a Friday, we're not required to abstain from meat (*or make an alternate sacrifice*).

We might think of "the saints" as just the canonized saints, such as the ones featured in this book—people whom the Catholic Church has officially recognized for their sanctity. My uncatechized twenty-something self once said at a book club meeting, "I don't need to be a *saint*; I'm fine with just barely making it into heaven." Well, I've got news for me: I'd better want to be a saint, because if I'm not, I'm not getting into heaven any which way.

The fact is, *everyone* in heaven is a saint. There are many, many times more saints whom we've never heard of than there are saints who appear on the calendar of feast days. This feast is the day we celebrate those saints: the secret saints, *our* saints, our saintly old neighbors, our grandmas who always prayed the Rosary and sprinkled us with holy water as we ran past, the celebrity who we happen to know made a good confession and had the last rites just before he died, babies and children and our disabled family members who we know died in a state of grace.

We celebrate the known saints too, and we can do that in confidence because the Church has proclaimed that they are in heaven. We can't be as sure about our noncanonized saints, of course. On some level it's still an exercise in hope because we can't presume to know the state of anyone's soul at his death. But hopefully we are all lucky enough to have known someone in real life who lived a life of heroic virtue before his death. There's no reason not to believe that person is in heaven.

Remember that when Catholics say we are "praying" to a saint, what we mean is that we are asking that saint to ask God for something on our behalf. We are not worshipping the saint as a god or instead of God. The word "pray" comes from the Latin *precari*, "to ask earnestly, beg, entreat"—as when Romeo says to Friar Laurence, "I pray thee, chide not."[29] Romeo isn't worshipping Friar Laurence; he's just asking him to quit making fun of him for falling desperately in love with every girl he meets. We can "pray" as in "ask earnestly" and expect that the saints will intercede for us with God, whom they now see face-to-face.

It can be a great comfort for a grieving person to ask for the intercession of his loved one who has died and to see that prayer answered. And even if the deceased family member isn't yet in heaven, or—God forbid—never will be, no prayer is ever wasted.

Pageants and Parades

Hopefully your kids have the opportunity to participate in a saints pageant. There has been no greater tool in our liturgical-year toolbox

[29] William Shakespeare, *Romeo and Juliet*, act 2, scene 3.

for really getting to know and love a saint than the saints pageant. If we didn't have the opportunity to participate in one through our homeschool group, I would definitely throw a party or a pageant myself—it's that good.

I'm sure there are many ways to do it, but in our group kids dress up as any saints they choose and take the stage (a.k.a. the top of the picnic table) one by one. Each child then gives three clues to the audience and then asks, "Who am I?" The audience calls out guesses until they get it right or are officially stumped.

Here is an example.

1. I was a princess and a third order Franciscan, born in the thirteenth century.
2. My husband supported my devotion to the less fortunate, and I often spun wool and baked bread for the poor.
3. After I became a widow, my father-in-law, the king, insisted that I stop sharing royal resources with the poor, so I saved my own food to give to them. One day, as I was leaving with a basket of bread to distribute, he stopped me and threatened to throw me in the dungeon. But when I lifted the cloth to show him the contents of the basket, it was miraculously filled with roses rather than bread.

Who am I?

The answer is St. Elizabeth of Hungary.

Here is an example for a younger child.

1. I was a priest in Mexico.
2. I dressed up as a mechanic to hide from the bad government.
3. I was killed by a firing squad.

Who am I?

The answer is Bl. Miguel Pro.

Another option is to have a saints parade. A grown-up can announce each saint as he comes by, and then everyone can sing "When the Saints Go Marching In".

After the pageant or parade, the older kids in the homeschool group put on a saints carnival for the little kids featuring games such as these:

- St. Peter's Fishing Pole: tie a clip to a string, and tie the string to a stick; the kids fling the fishing line over a sheet, and the kid working the booth attaches a small prize to the clip.
- St. Cecilia Musical Chairs: just like regular musical chairs.
- Pin the Arrow on St. Sebastian: just like pin the tail on the donkey.
- St. Thérèse's Shower of Roses: the kids try to toss roses into a basket or through a basketball hoop.
- St. Anthony's Finders Keepers: the kids stick their hands into a bowl of rice to find a hidden prize.
- Halo Toss: just like a ring toss.
- Saint Trivia Quiz: the kids answer a question about a saint and win a prize.
- Attributes Matching Game: on one side of a table, arrange cards with saints' names on them, and on the other side, arrange cards with pictures of attributes of those saints; the kids try to match the names and the attributes (e.g., St. Lucy and eyeballs, St. Peter and keys, St. Luke and a paintbrush and palette, St. Philomena and an anchor); kids who get one right win a prize.

An easy fun activity for a smaller group is a holy-card exchange. You can make holy cards featuring saints, or you can buy them online or at Catholic gift shops. The kids can store their holy-card collections in a dollar-store photo album.

Costume Ideas

It can feel overwhelming to come up with saints' costumes for your children. But as I said before, I really, *really* think it's worth it. The saints my kids know and love the best are the saints they have learned about and represented for All Saints' Day.

Focusing on a saint's attributes—the things that identify him in art—makes creating a costume simple. For instance, St. Cecilia usually carries a musical instrument. St. Dominic has a dog. St. Clare of Assisi holds a monstrance. St. Jude wears a giant medallion and usually has the flame of the Holy Spirit above his head. So, to create a costume for a saint, just find an image of him (usually a holy card will feature the traditional depiction of the saint), do your best to approximate the saint's religious habit or period dress, add the attribute props, and you're set.

It's fun to dress siblings up as saints who knew each other. Gus and Anita were once SS. Francisco and Jacinta of Fatima, and preschoolers Frankie and Lulu were their sheep. One year, I dressed as St. Juan Diego, and baby Mary Jane in a front carrier was Our Lady of Guadalupe on my tilma.

If you stock your dress-up box with some Jedi robes and some tunics and some capes, those can be the base of many saint costumes. A sheet makes an excellent toga. Big solid-color T-shirts can be adapted for lots of uses. Thrift stores and costume shops are great resources, and if, like me, you enjoy sewing, you can create anything!

Many saints costumes can be created from costumes you already have around the house or can easily find at a costume shop. The costume can represent a job or a hobby the saint had, or a profession that's associated with the saint. It doesn't always have to be a religious habit, even if the saint ended up as a religious. Here are some examples:

- King, queen, or princess saints: St. Edward the Confessor, St. Louis IX, St. Wenceslaus, St. Clotilde, St. Elizabeth of Hungary, St. Elizabeth of Portugal, St. Isabella of France, St. Helena, St. Margaret of Scotland
- Knight, soldier, or centurion saints: St. George, St. Francis, St. Ignatius of Loyola, St. Nuno, St. Joan of Arc, St. Martin of Tours, St. Michael the Archangel, St. Sebastian, St. Longinus, St. Hadrian
- Greek or Roman saints (toga or tunic): SS. Cyril and Methodius, St. Philomena, St. Luke, St. Barbara, St. Agnes, St. Paul, St. Mark (toga optional)
- Scandinavian or Viking saints: St. Olaf, St. Sunniva
- Farmer or shepherd saints: St. Isidore, SS. Jacinta and Francisco of Fatima, St. Patrick, St. Brigid
- Hiking or outdoorsy saints: St. Pope John Paul II, Bl. Pier Giorgio Frassati
- Doctor saints: St. Gianna Molla, St. Luke, SS. Cosmas and Damian, St. Camillus

- Egyptian saints: St. Catherine of Alexandria, St. Cyril of Alexandria, SS. Felix and Regula, St. Apollonia
- Japanese saints: St. Magdalene of Nagasaki, St. Paul Miki, Bl. Joannis Hattori Jingoro (a ninja saint!)
- Native American saint: St. Kateri Tekakwitha
- Hermit or wilderness saints: St. John the Baptist, St. Lazarus the Beggar, St. Anthony of the Desert, St. Kevin of Ireland, St. Syncletica of Alexandria
- Brown-robe or -habit saints: St. Anthony, St. Francis, St. John of the Cross, St. Thérèse of Lisieux, St. Teresa of Avila, Bl. Fra. Angelico, St. Clare
- White-robe or -habit saints: St. Catherine of Siena, St. Bruno
- Black-robe or -habit saints: St. Elizabeth Ann Seton, St. Isaac Jogues, St. Benedict of Nursia, St. Scholastica
- Bishop saints (have hat, will travel): St. Patrick, St. Augustine, St. Nicholas, St. Denis
- Suit-and-tie or Victorian-dress saints: Bl. Miguel Pro (or mechanic coveralls), Bl. Dina Belanger, SS. Louis and Zélie Martin, St. Giuseppe Moscati (or lab coat)
- Pajamas or nightgown saints: St. Maximilian Kolbe (concentration camp uniform), St. Anna Schäffer, St. Gemma Galgani

And, here are our personal favorites, the gruesome martyr costumes:

- St. John the Baptist: a homemade head-on-a-platter costume (from a tutorial online)
- St. Bartholomew: a red skin suit, a couple of yards of flesh-colored fabric, and a cardboard knife
- St. Peter, crucified upside down: a flesh-colored sweat suit— pants worn on top (cut eye-holes), shirt worn on the bottom with a print-out of St. Peter's face hanging from the neck of the shirt—a loincloth, and an upside-down cardboard cross
- St. Lawrence: a tunic with burn marks and a gridiron made of cardboard covered in foil, with cardboard flames, strapped over the shoulders
- St. Elmo (a.k.a. St. Erasmus): a barrel made out of cardboard, and a paper bishop's miter

- St. James the Greater: a skeleton costume and a boat for the bones to row themselves to Spain[30]
- St. Sebastian: a flesh colored T-shirt with abs and pecs drawn on, a loincloth, and some novelty arrows
- St. Lucy: a long white dress with a red sash, blacked eyelids, a palm frond, and a small plate with two foil-wrapped chocolate eyeballs on it
- St. Isaac Jogues and companions: hooded black robes, rope belts, crosses made of sticks and twine, and bloody cardboard tomahawks hot-glued to headbands
- St. Margaret of Antioch: a large cardboard or stuffed dragon, cut through the middle, with suspenders attached so it can be worn around the waist; the wearer's dress should trail out of the dragon's mouth
- St. Denis or St. Valerie (cephalophore—or head-carrying—saints): a homemade guy-carrying-his-head costume (from a tutorial online)

Now some of you, certainly, are thinking, "Wow, those costumes are awesome! My kids would love those and remember them forever. Let's do this." But perhaps others are thinking that they are insensitive or too scary or gory. And I get that. They are, admittedly, intense. But we never make them realistically gory; any blood is paint or construction paper. We're going for memorable, not horrifying.

We don't intend to be irreverent or insensitive, but to be fun and truthful. This is the reality of our faith. The blood of the martyrs is the seed of the Church.[31] Christians are still being martyred today. I wouldn't want to limit the saints that my kids can learn about and admire to those who died nice, tidy, nonshocking deaths. Some kids really love these saints and are inspired by the courageous (and sometimes spectacular) ways they died. St. Isaac Jogues wrote that he

---

[30] Legend says that the bones of St. James arrived in a boat from Jerusalem to northern Spain, where he was buried in what is now the city of Santiago de Compostela.

[31] Tertullian, *Apology*, in the *Ante-Nicene Fathers*, vol. 3., trans. S. Thelwall, ed. Alexander Roberts, James Donaldson, and A. Cleveland Coxe (Buffalo, NY: Christian Literature Publishing Co., 1885), rev. and ed. for New Advent by Kevin Knight, http://www.newadvent.org/fathers/0301.htm. Tertullian is not a saint, nor is he an official Church Father, as some of the things he taught are not in line with Catholic doctrine. He's got some good quotes, though.

was motivated to become a missionary—and, eventually, a martyr himself—by St. Jean de Brébeuf and the other Jesuit martyrs who went before him.

A recent concern when it comes to costumes is cultural appropriation, the adoption or use of the elements of one culture by members of another culture. This is an inevitable part of any multicultural society or institution and can be a way to bring people together. But it can also be divisive.

As Catholics, we share a common Catholic culture, no matter what our ethnicity or nationality may be. As such, it is appropriate to allow our kids to dress as anyone in the communion of saints. Cultural appropriation shouldn't be an issue if we are dressing as a particular individual, as we would be for an All Saints' Day pageant, rather than dressing up as a random member of another nationality or ethnicity. We avoid using makeup to try to look like a saint of a different ethnicity and focus on clothing and attributes instead.

But it's also important that our kids not be limited to saints of their own ethnicity. That would be terrible! Dressing up for All Saints' Day has been a great way for my kids to learn about and honor particular saints and to learn about other countries and other cultures. All Saints' Day costumes are created to honor the saint and educate and inspire the wearer and everyone around him.

COMMEMORATION OF ALL THE FAITHFUL DEPARTED (ALL SOULS): NOVEMBER 2

November is the month of the Holy Souls in Purgatory. If you aren't in the habit of hanging out in cemeteries and praying for the dead with your kids, well, you're really missing out. And so are your kids. *And* so are the dead.

As Christians, we believe that the dead are not gone. Their bodies have died, but their souls live on forever. We believe that Jesus will come at the end of time to judge all the people who have ever lived. This is called the general judgment (see *CCC* 1038–1041). But those who die before Jesus comes again face what is called the particular judgment (see *CCC* 1021–1022), which has three possible outcomes.

If our love for God has been perfected in this life, we will be taken straight to heaven. If we rejected God's love by mortal sin and died without repenting, we will be condemned to the everlasting torments of hell (not recommended). God is merciful, so he wouldn't send souls who love him to hell. But he is also just, and a soul who loves God imperfectly cannot justly enter heaven. So we need a third option: purgatory.

The *Catechism of the Catholic Church* defines purgatory as a "purification, so as to achieve the holiness necessary to enter the joy of heaven", which is experienced by those "who die in God's grace and friendship, but still imperfectly purified" (1030). In other words, this final purification is for those who are being saved by the mercy of God. It is completely different from the punishment of those who refuse God's mercy and choose hell instead (cf. 1031).

Purification is necessary because, as it says in the Bible, nothing unclean will enter the presence of God in heaven (Rev 21:27) and, though we may die with our mortal sins forgiven, there can still be many impurities in us, specifically, venial sins and the temporal punishment due to sins already forgiven. Purgatory is the gift of a loving, generous, merciful God.

It is a dogmatic teaching of the Catholic Church that a type of purification after death, which we call purgatory, exists. What it looks like, where it is, what happens when you're there—none of that is defined. But we know that, certainly, some of our loved ones are there and that they continue to be a real part of the Church.

The Church is divided into three parts:

1. The Church Militant: that's us, "militant" because we are fighting—against our inclination toward sin, against our fallen natures, against temptation, against the devil.
2. The Church Triumphant: that's the saints. Everyone who has died and gone to heaven is a saint. Some saints lived lives of such heroic virtue that the Catholic Church recognizes them by name and holds them up as models for us to emulate.
3. The Church Suffering: that's the Holy Souls in purgatory, whom we are praying for this month.

We refer to those in purgatory as the "poor" souls, because they can no longer pray for themselves, nor can they make sacrifices, do good deeds, or merit anything for themselves. They rely completely on us to make sacrifices, to pray, and to obtain indulgences on their behalf. They depend on us to help ease their suffering and quickly advance them through their purification so that they can join the saints in heaven.

Our prayers for the faithful departed please God, because he knows and loves these souls and wants them to get through the process of purification as soon as possible. It is an act of charity to pray for our deceased family members and friends. It's even more charitable to offer prayers for the poor souls who have no one to pray for them.

Explaining Death to Children

Death, dying, and the dead are all things we mostly try to keep far, far away from our children. I did, anyway. But I don't anymore. It turns out my kids are a lot more accepting of the afterlife than I gave them credit for.

When my oldest daughter, Betty, was three years old, my grandmother (for whom she was named) died. We lived an airplane ride away, and I was too pregnant to fly, so we weren't able to make it to her funeral. But we made a point to tell the kids she had died and to pray for the repose of her soul. A few days later, I was talking to my other grandmother on the phone. I asked Betty if she wanted to say hi. She very excitedly nodded and took the phone from me. "Hi, Nini!" she said. "Did you make it to heaven?"

I have found that, with my kids, presenting death as something to look forward to—on God's time, of course—has meant that they don't have a fear of death or dying. We know that death can be sad, because it means we will miss the people who have died. It can be hard on kids to see grown-ups crying at a wake or a funeral. But we don't keep them from that either. We want them to see that we come together as a community to mourn our loss but also to celebrate the hope that the person's soul is now in heaven, or at least on its way. And so praying for the dead, especially in November, *especially* this week, has become a really beautiful family tradition for us.

Praying for the Dead

One of the Spiritual Works of Mercy is to pray for the living and the dead. It truly is a beautiful act of charity to pray for these souls who cannot pray for themselves and to make sacrifices for them since they cannot make sacrifices for themselves. We've been saying special prayers for the dead every November for the past few years, and my kids love it. They really understand that these are people who need their help. It's something important and meaningful and useful that kids can do just as well as grown-ups—maybe better; at least with more enthusiasm.

On All Souls' Day, we visit a church and pray the Our Father and the Creed. Doing so gets us a plenary indulgence applicable to the souls in purgatory, if the usual conditions for indulgences are met.[32]

On as many days as we can manage it between November 1 and 8, we visit a cemetery and pray for the dead. Any time of the year, you can obtain a partial indulgence for praying for the dead in a cemetery, but this week you can obtain a plenary (or full) indulgence. You can obtain one on each of those days.

Also on All Souls' Day, we usually meet up with a few other families at a cemetery, and the children (devoutly) run around the cemetery, looking at the gravestones, praying for the dead by name, and leaving a flower at the gravestone of each person they pray for. It's beautiful and sweet and moving and fun.

We pray for a specific person by name using the prayer for eternal rest (*requiem aeternam*):

Eternal rest grant to them, O Lord, and let perpetual light shine upon them. May the souls of the faithful departed, through the mercy of God, rest in peace. Amen.

A partial indulgence, applicable only to the souls in purgatory, can be obtained every time we say it. It's a good prayer to recite anytime, but it's especially appropriate during November, and we add it after our Grace before Meals all month.

Another beautiful prayer for the Holy Souls is given to us by St. Gertrude the Great (feast day: November 16):

Eternal Father, I offer You the most precious blood of thy Divine Son, Jesus, in union with the Masses said throughout the world today,

---

[32] *Manual of Indulgences*, no. 29. See appendix B for more on indulgences.

for all the Holy Souls in Purgatory, for sinners everywhere, for sinners in the universal church, for those in my own home and in my family. Amen.

It's a great prayer. I recommend it. It's often associated with a promise that a thousand souls will be released from purgatory every time the prayer is recited. That claim does not appear in any of St. Gertrude's writings, however, and Pope Leo XIII issued a series of proclamations condemning this type of "prayer card promise".[33] So say the prayer, for sure. But if we want to help release souls from purgatory, we must follow the conditions for the All Souls' Day indulgences.

As an at-home activity for the month, we get a large, clear-glass votive candle, and write the names of all of our deceased loved ones on the glass with a permanent marker. It stays on our dinner table all month, and we light the candle when we say our family prayers.

And we make soul cakes! These are rather like round raisin scones. It used to be traditional to hand them out to people on All Souls' Day in exchange for their prayers for one's deceased loved ones. I make a big batch, and we share them with friends, eat them ourselves, and pray for the poor souls together. A perfect dinner for the day is eggs in purgatory, a quick and simple recipe in which eggs are poached in a simmering mixture of tomatoes and garlic, topped with cheese, and served over toast.

FEAST OF ST. MARTIN OF TOURS (MARTINMAS): NOVEMBER 11

Today is Veteran's Day in the United States, Remembrance Day in Canada and Australia, and Armistice Day in Europe. It is the day on which we commemorate the armistice of World War I that was signed in 1918 (on the eleventh day of the eleventh month, at the eleventh hour) that ended "the war to end all wars", which, unfortunately, it wasn't. Today, our nations gratefully remember everyone who has served in the military.

Coincidentally, or perhaps providentially, it is also the feast day of St. Martin of Tours, soldier and bishop. Martin was born in the

[33] Congregation for the Doctrine of the Faith, *Acta Sanctae Sedis* (Acts of the Holy See), vol. 31 (1898–1899), http://www.olrl.org/pray/apocryphal.shtml.

fourth century in Hungary and became a member of the Roman cavalry, like his father before him. As a young man, he converted to Christianity over the objections of his pagan parents. Christianity was legal at that time in the Roman Empire but was still frowned upon in Roman society, especially in the higher levels of the military.

Martin's faith, however, permeated every part of his life, including his military service. The most famous story about him says that one day, as he was approaching the gates of the city of Amiens on his horse, he met a scantily clad beggar. The beggar asked for alms in the name of Christ, but Martin had nothing with him but the clothes on his back. He took out his sword, cut his military cloak in two, and gave half to the beggar. That night, St. Martin had a dream in which he saw Christ, clothed in the half cloak Martin had given away.

When his military service ended, Martin was ordained a priest and ministered to the faithful from a hermitage in the French countryside. His superiors soon had grander plans for him, but he was uninterested in becoming a bishop. He was so uninterested that the archbishop had to trick him into coming to the city (he was asked to come pray with a sick man). When Martin figured out what was going on, he tried to hide from the archbishop in a barn, but the barn was full of geese, which started honking and gave him away. Thus discovered, he reluctantly became the bishop of Tours in 371. He served faithfully and well and died at the age of eighty-one.

Coat Closet and Other Ideas

In the spirit of St. Martin sharing his cloak with a beggar, I like to take this day to organize and clean out our coat closet. Over the year, we have often acquired more sweatshirts, coats, and jackets than we really need. As winter is beginning, it's the perfect time to donate our extra winter gear to friends or strangers who may need it more than we do. As St. John the Baptist said, "He who has two coats, let him share with him who has none" (Lk 3:11). Some years, I organize the coat closet, and it turns out that we really can use everything in there. And that's okay. Taking accounts is still a way to be good stewards of our resources.

In some parts of Europe, it's traditional for children to carve lanterns out of beets for Martinmas, but I can barely keep motivated to let my kids carve pumpkins for Halloween every year. The traditional food for the day is goose, after the hiding-in-the-barn incident, but as I related on Michaelmas, I'm not allowed to serve goose. So, if you're serving beet salad and roast goose, please invite me over.

In the meantime, a lantern walk of any kind is very appropriate and fun. Kids can make homemade lanterns out of paper, tissue-paper-covered glass jars, or punched "tin" cans, or just get out the camping lanterns and go for an evening walk with those.

For dinner, I like to make seven-can soup, sometimes called six-can soup, but these days mine is usually more like twelve- or fourteen-can soup. I plan to get the ingredients out of the cans and into a pot the night before so we can use the cans to make our lanterns.

Any size can will work for a punched-tin-can lantern craft. It involves tools and sharp implements and is therefore very exciting to children, but it is also manageable by even little kids (with some help). The night before the lantern making, remove the labels, wash the cans, fill them with water, and put them in the freezer. The next day, plan a design, and sketch it on paper, or draw it directly on the can. Or just wing it. Remove the can from the freezer, tape the pattern around the can, if you're using a pattern, and wrap a towel around the part of the can you're not working on. The towel keeps the can from rolling and catches the ice chips. Then use a hammer and an awl or a nail to punch holes in the can according to your pattern, about a quarter of an inch apart. Punch two holes near the rim to attach a handle.

When you're finished punching holes, soak the cans in hot water until the ice comes out, and attach a wire handle. Put a votive candle in there, and you're all set to go—after a nice bowl of soup, of course.

For dessert, I like to serve cookies. Any kind will do, but the catch is, you have to break each of your cookies and give half of it away.

FEAST OF ST. CATHERINE OF ALEXANDRIA: NOVEMBER 25

St. Catherine of Alexandria is another of the Fourteen Holy Helpers, about whom not much can be found in the historical record. But her story, found in *The Golden Legend*, speaks volumes. She was born at the end of the third century, the pampered daughter of the governor of Egypt, which was then part of the Roman Empire. She converted to Christianity at the age of fourteen and devoted the next few years to studying apologetics and theology.

The story goes that in the midst of the persecutions under Emperor Maxentius, she sought an audience with him through her father and rebuked the emperor for his cruelty to Christians. In response, he summoned his fifty greatest pagan scholars to debate her, hoping to disprove Christianity once and for all. She bested them. Several of her adversaries professed themselves Christians right then and there and were immediately put to death.

Catherine was arrested. During her imprisonment, she was visited by two hundred members of the emperor's court, including Maxentius' wife, Valeria Maximilla. Each converted to Christianity and was subsequently martyred. When Catherine couldn't be swayed by torture, Maxentius tried proposing marriage to her—as the position of his wife had recently become vacant—but she declined.

She was eventually sentenced to death by torture on the breaking wheel (now known as a St. Catherine's wheel), but it shattered at her touch, and she was beheaded instead. She was nineteen years old. More than a thousand years after her death, she was one of the saints who appeared to counsel another self-confident nineteen-year-old martyr, St. Joan of Arc.

St. Catherine's is a great story. I hope every word is true. But even if it's not, this is a story that has been told to Catholic children (and adults) for at least a thousand years. This is how our Church sees women. St. Catherine is held up to us as one of the many different examples of perfect Christian womanhood. If anyone ever tells you that the Catholic Church doesn't respect the intellects of women, *you* can tell the story of St. Catherine of Alexandria!

St. Catherine is traditionally invoked by women hoping to find a husband: "St. Catherine, St. Catherine, O lend me thine aid, and grant that I never may die an old maid." In France, unmarried women who had reached their twenty-fifth birthday were known as "Catherinettes" and were feted on this day—the twenty-fifth—with special parties, to which they would wear fancy hats of yellow (for faith) and green (for wisdom). If I were unmarried and over twenty-five, I would definitely hit the town in a crazy hat.

A fun dinner is a St. Catherine's wheel pizza with pepperoni spokes, and Catherine wheel cookies (a.k.a. pinwheel cookies).

SOLEMNITY OF OUR LORD JESUS CHRIST, KING OF THE UNIVERSE: LAST SUNDAY IN ORDINARY TIME

The feast of Christ the King was instituted in 1925 by Pope Pius XI as a response to the growing secularism of the Christian world, and as a reminder of Jesus' words to the eleven disciples after his Resurrection: "All authority in heaven and on earth has been given to me" (Mt 28:18).

This feast marks the end of the liturgical calendar. The new liturgical year begins next Sunday, with the advent of Advent. On this day, we take a last moment to dwell on Christ's supreme majesty, before we begin our preparations to celebrate his birth in a humble stable. As a reminder of this, the Te Deum is traditionally recited on this feast day.[34]

I like to serve chicken à la king for dinner. It's basically the inside of a chicken potpie, served over rice, pasta, or biscuits—or, if you're feeling really crazy, waffles. We'll have to have dessert, but that's a tougher one to figure out. I do wonder if Pope Pius XI took into account the fact that there is a king-cake season, and the end of November isn't in it. I suppose you could choose to live dangerously and make one for this feast. But I don't think I'll chance it. So far, we've just stuck with a Bundt-cake crown.

So, that's the whole year. Have I scared you off completely? I hope not. I hope and pray that adding a little or a lot from these liturgical-year celebrations will bring to your family the same joy and meaning they have brought to ours!

---

[34] See appendix B for more information on this and other indulgences.

ACKNOWLEDGMENTS

Like most books, this one wouldn't have been possible without the love, help, and support of a bunch of people.

Thank you to my husband, who works so hard to support our family and whose tireless efforts have allowed me to stay home with our children and pursue my dream of finally finishing this book. I love you forever. And someday I will get you to eat goose.

Thank you to my children, who have been my inspiration for all this liturgical living in the home. Thank you for always being excited about our feast-day traditions. Thank you especially to my big kids, who have cooked and cleaned and babysat so that I could sit and type. You weirdos are the best.

Thank you to my parents, who have always been a source of confidence and practical help. Thank you for always going above and beyond the call of grandparenting, for driving carpools and picking up takeout. And to my dad, a special shout out for proofreading and appreciating a book that really isn't aimed at seventy-year-old retired fighter pilots.

Thank you to my friend Micaela, who entertained my kids and pretended I was doing *her* a favor by letting them come over. This book wouldn't be finished without you.

Thank you to my proofreaders, perspective sharers, and sensitivity checkers: Karianna Frey, Molly Walter, and Ashley Woleben. If people read this book and are mad, that's on me, but if they're not, that's on you ladies.

Thank you to my bloggy friends and fellow lovers of liturgical living: Julia Harrell, Christy Isinger, Theresa Blackstone, Bonnie Engstrom, Mandi Richards, Kelly Mantoan, Micaela Darr, and Haley Stewart. Thank you for lending us all your unique voices and original perspectives on the liturgical year.

Thank you to my online community of readers and fellow bloggers. We've shared ideas and feedback together for going on five years now. This book is for all of us!

And thank you to my In Real Life community of Catholic friends. Thank you to the moms in our Rosary group and the Christ the King homeschool group for helping me along to this point in my journey. Thank you to the community of St. Monica Academy for the fellowship and all the rides for my kids. I totally owe you guys. And thank you to everyone who has come to our parties, bringing smiles and laughter and cupcakes and bottles of whiskey. Let's do it again really soon.

APPENDIX A

Days of Fasting and Abstinence

In the United States, the required days of fasting and abstinence are Ash Wednesday and Good Friday. Recommended days of fasting and abstinence are Holy Saturday and the Day of Prayer for the Legal Protection of Unborn Children. While the vigils of Christmas, Pentecost, the Immaculate Conception, and All Saints' Day no longer oblige Catholics to fasting and abstinence as they once did, the American bishops "suggest that the devout will find greater Christian joy in the feasts of the liturgical calendar if they freely bind themselves, for their own motives and in their own spirit of piety, to prepare for each Church festival by a day of particular self-denial, penitential prayer and fasting."[1]

On all Fridays during Lent, abstinence from meat (but not fasting) is required of Catholics. On Lenten weekdays (but not Lenten Sundays or solemnities) the American bishops "strongly recommend ... a self-imposed observance of fasting".[2]

On all other Fridays, in remembrance of Christ's death on the cross, abstinence from meat or a substitute sacrifice is required.

Friday should be in each week something of what Lent is in the entire year. For this reason we urge all to prepare for that weekly Easter that comes with each Sunday by freely making of every Friday a day of self-denial and mortification in prayerful remembrance of the passion of Jesus Christ.

---

[1] National Conference of Catholic Bishops, *Pastoral Statement on Penance and Abstinence* (November 18, 1966), no. 17, United States Conference of Catholic Bishops, http://www.usccb.org/prayer-and-worship/liturgical-year/lent/us-bishops-pastoral-statement-on-penance-and-abstinence.cfm.

[2] Ibid., no. 14.

Among the works of voluntary self-denial and personal penance which we especially commend to our people for the future observance of Friday, even though we hereby terminate the traditional law of abstinence binding under pain of sin, as the sole prescribed means of observing Friday, we give first place to abstinence from flesh meat. We do so in the hope that the Catholic community will ordinarily continue to abstain from meat by free choice as formerly we did in obedience to Church law.[3]

For Catholics in the other English-speaking countries, the rules are similar. The obligations are the same in Canada and Australia, except the Day of Prayer for the Unborn is not officially observed. In Canada the Holy Saturday Fast is required instead of optional. In England, Friday abstinence from meat is obligatory year-round, and no substitute is authorized. Obligatory fasting days are also observed on the vigils of the Immaculate Conception and Christmas, and on Holy Saturday.

If none of this sounds familiar to you, beyond maybe Ash Wednesday and Good Friday, you're not alone. I've been there, too.

Friday Abstinence and How It Got So Confusing

I was flabbergasted when I found out that we *are* still bound to observe Friday penance every week and that abstaining from meat is still the recommended penance. At that point I had been Catholic for more than thirty years. How had it never come up that this was something we were supposed to be doing? Let's break it down, shall we?

Canon law tells us, "The penitential days and times in the universal Church are every Friday of the whole year and the season of Lent. Abstinence from meat, or from some other food as determined by the Episcopal Conference, is to be observed on all Fridays, unless a solemnity should fall on a Friday. Abstinence and fasting are to be observed on Ash Wednesday and Good Friday."[4] So abstinence should be observed on all Fridays, unless a solemnity falls on a Friday,

---

[3] Ibid., nos. 23 and 23.

[4] *Code of Canon Law* (Vatican: Libreria Editrice Vaticana, 1983), cann.1250–1251, http://www.vatican.va/archive/ENG1104/_INDEX.HTM.

and abstinence and fasting should be observed on Ash Wednesday and Good Friday. Sounds pretty straightforward.

In 1966, however, the United States Conference of Catholic Bishops issued the *Pastoral Statement on Penance and Abstinence*, which acknowledges that, for some Catholics, the substitution of a different weekly penance, rather than abstinence from meat, would feel more penitential. Thus the bishops made permissible such substitutions while continuing to recommend abstinence from meat. They declared, "Let it not be said that by this action, implementing the spirit of renewal coming out of the Council, we have abolished Friday, repudiated the holy traditions of our fathers, or diminished the insistence of the Church on the fact of sin and the need for penance."[5] Unfortunately, it must be said: Friday got abolished. Holy traditions got repudiated.

But they seem to be coming back! Since 2011, British and Welsh Catholics have returned to an obligatory abstinence from meat on Fridays: "The Bishops wish to re-establish the practice of Friday penance in the lives of the faithful as a clear and distinctive mark of their own Catholic identity. They recognize that the best habits are those which are acquired as part of a common resolve and common witness. It is important that all the faithful be united in a common celebration of Friday penance."[6]

During the United States bishops' 2012 General Assembly, Cardinal Timothy M. Dolan, Archbishop of New York, suggested we consider doing the same in the United States. It's a slow Church, so we'll have to wait to see what becomes of it.

The Deal with Christmas Friday

For many years now, in our home, we have observed the traditional Friday abstinence from meat as a family alongside many of our Catholic friends. I have come to love that it is a penance we do in

---

[5] *Pastoral Statement on Penance and Abstinence*, no. 28.
[6] The Catholic Church in England and Wales, "Catholic Witness—Friday Penance", May 13, 2011, http://www.catholicchurch.org.uk/Home/News/2011/Catholic-Witness -Friday-Penance/(language)/eng-GB.

communion with other Catholics, all over the world and throughout time. We can nod knowingly at each other over our cheese pizzas and fish tacos. It's as if we're in a cool club with a secret handshake. And it makes us appreciate those Friday solemnities when they come. We get two for sure each year: Easter Friday and the feast of the Sacred Heart.

It also makes us notice when a Friday feels as if it should be a solemnity but isn't—such as the Friday of Christmas week. But, as I've found with everything I've wondered about in Catholicism, there *is* an explanation!

It's an unfortunate side effect of the 1969 reordering of the feasts on the liturgical calendar. Under the new liturgical calendar, in order to emphasize Sunday and solemnity Masses and the readings that go with them, those celebrations supersede lesser feast days. A saint's day that falls on a Sunday or during the Easter octave gets bumped only every few years, since Easter moves, but, if each day of the Christmas octave were a solemnity, the Christmas-octave saints' days would get bumped every year. To preserve the celebrations of the liturgies of the feast days that fall during the octave—St. Stephen, St. John, and the Holy Innocents—Christmas is celebrated as an octave, but as just one solemnity. It was the long tradition of the Church *not* to observe a day of penance during the octave of Christmas, but rules are rules, and solemnities are solemnities, and *not* solemnities are *not* solemnities. Thus, on Christmas Friday, which is *not* a solemnity, the rule of Friday penance applies.

For our family this means we usually abstain from meat on Christmas Friday. However, with most everyone on vacation, it could be a day for us to avail ourselves of the option to choose another form of penance. What always gets tricky for me, and why I prefer the unambiguity of just abstaining from meat, is that the bishops' suggestions for substitute penances are considerably more complicated for a large family with young children than making fish sticks for dinner:

> It would bring great glory to God and good to souls if Fridays found our people doing volunteer work in hospitals, visiting the sick, serving the needs of the aged and the lonely, instructing the young in the Faith, participating as Christians in community affairs, and meeting our obligations to our families, our friends, our neighbors, and our

community, including our parishes, with a special zeal born of the desire to add the merit of penance to the other virtues exercised in good works born of living faith.[7]

Because the actual obligation is just to make a single act of penance, the whole day I'm thinking, "I won't eat treats or watch TV. No, wait, I just won't eat treats. No, wait, I'll eat treats but I won't watch any *more* TV. Maybe I'll just be cheerful about doing the dishes." This is hardly the same as spending the day doing volunteer work in a hospital. I also prefer the community aspect of abstaining from meat. It's something the whole family does together. But it certainly *would* be a beautiful thing if, as the bishops suggest, we could take that Friday of Christmas vacation and spend it together in serving the poor or the sick or the elderly, in working at a food bank, or visiting a retirement home, or volunteering to clean the church or the rectory. Then we could come home and eat all the leftover Christmas meats we want!

What We Eat on Friday

Abstinence from meat on abstinence days is obligatory only for Catholics ages fourteen through fifty-nine. But it's something we observe together as a family, even the younger kids, as part of our family culture. We all eat our usual number of meals and our usual amount of food; we just don't eat meat. It's not usually a problem for me to abstain from meat even when I'm pregnant, but if it were, I would offer another sacrifice (say, the nausea and vomiting) and not worry about it.

On abstinence days, we eat pizza and pasta dishes with cheese; or egg-based dishes, such as frittatas or quiche; or Mexican dishes, such as bean and cheese burritos, quesadillas, and cheese tamales. Animal-derived products such as gelatin, butter, cheese, and eggs, which do not have any meat taste, are all okay. We eat soups. Broths made from meat or bones are allowed, as long as they don't have pieces of meat in them. We eat fish and shellfish. Abstinence permits all saltwater and

---

[7] *Pastoral Statement on Penance and Abstinence*, no. 27.

freshwater species of fish. We have never eaten alligator, frog, beaver, or capybara, but we *could*. Amphibians and reptiles are also allowed, as are mammals that spend the majority of their lives in the water.

At home or abroad, around our table or at a restaurant, special occasion or not, when dinner choices are up to us, we abstain from meat on abstinence days. If we are guests in someone's home, how-ever, we eat what's put before us and make an alternate sacrifice. As St. Josemaría said, "Choose mortifications that don't mortify others."[8] On Fridays in Lent, and on required days of fasting and abstinence, no alternate penance is allowed, so we avoid eating in the homes of people who wouldn't also be observing the day.

Fasting for Pregnant Ladies and Families

When fasting, a person is permitted to eat one full meal and two smaller meals (collations) that together are not equal to a full meal. The days of fasting are obligatory from ages eighteen through fifty-nine, but our older kids usually want to participate in an age-appropriate way, at least by avoiding snacks between meals, and often also choos-ing a smaller-than-usual breakfast and lunch.

The mentally, physically, and chronically ill are excused from fast-ing and abstinence, as are pregnant and nursing women.[9] As someone who has spent every day of the last sixteen years (and counting) preg-nant or nursing, or both, and has therefore *never* been obligated to fast the entire time I've been paying attention to things such as being obligated to fast, I have some thoughts on this exemption.

My first reaction is that *I don't like it*. I don't want anyone telling *me* I can't fast when everyone else is fasting. I'm tough. But then I realize that what *I* think and what *I* want aren't particularly important. "Behold, to obey is better than sacrifice, and to listen than the fat of rams" (1 Sam 15:22). So, even though it's more of a challenge to come up with alternate sacrifices on fasting days, and even though I don't

[8] Josemaría Escrivá de Balaguer, *The Way* (New York: Scepter Limited, 1953), no. 179.

[9] "Questions and Answers about Lent and Lenten Practices", United States Conference of Catholic Bishops http://www.usccb.org/prayer-and-worship/liturgical-year/lent/questions-and-answers-about-lent.cfm.

like feeling that I'm getting special treatment, I believe that taking the decision out of my hands (and out of my crazy pregnant brain) and erring on the side of obedience to my bishop is the right call.

If I can't observe a traditional fast, I can choose to abstain from meat, from salty or sugary snacks, from beverages other than water, from desserts, or from TV, computer, and phone screens. I can also offer Mass and the Rosary and some extra time in prayer. Just like most things done in a family setting, a feeling of penitence is possible, if we're willing to be creative.

Vigils

The vigils of Christmas, Pentecost, the Immaculate Conception, and All Saints' Day were, until 1983, required days of fasting and abstinence. Catholics observed these practices until they attended either Vespers, a vigil Mass, or a morning Mass celebrating the feast. This is shocking information to probably 90 percent of us. But it explains the French and Latin American tradition of having a big Christmas dinner in the middle of the night after Midnight Mass. They've been fasting all day on Christmas Eve and want to start feasting as soon as possible!

Even though we're late adopters of "the fast before the feast", as it's called, we've made meat-free dishes part of our own family traditions. Our children have come to expect baked mac and cheese before trick-or-treating on Halloween, and potato and dumpling soup on Christmas Eve.

Ember and Rogation Days

Before the Second Vatican Council, Catholics observed Ember and Rogation Days as special times of penitence. These days arose from the agrarian lifestyle of European Catholics and were linked with the planting and the harvest of certain crops. As of the 1983 *Code of Canon Law*, observance of these penitential days is no longer mandatory, and they are no longer universally marked on the General Roman Calendar. They do, however, still appear on the calendar for Masses according to the Extraordinary Form.

Although they are no longer required of Catholics, Ember and Rogation Days are making a comeback in some Catholic circles. As our family has dived deeper into liturgical living, and as we have found joy and truth and beauty in observing both feasts and fasts, I've felt called to explore these special days and to find ways of adopting them.

Ember Days

Ember Days were observed four times per year for three days over the course of a week: Wednesday, as the day Judas betrayed Jesus; Friday, as the day Jesus was crucified; and Saturday, as the day he was in the tomb. The traditional dates for the Ember Days were the Wednesday, Friday, and Saturday after these days:

1. St. Lucy's Day, December 13
2. The first Sunday of Lent
3. Pentecost
4. The feast of the Exaltation of the Holy Cross, September 14

Historically tied to agriculture, these days were for giving thanks to God for the seasonal harvests. The spring days were offered for the flower harvest and recalled baptism. The summer days were offered for the wheat harvest in thanksgiving for the Holy Eucharist. The fall days were offered for the grape harvest in thanksgiving for the Precious Blood. The winter days were offered for the olive harvest in anticipation of the holy oils used in anointing the sick. Priestly ordinations were traditionally performed on the Saturday Ember Days, so these days were also offered as a prayer for priests and for vocations.

Formerly, these were days of required fasting and abstinence, allowing one full meal and two collations, with meat allowed at the principal meal only, except on Fridays, when complete abstinence from meat was required.

Rogation Days

The major Rogation Day falls on the feast of St. Mark, April 25, and the minor Rogation Days fall on the Monday, Tuesday, and Wednesday before the Ascension. These seem like unlikely days for extra penance, as they fall during Eastertide, but they were offered to God during the spring planting season in the hope that the wheat crop would be protected from natural disasters. Because they fell during the Easter season, they were observed as days of abstinence from meat but were not days of fasting.

On the major Rogation Day Catholics recited the Litany of the Saints and walked in procession around the boundaries of the parish, blessing the crops. Those of us who live where parishes are big and crops are few can still offer our prayers and abstinence from meat for farmers and for the victims of natural disasters. We have a recent family tradition of walking around the edge of our yard, reciting the Litany of the Saints, and sprinkling our flowers and trees with holy water.

APPENDIX B

Indulgences

Indulgences! So much opportunity, so much confusion and misinformation. And that's just among Catholics. Within the main chapters of this book, I mentioned quite a few indulgences that are part of our family's liturgical-year observances. Here, I want to explain what indulgences are, and what they are not, and list how and when you and your family have opportunities to obtain them.

What Indulgences Are and What They Aren't

The rules and guidelines for obtaining indulgences are set out in the *Manual of Indulgences*, promulgated by Pope Paul VI in 1968 and revised in 1999, in which the system is much simplified from earlier years and indulgences are categorized as either partial or plenary (full). This replaced the earlier practice of assigning the worth of a particular act in terms of days, weeks, or years.

Part of the collateral damage of the Protestant Reformation and, more recently, the upheaval following the Second Vatican Council is that many Catholics have largely forgotten about indulgences. This is a huge loss for the Church, because indulgences are a beautiful, charitable, and efficacious practice for kids and grown-ups alike. Indulgences are good and just, and the bad press they've received is due to misunderstandings and abuses.

Indulgences are part of Church teaching. The Council of Trent stated that "the use of indulgences must be preserved because it is supremely salutary for the Christian people and authoritatively approved by the sacred councils; and it condemns with anathema those who maintain the uselessness of indulgences or deny the power of the Church to grant them."[1]

Indulgences aren't a money grab by villainous medieval bishops (although there was a time when indulgences were wrongly sold for money), and they aren't a get-out-of-hell-free card (indulgences do not apply to anyone in hell). What they are is the way the Church can exempt a member of the faithful from some or all of the temporal punishment due to his sins, after he has been forgiven of the eternal consequences of sin through the sacrifice of Jesus Christ.

The first thing to understand is that when we sin, we harm ourselves. After a Catholic confesses his sins, the priest gives him a penance (another word for temporal punishment). This is often a prayer or a good work that can help rebuild the person's moral and spiritual strength. In addition to the penances given in the confessional, we need to do penitential practices throughout our lives so that we become more and more like Christ and sin less and less. If we do not do enough penance during our time on earth, we go to purgatory until we are ready for full communion with God in heaven.

A long time ago, the Church used to give harsh public penances for grave sins. A person who confessed the sin of adultery, for example, might have been required to go on a long pilgrimage while barefoot, fasting, and wearing rough clothing. The Church would grant an indulgence, and lessen the severity of such a penance, if the penitent performed certain good works for that purpose. The Church also allowed the faithful to obtain indulgences for the souls in purgatory. Almsgiving (read money) was often involved, and corruption seeped into this practice.

Today, the penances given in the confessional are super easy compared with those given in the Middle Ages. But the Church still grants indulgences so that we will strive to do penance while we have the chance and shave off time in purgatory for ourselves and others.

Let's try an analogy. Say Johnny is playing baseball in the front yard, against known family rules, and breaks a window. He is truly

---

[1] Paul VI, apostolic constitution *Indulgentiarum Doctrina* (January 1, 1967), no. 8, quoting Council of Trent, Decree on Indulgences, https://w2.vatican.va/content/paul-vi/en/apost _constitutions/documents/hf_p-vi_apc_01011967_indulgentiarum-doctrina.html.

sorry and musters the courage to confess, and his parents forgive him. They do not kick him out of the house (eternal punishment), but they require that he pay to replace the window (temporal punishment, or penance), knowing that doing so will not only restore the window but also help Johnny become a more responsible person. Now say Johnny's parents allow him to do extra chores in order to reduce the amount he must pay for the window. That is like the Church granting an indulgence.

Stretching this metaphor further, let's suppose all the other kids in the neighborhood start doing odd jobs to raise money for the new window, and Johnny's parents deduct their contributions from the amount he owes. These efforts on Johnny's behalf are like the actions we perform in order to obtain indulgences for others. The only difference is that we can obtain indulgences for another person only after he has died and can no longer do acts of penance for himself.

Catholics believe that our prayers and sacrifices and good works go in together with the prayers and the sacrifices and the good works of Christ and the saints who have gone before us, and that these merits can be applied by the Church where the Church chooses, toward ourselves and others. As the *Catechism of the Catholic Church* explains:

> An indulgence is obtained through the Church who, by virtue of the power of binding and loosing granted her by Christ Jesus, intervenes in favor of individual Christians and opens for them the treasury of the merits of Christ and the saints to obtain from the Father of mercies the remission of the temporal punishments due for their sins. Thus the Church does not want simply to come to the aid of these Christians, but also to spur them to works of devotion, penance, and charity.[2] (1478)

The *Manual of Indulgences* covers specific things to do on specific days or in specific circumstances in order to lessen the punishments of ourselves or others. While the prayers and the practices recommended have indulgences attached to them, they are good in themselves. In other words, each indulgence is a twofer. We are decreasing the punishments our sins have brought upon us, and at the same time

---

[2] Cf. *Indulgentiarum doctrina*, 5.

we are growing in wisdom and prudence and virtue so that we are less likely to sin again. And that is the whole idea—to become more and more Christlike.

The Usual Conditions for Obtaining Indulgences

The following are the usual conditions for obtaining indulgences and a list of the indulgences available to Catholics as of the 1999 *Manual of Indulgences*. The suggested prayers must be approved versions or translations. For an expanded list of indulgences, more details about conditions and specific actions required, and the full text of the prayers, consult the manual itself.

- Indulgences can be plenary (full) or partial, so they remove either all or part of the temporal punishment due to sins.
- Indulgences can be gained for yourself or applied to the Holy Souls in purgatory, but not to another living person.
- To gain an indulgence, you must be a baptized Catholic, not excommunicated, and not in a state of mortal sin at the time of the actions performed for the indulgence.
- You must have the intention of gaining the indulgence and must perform the required actions in the required amount of time and in a devout manner.
- Each day, you can gain many partial indulgences but only one plenary indulgence, except at the point of death, when you may gain a second plenary indulgence.
- If the indulgence requires visiting a church or an oratory, you should devoutly recite the Our Father and the Creed during the visit.
- To gain a plenary indulgence you must be free from all attachment to sin, even venial sin. This does not mean that we never commit sins. This doesn't mean that we don't often find ourselves committing and confessing the same venial sins, especially those toward which we have habits and inclinations. It means that we do not love the sin or desire to commit it. It means that we must be willing to resolve not to commit the sin again, as we must do to make a good confession.

- You must perform the required actions, receive Holy Communion, make a sacramental confession, and pray for the intentions of the Holy Father.
- It is preferred that you receive Communion and pray for the intentions of the Holy Father on the day you perform the actions, but it is acceptable to do so within several days before or after the day. These must be performed for each indulgence sought.
- Confession should be made within three weeks before or after the actions for the indulgence. One confession can apply to many indulgences.
- The usual prayers offered for the intentions of the Holy Father are one Our Father and one Hail Mary.
- If all the conditions are not met, the indulgence becomes partial, rather than plenary.
- Things that we are obliged to do, such as attending Mass, are understood to confer graces and are not enhanced with indulgences.

Ways to Obtain Plenary Indulgences

- Spend thirty minutes or more in adoration of the Blessed Sacrament.
- Participate in the Stations of the Cross, using fourteen stations, marked at least by crosses, progressing from one to the next.
- Recite five decades of the Rosary in a church, religious community, or family, or while listening live to the Holy Father's Rosary.
- Read or listen to Sacred Scripture for at least thirty minutes; preference is given to reading.
- Make a three-day retreat.
- At the point of death, pray, ideally before a crucifix or a cross (this requires that you have been in the habit of praying during your life).
- Participate in a parish mission and its conclusion.
- Attend a ceremony in honor of a new saint during the first year after his canonization (available once).
- Attend a priest's first Mass or the jubilee celebrations for priests and bishops renewing their vocational promises (for priests and those in attendance).

- Visit the hosting church during a diocesan synod.
- Assist during a pastoral visit.
- Make a pilgrimage to one of the four patriarchal basilicas in Rome.

Plenary Indulgences Associated with Particular Feast Days

- Visit a basilica, cathedral, parish church, or approved shrine on its titular feast day.
- Receive the papal Urbi et Orbi blessing (usually given on Christmas and Easter) in person, on the radio, on TV, or online.
- Recite the Te Deum on December 31 in thanksgiving for the year.
- Recite the Veni Creator Spiritus on January 1 as a prayer for the beginning of the year or on Pentecost.
- Participate in special celebrations for days universally designated for particular intentions (such as the Day of Prayer for Peace on January 1, or Day of Prayer for Vocations on Good Shepherd Sunday, the fourth Sunday of Easter).
- Participate in the services of the Week of Prayer for Christian Unity, January 18–25.
- Recite the Prayer before a Crucifix ("Look down upon me, good and gentle Jesus ...") before a crucifix, after Communion on a Friday during Lent.
- Recite the "Tantum Ergo" on Holy Thursday before the Altar of Repose.
- Adore the cross on Good Friday.
- Renew your baptismal promises at the Easter Vigil or on the anniversary of your baptism.
- Take part in special services held on Divine Mercy Sunday, or, before the Blessed Sacrament on that day, pray the usual prayers and "Merciful Jesus, I trust in you."
- Participate in a eucharistic procession on Corpus Christi.
- Recite the Act of Reparation to the Sacred Heart of Jesus on the feast of the Sacred Heart in a church, a religious community, or a family.
- Use an article blessed by the Holy Father or any bishop on the feast of SS. Peter and Paul.

- Visit a basilica or a cathedral on the feast of SS. Peter and Paul.
- The Portiuncula Indulgence of St. Francis of Assisi: with a contrite heart, visit any church on August 2 (or the first Sunday of August if the church isn't open every day).
- Pray for the dead in a cemetery, November 1–8 (one plenary indulgence for each day, applicable only to the souls in purgatory).
- Pray for the dead in a church on All Souls' Day (applicable only to the souls in purgatory).
- Recite the Act of Dedication to Christ the King on the Feast of Christ the King in a church, a religious community, or a family.

Partial Indulgences

- Use a properly blessed crucifix, cross, rosary, scapular, or medal.
- Use pious invocations throughout the day, mentally or out loud (e.g., "Jesus, Mary, and Joseph", "Heart of Jesus, I trust in you", "Holy Mary, Mother of God, pray for us").
- Pray to the merciful heart of Jesus.
- Perform charitable works or charitable giving.
- Make a voluntary Christian witness to others.
- Teach or study Christian doctrine.
- Visit the Blessed Sacrament for any amount of time.
- Recite a Rosary alone, or recite a partial Rosary.
- Make an examination of conscience.
- Attend a monthly recollection.
- Spend time in mental prayer.
- Listen to preaching on the Word of God.
- Visit a cemetery and pray for the dead any time of year.
- Visit the catacombs.
- Make the sign of the cross using the customary words.
- Renew your baptismal vows at any time.
- See the *Manual of Indulgences* for dozens of prayers recommended to obtain partial indulgences.

So, there you go: everything you never knew you wanted to know about indulgences. Over the past few years, we've been slowly incorporating them more and more into our family's liturgical-living traditions. My big takeaways in what I've learned so far about indulgences are these:

1. Attempting to obtain indulgences is like following a Vatican-approved training program for strengthening your faith while getting the amazing free bonus of time out of purgatory.
2. Obtaining indulgences for the poor souls in purgatory is probably the single most charitable thing you could possibly do in your lifetime.
3. If your goal is quantity: daily Mass, monthly confession, and a daily family Rosary, including prayers for the Holy Father, will get you a plenary indulgence (or at least a partial one, depending on your attachment to sin) every day of the year, in about an hour a day.
4. If you are looking for a Whole Catholic Living approach: incorporating any or many of the yearly indulgences into your family's annual traditions is a beautiful way to share in the deep history and universality of our Catholic faith.

APPENDIX C

The Canonization Process and Favorite Saints

How did the saints get to be the saints, anyway? Well, that depends.

In the earliest days of the Church, only martyrs (people known to have been killed for professing their faith in Jesus Christ) and the Virgin Mary were venerated as saints. By the fourth century, confessors (people who had shown their dedication to Jesus not by their deaths but by *confessing* their belief through their lives and their words) also began to be venerated and held up as examples. Christians honored the tombs and relics of martyrs and confessors alike, but since the holiness of a confessor wasn't as easy to know as the holiness of a martyr, the Church began to require that saints be publicly venerated only with the approval of the local bishop.

Those saints were recognized only locally, unless their holiness was also approved by the pope, in which case the "cult" of the saint became a part of the universal Church. By the twelfth century, papal approval was required for all canonizations, and a multistep process was created.

In 1983, Pope St. John Paul II simplified the procedural side of the canonization process. Postulators for the cause of the canonization of an individual come from his home diocese to present evidence of his holiness. An official Vatican Promoter for the Faith, colloquially known as the devil's advocate, looks for reasons why the person in question might not be worthy of public veneration. In previous eras, there was a rather adversarial trial process, but these days it's just a process of gathering information on both sides.

Four Steps

There are four steps on the way to canonization.

1. Servant of God

The process begins with the faithful. If people believe that a particular person who has died is a saint in heaven, they may petition the local bishop, usually of the place where the candidate is buried. The bishop can then give permission for an investigation to be opened. This begins five years after the person's death, unless the pope waives the waiting period. Evidence about the person's life, including eyewitness accounts, writings, speeches, sermons, and so forth, is collected. If the bishop believes that the cause should go further, he presents the information to the Congregation for the Causes of Saints in Rome. If accepted into the process, the candidate is now called Servant of God and is assigned a postulator. The body is exhumed and examined, and relics are collected and preserved.

2. Venerable

Once all the evidence has been reviewed, the Congregation can vote to recommend that the pope proclaim that the Servant of God has lived a life of "heroic virtue". The person must be known to have lived the theological virtues of faith, hope, and charity and the cardinal virtues of prudence, justice, fortitude, and temperance to a heroic degree. At that point, the person is called Venerable, and the faithful are encouraged to pray for a miracle wrought by his intercession.

3. Blessed

The next step in the process is beatification. This is a declaration by the Church that it is "worthy of belief" that the Venerable is in heaven and saved. For a martyr to reach this step from Venerable requires that the pope certifies that the Venerable gave his life voluntarily as a witness of the faith or in an act of heroic charity for others, or both. For a confessor, proof is required of the occurrence of a miracle through the intercession of the Venerable; that is, someone has prayed for the intercession of the saint and has received a miracle from God, which suggests that the Venerable is, in fact, in heaven.

The miracle is almost always a cure of an ill or injured person that cannot be explained by medicine. Once a person is declared Blessed, a feast day is assigned in his honor, which is not normally permitted to be publicly celebrated out of the Blessed's home diocese.

4. Saint

Finally, the person can be canonized a saint. It traditionally takes fifty years from a person's death to reach the canonization stage. This is a declaration by the Church that the person certainly enjoys the Beatific Vision of heaven and is worthy of being held up as an example of sanctity to the faithful. To move from Blessed to Saint usually requires another certified miracle attributed to the intercession of the saint. The saint's feast day is confirmed and may be celebrated anywhere in the universal Church, but it is not necessarily added to the General Roman Calendar. Churches may be dedicated in the saint's honor, and statues, and prayer cards, and medals encouraging devotion to the saint may be distributed.

Doctors of the Church

But wait, there's more. There's one rank beyond "just" saint. As of this writing, thirty-six saints have been proclaimed Doctors of the Church. There are three requirements that must be fulfilled to merit being included among these super saints:

- holiness that is truly outstanding, even among saints
- depth of doctrinal insight
- an extensive body of writings that the Church can recommend as an expression of the authentic and life-giving Catholic Tradition

The two popes included among the Doctors of the Church, Pope St. Gregory and Pope St. Leo, are both called "the Great". So are bishops St. Basil and St. Albert. This isn't a title officially bestowed by the Church. Rather, it's awarded first by the faithful at a grassroots level and is then agreed upon by an unofficial consensus of Church historians and so becomes common usage. There has been talk since Pope St. John Paul II's death and canonization of whether he will be added to the ranks of the "greats." If we want him to be Pope St. John Paul the Great, all we have to do is start calling him that. History will take care of the rest.

Saints and More Saints

The saints on the General Roman Calendar are just a fraction of all the canonized saints who are recognized by the Catholic Church and considered worthy to be honored by the faithful. We are welcome to celebrate any saint with a feast day, but the saints with universal feasts are presented to us by the Magisterium as especially worth getting to know.

While newly canonized saints have continued to be added at the discretion of the current pope, the most recent significant revision of the General Roman Calendar happened in 1969 under Pope Paul VI. Saints without a reliable historical footprint were largely removed from the calendar (but not "de-sainted" or anything), and the current ranking system of solemnity, feast, memorial, and optional memorial was implemented.

Solemnities rank the highest and are reserved for celebrations of the most important people and mysteries of our faith. Feasts come next in importance, then memorials, then optional memorials. The practical difference between the categories, however, has to do with how the day's Mass is celebrated. Since those differences don't affect how we might choose to observe the feasts in our homes, and since "feast", while one of the specific categories, is also the general term, I've chosen to label the days in this book as either "solemnity of ..." or "feast of ..."

The revision sought to emphasize the importance of the celebration of the Sunday liturgy. Therefore, feast days that fall on a Sunday are outranked by the Sunday and don't show up on the liturgical calendar for that year. Solemnities that would have fallen on a Sunday are moved to another day (unless they are celebrated as a specifically Sunday solemnity).

It's worth noting, however, that this issue really has to do with the Sunday liturgy and the cycle of Sunday readings. The Magisterium determined that the faithful were better off getting to hear the usual rotation of readings for Mass on Sunday, rather than the readings and prayers proper to a particular saint's feast day. This doesn't mean, of course, that it would be inappropriate for the faithful to observe a special meal or activity or prayer or blessing at home in honor of a particular saint, even if his Mass has been bumped.

Some feasts are classified differently in different countries. Some feasts are celebrated on different dates in different Catholic rites. The dates of some feast days have been moved. I've listed them in the text according to their United States classification and their current Latin Rite date. If you're outside the United States or outside the Latin Rite, check with your bishops' conference to find your particular classifications and dates.

The Fourteen Holy Helpers

The Fourteen Holy Helpers are the fourteen favorite saints of the fourteenth century. They were basically the Justice League of the late Middle Ages, invoked separately as patron saints against the most pressing concerns of the era, and invoked together as a force of intercessory prayer against the bubonic plague. They are associated with some of the most fantastic legends of all the saints. Even though in many cases we think that their stories are meant to be understood allegorically rather than literally, they are still fun to share with kids. These hagiographies (the official fancy word for stories of the lives of the saints), along with many others, are included in *The Golden Legend*, a book compiled by Archbishop Bl. Jacobus da Voragine. It was published in Italy in 1260, was soon translated into all the languages of Europe, and was the second most widely read book of the Middle Ages (after the Bible).

These are the Fourteen Holy Helpers:

St. Barbara (December 4), patroness against fever and lightning, and of artillerymen: she is said to have been imprisoned in a tower, Rapunzel-style, by her father to keep her away from the world. She was converted to Christianity by the song of a priest who passed beneath her tower window. When her father discovered that she had been secretly baptized, he denounced Barbara to the emperor and carried out himself her sentence of beheading. On his way home, he was struck by lightning and killed; hence St. Barbara's associations with lightning and explosions.

St. Blaise (February 3), patron against illness of the throat: see chapter 4 for more about St. Blaise.

St. George (April 23), patron of England, knights, soldiers, and the health of domestic animals: see chapter 4 for more on St. George.

St. Agathius (May 7), patron against headaches: according to Christian tradition, he was a Cappadocian Greek centurion of the Roman imperial army who was martyred. He was scourged and then beheaded, which is a surefire cure for a headache.

St. Erasmus (a.k.a. St. Elmo; June 2), patron against intestinal ailments: St. Erasmus was bishop of Formia, martyred by the Roman emperor for refusing to worship idols. If you've got boys who like this kind of thing (I do), wait until you hear about his tortures. He was put into a barrel of spikes and rolled down a hill. When that didn't kill him, he was whipped, beaten, tarred, set on fire, and, finally, his intestines were wound up on a winch. I love the idea that some guy, at some point, had a terrible stomachache, and some other guy told him, "You know who you should pray to? St. Erasmus. For sure. He got his intestines wound up on a winch. He'll know what to do."

St. Vitus (a.k.a. St. Guy; June 15), patron against epilepsy and oversleeping: as a child of seven, he was converted to Christianity by his tutor and then martyred with him for refusing to apostatize. Because of a European tradition of celebrating his feast day by dancing before his statue, he is also the patron saint of dancing and entertainers.

St. Margaret of Antioch (July 20), patroness of safety in childbirth and escape from devils: if professional wrestling needs a patron saint, they should call her. St. George gets all the press when it comes to dragons. But we gals have an (allegorical) dragon slayer too! Margaret was jailed at age fifteen for being a Christian and for refusing an offer of marriage from the provost. Satan appeared to her in prison to tempt her, but she refused to listen to him. At that point he turned into a dragon and swallowed her. But the crucifix she held in her hand allowed her to burst, alive, out of the dragon's belly. (Hence the childbirth thing. Ouch.) Satan turned into a man again, and Margaret, after kneeling to pray, caught him by the head and flipped him to the ground, holding him down with her foot on his neck and taunting him about being whupped by a girl. And she sent him away. Later, she was martyred.

St. Christopher (July 25), patron of transportation and travelers: it is said that he was seven and a half feet tall, strong, and fierce to behold. Christopher asked a skinny old holy hermit how he could serve Christ, and the hermit suggested fasting, of course. Christopher didn't think he would be good at that, so the hermit proposed that he help people to cross a dangerous river instead. One day a child came and asked for his help. With each step across the river, the child on his shoulders grew heavier and heavier, and Christopher barely made it to the other side. The child told Christopher that the weight on his shoulders had been the weight of the whole world, and the one who made it. Christ, for that is who the child was, said that by using his strength to serve others, Christopher was serving God. I love this reminder that we are not all called to serve in exactly the same way.

St. Pantaleon (July 27), patron of physicians and against cancer and tuberculosis, and officially invoked as the "helper of crying children": he was the pagan physician to the Roman emperor. When Pantaleon converted to Christianity, the emperor attempted to have him killed, but it was easier said than done. They tried to set him on fire, but the torches went out. They tried to put him in a cauldron of molten lead, but it cooled and hardened. They tried to feed him to the wild beasts, but the wild beasts just wanted to cuddle. Finally, after forgiving his executioner, St. Pantaleon allowed himself to be beheaded.

St. Cyriacus (August 8), patron against deathbed temptation: he was a bishop said to have exorcised demons from two girls, one of whom was a Persian princess. As a result, the king and his whole household converted to Christianity.

St. Giles (September 1), patron of beggars, cripples, and breastfeeding: he's a prince and a hermit who is also the patron saint of breastfeeding. I'll bet you didn't see that one coming. The legend says his sole companion in his hermitage in the woods was a deer, who sustained him with her milk. He took a hunter's arrow meant for the deer and became crippled but lived to an old age. In the Middle Ages, churches named for St. Giles were built to be handicapped-accessible.

St. Eustace (September 20), patron of family togetherness: he was a wealthy Roman general who converted to Christianity after seeing, while out hunting, a vision of a stag with a crucifix between its antlers. After his conversion, he was robbed of his estate, his wealth, his wife, and his two children in succession. But he remained firm in his faith, and all was restored to him before he was martyred for refusing to offer a sacrifice to the pagan gods.

St. Denis (October 9), patron against headaches (this was before Tylenol, so we needed two such patrons): he was the bishop of Paris in the third century. The stories say his preaching was so effective that hardly anyone could hear him speak without converting. The furious Roman governor sent an executioner to behead him while he was speaking atop Montmartre, the highest hill in the city. Unfazed, Denis picked up his head and walked six miles down the hill to his church, finishing his sermon on the way.

St. Catherine of Alexandria (November 25), patroness of lawyers, apologists, unmarried women, and milliners and against sudden death: see chapter 8 for more on St. Catherine of Alexandria.

The Fourteen Modern Mentors
(Twentieth-Century Saints)

If it was good enough for those medieval types, it's good enough for us, right? Well, not the plumbing. But I figure *we* could use a posse of fourteen saints of our own. Because they all lived in the twentieth century, there is a *ton* of available information about these saints. I encourage you to look them up (in a good book or on a reliable Catholic website) and learn their inspiring stories and see their photographs! Here are my recommendations for the Fourteen Modern Mentors:

St. Marianne Cope (1838–1918; January 23), patroness of Hawaii and against AIDS and leprosy: St. Marianne enthusiastically answered a request by the king of Hawaii for volunteers to care for the people of the islands suffering from leprosy. She spent over twenty years attending to the physical and spiritual needs of the community, including caring for St. Damien of Molokai in his final illness, but never contracted leprosy herself.

St. Josephine Bakhita (1869–1947; February 8), patroness of Sudan and against human trafficking: see chapter 4 for more on St. Josephine Bakhita.

St. Katharine Drexel (1858–1955; March 3), patroness of philanthropy and racial justice: Katharine Drexel was a socialite of enormous personal wealth whose decision to become a nun made headlines in Philadelphia newspapers. She founded a religious order and dedicated herself to work among Native Americans and African Americans in the western and southwestern United States.

St. Gemma Galgani (1878–1903; April 11), patroness of students, parachutists and against back pain, migraines, and temptations to impurity: Gemma was a young Italian mystic and stigmatist who had been studying to become a pharmacist before contracting tuberculosis and dying at the age of twenty-five.

St. Gianna Molla (1922–1962; April 28), patroness of physicians, wives, mothers, and unborn children: see chapter 7 for more about St. Gianna Molla.

St. Josemaría Escrivá (1902–1975; June 26), patron of Opus Dei, diabetics, job seekers, and the sanctification of ordinary work: see chapter 8 for more about St. Josemaría Escrivá.

St. Maria Goretti (1890–1902; July 6), patroness of sexual assault victims and other crime victims: Maria was an Italian virgin martyr and is one of the youngest canonized saints. When she was eleven, a nineteen-year-old neighbor made sexual advances toward her. When she tried to fight him off, he stabbed her fourteen times. She was taken to the hospital but died of her injuries, forgiving her attacker and saying she hoped he would make it to heaven. He was arrested, convicted, and sentenced to thirty years in jail. After three years he repented, writing a letter to the local bishop, saying that Maria had appeared to him in a dream. When eventually released from prison, he visited her mother to beg forgiveness, which she granted. He later became a lay brother in a monastery and was present at Maria's canonization.

St. Teresa Benedicta of the Cross (Edith Stein) (1892–1942; August 9), patroness of Jewish converts and those who have lost parents: Edith Stein was born into an observant Jewish family in Poland, received a doctorate in philosophy in Germany, became an atheist, converted to Catholicism, and became a Carmelite nun, taking the name Teresa Benedicta of the Cross. During World War II she was arrested by the Nazis because of her Jewish heritage, imprisoned in Auschwitz concentration camp, and executed in the gas chamber.

St. Maximilian Kolbe (1894–1941; August 14), patron of political prisoners, publishing, and amateur radio and against drug addiction:

Maximilian was a Polish priest, missionary, and ham radio enthusiast, who was sent to Auschwitz for publishing anti-Nazi publications and for refusing to cease his work as a priest. Once there, he volunteered to take the place of a husband and father who had been sentenced to starvation along with nine others, as a punishment for the escape attempt of another prisoner. When he was still alive after ten days, he was killed by a lethal injection.

St. Pio of Pietrelcina (1887–1968; September 23), patron of teenagers and against stress: Padre Pio was an Italian friar, priest, stigmatist, and mystic, known in his lifetime as a gifted confessor and miracle-worker. He was so famous that the Vatican, fearing the celebrity that grew up around him, forbade him, for more than ten years, to celebrate the sacraments publicly. He humbly submitted to the censure, and eventually the pope removed all sanctions and publicly declared support for him. His motto, "Pray, hope, and don't worry", still inspires the faithful.

St. Teresa of Calcutta (1910–1997; September 5), patroness of the Missionaries of Charity and World Youth Day: see chapter 8 for more about St. Teresa of Calcutta.

St. Faustina Kowalska (1905–1938; October 5), patroness of Divine Mercy: Faustina was a Polish nun and mystic who had visions of Jesus throughout her life. Jesus' messages to her of love and mercy resulted in the Divine Mercy devotion and its feast day.

Pope St. John Paul II (1920–2005; October 22), patron of families, young Catholics, and World Youth Day: see chapter 8 for more about Pope St. John Paul II.

St. Frances Xavier Cabrini (1850–1917; November 13), patroness of immigrants and hospital administrators: born in Italy, Frances became a nun and was sent as a missionary to tend to the Catholic immigrant population of the United States. She founded a religious order and sixty-seven orphanages, schools, and hospitals She eventually became an American citizen.

The JV Squad (Fourteen Blesseds to Get to Know before They Hit the Big Time)

Bl. Charles de Foucauld (1858–1916; December 1): Charles was an officer of the French army in North Africa, who became a Trappist monk and priest and lived as a hermit in Algeria until he was martyred by local bandits in 1916.

Bl. Solanus Casey (1870–1957; July 30): Solanus was a Capuchin priest in Detroit, Michigan, well-known in his lifetime for his devotion to the sick, for whom he celebrated special Masses, and for the many healings that resulted from his prayers. He was an enthusiastic—but terrible—singer and violin player.

Bl. Sára Salkaházi (1899–1944; December 27): Sára was a Hungarian Catholic nun who saved the lives of more than a hundred Hungarian Jews during World War II. She was captured and executed in 1944.

Bl. Cyprian Michael Iwene Tansi (1903–1964; January 20): as a child, Cyprian was blinded in one eye by mud. He became one of the first native Nigerian priests and was known in his lifetime for his austere lifestyle and advocacy of women's rights in Africa. He died at a Trappist monastery in England in 1964.

Bl. Ceferino Giménez Malla (1861–1936; May 4): Ceferino was born in Spain into a Catholic Roma family and was respected by members of both communities for his wisdom and piety. He was a catechist and an advocate for Roma causes and was martyred in 1936 while defending a priest during the Spanish Civil War.

Bl. Imelda Lambertini (1322–1333; May 13): although the custom of the time was to receive First Holy Communion at the age of fourteen, Imelda began to ask to receive at the age of five. She joined a Dominican cloister at the age of nine. In 1333, after years of refusing her requests, a priest saw the Blessed Sacrament floating above her head while she was in prayer and agreed to let her receive. Afterward, she died of joy.

Bl. Margaret Ball (1515–1584; June 20): Margaret was the wealthy widow of an Irish nobleman, denounced and imprisoned by her eldest son for being a Catholic during the religious persecutions of Elizabeth I. She died in Dublin Castle in 1584.

Bl. Pier Giorgio Frassati (1901–1925; July 4): Pier Giorgio was born into an agnostic Italian family, active in national politics. He enjoyed hiking and the outdoors, and as a student he became Catholic and was involved in charity and social activism. He died of polio in 1925 at the age of twenty-four.

Bl. Peter To Rot (1912–1945; July 7): Peter was born in what is now Papua New Guinea and became a lay catechist, husband, and father. When foreign missionaries were expelled from the country by the occupying Japanese forces in 1942, he secretly continued to serve the Catholic community. He was arrested and martyred by lethal injection in 1945.

Bl. Titus Brandsma (1881–1942; July 27): Titus was a Dutch Carmelite priest, doctor of philosophy, and magazine publisher, imprisoned in the Dachau concentration camp for continuing to agitate for freedom of education and of the press in the face of Nazi oppression. He was subjected to the medical experimentation done on prisoners and died in 1942 as a result.

Bl. Stanley Rother (1935–1981; July 28): Stanley was a farmer from Oklahoma who became a priest and missionary to Guatemala, learning not only Spanish, but also the native Tzutujil language. He is believed to have been martyred in 1981 by members of a right-wing-extremist death squad attached to elements of the Guatemalan armed forces.

Bl. Dina Belanger (1897–1929; September 4): Dina was a Canadian nun and mystic, and a talented concert pianist. She died of tuberculosis in 1929.

Bl. Chiara Luce Badano (1971–1990; October 29): Chiara was an Italian teenager involved in the Focolare Movement when she was diagnosed with bone cancer. She died after a two-year battle with the disease.

Bl. Miguel Pro (1891–1927; November 23): Fr. Pro was a Mexican priest known for his piety and innocence, but also for his wit and practical jokes. Under relentless persecution from the government under President Calles, the Catholic Church was forced to go underground. To continue to offer the sacraments, Fr. Pro would disguise himself as a businessman or a mechanic, until he was arrested and martyred by firing squad in 1927.

Your Family Fourteen

You can play along at home by creating a Family Fourteen—the fourteen saints that are most meaningful to your family. A Family Fourteen could include your name saints, the patrons of your professions and hobbies, perhaps the patron of your city, or just saints for which your family has a particular affinity. These days our family has pretty much outgrown just fourteen favorite saints. We need, say, thirty.

But I still love the concept. Choosing specific family saints is a great way to narrow down the liturgical-year possibilities a bit. You can even print out a special litany to your family saints for your altar table and say it as part of your evening prayers: Pope St. John Paul II, pray for us. St. Elizabeth of Hungary, pray for us. St. Robert Bellarmine, pray for us. And so forth.

APPENDIX D

Quick Reference Guide to the Feasts in This Book

You're busy. I know. So here's a reference guide to help you quickly and easily find suggestions of feasts to celebrate, and prayers, activities, and foods to make the day fun and memorable. For anecdotes, explanations, and backstories, please see the page numbers referenced.

I've listed suggestions for prayers, especially when there are partial or plenary indulgences associated with their use on particular feast days. The Magisterium encourages us to make prayer a part of every saint's day celebration. Prayers in honor of each saint on the universal calendar can be found in the Roman Missal and are available on the Vatican and USCCB websites, in Catholic prayer books, and from reliable Catholic online sources, such as CatholicCulture.org and EWTN. Mass and a family Rosary are excellent complements to every feast-day celebration.

November 30: St. Andrew, apostle (feast), patron of Scotland, fishermen, pregnant women, and against sore throats—Christmas Anticipation Prayer; haggis, *neeps*, *tatties*, a dram, shortbread cookies (page 40).

First Sunday of Advent: Stir-Up Sunday (Sunday, holy day of obligation)—Christmas baking; Advent wreath and prayers; Straw for Baby Jesus; choosing family saints (page 44).

December 6: St. Nicholas, bishop (optional memorial), patron of children, sailors, and merchants—Nicene Creed; letters to Santa; leave shoes by the door; *speculaas, bishopswyn* (page 46).

December 7: St. Ambrose, bishop and Doctor (memorial), patron of Milan, students, beekeepers, and candlemakers—Penitential Prayer of St. Ambrose of Milan; recommended fasting and abstinence for the vigil of the Immaculate Conception; candle craft; minestrone soup, ambrosia salad (page 56).

December 8: Immaculate Conception of the Blessed Virgin Mary (solemnity, holy day of obligation, United States), patroness of the United States—Litany of the Blessed Virgin Mary (Litany of Loreto), Immaculate Conception Prayer; family Marian procession; all-white dinner (page 58).

December 9: St. Juan Diego Cuauhtlatoatzin (optional memorial), patron of indigenous peoples—tilma making; tacos and *polvorones de canele* or snickerdoodles (page 60).

December 10: Our Lady of Loreto (historical), patroness of air travel— Litany of the Blessed Virgin Mary (Litany of Loreto); gingerbread houses; Italian food (page 63).

December 12: Our Lady of Guadalupe (feast), patroness of Mexico and the Americas—Litany of the Blessed Virgin Mary (Litany of Loreto), John Paul II's Prayer to the Virgin of Guadalupe; hair braiding; tamales, hot chocolate, Mexican wedding cookies (page 60).

December 13: St. Lucy, virgin and martyr (memorial), patroness of writers and the blind—winter Ember Days (on the Wednesday, Friday, and Saturday after St. Lucy's Day); making crowns; Christmas lights; Swedish *lussebullar* (page 66).

December 14: St. John of the Cross, priest and Doctor (memorial), patron of contemplatives—read the *Spiritual Canticle of the Soul and the Bridegroom Christ*; veneration of the cross; salt fish, *sopa de ajo*, peanut butter kiss cookies (page 68).

Third Sunday of Advent: Gaudete Sunday or Bambinelli Sunday (Sunday, holy day of obligation)—wear pink; blessing of the baby Jesus; setting up the Nativity scene; meat pie, pink sugar cookies (page 70).

December 24: Christmas Eve and feast of SS. Adam and Eve (historical)— read Genesis 2:4–3:24; recommended fasting and abstinence for the vigil of Christmas; put on a Paradise Play; decorate the Christmas tree; place baby Jesus in the Nativity scene; apples, *ensalada de Nochebuena*, *spaetzle kartoffelsuppe* (page 76).

December 25: The Nativity of the Lord (Christmas) (solemnity, holy day of obligation)—read Luke 2:1–20; watch the papal Urbi et Orbi blessing on TV or online (plenary indulgence); exchange gifts; put on a Nativity play; birthday cake (page 83).

December 26: St. Stephen, first martyr (feast), patron of deacons—read Acts 6:1–7:60; deliver Boxing Day boxes of cookies to neighbors; leftovers (page 92).

December 27: St. John, apostle and evangelist (feast), patron of priests, theologians, and friendships—read John 1:1–18; blessing of wine; drinking the love of St. John; wine, deep-fried anything (page 95).

December 28: The Holy Innocents, martyrs (feast), patron of children and altar servers—read Matthew 2:13–18; "Coventry Carol"; blessing of children; pranks; kids in charge; "baby food": cream of wheat or grits (page 98).

Sunday after Christmas (or December 30 if Christmas is on a Sunday): The Holy Family of Jesus, Mary and Joseph (feast), patrons of families— read Luke 2:39–52; consecration to the Holy Family; family outing; family potluck (page 103).

January 1: Mary, Mother of God (solemnity, holy day of obligation)— Litany of the Blessed Virgin Mary (Litany of Loreto); Veni Creator Spiritus (plenary indulgence); Te Deum (recited on December 31 for a plenary indulgence) (page 104).

January 3: The Most Holy Name of Jesus (optional memorial)—read Luke 2:21 and Philippians 2:9–11; Litany of the Holy Name; discussion about respect for the God's name; alphabet soup (page 106).

January 4: St. Elizabeth Ann Seton, religious (memorial), patroness of Catholic schools—hug a Catholic school teacher; New York pizza, New York cheesecake, Maryland blue crabs, black and white cookies (page 107).

January 5: St. John Neumann, bishop (memorial), patron of Catholic education—hug a Catholic school administrator; Philly cheesesteak sandwiches (page 108).

January 6 (or the Sunday after January 1): The Epiphany of the Lord (solemnity)—read Matthew 2:1–12; Epiphany house blessing; leave out shoes for the Wise Men; treats and camel spit; King or Queen of Epiphany; Wise Men arrive at Nativity scene; Twelfth Night white elephant gift exchange; take down Christmas tree and put Christmas decorations away; king cake, international potluck (page 108).

Sunday after Epiphany or January 9: The Baptism of the Lord (feast)—read Matthew 3:13–17; renewal of baptismal promises; winter swim; godparents get-together; fondue (page 115).

January 20: St. Sebastian, martyr (optional memorial) patron of soldiers, archers, and athletes; have a team party; shish kebabs (page 120).

January 21: St. Agnes, virgin and martyr (memorial), patroness of engaged couples, chastity, and girls—lamb, lamb cake (page 121).

January 22: Day of Prayer for the Legal Protection of Unborn Children— recommended fasting and abstinence; walk for life; pray a Rosary outside an abortion clinic (page 122).

January 23: St. Vincent of Saragossa, deacon and martyr (optional memorial), patron of winemakers—wine tasting; wine (page 126).

January 25: The Conversion of Saint Paul the Apostle (feast), patron of the missions, publishers, and theologians—read Acts 9:1–22; blindman's buff; hummus, falafel (page 127).

January 28: St. Thomas Aquinas, priest and Doctor (memorial), patron of academics, students, and chastity—"Pange Lingua Gloriosi", "Adoro Te Devote", "Tantum Ergo"; chastity talk; oxtail soup (page 128).

February 1: St. Brigid of Ireland (optional memorial), patroness of dairy-maids, poultry raisers, and children; make butter; weave a cross of rushes (or pipe cleaners); scones with butter and jam (page 130).

February 2: Candlemas and the Presentation of the Lord (feast)—read Luke 2:22–38; blessing of candles; avoid using electric lights; put away Christmas decorations; crepes (page 131).

February 3: St. Blaise, bishop and martyr (optional memorial), patron against illness of the throat—blessing of throats; whole fish (page 136).

February 5: St. Agatha, virgin and martyr (memorial), patroness of bell makers and against breast cancer—*minni di virgini* (page 137).

February 6: St. Paul Miki and companions, martyrs (memorial), patrons of Japan—sushi, Japanese curry, castella cake (page 138).

February 8: St. Josephine Bakhita, virgin (optional memorial), patroness of Sudan and against human trafficking—discuss human trafficking; Sudanese or Italian food (page 140).

February 11: Our Lady of Lourdes (optional memorial), patroness of the sick—Litany of the Blessed Virgin Mary (Litany of Loreto); Rosary; family pilgrimage; French picnic (page 142).

February 14: SS. Cyril, monk, and Methodius, bishop (optional memorial), patrons of Europe; and St. Valentine (historical)—family bistro; Slavic food (page 144).

February 22: The Chair of St. Peter the Apostle (feast)—read Matthew 16:13–20; write a letter to the pope; cookie chairs (page 148).

March 7: SS. Perpetua and Felicity, martyrs (optional memorial), patronesses of mothers and expectant mothers—read *The Passion of Saints Perpetua and Felicity*; fancy hairdos; *stracciatella alla Romana* (Roman egg drop soup) (page 149).

March 9: St. Frances of Rome, religious (optional memorial), patroness of homemakers and automobile drivers—attention to homemaking; soft pretzels, soup (page 152).

Forty-seven days before Easter: Fat Tuesday (Mardis Gras)—King or Queen of Mardi Gras; *paczki*, pancakes, king cake, jambalaya or *étouffée*, all the treats in the house (page 155).

Forty-six days before Easter: Ash Wednesday—required fasting and abstinence; spring Ember Days (Wednesday, Friday, and Saturday after

Ash Wednesday); receive ashes; bury the Alleluia; choose Lenten disciplines; bean jar; decorate for Lent; meat-free soup, eggs, fish, alligator, beaver (page 169).

March 17: St. Patrick, bishop (optional memorial), patron of Ireland and engineers, and against snakes—read St. Patrick's Breastplate; hooley or tea party; use a shamrock to discuss the Trinity; corned beef and cabbage, shepherd's pie (page 172).

March 19: St. Joseph, Spouse of the Blessed Virgin Mary (solemnity), patron of the Catholic Church, fathers, workers, and a happy death—read Matthew 1:18–23; Litany of St. Joseph; seven Sundays of St. Joseph; wear red; St. Joseph's Table, Pasta un Gobola Tabola; pasta, St. Joseph's *sfinge* (cream puffs) (page 174).

March 24: St. Catherine of Sweden (optional memorial), patroness against miscarriage—Requiem Aeternam (Eternal Rest prayer); remembering babies lost to miscarriage and stillbirth; one-on-one outing with an older child; Swedish meatballs (page 177).

March 25: The Annunciation of the Lord (solemnity)—read Luke 1:26–38; the Angelus; *Våffeldagen*; "It's a boy!" party decorations; Annunciation puppet show; waffles (page 180).

Fourth Sunday of Lent: Laetare Sunday (Sunday, holy day of obligation)—read Isaiah 66:10; pilgrimage to your "mother church" on Mothering Sunday; wear pink; pink steak, pink cake (page 182).

Fifth Sunday of Lent: Passion Sunday (historical, Sunday, holy day of obligation)—veil statues (see John 8:59); go to confession; purple dinner (page 183).

Sixth Sunday of Lent: Palm Sunday (Sunday, holy day of obligation)—read Mark 11:1–11; blessing of palms; wear red; hearts of palm salad, falafel, hummus (page 186).

Holy Week: Monday and Tuesday—read Mark 11:12–25, 14:3–9, and John 12:23–25; Holy Week cleaning; Easter meal prep, big pot of soup (page 187).

Holy Week: Spy Wednesday—read Matthew 26:14–16 and Luke 22:3–6; Holy Week cleaning; thirty pieces of silver; Tenebrae dinner, big pot of soup (page 189).

Holy Week: Holy Thursday—"Tantum Ergo" (plenary indulgence); read John 13:1–20 and Matthew 26:17–29; Seven Churches Visitation; Mass; family foot washing; watch *The Prince of Egypt*; Last Supper dinner, Rice Krispies Treats lamb cake (page 194).

Holy Week: Good Friday—read Mark 14:26–15:27; required fasting and abstinence; veneration of the cross (plenary indulgence); Prayer before a Crucifix (plenary indulgence after Communion on any Friday of Lent);

Divine Mercy Novena begins; wear black; quiet from noon until three o'clock; Stations of the Cross; hot cross buns, fish fry (page 198).

Holy Week: Holy Saturday—recommended fasting and abstinence; maintain the great silence; prepare for Easter; dye eggs; soft pretzels (page 204).

Easter Sunday of the Resurrection of the Lord (Sunday, holy day of obligation)—read John 20:1–23; watch the papal Urbi et Orbi blessing on TV or online (plenary indulgence); "O Filii et Filiae" ("Ye Sons and Daughters"), "Jesus Christ Is Risen Today"; attend the Easter Vigil and Easter Sunday Mass; jelly bean jar; braided Easter bread, New Covenant Easter dinner: ham, shrimp, cheesy potatoes (page 209).

Easter Week: Monday through Saturday—Regina Caeli; daily Mass; water fights (Monday); Easter greeting: "He is risen", "He is risen, indeed!"; *paczki*, Meat Friday (page 213).

Second Sunday of Easter: Sunday of Divine Mercy (Sunday, holy day of obligation)—participate in a Divine Mercy service, or, before the Blessed Sacrament, recite the Our Father and the Creed and pray "Merciful Jesus, I trust in you!" (plenary indulgence); the Chaplet of Divine Mercy; heart-shaped waffles, Polish borscht soup, Divine Mercy sundaes (page 215).

April 23: St. George, martyr (optional memorial), patron of England, knights, soldiers, and the health of domestic animals—cardboard-sword fights; bangers and mash, dragon-shaped anything, St. George's Cross fruit crumble (page 217).

April 25: St. Mark, evangelist (feast), patron of Venice, barristers, and notaries—read Mark 14:48–52; Litany of the Saints; major Rogation Day; pray for farmers and those affected by natural disasters; process around the boundaries of the parish; lion's head veggie pizza (page 219).

April 28: St. Gianna Beretta Molla (optional memorial), patroness of physicians, wives, mothers, and unborn children; moms' night out; Italian, takeout, or anything moms don't have to cook (page 220).

April 29: St. Catherine of Siena, virgin and Doctor of the Church (memorial), patroness of Europe, Italy, and against illness; Airing of Grievances; Italian food, tiramisu (page 221).

May 1: St. Joseph the Worker (optional memorial), patron of workers, employers, and employment; Litany of St. Joseph; a hands-on project; pray for laborers and for the conversion of communist nations; Italian food (page 225).

May 13: Our Lady of Fatima (optional memorial)—Litany of the Blessed Virgin Mary (Litany of Loreto); Rosary; Portuguese-style mussels, dancing-sun cupcakes (page 225).

May 21: Mexican Martyrs (optional memorial), patrons of Mexico—piñata; tacos, tres leches cake, Mexican Cokes, margaritas (page 226).

May 22: St. Rita of Cascia, religious (optional memorial), patroness of lost and impossible causes, difficult marriages, and baseball; baseball game; hot dogs and margaritas (page 227).

May 30: St. Joan of Arc, virgin and martyr (optional memorial), patroness of France and soldiers—wear pants; croque madame, torched crème brûlée (page 228).

May 31: The Visitation of the Blessed Virgin Mary (feast)—read Luke 1:39–56; Litany of the Blessed Virgin Mary (Litany of Loreto), Hail Mary, Magnificat; prepare a meal for a friend who is pregnant or has a new baby (page 229).

Forty days after Easter (a Thursday) or Seventh Sunday of Easter: The Ascension of the Lord (solemnity, holy day of obligation)—read Acts 1:6–11; Pentecost Novena begins on Ascension Thursday; lesser Rogation Days (Monday, Tuesday, Wednesday before the Solemnity of the Ascension); mountain climbing; outdoor picnic; popovers (page 230).

Fifty days after Easter: Pentecost (Sunday, solemnity, holy day of obligation)—read Acts 2:1–4; Come, Holy Spirit; summer Ember Days (Wednesday, Friday, and Saturday after Pentecost); recommended fasting and abstinence on the vigil of Pentecost; bonfire; pin the tongues of fire on the apostles; donuts, birthday cake, hot dogs, s'mores (page 233).

Monday after Pentecost: Blessed Virgin Mary Mother of the Church (memorial)—Rosary, Litany of the Blessed Virgin Mary (Litany of Loreto); meatloaf, apple pie (page 235).

Sunday after Pentecost: The Most Holy Trinity (Sunday, solemnity, holy day of obligation)—Athanasian Creed, Lesser Doxology (Glory Be); discuss symbols of the Trinity; Turducken, three-meat chili, cloverleaf rolls, trinity cream (page 237).

Second Sunday after Pentecost: The Most Holy Body and Blood of Christ (Corpus Christi) (Sunday, solemnity, holy day of obligation)—read John 6:52–59; eucharistic procession (plenary indulgence); Act of Spiritual Communion, "Tantum Ergo"; begin the practice of making the sign of the cross whenever passing a Catholic church; visit to the Blessed Sacrament; Last Supper dinner (page 241).

Friday after Corpus Christi: The Most Sacred Heart of Jesus (solemnity)—publicly recite the Act of Reparation to the Sacred Heart of Jesus (plenary indulgence); Meat Friday, red Jell-O heart (page 244).

Saturday after Corpus Christi—The Immaculate Heart of the Blessed Virgin Mary (memorial)—Litany of the Blessed Virgin Mary (Litany of Loreto); heart-shaped food (page 244).

June 13: St. Anthony of Padua, priest and Doctor (memorial), patron of lost items, lost people, lost souls, the elderly, and mail—St. Anthony box; rye bread (page 245).

June 22: SS. John Fisher, bishop, and Thomas More, martyrs (optional memorial), patrons of lawyers and stepparents—fish, s'mores (page 247).

June 24: The Nativity of Saint John the Baptist (solemnity)—patron of builders, tailors, printers, baptism, and against seizures; read Luke 1:57–80; vigil bonfire; locusts, wild honey, grasshopper pie (page 248).

June 26: St. Josemaría Escrivá, priest (optional memorial), patron of Opus Dei, diabetics, job seekers, and the sanctification of ordinary work—consider ways to grow holier in daily life; tortilla, paella, flan (page 249).

June 29: SS. Peter and Paul, apostles (solemnity)—"Holy Apostles, Peter and Paul, intercede for us" prayer; use an article blessed by the pope or a bishop (plenary indulgence); camping, fishing, or a picnic; cookie tents, candy fish (page 250).

July 14: St. Kateri Tekakwitha, virgin (memorial), patroness of Native Americans and the environment—three sisters stew, fry bread, maple taffy (page 253).

July 16: Our Lady of Mount Carmel (optional memorial), patroness of Carmelites and deliverance from purgatory—Litany of the Blessed Virgin Mary (Litany of Loreto); investiture with the Brown Scapular; caramel brownie sundaes (page 254).

July 22: St. Mary Magdalene (feast), patroness of converts, hairdressers, and penitent sinners—egg tapping game; red eggs, curry, spice cake, 7 Up (page 255).

July 23: St. Bridget, religious (optional memorial), patroness of Sweden and widows—Swedish meatballs, Swedish Fish candy, lingonberry jam (page 256).

July 26: SS. Joachim and Anne, parents of the Blessed Virgin Mary (memorial), patrons of grandparents, homemakers, and lace makers—do something special with or for grandparents; lobster, Florentine lace cookies (page 257).

August 2: Feast of Our Lady Queen of Angels (memorial), patroness of Los Angeles—Litany of the Blessed Virgin Mary (Litany of Loreto); visit a church on the feast day or the following Sunday for the Portiuncula Indulgence of St. Francis of Assisi (plenary indulgence) (page 258).

August 6: The Transfiguration of the Lord (feast)—read Mark 9:2–8; toad in the hole, transformed leftovers, whipped cream (page 259).

August 10: St. Lawrence, deacon and martyr (feast), patron of librarians, comedians, cooks, and roasters—comedy showcase; barbecue (page 261).

August 11: St. Clare, virgin (memorial), patroness of television and embroiderers—family movie night; veggie pizza, éclairs (page 262).

August 15: The Assumption of the Blessed Virgin Mary (solemnity, holy day of obligation)—Litany of the Blessed Virgin Mary (Litany of Loreto); Blessing of Herbs; drying herbs, herb sachet; herb roast, herb salad, blackberry basil tart (page 263).

August 22: The Queenship of the Blessed Virgin Mary (memorial)—Litany of the Blessed Virgin Mary (Litany of Loreto); Marian procession; Marian tea party: queen cakes, tea, coronation chicken salad sandwiches (page 264).

August 24: St. Bartholomew, apostle (feast), patron of bookbinders and butchers; skinning apples; applesauce, skinless chicken breasts (page 266).

August 27: St. Monica (memorial), patroness of difficult marriages and difficult children—pray for family members away from the Church; couscous, tagine, salted caramel (page 267).

August 28: St. Augustine, bishop and Doctor (memorial), patron of brewers, printers, and theologians—Holy Spirit Prayer of St. Augustine; dig a hole at the beach; beer, root beer, pastilla (meat pie) (page 267).

August 29: The Passion of St. John the Baptist (memorial)—patron of builders, tailors, printers, baptism, and against seizures; read Mark 6:14–29; avoid platters, knives, and round foods, or just go with it and serve a head (of lettuce) on a platter, lettuce wraps (page 269).

September 5: St. Teresa of Calcutta (optional memorial), patroness of the Missionaries of Charity and World Youth Day—pray for the poor; serve the poor; almsgiving; Indian food, blue Jell-O (or white Jell-O with blue stripes) (page 270).

September 8: The Nativity of the Blessed Virgin Mary (feast)—Litany of the Blessed Virgin Mary (Litany of Loreto); birthday party; blue-cornchip nachos, blueberry cornbread, blue crabs, blue cheese, blue birthday cake (page 272).

September 14: The Exaltation of the Holy Cross (feast)—read 1 Corinthians 1:23–25; Prayer before a Crucifix; veneration of the cross; fall Ember Days (Wednesday, Friday, and Saturday after the feast of the Exaltation of the Holy Cross); basil foods: caprese salad, pesto pasta with shrimp, strawberry basil lemonade (page 273).

September 15: Our Lady of Sorrows (memorial), patroness of Poland— Litany of the Blessed Virgin Mary (Litany of Loreto); sour-candy Seven Sorrows of Mary; sweet-and-sour dish, 7 Up (page 273).

September 21: St. Matthew, apostle and evangelist (feast), patron of accountants and bankers—read Matthew 9:9–13; silver dollar pancakes (page 275).

September 29: SS. Michael, Gabriel and Raphael, archangels (Michaelmas) (feast), patrons of police officers, the military, firefighters, and paramedics (Michael); messengers, radio, and postal workers (Gabriel);

nurses, pharmacists, and physicians (Raphael)—read Revelation 12:7–9; St. Michael Prayer; wear leggings; beat the devil (piñata) with swords; blackberries, goose, game hen, asparagus spears, deviled eggs, angels on horseback, devils on horseback, Flamin' Hot Cheetos, angel food cake, devil's food cake (page 276).

October 1: St. Thérèse of the Child Jesus, virgin and Doctor of the Church (memorial), patroness of France, florists, and loss of parents—sacrifice beads; vegetable rose tart, French onion soup, puff-pastry apple roses, strawberry roses (page 280).

October 2: The Holy Guardian Angels (memorial)—read Matthew 18:10; Guardian Angel Prayer; say good morning to your guardian angel; angel hair pasta, angel food cake (page 281).

October 4: St. Francis of Assisi (memorial), patron of Italy and animals— "Canticle of the Sun"; blessing of pets; make a bird feeder; visit the zoo; ants on a log, animal crackers, bird's nest cookies, bear claw cookies, gnocchi (page 284).

October 7: Our Lady of the Rosary (memorial)—Litany of the Blessed Virgin Mary (Litany of Loreto); Rosary; edible rosaries (page 286).

October 18: St. Luke, evangelist (feast), patron of artists, physicians, and surgeons—Magnificat, Benedictus, Nunc Dimittis; visit an art museum; hug a doctor; burgers, steaks, oxtail soup, Banbury cakes, Fig Newtons (page 288).

October 22: St. John Paul II, pope (optional memorial), patron of families, young Catholics, and World Youth Day—JPII's Act of Entrustment to Mary; hike; watch an online video of JPII speaking; Polish sausage, pierogies, *kremówka papieska* (papal cream cake) (page 289).

October 31: All Hallows' Eve—recommended fasting and abstinence for the vigil of All Saints; contemplate your mortality; carve a jack-o'-lantern; go trick-or-treating; spooky baked macaroni and cheese, candy (page 291).

November 1: All Saints (solemnity, holy day of obligation)—Litany of All Saints; pray for the Holy Souls in a cemetery each day from November 1 through November 8 (plenary indulgence each day, applicable only to the souls in purgatory); All Saints' Day pageant (page 294).

November 2: The Commemoration of All the Faithful Departed (All Souls' Day) (memorial)—Requiem Aeternam, St. Gertrude Prayer; pray for the Holy Souls in a church (plenary indulgence); pray for the Holy Souls in a cemetery each day through November 8 (plenary indulgence each day, applicable only to the souls in purgatory); write the names of deceased loved ones on a candle; put photos of deceased on home altar table; soul cakes, eggs in purgatory (page 301).

November 11: St. Martin of Tours, bishop (Martinmas) (memorial), patron of soldiers and against poverty—donate coats that are no longer used; lantern making; lantern walk; pray for the poor; seven-can soup, cookies (broken in half and shared) (page 305).

November 25: St. Catherine of Alexandria, virgin and martyr (optional memorial), patroness of lawyers, apologists, unmarried women, and milliners and against sudden death—pray for a husband and for the unmarried "Catherinettes"; wear fancy hats; Catherine's wheel pizza, pinwheel cookies (page 307).

Last Sunday in Ordinary Time: Our Lord Jesus Christ, King of the Universe (Sunday, solemnity, holy day of obligation)—Te Deum (plenary indulgence); chicken à la king, Bundt cake (page 309).

INDEX OF FEAST DAYS